The Writer's
Legal Companion

The Writer's Legal Companion

Third Edition

Brad Bunnin

with a chapter on
The Author and the Business of Publishing
by Peter Beren

PERSEUS BOOKS
Reading, Massachusetts

Library of Congress Catalog Card Number: 98-86943

ISBN 0-7382-0031-X

Perseus Books is a member of the Perseus Books Group

Cover design by Andrew Newman
Set in 10 point Palatino by Vicki L. Hochstedler

1 2 3 4 5 6 7 8 9 10—DOH—0201009998
First printing, September 1998

Our book is dedicated to Nenelle, Erika, Andrew, and Francesca, who helped when it mattered most, and to Susan, whose support and understanding never faltered.

ACKNOWLEDGMENTS

Dozens of people share the credit for this book—clients and adversaries, and the writers and publishers who attended classes, seminars, and workshops we've conducted during the last several years.

Those to whom we owe special thanks include:

Bernard Taper
Alan Rinzler
Annette Dornbos
Alma Robinson
Jeremy Tarcher
Gloria Frym
Sayre Van Young
Helen Palmer
Della van Heyst

And Stephanie Harolde not only is a terrific client and a warm friend; she also saved us weeks of drudgery by converting this book from its original computer format to its usable Macintosh format. Our book is dedicated to our clients and our friends in publishing, who have taught us that we—and they—should never take "no" for an answer.

CONTENTS

INTRODUCTION

You, a writer, want to devote your time and energy to the creation of high quality, publishable work, not hassles with publishers, editors, agents, lawyers, or even the occasional reader who claims he's been libeled. But in today's publishing business, you can't avoid the legal implications of your professional decisions. You can, however, understand the major ways in which the legal system impinges on your work and incorporate this knowledge into your decision-making. Done sensibly, this will enable you to sidestep many potential legal problems and minimize the effect of those that can't be absolutely avoided.

What problems are likely to beset you? Here's a sample:

- Your publisher insists that you revise your last book and doesn't seem to care that you're in the middle of your next one. Must you turn your life upside-down just because he says so? What will it cost you if you say it can't be done for six months?
- Your friend at the library says it's legal to use five lines (or ten, or two) from someone's poem in your new book without getting the poet's consent. Are you a literary thief if you do?
- Your royalty statement and check are five weeks late. So is your rent. Should you sue your publisher before your landlord sues you?

It's wise to stand back and think through how the larger ecosystem works before you identify and deal with each legal tree in the publishing forest. You'll discover that you as a writer are a part of the whole. You share the terrain with all sorts of others, including agents, publishers, lawyers, accountants, bookstore owners, critics, and, we hope, readers. Each of these groups operates in a different setting, according to different rules, and is motivated by interests that often compete. Because a clear understanding of how these various interests coexist and conflict can be as important to you as knowing how any particular law affects your rights, this book emphasizes how the legal interests of those around you affect your rights.

To illustrate, suppose for a moment you're writing a novel. You're beginning to get a feel for your main character, several of whose superficial characteristics you have borrowed from a living person. What, if any, legal dangers threaten if your efforts at disguising your protagonist aren't foolproof? Or, to ask the question more directly, should you be worried about libel law and invasion of privacy? When author Gwen Davis and the Doubleday Publishing Corporation were successfully sued by a California therapist, they found out the hard way that they should have.[1]

While often fascinating, libel law problems are far less common than those arising from the legal relationships inherent in the publishing business itself. You can minimize problems by knowing in advance the potential legal consequences of the agreements you make. For example, arrangements with agents often seem so simple and straightforward that many agents don't even bother asking writers to sign a written agency agreement. But what happens if you become unhappy with your agent, terminate the arrangement, and make your own deal with a publisher? Are you obligated to pay the agent's commission? What if you make your deal with a publisher your agent had already contacted? A clear written agreement will help avoid costly uncertainties about your obligations to your agent.[2]

Relationships with agents are only one area where a knowledge of contract law can be extremely helpful. Signing a publishing contract is even more important. It's here that the average author with little legal and practical knowledge about the publishing business is most apt to make costly mistakes. This is understandable, because the typical publishing contract is a complicated document that tends to be hard to read. Many authors, thoroughly intimidated, simply sign on the dotted line. Of course, by proceeding without fully understanding what you are signing, you play into the publishing company's hands. The publisher hopes that in your flush of success (after all, how many writers even get

---

1.   See Chapters 5 and 6 for the details of this case, *Bindrim v. Mitchell,* 92 Cal.App.3d 61 (1979).

2.   Chapter 4 describes how to structure an agency relationship.

published?) you may not take the time to understand each clause and may not even know that publishing contracts, like your manuscript, almost always need knowledgeable editing.

Take heart. We've designed this book to show you how to understand each separate part of your publishing contract. Armed with this knowledge, you should know what contract changes to ask for. Whether you get what you want depends on your bargaining power and negotiating skills, or those of your agent or lawyer. Obviously, however, you can't negotiate effectively if you don't understand what the contract means. We haven't hesitated to tell you what we think is best, and we've even advised you about tactics to get what you want. But please use your good judgment and common sense when you negotiate. Don't expect to get everything you ask for, and prepare yourself for effective compromise. And be reassured: Even the first-time authors we've worked with— newly fledged and lacking clout—have *all* been able to win a better contract through negotiation.

If you've never had to deal with a written publishing agreement before, you're going to encounter a new language and new concepts: "second serialization," "reserve against return." Don't be intimidated. Each strange word is defined—in the text, if you'll be patient, in the Glossary (Appendix A) if you won't.

The Writer's Legal Companion deals with the laws of an industry in flux. The industry bears small resemblance to that of even ten years ago. Despite its proverbial conservatism, and its long-standing but now inaccurate reputation as a "gentleman's trade," the publishing business is dynamic and highly competitive. So it's our goal to help you not only to understand the fundamental nature of the publishing business, but also to grasp the legal implications of the trends that are sure to lead in new directions.

No book can make you a self-sufficient legal expert. This one makes no such claim, but it will alert you to the need for help when help is what you need. Don't try to "learn" the book's contents. Read it for a sense of how law and legal relationships are important to you. Then keep it next to your thesaurus and use it as a reference.

Finally, we should explain who "we" are. One of us is Brad Bunnin, a lawyer in practice for over a decade and a half, the last half-decade devoted to the law of writing and publishing. Brad wrote the text of the book except for Chapter 12, which was written by Peter Beren, a writer and a publishing professional since 1969, with extensive experience in book marketing, publicity, and editorial development.

Brad Bunnin
Peter Beren
Berkeley, California

1 THE PUBLISHING CONTRACT

INTRODUCTION: ABOUT CONTRACTS AND INTIMIDATION

This chapter is a guide to effective negotiating for the author who has something to sell—the right to publish his or her work—to a publisher who wants to buy it. The chapter is about power and money. The author has the power to sell or not to sell. The publisher has money to pay for the author's exercise of that power. The publishing contract is the legal means by which power and money change hands.

Most authors, even those with a great deal of publishing experience, doubt their power. They often feel compelled to sign any agreement the publisher submits, without negotiating, afraid that the publisher will back out of the deal at the first sign of ingratitude. This is simply not true. It evidences the author as the victim of his or her own imagination, of self-intimidation. Virtually without exception, publishers willingly change contracts at the author's request, whether the author speaks directly or through an agent or attorney. A new author may lack the bargaining strength of an established money-maker, but publishers take reasonable requests seriously even when a rank beginner makes them, because even the novice has power.

The time to use that power is *before* you sign away your rights in the publishing contract, while you still have something your publisher-to-be wants.

The Myth of the "Standard Contract"

Because the publishing business follows certain predictable patterns, publishing agreements tend to resemble each other in outline. But they also differ from one another in significant ways. There's no such thing as a "standard contract." Although the printed eight-page form that daunts you may look immutable, it isn't.[1] New contract language can be added to the agreement in the margins, between the lines, and in a rider attached to the end of the contract document.

Of course, the editor buying your work will react with delight if you accept what's offered, without negotiating; that editor will make you a better deal with equal delight. To negotiate a contract that fits you like a glove instead of handcuffs, you must understand your publisher's need to solve its editorial, production, and economic problems. You also need to understand how you can successfully bargain for modifications to protect and advance your interests. To help you do this, we'll first look at the true nature of contracts, what they do, and why it's crucial that they be in writing. We'll follow with some advice on contract negotiation. Then we'll review typical contract provisions and the common variations that publishers often use. We'll discuss the issues raised by each significant provision and suggest various possible modifications. We'll use a trade book[2] contract as our model because it tends to be the most comprehensive. But we'll also comment on textbook contracts and those for mass market paperbacks, where they differ in important respects from the trade book contract.

What Do Contracts Do?

Contracts deal with the future. They provide solutions in advance for uncertain events that haven't yet occurred. The contract says, "Here's what I'll do, and here's what you'll do, *if* your book needs revising, or

---

1. See Appendix C for sample publishing agreements. These samples aren't model forms; we include them to show you what a variety of contracts looks like.

2. You'll find a glossary of publishing business terms in Appendix A. *Trade book* is a term that can be particularly confusing because it his more than one common meaning. In the broad sense (this is the way we use it here), it means all hardcover and softcover books meant primarily for the bookstore market, except mass market paperbacks, which are always 4" by 7" and designed to fit in the book racks you find at drugstores or supermarkets. The confusion over the term *trade book* develops in the area of oversized paperbacks (everything from odd-sized joke books to an 8½" by 11" paperback on how to grow snapdragons). These are most often called trade paperbacks, although they are sometimes called trade books by people who think that if you are referring to a hardcover book, you should call it one.

if it sells 1,000,000 copies, or if you decide to write another book, or *if* someone sues us because of what you wrote." The publisher puts money into publishing a book (bets might be as good a term), often paying the author an advance against possible future earnings; the author works for months or years, hoping that in the future the book sells by the ton. Both invest time and financial resources with no assurance that events will ever justify the investment. The book contract is an imperfect attempt at a fair division of the cost of losing and the rewards of winning. The considerable uncertainty as to whether a book will return ten cents or ten million dollars is a principal factor allowing room for contract negotiation.

What Is a Contract?

Lawyers say that a contract is a legally enforceable agreement between two or more parties consisting of reciprocal promises. In our context, this simply means that if you promise to write a book and let Random House publish it, and Random House, in return, promises to do so and pay you, you and the publisher have a contract. If you don't write the book, Random House doesn't have to pay you. If Random House doesn't pay you, you don't have to let it publish your book. And either party to the contract, given sufficient time and money, can get an arbitrator or a court (depending on the contract terms) to help make the other one keep its promises or pay damages for failing to do so.

Note on terminology: We use the words *contract* and *agreement* interchangeably. Most lawyers do.

Why Bother with a Written Contract?

When you deal with an established publisher, you will almost always find yourself presented with a long, detailed written contract. New, small publishers sometimes don't bother. That's a grave mistake for both publisher and author.

The compelling reason for a contract is to aid clarity and prevent misunderstanding between author and publisher about the terms of their agreements. By referring to the contract when questions or disputes crop up, each party should be able to understand what's to be done, when, and how. There is a corollary to this principle, which is "Write it down!" in theory, many publishing contracts may be enforceable, even if they are oral, but the obvious problems inherent in proving oral understandings make them almost worse than no contract at all. The question of enforceability aside, all oral contracts raise an obvious problem:

who is to decide what the parties agreed? The usual answer—painful and expensive—is a court.

Some unwritten mutual promises are not enforceable, even if other evidence exists that the parties actually agreed. That is, a court won't force a party to comply with the terms of the agreement. The rules vary from state to state, but in general, a contract to be performed more than a year in the future, or one calling for the payment of a large sum of money—say $5,000 or more—must be in writing to be enforceable. The reason the law demands a written agreement in these circumstances is to minimize the likelihood of fraudulent claims for large sums of money or those based on promises made long ago.

There are times when authors learn, to their dismay, that a document that looks like a contract, feels like a contract, and reads like a contract isn't one. For this reason, be sure you understand the difference between a valid publishing contract and the publisher's unenforceable promise.

Most publishing agreements are enforceable only when both author and publisher have signed them, even if you've agreed to most of the terms. You and the senior editor of Mountain Molehill Press are in accord that it should publish your new book. In due course, she sends you a printed form headed "Publishing Agreement." Her cover letter asks that you sign the agreement and return it to her for the publisher's countersignature. You note a place for the publisher's signature, but the signature isn't entered. You sign the agreement and send it back to the editor. A month later, the editor writes to say she's decided not to publish your book after all. Can you get a court to force Mountain Molehill to publish or pay you damages for breach of contract? Unfortunately, you cannot. The cover letter implies a requirement that the publisher sign before the agreement is enforceable.

Easy Ways to Change a Contract

A common mistake made by publishers and authors alike is to rely on oral promises—or even letters—that add to or change the written contract. As a general rule, oral modifications to a written contract are worse than useless. Most contracts state that enforceable modifications must be in writing signed by both parties, or by "the party to be charged"—the one who bears the burden of the change. Oral modifications, or written ones not signed by the party to be charged, create expectations on which you can't legally rely. So if you call your editor, and explain why this or that contract clause must be modified, and get her agreement over the phone, be sure to follow up and put the change in writing. There are three ways to accomplish this:

1. You can send a letter summarizing your understanding, proposing language to accomplish the changes you've agreed to by telephone, and asking your publisher to sign and return a copy of the letter. An example appears on the following page.
2. You can incorporate the contents of the letter into a more formal agreement by reference, adding language like the following to the publishing agreement:

> The attached letter from Arthur Author to Sally Bowles, dated December 1, 20__, is hereby made a part of this agreement by this reference as if fully set out in it.

3. You can change the language of the publishing agreement to reflect the negotiated terms. You may type the changes or write them in ink on the face of the agreement, with the usual arrows or other symbols to show where they go. Or you may use a rider, a separate piece of paper attached to the main agreement that refers to it, states the changes, and tells what sections the changes affect:

> *RIDER*
>
> This rider amends the publishing agreement between Mountain Molehill Press, Inc. ("Publisher") and Arthur Author ("Author"), dated November 22, 20___.
>
> 1. Section 5 is amended by adding the following words:
>
> Publisher's first edition of the Work shall remain in print and not be remaindered for at least eighteen months after its publication.
>
> 2. In all other respects, the agreement shall remain in full force and effect.
>
> Dated:
>
> _____
>
> Arthur Author
>
> Dated:
> Mountain Molehill Press, Inc.
>
> By: _____

December 1, 20___

Ms. Sally Bowles, Editor
Mountain Molehill Press
1 Park Avenue
New York, NY 10001

Dear Sally:

I was delighted you and I were able to resolve the issues that made your offered publishing contrast less than perfect for me. I thought it would be a good idea to state my understanding of the changes we agreed to, for the sake of clarity and to be sure we understand one another.

First, you agree to raise my royalty rate from 7 percent to 8 percent when the softcover trade edition of my book has sold 25,000 copies.

Second, you guarantee that my book will remain in print and not be remaindered for at least eighteen months after publication.

Third, you agree that I reserve all rights to license publication in the British Commonwealth nations because of my connections in England, and I agree to share my income from any of those licenses with you, splitting my income 10 percent to you and 90 percent to me.

If this letter states our agreement accurately, and if you agree that these terms are hereby made part of our publishing contract, please sign the enclosed copy of this letter where I've indicated and return it to me.

It's a pleasure dealing with you, and I am confident and excited about the future of my book with you.

Sincerely,

Arthur Author

Agreed and accepted:
Mountain Molehill Press, Inc.

By: _____

Dated:

NEGOTIATING YOUR PUBLISHING CONTRACT

Expert Help

Publishing is a business. For its better practitioners, it's an art and a passion as well, but it remains fundamentally a business. Successful publishers have learned to keep their art and craft separate from the day-to-day realities of business. You must do the same when you deal with them. One way is to hire someone to handle the business side of your career for you, either an agent or a lawyer. These professional advisors and representatives, when they're good, put their knowledge, skill, and contacts to work for you. They also buffer the relationship between you and your publisher, freeing you to concentrate on its happier aspects. But the choice and use of an agent or a lawyer (or both, because they serve different functions) must be done with care.

Your agent should know the market, be skilled at negotiation and contract analysis, and represent your best interests. But you should always bear in mind that agents make a living by selling literary property to publishers and taking a cut of the income the sale generates. In some situations, the agent may be motivated to make a deal, even when it's not in your best interest. We talk more about choosing and working with agents in Chapter 4.

Lawyers are in a different position, largely because they normally get paid whether your book sells or not. For this reason, they are likely to be more objective. But if you do consult a lawyer, retain one who knows something about publishing. Be more sensible than our poet friend who took her book contract to a labor lawyer. He swallowed, cleared his throat, and asked our friend if she knew how long a copyright lasted these days. She, failing to recognize the sounds of a man drowning in his ignorance, left his office with a list of demands that no rational publisher could accept. We discuss how to find and use lawyers who know what they're doing in Chapter 11.

Fundamentals of Contract Negotiation

To prepare for your book contract negotiations, engage yourself in a dialogue and decide what you absolutely must have, what you want badly, and what you'd like to have but could live without. If you've found an agent or a lawyer to champion your cause, you'll further it by making your needs clear before negotiations begin. If you're a do-it-yourself negotiator, you can stand the rehearsal.

Understand at the outset that compromises are inevitable; you won't get everything you want.

Remember always that even in a "standard" publishing contract, many provisions can be altered to fit, if you make convincing arguments. These arguments should be based on both your needs and the publisher's. The relationship between author and publisher may at times appear adversarial, but it also works as a collaboration.

You're far more likely to negotiate a sound publishing contract if you know how to analyze the clauses that make up the contract and understand why they appear as they do. Reading a contract "cold" is an exercise in boredom and frustration, best avoided unless you're a lawyer, who's paid well to be bored and frustrated. But with a little background about what each clause means, and some suggestions about how to improve them, you should find your publishing contract to be very interesting indeed. After all, the contract may well determine whether the publication of your book is a pleasure for you or a conflict-ridden failure.

PUBLISHING CONTRACT TERMS

Enough preliminaries. To help you find your way through the contract's legal thicket, we'll describe what a typical one contains before jumping off. Then we'll plunge into the details. Most contracts will contain most of the provisions we're about to describe, although organization, wording, and many substantive details will vary. We include samples of complete contracts in Appendix C, but we suggest you read this chapter carefully before examining them closely. Take an advance look now, for an overview.

The Structure of the Publishing Agreement

Although every publishing house produces a different contract form, based on its experience, its personality, and its lawyer's drafting style, publishing agreements share many characteristics. The agreements usually begin with a preamble, in which the parties are named and the book described. More than 100 clauses may follow (in the Simon & Schuster agreement, for example), but most agreements contain about twenty-five. The agreement ends with signature lines.

At the very least, a publishing agreement will usually contain clauses covering the following:

- Who is signing the agreement and is therefore legally obligated by it?
- When does it take effect? When does it end?
- What rights is the author granting the publisher?
- What and when is the publisher paying for those rights?
- What happens if someone claims the author did something wrong, such as infringe a copyright?

As you'll see in the next couple of dozen sections of this chapter, a carefully drafted agreement is likely to include much more.

The Title and the Introductory Clauses:
Parties, Effective Date, and Location

Most contracts have a title, such as "Publishing Agreement" or "Publishing Contract." Sometimes the document is merely headed "Agreement."

Below the title appears the introductory paragraph, which usually names the parties and their geographical location, and recites the fact that the parties have agreed to something, as of a certain date.

> *PUBLISHING AGREEMENT*
>
> This Agreement is made in New York, New York, by and between Danae Publishers, Inc., a New York corporation, having its principal offices at 2505 Park Avenue South, New York, NY 10001 (hereinafter called "Publisher"), and Della D. Rhodes (hereinafter called "Proprietor"), of Oak Park, IL, as of March 1, 20__. In consideration of the mutual covenants contained herein, the parties hereby agree:

The language need not be so formal to produce the same legal effect:

> *PUBLISHING AGREEMENT*
>
> This agreement is made as of March 1, 20__, between Danae Publishers, Inc. ("Publisher"), and Della D. Rhodes ("Author"), at New York, NY. The parties agree:

The difference between these two clauses is purely one of style.

Every contract needs to be dated so the parties can know when the contract begins. Ordinarily, the contract relationship legally begins when the last person signs the contract. But the contract may specify another date, different from the date of signing. It's often convenient to pick an "effective contract date" for reference purposes, especially when the parties are in different cities and can't both sign on the same day. If the contract relationship begins at some time other than the date of signing, the contract should say so.

Most of us grew up hearing bad jokes about what "the party of the first part" did to "the party of the second part." The term *party* is a lawyer's shorthand way of identifying the person or business bound by a contract. The names that appear in the contract establish who is legally liable to do what the contract says. For convenience, many publishing contracts first identify each party by name and then refer to them as "Author" and "Publisher."

Where the parties live and work may affect which state's laws apply and which state's courts are available for a lawsuit.[3] Stating these geographical facts in the agreement makes them clear.

Recitals

Some lawyers like to include recitals of facts that underlie the agreement. These recitals, also called the "whereas" clauses, read like this:

> WHEREAS Author has submitted a proposal for a novel about life along the Trans-Siberian Railroad to Publisher; and
>
> WHEREAS Publisher desires to publish the same; and
>
> WHEREAS Author and Publisher believe it to be in their mutual interest that Publisher publish the same;
>
> NOW THEREFORE, the parties hereto agree to the following terms and conditions:

Recitals aren't found frequently in publishing agreements; if you find them, read them with care to be sure they state the facts accurately.

The Description of the Work

Unfortunately, many publishing contracts do not define "the Book" or "the Work" that the author intends to write with any degree of detail, relying instead on a general statement about subject matter. All too often this leads to a situation where writer and publisher discover, only after the book is well along toward completion, that each had a very different idea about its form and content.

---

3.   See page 67, "Governing Law," for more.

How can you, as the author, define your "work" so that your publisher really understands and is enthusiastic about the book you plan to write? If you've submitted an outline or a detailed proposal, consider asking that it be incorporated into the publishing contract, to provide a definition of "the Work."

The usual, undefined, delivery clause includes language like this:

Author will deliver a book-length manuscript tentatively entitled *The Field Guide to Field Guides,* which will catalog major field guides.

Obviously, this doesn't tell you much. For example, it has not established the book's length, or what is to be covered in the book. You could add the following:

. . . and will contain approximately 60,000 words. An outline of the Work is attached to this agreement and made a part of it by this reference.

A better clause would read:

Author will deliver a manuscript of approximately 60,000 words, describing the variety of field guides available for outdoor activity in North America, concentrating on field guides for backpackers, rock climbers, and nature enthusiasts. It will include a comprehensive review of material of interest to bird, animal, insect, and plant hobbyists. At least 500 field guides will be cataloged following the format set forth in pages 2 and 3 of Author's "Field Guide Proposal" of April 7, 20__. The style of the Work shall, in general, be like that of the proposal.

Be careful of clauses that define the length of the work in printed pages. The number of words that will fit on a printed page depends on the size of the page, the margins, the type font, and the type density. Startling variations exist.

The Grant-of-Rights Clause

Initially, the author of a written work has absolute legal control over the use of the material. This includes the right to reproduce the work or to sell it to a publisher, filmmaker, theatrical producer, or anyone else. Taken together, these various rights are called the "copyright" (see Chapters 7 through 9 for much more about copyright). Here we are primarily concerned with the legal way the author transfers some or all of the ownership of the work to a publisher. This is, of course, done as part of the grant-of-rights clause of the publishing contract. This clause defines all the things the publisher acquiring rights can do with the copyrighted work.

Let's spend a little more time on the concept of rights. Understanding it is central to your success in negotiating a sound contract. The key thing to understand at the outset is that the word *rights* has an *s* at the end. The author starts with a number of different rights. Depending on how the publishing contract reads, he may transfer all, or a substantial number, or very few of these rights to the publisher. An important issue in any publishing contract is whether the grant of rights to the publisher is complete and exclusive or is limited in one or more ways. The duration of the grant of rights, the territory in which the publisher may exercise the rights, and the publisher's right, in turn, to grant rights to others are also issues that must be fully understood and resolved. Let's take the grant-of-rights clause apart and examine its constituent elements one by one.

Duration of the Grant of Rights

Most trade book publishers will ask at least for the exclusive right to "print, publish, and sell" a trade edition in the English language in the United States, for the full initial term of the copyright and all renewals and extensions. Asking for the full term of copyright is a publishing tradition, supported in part because some books can be marketed for a long time and become major back-list sellers. Strunk and White's *Elements of Style* is one of any number of possible examples.

It is possible, however, for authors to negotiate a shorter grant-of-rights term, or a conditional one. If, for example, the publisher is in breach of its agreement, the author should be able to terminate the agreement and get his rights back. Failure to keep the book in print (see page 58) should lead to termination and reversion of rights. So should failure to pay royalties. And if, for example, you feel strongly that your book on prescription drugs for parakeets must be revised often to maintain its accuracy and marketability, you may want to insist that your publisher either publish a revised edition within, say, three years, or restore publication rights to you so you can find another publisher or publish it yourself.

Copyright Ownership

Surprisingly, ownership of the copyright itself is not a major concern to most trade book publishers. All they really need is the legal right to publish, which an author can give them by various means. One way to do this is for the author to keep copyright ownership in his name and grant the publisher a license to exercise the rights the publisher needs. This occurs routinely. The author's name will appear on the copyright page, even though the license or right to publish the book has been transferred to the publisher.

The other approach to copyright ownership, commonly used by textbook publishers, is for the publisher to obtain copyright in its own name and provide for copyright to revert to the author when specified events occur (when the book goes out of print or the publisher's right to publish the book ends for some other reason). To repeat, copyright ownership, in the sense of whose name is on the copyright certificate, usually doesn't matter very much. What does matter is who has legal control over how the copyright may be used (who has what rights) and how the proceeds are divided (what royalties are to be paid). Defining these relationships are what much of the publishing contract is about.

Subsidiary Rights

Most publishers in the United States consider the right to publish a book here, in English, the most important right. That right is the primary publishing right. There are other rights, usually called "subsidiary rights" ("sub rights" for short) or "secondary rights," because they were traditionally less important than the primary right to publish. Subsidiary rights have value, sometimes far more than the primary right. They are valuable because the publisher can sell them to others, for a license fee, or exploit them itself, for extra income.

Here is a list of subsidiary rights, with definitions where the meaning isn't immediately apparent:

FIRST SERIALIZATION • The right to publish all or part of the book in a serial publication (such as a newspaper or magazine) before the book is published. First serial rights are sometimes called first periodical rights. They can be valuable. A potential best-selling memoir by a recent president (or the star of a nighttime soap opera—take your choice, American readers) may be worth tens of thousands of dollars. First serial publication can boost book sales dramatically, even before copies reach the stores. These advance sales make publishers happy, so they are eager to make first serial sales even if payment isn't much. Sometimes publication of a book is delayed to allow a magazine to exercise its first serial rights and sales interest in the book to build.

SECOND SERIALIZATION • The right to publish all or part of the book in a serial publication (such as a newspaper or magazine) after the book is published. Second serial rights aren't as valuable as first serial rights.

NEWSPAPER SYNDICATION • The right to allow publication of all or part of the book in many newspapers, usually exercised by a syndication service. No one newspaper pays much, but the income can be substantial if enough buy rights.

REPRINT RIGHTS • The right to allow another publisher to publish an edition of the book that differs in quality and price from the original version. In the old days, the reprint was often a "cheap edition," an appellation that does little for an author's ego and not much more for his bank account. Cheap editions were published in hard cover on brittle, unpleasant paper. With the advent and growth of the mass market paperback house, such as Pocket, Bantam, and Dell, reprint rights became more and more valuable. Many hardcover trade books probably wouldn't be published if it weren't for the prospect of a mass market paperback rights deal. Income from mass market reprint rights frequently exceeds the trade publisher's earnings from its own edition.

As mergers join trade publishers with mass market publishers in unholy wedlock, and as unmerged houses respond by publishing in formats formerly published by the other kind of house, the "hard/soft deal" or "volume rights deal" is becoming more common. In a hard/soft deal, the publisher acquires the right to publish the book in any format, and does so. There is, therefore, no sale of mass market rights; instead, the trade publisher produces a mass market edition itself.

Sometimes a mass market publisher acquires the right to publish an original work, not a reprinted one. If the mass market publisher then sells trade rights to a trade house, the sale is called a "back sale."

DRAMATIZATION, MOTION PICTURE, AND BROADCAST RIGHTS • The rights sometimes grouped as "performance rights." Most novelists I know dream of a sale to Hollywood, and then worry about what will happen to their integrity if the dream comes true. Productive worry is about things we can control. A sale of motion picture or television rights always costs the author control of his work, so there's no use worrying.

SOUND REPRODUCTION AND RECORDING RIGHTS • Rights that are sometimes defined to distinguish between dramatization and nondramatic reading of the work. Although most grants of rights in publishing are exclusive, which means only one licensee at a time can own and exercise them, audiotape rights are frequently nonexclusive, which means more than one tape producer may sell a tape based on the same book.

DIRECT MAIL OR DIRECT SALE RIGHTS • The right to sell directly to customers without bookstores. The medium of sale is a coupon in a magazine, newspaper, brochure, or advertisement in another book published by the publisher.

BOOK CLUB RIGHTS • Interesting, because money isn't usually the publisher's motivation to sell rights to a book club. Instead, the endorsement of the book and the free publicity it gets in book club ads induces the sale. Book clubs pay in one of two ways: a royalty or an inclusive price based on the manufacturing cost of the book.

TRANSLATION RIGHTS AND FOREIGN RIGHTS • Rights dealing with publication in languages and countries different from those in which the book is originally published. These rights can be valuable. Major publishers, and some smaller ones, have rights departments that sell these rights. Some agents specialize in them.

COMPUTER AND OTHER MAGNETIC AND ELECTRONIC MEDIA RIGHTS, INCLUDING "THOSE NOT YET KNOWN BUT LATER DISCOVERED" • Rights of unknown value, but of value nonetheless. As technology and markets change, so do the nature and value of subsidiary rights. A few years ago, the right to produce an audiotape version of a book was of principal interest to one producer, Caedmon. Today the competitors for tape rights include major book publishers, a chain bookstore, and dozens of producers. And the proliferation of personal computers created a new right: to express a work in computer media, such as CD-ROM.

CONDENSATION, DIGEST, AND ABRIDGMENT RIGHTS • Rights of limited monetary value; even if acquired by *Reader's Digest.*

ANTHOLOGY RIGHTS • Ditto.

SPECIAL (SCHOOL OR LIBRARY) EDITION RIGHTS.

BRAILLE OR TALKING BOOK RIGHTS • Rights exercised by the Library of Congress for the benefit of those whose sight or hearing is impaired, as an act of generosity, without payment to publisher or author.

MICROFILM AND FILMSTRIP RIGHTS • A somewhat specialized right, primarily of value to the educational market.

COMMERCIAL RIGHTS • The right to allow Coleco to create dolls in the author's image, and other merchandising rights, covering such items as T-shirts. Wouldn't you buy the word processor Joyce Carol Oates uses?

Sometimes the publisher either has little interest in certain subsidiary rights or recognizes that the author or his agent can do a better job of marketing them. Very small or very specialized publishers may well allow the author to handle subsidiary rights in areas outside their concern. But as a general rule, the financially marginal nature of the publishing business demands that a publisher make money any way it can. Often the difference between red ink and black on a particular title is the sale of subsidiary rights, and most publishers aren't about to overlook any marketing possibility, no matter how remote. At the same time, an informed author may well want control over, and the lion's share of income from, subsidiary rights sales. So subsidiary rights negotiations often become a real struggle for economic position and advantage.

Publishers have no divine mandate to sell your work to third parties. The publishing contract sets out the negotiated details of ownership, control, and how income is to be divided. You, the author, start out with all the rights. The publisher receives only what you grant by contract. If your publisher has the right to license your book on motorcycle repair for translation into Serbo-Croatian, it's because you granted it.

Contract language covering the grant of subsidiary rights ranges from simple, all-inclusive grants to lengthy, detailed lists. An example of each follows:

Simple clause: The Author grants the Publisher all rights in and to the Work, including the sole and exclusive right to print, publish, sell, and distribute the Work for the duration of copyright in the Work, together with all renewals and extensions, in all languages throughout the World.

Complex clause: Author grants Publisher the right, solely and exclusively, to print, publish, distribute, and sell the Work, and to dispose or license the disposition of the subsidiary rights in and to the Work described herein:

a. Periodical or newspaper publication prior to book publication;
b. Periodical or newspaper publication subsequent to book publication;
c. Book club publication;
d. Publication of editions for premium or special use or for direct sale to consumers through mail order;
e. Foreign language publication;
f. English language publication outside the United States and Canada;
g. Paperback reprint editions;
h. Hardcover reprint editions;
i. Motion picture, television, radio, and live-stage dramatic adaptation, commercial and/or merchandising;

j. Nondramatic audio and/or visual adaptation, and similar adaptation by whatever means made or transmitted, whether now in existence or here-after invented, including but not limited to microfilm, microfiche, information storage and retrieval systems, filmstrip, cassette, disc, tape and wire recording, photocopying, electronic transmission, transparencies, and public reading; and

k. Braille, Talking Book, large-type, and other editions for the handicapped.

The first, simple clause grants everything to the publisher. The author retains no rights, so the failure to list all possible subsidiary rights doesn't diminish the publisher's complete control over them. The second, specific clause must list all those rights the author grants to the publisher. Those not granted are automatically reserved to the author by the Copyright Act (see Chapter 7).

In deciding whether to let a publisher run the entire subsidiary rights show, including attempts to market movie rights, foreign rights, sales of excerpts to magazines, and so forth, or to try to do it yourself, you must weigh several factors. Perhaps the most obvious is whether you believe you—or your agent—can do better than your publisher. Many publishers, especially smaller ones, don't know very much about anything but trade book publishing, and their efforts to sell subsidiary rights are less likely to succeed than yours. Do a little research if you have doubts. Ask the editor you're dealing with about the publisher's subsidiary rights department and, specifically, about arrangements the house has negotiated in the recent past. If you're particularly interested in selling your book in Holland, for example, ask whether the publishing company sells Dutch rights on a regular basis. Request specific examples, not vague assurances. If you're concerned about movie rights, check *Variety* or look through the "Rights and Permissions" column in *Publishers Weekly* for the last year, to get a good idea of who is making movie sales.

CONTROLLING SUBSIDIARY RIGHTS • Although the publisher may feel strongly that it wants to control subsidiary rights, you may be able to exercise some control yourself by asking for the right to review and approve the publisher's exercise of rights, or by asking that all or select rights revert to you if the publisher doesn't exercise them within a stated period, perhaps one to three years after publication. You should also insist that the publisher notify you promptly, in writing, whenever a subsidiary rights sale takes place except for second serial rights deals, which aren't likely to be of much consequence.

Once you negotiate a reservation of subsidiary rights, then you or your agent can try to sell them. This can be a difficult, often impossible, job for a person with no experience in the area. Movie rights are particularly tricky, and your literary agent may be no more adept at selling them than your publisher. Specialist agents exist whose main function is to sell books to Hollywood, and you may want to contact one of them if you hold onto these rights. But be warned: of the tens of thousands of books published each year, only a few make it to the option stage (when a producer pays for the right to buy film rights within a certain time) and an even smaller number are actually picked up for production. The proportion of books that are ultimately turned into films released to the market is statistically almost nonexistent.

Of course, you may have developed a number of your own contacts. This is particularly likely if you are an expert in an area that has an extensive network of people likely to be interested in buying your material. Examples abound. One client, a British scholar, had already established herself and been widely published in Great Britain. She objected to the publisher's insistence on controlling British rights, and won. She had to compromise, however, by allowing the publisher to sell British rights if she wasn't able to within a year after publication.

It's important. to understand what the publisher will accept. If you insist on keeping so many sub rights that your book isn't published, you've gained nothing. You can maintain a real measure of control, however, by retaining the right to approve the publisher's sale of subsidiary rights.

Dividing Income from Subsidiary Rights

For certain types of material, subsidiary rights may prove immensely valuable, perhaps far more so than the right to publish in traditional book form. One client, even after the rights agent took 10 percent and the publisher half of the remaining 90 percent, earned almost $100,000 from a mass market reprint rights sale—for a book that the original publisher acquired for a $500 advance!

Although most publishing agreements offer a fifty-fifty split of income from subsidiary rights, it is common for the author to get a different share for different types of subsidiary rights. The split for most rights is almost always negotiable. No universal formula dictates how much the author receives and how much the publisher withholds for each type of right. The normal range of the publisher's share extends from nothing at all to 50 percent, the percentage depending on industry tradition, the nature of the right, who owns or controls it, the amount of work the publisher (or the author) will do to sell the right, and the author's bargaining strength. Even when the publisher agrees that the author should control and exploit specific subsidiary rights, the author should expect to share the proceeds with the publisher. If the book is the main economic entity (and not just a spin-off from TV or film, for example), a publisher who has invested in and promoted the book feels fairly entitled to share in the proceeds from nonbook markets.

SUBSIDIARY RIGHTS INCOME SPLITS

	Range of Income Splits	
Nature of Right	*Author*	*Publisher*
Mass market reprint	50%	50%
Film, TV	75–100%	25–0%
Foreign		
British Commonwealth	50–75%	50–25%
Elsewhere	75%	25%
First serial	90–100%	10–0%
Second serial, book club, audio, and most other rights	50%	50%

DEFINING "NET" • Some publishers pay the author's share of rights income out of "net revenues/receipts/income." Make sure you know what "net" means in your contract, so you won't be shocked when your share is reduced by agency commissions or other charges.

The Delivery-of-Manuscript Clause

The delivery-of-manuscript clause is the single most important and most misunderstood clause in the contract. And it causes more anguish, in our experience, than all the other clauses combined. The clause consists of several elements:

- A description of the work the author is to deliver
- The date the author is to deliver the work
- A statement of what happens if the author doesn't deliver the work at all, on time, or to the publisher's satisfaction

A typical clause reads like this one:

> Delivery of Manuscript. The Author shall deliver to the Publisher two complete, clean, typewritten copies of the Work, ready for the printer, in form and content satisfactory to the Publisher, no later than September 1, 20__. If

the Author fails to deliver the manuscript as this paragraph requires, the Publisher may terminate this Agreement, and the Author shall immediately repay to the Publisher any and all sums already paid to the Author by the Publisher, and shall not be free to publish the Work elsewhere until such sums have been repaid.

Delivery Date

The manuscript delivery date is extremely important to both the writer and the publisher. If an author fails to deliver a manuscript on time, the publisher has the right, under many contracts, to terminate the contract and insist that the writer return any advances already paid. At the very least, a confrontation about a seriously late manuscript causes bad feelings. At the worst, it can turn into a financial disaster for a writer unable to return an advance.

In agreeing to a delivery date, be realistic and responsible to yourself and to your publisher. Acknowledge to yourself when you're negotiating the contract that your book may take more time to write than you plan. Never sign a contract with an unreasonably short delivery date just to be sure you clinch the deal, when you know you can't fulfill your commitment. And understand that publishers face real deadlines. There are catalogs to print, trade shows to plan for, promotion and advertising campaigns to construct, sales to be made and honored, and work schedules to devise. All of these are designed to sell your book. If you ignore your delivery responsibilities, the entire plan must be rescheduled, a major irritant to your publisher, likely to add to the cost of publishing and selling your book. It may make the publisher less enthusiastic about your book when it finally does show up—or it may forfeit the book's publication.

On the other hand, editors who propose an uncomfortably early delivery date may well accept a later one. And despite a firm contract delivery date, some publishers do not insist that an author stick rigorously to the delivery date if there is a good reason to be late. But you can't count on this liberal treatment. It's especially important to keep your publisher informed if you know you're going to be late. If your editor agrees to a new delivery date, get it in writing, as a modification of your publishing contract (see page 8 on how to modify contracts).

Satisfactory Manuscript

A publisher faces a dilemma. When it signs a publishing agreement to acquire the right to publish a book, the book often doesn't yet exist. The decision to acquire the book is based on a proposal that describes the book and includes a couple of sample chapters.[4] The author may not complete the book for months, even years, after the parties sign the publishing agreement. Because the publisher can't be sure the author will write a publishable book, most publishing contracts contain a ticking time bomb for the author that requires delivery of a manuscript "satisfactory in form and content." Usually a part of the delivery-of-manuscript clause discussed just above, it typically reads:

1.   The Author shall deliver two complete typewritten copies of the Work on or before July 1, 20___, *satisfactory in form and content to the Publisher.*

Sometimes the clause expressly allows the publisher to exercise "its sole judgment" in determining whether the manuscript is satisfactory. Sometimes the words "in form and content" are omitted, making the publisher's power to reject or accept even more broad.

This clause is the publisher's nearly foolproof exit from your contract if it decides at some later time that you haven't done your job, or that the book, no matter how well written, is no longer publishable. The clause allows the publisher to reject a finished manuscript as "unsatisfactory" for any "good faith" reason. Good faith reasons include the publisher's feeling that the manuscript is poorly written or researched, or would cost too much or take too much time to revise into publishable form; that publication might subject the publisher to a lawsuit for defamation; or that there's something else, not so well defined, that legitimately causes the publisher to resist publication.

Isn't this sort of open-ended clause seriously unfair to authors? Doesn't it potentially allow an unscrupulous or uncommitted publisher to escape from a valid contract even when the manuscript submitted is excellent? Of course. The satisfactory-in-form-and-content clause has done more to convince generations of authors that publishing contracts are inherently unfair, one-sided instruments, designed to oppress them, than has any other aspect of the publishing transaction. Nevertheless, most publishers wouldn't delete it even if William Shakespeare rose from his grave in the Stratford churchyard tomorrow and appeared in their office with a proposal for *Hamlet II: The Ghost Returns.*

An author can reduce—but not eliminate—the adverse impact of this clause by adding a few words that obligate the publisher to ask the author to make specific changes if the manuscript is unsatisfactory, or

---

4.   Novelists without a successful record of producing books that sell usually must submit a complete manuscript, but the clause is equally applicable to them because the manuscript more likely than not will require revision. It won't be accepted until the revisions are done.

even to retain another writer to make these changes at a reasonable fee. And some contracts allow the author to retain any advances already received from a publisher when a project is found to be unsatisfactory. A variant of this approach is to allow the author to delay repayment until another publisher picks up the project and provides an advance, the so-called first-proceeds clause.

Here's the way such a modified clause might look:

> 2. Author shall deliver to Publisher on or before July 1, 20__ two complete copies of the Work, double-spaced and typewritten, ready for the printer. The Work shall be approximately 500 typewritten pages in length. The manuscript of the Work must be satisfactory in form and content to the Publisher. If, within ninety days after receiving the manuscript, Publisher notifies Author that the manuscript is unsatisfactory, Author shall have thirty days after receiving that notice within which to make those changes Author believes are required. If those changes do not render the manuscript satisfactory, or if Author fails to make such changes in the time provided, this agreement shall be terminated by Publisher's notice to Author and Author shall repay any sums advanced hereunder out of the first proceeds of any subsequent sale of the Work.

This clause can be further improved by limiting the publisher's right to reject the manuscript for market reasons:

> 3. The manuscript of the Work must be satisfactory in form and content to the Publisher, *but may not be rejected because of changes in the market for the Work.*

The recommended language from the Authors Guild[5] trade book contract is much more complicated and somewhat more favorable to the author. The Authors Guild provision extends the time of delivery if the author is slowed by "illness, accident, or military service." Once the manuscript has been delivered, the publisher must notify the author within sixty days, in writing, "of the respects in which Publisher maintains the manuscript of the Work is not, in style and content, professionally competent and fit for publication." The author then has sixty days to cure the problems, with the publisher's "written editorial assistance." If the publisher remains unsatisfied, it may terminate the con-tract, by written notice, and require the author to repay an agreed portion of any advance, but only from another advance received from another publisher.

The first sample clause (the publisher's version) implicitly allows the publisher to reject your manuscript for a "good faith" reason, as we

---

5.   The Authors Guild, Inc., is located at 330 W. 42nd Street, New York, NY 10036. The organization provides a great deal of support to its members through its model contracts and informative newsletters and reports.

mentioned above. The Authors Guild provision requires the publisher to meet a somewhat more stringent standard of reasonableness. Despite the absence of a definition of what is professionally competent and fit for publication, the Authors Guild clause clearly requires more of the publisher than an exercise of good faith.

What happens if a publisher rejects a manuscript without justification? Courts have most often sided with publishers when authors have challenged publisher discretion under the satisfactory-in-form-and-content clause. Occasionally, a court or an arbitrator has permitted an author to keep the advance, if the author has worked diligently and for a long time preparing a manuscript that seems sound. More often, however, the author has been compelled to return the advance, either at once or when he later sells the book to another publisher (an obligation stated in the first-proceeds clause, requiring the author to repay the advance out of the first money he receives from the later sale).

You can take some practical steps to prevent your publisher from pulling the plug after one year's work, or two, or three:

- Correspond with your editor regularly, and provide opportunities for the editor to express enthusiasm for your work, in writing, as you submit it. A file full of praise for the quality of your manuscript will help you establish that the publisher's last-minute decision to reject was made in bad faith.
- Ask your editor to tell you in writing if the work presents problems of quality or marketability. If it does, ask for guidance in making changes. Involve your editor in the revision process and document that involvement with letters.

Evidence that your publisher thinks your work is good throughout the process of writing—or evidence that the publisher didn't allow you a chance to cure problems—will make it easier for you to insist on keeping your advance if the publisher pulls the plug. But in the last analysis, you can't do much to protect against the publisher's sudden loss of enthusiasm for your book. This is true even if the decision to reject your manuscript has little or nothing to do with your work and a great deal to do with your editor's move to a rival publishing house two blocks down Fifth Avenue.

The first-proceeds clause, which requires that you return the portion of the advance paid you if the publisher rejects the manuscript, is your best protection against utter financial disaster. You may not be paid more for writing your book, but at least you won't have to mortgage the homestead to repay the advance. Not all publishers offer a first-proceeds clause, although they will add one to the contract on request. Some refuse outright, insisting on their right to repayment, no matter what the hardship for the author, no matter how hard he worked to comply with the contract. And some add a twist: the author is obligated to pay back the advance out of first proceeds but must use his best efforts to sell the work for a year. If he's unsuccessful, then he's obligated to pay at the end of the year.

The Front-and-Back-Matter-and-Illustrations Clause

Usually, a publishing contract makes the author responsible for providing all illustrations, introductions, forewords, tables of contents, and indexes, at the author's expense.

Indexing isn't cheap. A professional indexer may charge $500, $750, or even more for a book-length manuscript.

The cover illustration should be the publisher's responsibility, not the author's. Interior illustrations can cost very little or a great deal, depending on their kind, quality, and number. If the publisher wants to add decorative illustrations to your book, negotiate for the publisher to pay for them. If the illustrations are editorial—that is, if they are a necessary part of the content of the book—you may be able to get the publisher to cover some of the costs. You may have to pay an artist or a photographer for original illustrations, or you may need to pay permissions fees for the right to use material that already exists (see Chapter 7 for a discussion of permissions).

You can ask for a grant, money that you needn't repay, to obtain illustrations. Bargaining for at least a partial production grant should especially be considered when costs are likely to be large—when a book needs many charts, illustrations, or photographs, for example. But your publisher is more likely to advance the money for indexes and illustrations if it has the right to deduct these costs from eventual royalties (see page 36 for more on advances).

NOTE ON PRODUCTION GRANTS • Don't expect or demand a production grant unless you have special production needs. With book production costs already high and climbing, publishers are unlikely to be sympathetic to authors who make unreasonable demands. But if you have special problems, state them clearly when you negotiate your contract. For example, if you plan to write a cookbook and you need to test a hundred recipes, your food costs may be substantial. Ask for a production grant to help defray them.

Royalties

Royalties Defined

A royalty is a payment based on the sale of your book, the rights to which you have licensed to your publisher by a contract. In other words, in exchange for your granting the publisher the right to publish your work, you are given certain payments. Occasionally (almost always, in the case of a poem or a magazine piece), an author sells rights to a work for a one-time payment, in which case there is no continuing right to receive a royalty. But in the strong tradition of the book publishing business, the publisher calculates the royalty and pays it as a percentage of the cover price or the publisher's income from sales of the book.

How is a royalty computed? Publishers use a variety of formulas. Let's start with trade books (hardbacks and paperbacks sold in bookstores) and mass market books (4" by 7" paperbacks sold principally at newsstands and in supermarkets, drugstores, and airports, usually from wire racks).

To figure royalties under most trade and mass market contracts, multiply the author's royalty percentage by the cover price (sometimes called "suggested retail price" or "list price"). This calculation yields the author's income for each book sold. Then multiply that amount by the number of books sold to determine the dollar amount the author receives. In mathematical terms, the royalty calculation looks like this:

cover price × royalty percentage × number of books sold = author's royalty

As you'll see, the royalties an author actually receives are likely to differ considerably from the results of this simple, straightforward calculation because of complicated royalty schedules, the effect of books returned unsold, and other factors.

One relatively minor but confusing complication is the "freight passthrough" or "freight allowance." This pricing method, used by some publishers, is designed to help booksellers recover the cost of having books shipped to their stores. It works like this: A book that normally would be priced at $14.95 is priced instead at $15.70. The difference is the freight allowance, which the bookstore keeps. You must exclude the freight amount when multiplying the cover price for royalty purposes. In other words, the author receives no royalty on the freight passthrough component of the price, only on the underlying price of the book itself, usually called "invoice price," defined as the retail price less the freight passthrough amount.

EXAMPLE 1, A TRADE BOOK • *Escargot Cooking*, a trade hardcover book, sells 4,000 copies at a retail price of $10.70, including freight passthrough. The passthrough is $.70. Your royalty rate is ten percent. Your royalty per book is ten percent of $10.00, or $1.00. Your royalty income should be $4,000.

EXAMPLE 2, A TEXTBOOK • *Hotel Cooking*, a textbook designed for hotel schools, sells 6,000 copies. One thousand are sold directly by the publisher at the full price of $20, for publisher's net receipts of $20,000. The rest are sold to school bookstores, distributors, and others at a discount of 20 percent off cover price, or $16, for additional publisher's net receipts of $80,000. The total publisher's net receipts are $100,000, and the author's 15 percent royalty rate is multiplied by this amount to calculate the author's royalties: $15,000.

Royalty Rates

Royalty rates depend on the kind of book to which they apply, the book's format, the book's sales, and the success of your negotiations. The royalty rates for trade hardcover books, for example, begin at 10 percent of cover price. As sales increase, so does the royalty rate: to 12½ percent for each copy sold over 5,000 copies, and to 15 percent for each copy sold over 10,000 copies. This pattern of increasing royalties is called "escalation."

Royalty rates for trade paperbacks are commonly lower than those for hardcover trade books. Some publishers offer as little as 6–7 percent, but many are willing to give an author 10 percent, or even more in rare cases, if they really want the book. The royalty rates escalate, but not as dramatically as for hardcover books. If the basic royalty rate is 7 percent, it might climb to 8 percent at 25,000 copies. If the basic royalty rate is 8 percent, it might reach 10 percent at 25,000 copies. Some publishers that specialize in trade paperback books offer more generous royalties, as much as 10 percent rising to 12 percent at, say, 20,000 copies. But because the margin of profit is smaller for trade paperbacks than for hardbound books, the royalty usually is, too.

Mass market paperback royalty rates begin at about 5 percent. Again, the negotiated rate depends on the book and the author. We have seen mass market contracts pay as little as 4 percent of the cover price; others, especially for mass market originals, pay 10 percent or more.

Textbook royalties are calculated on "publisher's gross (or net) receipts" from sales of the book (typically about 60–80 percent of the retail price). Because the price used to figure royalties for textbooks is considerably less than that for trade books, the basic textbook royalty rate often starts at 15 percent, climbing to 18, 20, even 25 percent as sales increase.

Publishers will usually be reasonable in allowing authors larger royalties if sales are strong, because the low initial rate allows the publisher the chance to recover the initial investment in the author's advance, editing, typesetting, graphics, and so on. Once those costs have been recovered, the publisher should be willing to give the author a larger share.

The Many Ways Royalties Are Reduced

Basic royalty rates apply only to regular book sales. The publishing contract also creates a whole structure of royalties for other kinds of sales, and those royalties are always less than those for regular sales. In extreme cases, far fewer than half a book's total sales bring in full regular royalties. Authors and agents pay insufficient attention to these reduced royalty provisions. It's up to you to understand what each contract provision means. When you do, you can bargain to get the most destructive clauses modified.

The Effect of Discounts on Royalties

Trade publishers assign each title a retail price, and most sell them to wholesalers and bookstores at a discount from that retail price. If, for example, a book carries a cover price of $19.95, the publisher may sell it to a bookstore at a discount of 44 percent, or $11.17. These trade discounts range from 20 percent for very small orders (one to five books), to the more typical 40–42 percent for small orders, to as much as 46–50 percent for larger ones. Publishers allow booksellers to mix titles when they order, to take advantage of the larger discount.

Discount schedules have been the subject of much experimentation in the last few years, as bookstores have demanded larger profit margins for the sake of their survival. Freight passthrough pricing, larger discounts in exchange for curtailed return privileges, and a number of other plans, have had an impact on pricing. Generally, though, publisher sales to bookstores are still made at a discount of 40–50 percent from cover price.

The regular royalty rate schedule is tied to publisher's sales at these normal discounts. If the publisher sells books at a larger discount, called an "excess discount," the publisher's profit per book sold diminishes. When that happens, the author's contract usually reduces the author's royalty.

The most common excess discount sale occurs when the publisher uses a wholesaler to distribute its books to the trade. The wholesaler will resell books to stores for nearly the same discount that the publisher offers when it sells directly. The wholesaler makes money by buying books from the publisher for a larger discount. The difference is the wholesaler's income.

Other excess discount sales are those made to the buyer who buys a large quantity of books, much larger than the characteristic sale to a bookstore, as a special sale or to offer as a premium. For example, the International Society of Reptile Fanciers might buy a new dictionary of lizards and make it available at low cost to new members. The premium buyer usually negotiates a better discount on these "special sales," and, as a result, the publisher's per copy profit margin is reduced.

Some publishers treat all excess discount sales alike, reducing the author's royalty rate for all of them. Others distinguish between sales made to wholesalers and those made to premium and special buyers. Most often, the publisher's response is to reduce the royalty rate to about half the full royalty rate. The publisher will sometimes base the excess discount royalty rate on the publisher's "net receipts" from these sales instead of on the cover price of the books. You can recognize an excess-discount clause from its reduced royalty for certain defined sales. Examples of the breed look like this:

> 1.   The Author shall receive the following royalties: 5 percent of the Publisher's dollar receipts from sales of the regular edition sold in bulk quantity, at special discounts, for premiums and other special sales incentives, to professional groups and industry.

Or this:

> 2.   The Publisher agrees to pay to the Author as follows: On copies sold at a discount of 50 percent or more of the catalog retail price, the prevailing royalty less one-half of 1 percent for each 1 percent discount of more than 49 percent.

The first of these clauses doesn't apply to sales through wholesalers and calculates the royalty on publisher's receipts. Measured by cover price less discount, these receipts will likely be less than half cover price. And the royalty rate is also considerably less than the regular royalty rate, which in this contract was 8 percent.

The second clause covers all excess discount sales, including those to wholesalers, and uses a formula to determine the royalty for excess discount sales. The royalty goes down by one-half percent for each full percent the discount exceeds 49 percent. If the regular royalty rate is 10 percent, a 52 percent discount reduces it by 1½ percent to 8½ percent.

Because books sold to bookstores through wholesalers reach the same ultimate buyers at the same purchase price as books the publisher sells directly to bookstores, and because the publisher saves money by not having to fulfill orders from its own warehouse with its own staff, there is a strong argument that wholesale sales shouldn't reduce royalties. Many publishers don't penalize royalties for sales through wholesalers, no matter how big the discount; they apply the clause only to premium or special sales, outside normal trade channels. Others limit the effect of the clause by applying it to a stated maximum percentage of books sold, perhaps 20 percent.

If the contract provides that you will be paid a percentage of the publisher's net receipts, make sure the term *net receipts* is defined. Make sure, too, that only direct costs of sale (for example, commissions) are deducted from the publisher's gross receipts to calculate its net. You shouldn't be paying part of your publisher's overhead by way of a deduction from your royalty base.

EXAMPLE • Consider the mythical case of *The Great Big Book of Shrimp*, a regional cookbook with modest sales until the Universal Shrimpers Association decided to make it a promotional premium given to fish markets coast-to-coast. The publisher shipped 50,000 trade paperback copies in a year, for $2 each. The author's contract carried a basic royalty rate of 8 percent, escalating to 10 percent at sales of 20,000 copies, based on a suggested retail list price of $7.95. "Whoopee," exulted the author. "It's jumbo prawns from now on!" Then he read the special-sales clause. Unfortunately for him, the royalty on special sales was fixed at 10 percent of the publisher's net receipts, for a royalty of $10,000, not the $36,570 that would have been payable for normal retail sales. The result: one more year of imitation crab.

SMALL-PRESS WARNING • If you are dealing with a small publishing house, you should review the details of any discounted royalty provision with particular care. Most publishing companies with gross sales of less than $1,000,000 or so don't have their own salespeople or commissioned reps. This means they rely heavily on wholesalers such as Bookpeople, The Distributors, Ingram, Pacific Pipeline, Book Carrier, Publisher's Group West, and many others; and they sell a high percentage of their books at a discount of more than 50 percent. So a nominal 10 percent royalty may end up being little more than half the royalty you expect. But some trade publishers, and most textbook and professional book publishers, don't base royalties on cover or invoice price. Instead they pay royalties on the money they receive from the sale of books, which they call publisher's gross receipts, publisher's actual receipts, publisher's cash receipts, or publisher's net receipts (if certain costs of sale are deducted). Royalties based on these publisher's receipts are not paid on the cover price unless a book is sold for full price. More often, royalties are based on the wholesale price the publisher gets from a bookstore or distributor. To figure the royalty, you must multiply the aggregate amount the publisher receives by the royalty rate.

NOTE ON EXPORT SALES • If your publisher is likely to sell significant quantities of your book abroad, pay special attention to the contract provision that sets royalties for these sales. It usually sets them at about half the royalty you'd expect. The publisher faces special problems when exporting books (customs duties, for example), but some publishers nevertheless find it more profitable to export books (especially to English-reading countries) than to sell a license for publication there.

Limitation of Royalties—the Spreadforward

Some authors agree with their publisher to limit royalties to a stated amount each year, no matter how much their books earn, by a device called "royalty spreadforward." The ostensible reason is to prevent royalty income generated by a best-selling book from driving the author into a higher tax bracket. We should all have such problems.

No matter what your tax position, you are almost always better off taking your earnings and solving your own tax problems than allowing your publisher to hold the funds for you. When you're earning enough for this issue to matter, you'll also be able to pay for first-rate tax advice. Be sure to discuss any sort of deferred compensation deal with your tax advisor, lawyer, or accountant before agreeing to it. Our advice, in general, is to take every penny you can get, as fast as you can get it. Here's what happened to one wildly successful author who didn't. Nancy Friday agreed with her publisher to limit royalties to $25,000 a year, although her books, such as *My Mother, My Self* and *A Secret Garden*, have sold millions of copies. She brought suit to set aside that provision of her contract. In the meantime, her publisher had the use of thousands of dollars that belong to Ms. Friday, who essentially made a large, interest-free loan to her publisher.

Returns

The publishing industry has traditionally been one of the few where the manufacturer (the publisher) will take back unsold merchandise for full credit. Recently, some publishers have restricted or eliminated the right of bookstores to return merchandise, offering instead a higher discount rate. But for most publishers, some sort of return privilege is still the rule.

The publishing contract usually provides for an author's royalty payments to be figured "less returns." These two words mean that the publisher need not pay a royalty on books sold to booksellers if those copies are later returned because they failed to sell. How do returns affect payments to authors? The publisher is always afraid that if royalties are paid on the basis of books shipped, large quantities of unsold books may be returned months later. In theory, this would give the publisher the right to ask the author to return royalty payments already made, because what looked like sales turned out not to be. We say "in theory" because, not surprisingly, publishers are wary about an author's ability or willingness to reimburse overpaid royalties. To deal with this problem before it occurs, publishers withhold part of the author's royalties from the start. The withheld royalties are called a "reserve against returns." Some contracts specify the percentage the publisher may withhold, which can be as high as 35 or even 50 percent. Others allow the publisher a "reasonable reserve." The industry average on returns is about 15–25 percent of trade books shipped, somewhat higher for mass market paperbacks. Front-list books (those just published for the first time) tend to produce higher returns than back-list books with a proven sales history. It isn't wise to sign a contract with an unspecified reserve, or one much larger than industry averages, although some entirely reputable publishers won't negotiate a ceiling on the size of the reserve. Negotiations should be based on the kind of book and the rate of returns for similar books.

The reserve-against-returns provision of your contract should also restrict the reserve to a specific period of time. This is particularly sensible when you understand that most publishers allow bookstores to return books for only a limited period. The return period varies with the type of book, anywhere from a few months to a year or more. Unfortunately, if you have no language to the contrary it may take months—or even years—before the publisher is ready to pay royalties out of the reserve account. In a world where money is perennially tight, a few publishers are unwilling to release money until they absolutely must. This sort of abuse is inexcusable, but it does occur. Therefore, be sure to insist that the publisher credit you for all accumulated, unused reserves in the third accounting period after the reserved royalties were earned. That means the publisher has a year to ship the books and determine whether they stay sold, and several months more to pay you. A fair clause reads as follows:

> Publisher may establish a reserve against returns based on the returns history of the Work but not to exceed 20 percent of amounts earned through normal retail sales, and shall pay Author any royalties reserved but not applied to returns with the payment due for the third royalty accounting period after the reserved royalties have accrued.

The Advance

Because publishers know that authors need money to live on while writing, they are often willing to pay authors some portion of royalties long before the manuscript is finished. These payments are called "advances." The payment of advances is usually scheduled in the contract, which means that the publisher pays them in installments. Here are two typical advance schedules:

> The advance shall be paid one-third upon signing the publishing contract, one-third upon acceptance of the completed manuscript, and one-third upon publication.

> Author shall be paid her advance one-half when this contract is signed and one-half when she delivers a satisfactory, complete manuscript of the Work to Publisher.

An experienced writer who knows that long delays—often one, two, or even three years—may occur between submission of the manuscript and publication will negotiate to get the largest possible share of the advance before publication. On the other hand, in this era of the blockbuster book and advances big enough to be front page news, publishers negotiate the payment of advances in a number of smaller portions, the last of which may not be payable until a year after publication! The larger the advance, the more likely the publisher will insist on this approach.

Advances are almost always *nonreturnable*, but they are almost always *recoupable*. Understanding the difference between these terms is crucial.

The publisher that pays a recoupable advance assumes the risk that the book (once accepted for publication) will never earn back its advance. Here's how it works. Money the author receives as an advance is his to keep no matter how many books are sold. However, the author doesn't get more money until his earnings from royalties and subsidiary rights income equal the amount of the advance. Thus, if Arthur Author writes a book for a $10,000 advance, and the royalty rate is 10 percent of the $9.95 cover price, his book must sell 10,051 copies before he is entitled to any further payment.

A large advance is almost always better than a small one. It's money in hand now, not a promise of future payment. And in addition to relieving financial pressure on the author, it establishes the publisher's substantial investment in your book. In an age when publishers pump out too many books, editors change from company to company willy-nilly, and whole companies pass from one conglomerate to another, the fact that a publisher has made a substantial initial investment in your book can mean the difference between an active sales and promotion effort and an unsupported, sink-or-swim release of your work. (See Chapter 12 for many ways to help your publisher promote your book and to do some effective promotion of your own.)

Joint Accounting

A joint-accounting clause allows the publisher to use money an author earns from one book published by that publisher to pay back money the author owes the publisher from another book. It pools all the author's advances and debts, and offsets them with all the author's income from any books published by his publisher.

Suppose you publish two books (or more) with the same publisher. And suppose you were paid an advance of $15,000 for your first book, which earned back only $5,000. Your second book, for which you also received a $15,000 advance, has just made the *New York Times* bestseller list. With trembling hands, you open your first royalty statement, anticipating the heady feeling of having enough money to dine at a restaurant with tablecloths. Don't be too quick to order pheasant under glass, however. If your publishing contract contains a joint-accounting provision, those lovely royalties from your second book will repay the unearned advance of $10,000 from the first book, before they begin to cover the $15,000 advance for book number two. You'll be ingesting Big Macs for a while longer.

Some joint-accounting clauses are straightforward:

> All monies from this Work shall be accounted for jointly with any monies earned under any other agreement between Publisher and Author.

Others are not; they look like this:

> If the Work has not earned the amount of royalties advanced, or if there are sums owing to Publisher under this or any other Agreement between Author and Publisher, Publisher may deduct the same from any sum due Publisher under this *or any other agreement* with Author.

The joint-accounting signal is "or any other agreement." Even if the clause doesn't contain the words *joint accounting,* the effect is to pool income and deductions. The signal words may appear in many places throughout the agreement, so search them out with care wherever money is involved in a clause.

Joint accounting is too big a burden on an author to be acceptable in any publishing contract. Predictably, many publishers disagree, because the effect of joint accounting is to reduce the publisher's financial risk. Despite its obvious attraction for publishers, most are willing to delete joint accounting provisions on request. Some will compromise, insisting on the power to tap any source of income to repay the author's debts to the publisher, such as the cost of books purchased by the author, but giving up joint accounting for advances. The compromise means that one book's earnings can't be used to repay the unearned advance for another. For most authors, this solution is acceptable.

The Revision Clause

The Burden of Revision

Publishers often insist that an author promise to revise certain types of books when and if the publisher thinks it necessary. Of course, for educational and other topical sorts of books, such as this one, regular revisions are essential.

Publishers usually resist paying authors for the additional work of a revision, figuring if the book is selling well enough to justify redoing, the author ought to be delighted with continuing royalties and not demand more. However, a publisher that wants to keep a work in print may be willing to negotiate an additional advance for revisions and sometimes even to pay a small amount of money for an author's out-of-pocket expenses, which need not be reimbursed out of royalties.

At the very least, it's important for an author of topical material to pay attention to the revision issue. Think about how much you're willing to be burdened with revising your book, and set some sort of reasonable maximum as part of the contract. One way to do this is to bargain to limit the page count of revisions to a stated percentage of the text. Or you can insist on a contract provision that regulates the interval between revisions.

A typical revisions clause reads:

> If the Publisher determines that a revision is desirable, it shall request the Author to prepare the revision and the Author shall advise the Publisher within ninety days whether he or she will do so. If the Author is unwilling or unable to prepare the revision within a reasonable time, the Publisher may arrange with others for the preparation of the revision and to share the Author's royalties with the revisers.

Language to set limits on the publisher's rights reads:

> The Publisher may not request a revision sooner than two years after publication of the then-current edition of the Work. The Publisher shall pay the Author an additional advance against royalties to be negotiated in good faith having regard for the extent, complexity, and research required for the revision, if it will exceed 20 percent of the text of the then-current edition of the Work.

The Benefits of Revision

Authors sometimes feel unfairly harassed by the necessity to revise a book. More commonly, however, they find their interests compromised by their publisher's failure to revise material. For example, a local author wrote a self-help book that sold 35,000 copies out of a print run of 40,000. By this time, the book was seriously out-of-date and its sales had sharply diminished. The author wanted to revise, feeling certain that the book would sell as well as ever if it were current. The publisher, who wanted to hold onto remaining inventory until it was sold out, refused, basing the refusal on the lack of a contract provision requiring regular revisions. The publisher also refused to restore rights to publish the book to the author, apparently reasoning that since the book was still selling a little, some income was better than none.

If you are worried about a publisher failing to revise topical material (and you should be if you aren't), one way to prevent trouble is to demand that a book be regarded as out-of-print (see page 58) if the publisher is not willing to publish a revised edition within a certain time, measured from initial publication. One author we work with got a major house to accept a provision saying that if the publisher failed to publish a revised edition within three years of initial publication, rights would revert to the author. Another approach gives the publisher a set period of time, say six or nine months, to agree to publish a revised edition after a written request from the author. This request can't ordinarily be made until at least two years after initial publication. If the publisher refuses the author's request, rights revert to the author.

Cumulative Sales of Revised Editions

Do all you can to make certain you don't lose the benefit of the royalty escalation clause when a revised edition is published. This is a particularly insidious example of how the fine print of a publisher's contract can take income out of an author's pocket. Here's how it happens. The revision clause says:

| Sales of copies of revised editions are not cumulative.

or

| The provisions of this agreement shall apply to each revision of the Work as though that revision were the Work being published for the first time under this agreement.

These rather obscure words allow the publisher to start counting sales of the revised edition over again for royalty purposes, as if it had never sold a copy of the original edition, even though the contract contains an escalation clause. The result is that the royalty rate reverts to its lowest level every time a new edition is published. Note the irony: Author (and publisher) work hard to make the book more saleable, and when their efforts bear fruit, the publisher pays royalties as if the book had never previously been published and sold successfully! Fight hard to avoid signing a contract that requires revisions and contains an escalation of royalties clause unless you also get a clause that accumulates all sales for royalty purposes

Recently we worked with an author who almost swallowed a "noncumulative" provision for a book that will almost certainly have to be revised every two years. The author successfully insisted that the publisher allow frequent revisions because the book deals with financial markets and investments, and rapidly changing economic conditions will surely make it of small value if not updated. He accepted a rather modest initial royalty rate but bargained for a generous escalation clause that called for a royalty rate of 15 percent when sales exceeded 15,000 copies. Delighted, he called us to relay the good news. When we pointed out that because the contract had a clause saying that royalties for each edition were "not cumulative," and each revised edition would start his royalty rate at the lowest rung of the ladder, his delight rapidly faded. Fortunately, he went back to the bargaining table and was able to convince the publisher that revisions would sell lots of books without imposing significant production costs on the publisher. The publisher eliminated the noncumulative-royalty provision but insisted on a less damaging provision allowing a reduced royalty rate if production costs exceeded an agreed amount.

Here is a sample of contract language that protects an author's interests in a revision situation:

| Sales of revised editions of the Work shall be cumulative for royalty calculation and payment under this agreement.

Editorial Control

If author and publisher agree about the content and style of a book, the question of control never arises. But when they disagree, someone must have the final say to avoid an impasse. Most publishing agreements contain a set of clauses that defines who has the final say about what appears on the printed page. Usually it's the publisher.

Understandably, most writers don't like this sort of open-ended provision, even though they realize, or should realize, that a good editor can do much to make a good manuscript better. Authors fear, often with good reason, that they may end up with a bad editor who insists on making unnecessary changes for all the wrong, "commercial" reasons,

Unfortunately, especially for a writer who is not yet established, it may be impractical to hold out for final editorial control, or even mutual consent to changes. At the very least, however, you should demand that the sense of your work remain unaltered and that the editor consult with you about all changes, including alterations to the title. You'll find most publishers reasonable in negotiating about these problems, as did an author-photographer who cared a great deal about the visual quality of her book. She was worried by the usual language in her publishing contract, giving the publisher an unrestricted right to make all production decisions:

> Publisher shall, in its sole judgment, determine the size, style, quality, and price of the Work, and may make such editorial changes as it deems necessary.

She asked for changes. The publisher was enlightened, and when the author explained that she had a strong design background and that good visual quality was essential to the success of the work, the publisher listened. Author and publisher agreed on certain detailed specifications for the quality of the book and included them in the contract. Quality was so important to the author that even specification of the weight and gloss of the paper stock on which the book was to be printed were included in the contract.

The range of clauses covering editorial control includes the following:

1. Publisher and Author shall consult on questions of style and substance, but the decisions of Publisher shall be final.
2. Publisher and Author shall agree to any changes in the manuscript, and neither shall withhold consent unreasonably.
3. Publisher may make changes in the manuscript so that it conforms to Publisher's house style, but shall otherwise make no changes without Author's approval.

4. Publisher shall make no changes in the manuscript, once accepted in final form, without first obtaining Author's written consent.

Any of these clauses is better than the usual provision giving the publisher complete control over the style and content of the book.

Corrections and Alterations to the Manuscript

There is another important aspect of manuscript alterations customarily covered in a publishing contract: corrections. Once the back-and-forth process of editing the submitted manuscript is done, the publisher will begin the final production process. That process usually requires the author to proofread and correct galley proofs. The author must return the corrected proofs within a short time to help the publisher make the publication schedule.

Occasionally the publisher fails to give the author a chance to read proofs before going to the printer. As if by divine plan, this practice guarantees that the book will contain serious errors that the author would have easily caught. Errors of this kind can jeopardize careers. A scientist of world renown didn't see the galleys for his contributed chapter in a major new textbook because he was in Europe when (months after he submitted his chapter) the galleys were pulled. When he finally saw what had happened to his work, he was appalled to find errors that took him five single-spaced pages to describe. Because his publishing contract required his review of galleys before publication, he could insist that an errata sheet, with a brief but pointed explanation of how the errors occurred, be inserted in every copy of the book in inventory, and that it be sent to each of the thousand peers who had received a review copy of the book.

This instructional tale shows why the author should add an affirmative duty to the publishing agreement, to require the publisher to send galley and page proofs for review:

> The Publisher shall deliver a copy of each galley and final proof of the Work to the Author, who shall promptly return it with his corrections and changes.

By contract, the publisher bears the cost of production, including typesetting. But if the author has second thoughts about the manuscript at the galley stage and wants to do a major rewrite, the cost of the changes, if it exceeds 5 or 10 percent of the total cost of composition (typesetting), is the author's responsibility. Most publishers will charge the cost against the author's royalties. This practice is reasonable. It is expressed in clauses like this one:

> If alterations in the proof are made at the Author's request that cost more than ten percent of the cost of composition, exclusive of the cost of correcting printer's errors, the Author be charged for such costs. The Publisher may, at its option, either charge such costs against the Author's income under this or any other agreement with the Publisher, or bill the Author for them, in which case the Author shall promptly pay them.

The Obligation to Publish

Although publishers traditionally have insisted on the right to decide whether to publish even an acceptable work, the courts have begun to obligate them to do so. In *Zilg v. Prentice-Hall, Inc.*, 717 F.2d 671 (2d Cir 1983), the court opined that a publisher has an implied good faith obligation to publish and promote an accepted manuscript. And Harcourt Brace Jovanovich settled out of court by paying author Deborah Davis a reported $100,000 for refusing to keep her book, *Katharine the Great* (about the chairwoman of the Washington Post Company), in the stores.

Relying on lawsuits, however, makes far less sense than negotiating a contract that obligates the publisher to publish your book reasonably promptly once it has accepted the manuscript. Traditionally, "reasonably promptly" has meant within twelve to eighteen months. However, changes in typesetting and printing technology, as well as improvements in transportation, now make it possible for a publisher to get a book out within a few months (in extreme cases, within a few weeks) after all parties approve a manuscript. For certain kinds of books, speed is obviously of the essence.

Accordingly, you should insist on a contract provision that binds the publisher to have books ready to ship within a reasonable time after acceptance of the manuscript. What's reasonable depends on the size and editorial difficulty of the book, the size of the publisher's staff, and the way the book fits into the seasons of publishing. Small publishers are often far more flexible than are large houses, many of which plan lists of new books over a year in advance.

If the publisher fails to publish within the contractual time limit, most agreements require the author to demand in writing that the publisher publish the book; the publisher then has six months, typically, to do so. It's far better for the author to have the right to terminate the agreement and take back all rights granted to the publisher, without further delay.

Many clauses also restrict the author's compensation for the publisher's failure to publish, usually to any money (the advance and grants, if any) already paid. If no such restriction existed, the author could sue the publisher for breach of contract, and a successful author might win substantial damages if he could show that the delay cost him a provable loss. But most houses won't modify an agreement to delete or narrow this limitation on the author's recovery.

Here's an example of an acceptable clause:

> Publisher agrees to publish the Work, and to make it available for distribution through normal retail outlets, no later than twelve months after accepting the manuscript. If Publisher fails to do so, Author may demand in writing that it be done within thirty (30) days. If Publisher fails to comply, Author may immediately terminate this agreement and all rights granted hereunder shall revert to Author. Author shall keep any money paid him under this agreement but shall be entitled to no further payments.

Publicity and Promotion

Most books don't just sell; they have to be sold. The publisher's marketing expertise and commitment to use it become supremely important (see Chapter 12). As we discussed earlier in this chapter, one assurance of a publisher's commitment to aggressive marketing is the amount of the author's advance. In some situations, an author may want to gamble and trade a reduced advance for the publisher's larger, explicit commitment to promotion and advertising. There can be merit to this approach. But the author who considers trading upfront money for after-publication promotions should be absolutely sure the publisher really will spend the promotion money on a stated schedule, in agreed-upon ways. If the publisher is willing to make an additional contractual commitment to spend money on publicity and advertising, so much the better.

To mean anything, the marketing commitment should be part of the written contract. Editors often promise much while they court an author, only to change their mind as publication day nears. Early optimism gives way to an understandable reluctance to spend money promoting a book whose advance sales aren't promising. The decision not to promote because sales aren't likely to be strong is even more likely to be a self-fulfilling prophecy. If the publisher refuses to include the marketing commitment in the contract, try instead for a letter from the acquiring editor describing what the house is willing to do. Even a general statement of intentions is better than nothing; it may be useful to embarrass the publisher into doing more than it would otherwise.

If the author has good ideas about ways to market his book, they should become part of the marketing plan. Just binding the publisher tospend a set amount of money may not make much sense. For example, one ad in the *New York Times Book Review* can use up a substantial part of the promotion budget without reaching the audience most likely to buy the book. An author who believes a mailing to every member of a certain special interest group might be more helpful should insist that the publisher's obligation for the mailing be included in the contract. One useful way to negotiate for effective promotion and publicity is for the author to list the specific types of promotion he considers crucial to the success of his book. The author might also want to arrange for review copies to be sent to an extensive list of reviewers. (For some advice about what works, see Chapter 12.) The author should present the plan to the publisher and ask that it be made a part of the contract.

If you succeed in getting the publisher to incorporate a marketing commitment in the publishing agreement, the clause might look like this one:

> Publisher agrees to prepare and mail, at its expense, a flyer describing the Work to all members of the American Stock Breeders Association. Publisher also agrees to send a review copy of the Work to each reviewer named on a list provided by Author, the number of reviewers not to exceed 250. Publisher shall also place at least one quarter-page display ad for the Work in *Stockman*, the official magazine of the American Stock Breeders Association.

Sometimes the problem isn't too little publicity, but too much. Part of the publisher's technique for promoting a book is to use the author's face (if well known, attractive, or expressive), body (through appearances at bookstore signing parties and TV talk shows), and personal history (in press releases). The publishing contract typically gives the publisher these rights. Of course, intensive publicity techniques, including author tours, book-signing parties, and the like, have been known to sell a lot of books. What's more, the application of a little common sense and humanity to a tour schedule can make it a pleasant opportunity to meet interesting people and talk about the book at the publisher's expense. So instead of arguing with your publisher about what you won't do, you might be wise to expend the same energy working out a publicity plan that feels comfortable to both parties. (For some pointers on how to do this, see Chapter 12.) But a shy author, or one who has no wish to be interviewed by people who have barely read the back cover of his book, should negotiate hard for freedom from these burdens. The best way to do this is to include language in the publicity-and-promotion provision of the contract setting forth exactly what the author will and will not be expected to do. An alternative is to require mutual consent to promotion. These sample clauses show how:

1.   Author grants Publisher the right to use Author's name, likeness, and biographical information to promote the Work. Author shall make himself reasonably available for promotional and marketing activities to benefit the Work, the travel, food, and lodging expense of which shall be borne entirely by Publisher. Publisher shall arrange a ten-city tour for Author to promote the Work, to cover the following major markets and others to be determined by Publisher: New York, Chicago, Atlanta, Dallas, Los Angeles, and San Francisco. The schedule for that tour shall be designed to minimize any disruption in Author's professional life.

2.   The Publisher and the Author shall plan and execute promotional activity for the Work by mutual consent. Such activity shall be at the Publisher's sole expense.

NOTE FOR ACADEMIC WRITERS ON THE TEXTBOOK/TRADE BOOK MARKETING PROBLEM • Most publishers who publish both textbooks and trade books draw a strong, often complete distinction between the two categories, creating entirely separate editorial, distribution, and marketing organizations for each. That's fine, unless you happen to write a textbook with prospects for a broad, popular market. We struggled on behalf of one such client—unsuccessfully—who discovered commercial promise in her work-in-progress after she'd signed a textbook contract. Neither she nor we could convince her publisher that the contract should be rewritten to allow for trade book treatment. The consequence was the loss of the chance to sell many more copies at half again as high a royalty. If you think your book belongs in both the text and trade categories, choose a house that publishes both (or books that are sold in both markets, although not identified exclusively as either), and prepare for difficult negotiations.

Author's Copies

Most publishing contracts contain a clause stating how many complimentary copies an author is entitled to receive for personal use. By custom, the author is offered a number of free copies, usually ten, for personal use, not resale. Most houses will gladly increase the number of author's copies: twenty to fifty for a trade book and fifty or more for mass market paperbacks. Ask for copies of each edition of the work; some agreements limit the giveaways to the first edition.

If you decide that you'd like to send copies to reviewers and other opinion-makers, your publisher might be willing to accept a list of recipients and handle this task for you, without taxing your supply of free copies.

More important to some authors, especially those who lecture, put on workshops, or run their own mail-order business, is the price at which they can buy additional copies for resale. This purchase price should be set in the contract. You may or may not get royalties on these copies. Standard clauses often allow an author no more than a 40 percent discount, without royalty. You can probably do better. If you receive royalties on books you buy for resale, your price should be the best price regularly available to booksellers (usually 40–50 percent below retail list, depending on the quantity purchased). If the discount follows the schedule for trade accounts, these books—bought, after all, not given away—should carry a full royalty. But if you negotiate a clause that gives you an extremely generous discount (say, 55–65 percent), don't be greedy and expect royalties on books you sell yourself, at a profit.

From the publisher's point of view, it is reasonable to ask that you not compete unfairly in the same markets served by bookstores or other outlets.

Here's a usual clause:

> The Publisher shall give to the Author ten free copies of the first edition of the Work on publication, and the Author shall have the right to purchase copies for personal use, but not for resale, at a discount of 40 percent of the retail catalog price. Such purchases shall be paid for within thirty days after the date of the Publisher's invoice to the Author, or may be charged against the Author's royalty account, at Publisher's option.

And here's a clause much more beneficial to the author:

> Publisher shall provide Author twenty-five free copies of each edition of the Work on publication, for his own use. If Author provides Publisher a list, not to exceed fifty names, of persons whose receipt of a copy of the Work would benefit its sale, Publisher at its own expense shall send a copy to each such person. Author may purchase additional copies of the Work at the normal trade discount for resale at his workshops, seminars, and other public appearances, but shall not dispose of them through normal wholesale or retail outlets. Publisher may either invoice Author for copies purchased for resale, or charge their cost against Author's royalty account under this or any other agreement with Publisher.

Note that this is one instance when joint accounting (see page 37) is justified.

The Free-Goods Clause

Your publisher will want the right to send out free books as review copies and to provide booksellers bonus or promotional copies for orders of a certain size. Normally, the contract allows the publisher to do so without paying royalties on free goods. This practice is almost always reasonable, and, for obvious reasons, publishers don't abuse the right. If you are concerned about giveaways, however, you should be able to limit the number of or purpose for free books in the contract, by asking for the second of these sample clauses:

1. On copies furnished free to Author, or for review, sample, or promotion of the Work, no royalties shall be paid.

2. No royalties shall be paid on copies of the Work given away to the Author, or for sales promotional use not to exceed 500 copies.

Some publishers throw in free copies of one book to promote sales of another. For the author's full protection, the second clause above could be modified to read:

2. No royalties shall be paid on copies of the Work given away to the Author, or for sales promotional use *to benefit the Work* not to exceed 500 copies.

Permissions

The publisher's contract usually makes the author responsible for arranging for permission to use material that belongs to someone else:

Author shall deliver the manuscript, including all illustrations, charts, tables, indexes, *permissions, and consents for use*, no later than_____, 20___.

The author's responsibility includes financial responsibility if a legal problem ensues; see page 49, "Warranties and Indemnities."

Generally speaking, permission must be obtained for all material still under copyright, although occasionally you may be able to use short excerpts from another person's work under the "fair use" doctrine (see Chapter 9). Resting this responsibility on the author makes sense. The author, after all, is the one who knows best what material he has borrowed. If a particular permission proves hard to get, publishers will sometimes help. But it's important to realize that the publisher's voluntary assistance doesn't relieve the author of legal responsibility.

Because no prudent publisher will publish a work until all permissions are in hand, it is best to obtain them early. If doing this is likely to be a problem, and you want the publisher's help, discuss the matter during negotiations and be sure the publisher's obligations are clearly stated in your contract. For example, you might want to add language like this to the standard permissions clause:

> Publisher shall use reasonable efforts to obtain permission to use excerpts not exceeding ten lines from songs published in *The Beatles Songbook*, for use in the Work, from the owner or owners of those rights, but Author shall be responsible for any payments required to obtain those rights. Publisher shall advance any such payments and may charge those amounts paid against Author's royalties under this agreement.

Most publishers will supply permission forms that they expect you to use. Some will provide you with a kit, containing forms, instructions, and suggestions for how to proceed (see Appendix E for a typical kit). Take your publisher's advice seriously; it's likely to be based on long experience in dealing with rights and permissions.

Warranties and Indemnities

An author's warranties and representations are statements of fact and promises. They are of special legal importance. In most publishing agreements, the author warrants and represents that he has all the rights necessary to bring the work to the public without interfering with anyone else's rights. Some contracts require the author to preserve his notes and working papers, including tape recordings, for a period of time after first publication, and to make those materials available to the publisher if the need arises.

Usually, the warranty clause includes provisions like these:

> The Author warrants and represents that he is the sole author of the Work and owns all the rights granted to the Publisher under this agreement; that he has the full power to execute the agreement; that the Work has not been published in any form; that the Work will not infringe any copyright or other proprietary right, including the right to privacy, or to be free of libel; that he has obtained all permissions necessary for publication of the Work; and that the Work contains no recipe or instructions that are injurious to any person.

The author's indemnities constitute the author's promises to pay the publisher for any loss caused by the author's breach of his warranties. In most contracts, indemnification includes a promise to pay to defend claims falling within the warranty, even if groundless.

Indemnity clauses resemble this one:

> Author shall indemnify Publisher, its officers, employees, agents, licensees, and assigns, and hold them harmless, against all loss, damage, injury, and expense, including attorney's fees, arising out of or in connection with any

claim, demand, action, or proceeding for any actual or alleged breach of Author's warranties and representations hereunder. Publisher may withhold the amount of any such claim from amounts owing Author under this or any other agreement with Publisher until such claim, demand, action, or proceeding is finally resolved. Author shall cooperate fully in the defense of any such claim, demand, action, or proceeding, and may retain counsel of his own choosing, at his sole expense.

If someone makes a claim of infringement of copyright or defamation against the author and the publisher based on publication of the contents of the work, the indemnity clause usually puts the entire financial burden on the author. It also frequently leaves control over legal defense or settlement of the action to the publisher. The author can wind up owing the publisher the amount of a court judgment or negotiated settlement even when he doesn't agree with the publisher's defense strategy. What's worse, the author may even be responsible for legal defense costs for claims that are obvious phonies. Worst of all, the publisher may have the right (as in the sample clause above) to withhold all the author's royalty earnings until a legal claim is resolved, whether or not the claim is for an amount as large as the accumulated earnings.

Some publishers attempt to justify these Draconian measures on the theory that since only the author can know whether he has wronged another, the author should bear the entire burden. That theory ignores the fact that the publisher is in the business of publishing, and part of the risk of this business is the obvious risk of infringing on another's rights. For this reason, some publishers don't invoke the indemnity provision, even if they have the legal right to, except in extreme circumstances.

What can an author do to negotiate a more equitable warranties-and-indemnities clause? First, ask for a contract provision that limits financial liability to claims determined to be valid by a final court judgment or by a settlement agreement to which he agrees. If a claim is unfounded, the contract should make the publisher responsible for the entire expense of dealing with it (or at least, half the cost). In addition, the contract should provide that a publisher can withhold royalties only in an amount reasonably sufficient to satisfy a claim that is reasonably likely to be found valid. What's more, the author should have a good deal to say about the way any claim is defended, including the choice of lawyer and the terms of any settlement. Keep in mind that this clause is not one the editor can tamper with; the publisher's lawyer wrote it, and the publisher's lawyer will review any author's request that it be softened.

A better indemnity clause is the following:

> Author shall indemnify Publisher, its officers, employees, agents, licensees, and assigns, and hold them harmless, against all loss, damage, injury, and expense, including reasonable attorney's fees, from any breach of Author's warranties and representations hereunder finally determined or settled with Author's consent. Author shall cooperate fully in the defense of any such claim, demand, action, or proceeding, and may retain counsel of his own choosing, at his sole expense.

Publishers can buy defamation and liability insurance for themselves. It's called "publisher's special perils insurance," and it's expensive. Most authors can't afford it. This insurance also carries a high deductible (often $100,000 per claim). The insurance company pays any judgment or settlement against the publisher that exceeds the deductible.

Historically, publishers did not arrange for authors to be protected by this insurance. But in 1982, a major New York house broke new ground by voluntarily including authors under its policy. Since then other publishers have followed. Insurance companies that write this insurance don't charge much, if any, additional premium to include authors. Authors and agents should routinely ask for insurance coverage. Most publishers that carry the insurance will routinely provide it, through a rider attached to the publishing agreement.

The insurance clause is usually not negotiable, and the protection it offers isn't perfect. Although the clause limits the author's liability to the amount of the publisher's loss that isn't covered by insurance, it requires the author to share the deductible, either equally or up to the amount of the advance, or, for a lucky few, up to a stated amount lower than either. It provides that if the aggregate payments under the insurance policy exhaust its coverage (usually several million dollars) in a given year, the author whose liability is established after the insurance is exhausted receives no benefit from it. Despite its imperfections, special perils insurance protects against the possibility of ruinous judgments or settlements. So ask for it, if even a remote chance of an action against you exists.

If your publisher chooses not to buy insurance (many small ones don't), plead that your liability should be no more than the amount of your advance, and less, if possible.

A sample clause incorporating defamation insurance provisions looks like this:

> Publisher shall arrange for Author to be a named insured in each insurance policy insuring Publisher against liability to third parties. Publisher agrees that the proceeds of such insurance shall satisfy Author's obligations to

indemnify, as provided in this agreement, except that Author shall indemnify Publisher up to the lesser of Author's advance or advances made under this agreement, or an amount equal to one-half Publisher's deductible under such policy of insurance in effect at the time this agreement is made, if any claim, action, or proceeding is settled adversely to Publisher, or results in a final judgment against Publisher, based on allegations which, if true, would constitute a breach of Author's warranties under this agreement. If Publisher declines to purchase such insurance, or if the amount of such insurance is insufficient to satisfy any such judgment or settlement, or if the coverage of such insurance is exhausted, Author's liability to Publisher shall be the lesser of Author's advance or advances under this agreement or the sum of $_____. Publisher agrees to provide Author a copy of any such insurance policy, together with any amendments to it which may be made from time to time, and to arrange for Author to be notified of the policy's cancellation at least thirty days in advance. Publisher's agreement under this paragraph shall survive the termination of this agreement.

A good discussion of publisher's liability insurance appears in Stuart Speiser's article, "Insuring Authors: A New Proposal," in *Publishers Weekly*, May 7, 1982, page 26.

Accounting and Payment

In a perfect writer's world, an author would receive the agreed-upon royalty payment immediately every time a copy of his book was sold. In a perfect publisher's world, the publisher would pay the author accumulated royalties about once a decade. Not surprisingly, the real world isn't perfect for either. The compromise most trade publishers adopt is to pay royalties every six months, but a few medium-sized West Coast publishers pay four times a year, and textbook publishers typically pay once a year.

Royalties may be calculated on cover price, stated in the publishing agreement as "suggested retail price," "list price," or "cover price." Or they may be calculated on what the publisher receives for the book: "Publisher's net receipts," "Publisher's actual cash receipts," "Publisher's gross receipts." See page 29 for more about royalties.

Some publishers pay royalties on books sold, which means the publisher—given the long time between shipping books to bookstores and getting paid for them—may not have been paid for all the books for which the author gets royalties. Other publishers pay only when they are paid.

The contract usually obligates the publisher to pay the amount of accumulated royalties earned, but allows the publisher to hold back a reserve against returns (books sold to bookstores or wholesalers, but later returned to the publisher for credit; see page 34, for a discussion of the reserve against returns).

Publishers usually pay their authors 90 or 120 days after the accounting period for which the royalty is calculated. Thus, under most contracts, royalties paid on March 31 of a given year were earned between July 1 and December 31 of the previous year.

The contract may give the author the right to ask for a detailed royalty statement (more detailed than the one the publisher will send if the author doesn't ask). We've suggested amending the contract to require the detailed statement, but savvy editors suggest that the author trigger this obligation with a letter to his editor; the royalty accounting department won't know about your request if you bury it in the contract.

NOTE ON LATE ROYALTIES • Not all publishers are scrupulous about getting royalty checks to you on time. If your contract requires the publisher to pay interest on late payments, there's some incentive to meet its obligations. But the publisher's controller knows that you're not likely to sue if your check is a little late, especially if it's small. The best way to combat this perennial problem is to build even stronger incentives into your contract. You can try to define a material breach of the contract to include late royalty payments, with a brief grace period after which some or all your rights revert to you. Even if the publisher won't accept your proposal, it may provoke a response that improves your chances of getting paid when you're supposed to. For example, you might condition the publisher's exercise of a right of first refusal (see page 62), or of control over subsidiary rights sales (see page 17), on timely royalty payment.

If your contract doesn't contain provisions like these, what can you do to get paid on time?

- Start with your editor. Sometimes the editor's voice, speaking on your behalf, can pry loose a check.
- If you have an agent, borrow some of her clout.
- Try a dignified letter demanding payment (see following page).

If a letter on this model doesn't produce results, you should consider a lawsuit in small-claims court. The maximum you can sue for in small-claims court varies from state to state, but if your claim falls within the limit, this "people's court" is the place to be.

If you're uncomfortable stepping into the toils of the legal system alone, you might ask a lawyer to write a stern, uncompromising letter threatening dire consequences for continued fiscal rebuffs. Make sure,

December 7, 20__
Missoula, Montana

Robert Tardy, Publisher
Tardy Press, Inc.
6500 Park Ave., 13th Floor
New York, NY 10000

Dear Bob,

Through some oversight, you have sent me neither my royalty statement nor my check, both due December 1. I was counting on the check to pay a number of current bills.

Please direct your accounting department to send me the statement and the check immediately. If I haven't received it by December 15, 20____, I'll have to look for help elsewhere. Thanks in advance for your assistance.

Sincerely,

Tom Manly

though, that you and the lawyer reach a clear understanding about the scope and cost of his work. And be aware that unless the amount you're owed is large, measured in the tens of thousands, it probably won't be worthwhile to sue, because lawsuits are incredibly expensive. See Chapter 11 for advice about choosing and using a lawyer.

Audits and Examinations of the Publisher's Books

Sometimes publishers make mistakes when they prepare royalty statements. A few (not many) are dishonest. The author's only hope of verifying whether either of these conditions exists is to examine the publisher's books. Accordingly, every publishing contract should give the author this right. Under most contracts, the author is entitled to one inspection per twelve-month period, must give the publisher reasonable notice, and must perform the examination himself or through a qualified representative (an agent, accountant, or lawyer is qualified). Some publishers grant authors much more generous audit rights, however. And in fairness, we should note that despite more restrictive contract clauses, many publishers will allow their authors almost unlimited reasonable access to the pertinent books, if the author gives reasonable notice and isn't a pest.

A typical clause imposes a time limit on the author's right to sue for a discovered short payment, usually to two years from the time the author receives his royalty statement. Because the law of most states allows a lawsuit for breach of a written contract to be filed anytime within four years, these two-year clauses impair the author's rights significantly. The publisher can't argue that it keeps records for only two years, because income tax law requires a longer retention period.

Every audit clause should state that if the author discovers discrepancies in the publisher's favor of more than a stated percentage—usually 5 percent—the publisher should pick up the cost of the audit. Otherwise, the financial responsibility is entirely the author's, and the cost can be substantial. Recently, publishers have begun to limit their payment for an audit that reveals errors to the amount of the underpayment plus the cost of the audit up to an amount equal to the underpayment.

A typical audit clause, before negotiation, looks like this:

Author may arrange for examination of Publisher's books and records for the sale of books under this agreement by a certified public accountant, not more than once each year, on thirty days' written notice to Publisher, during normal business hours, at Publisher's offices. The examination shall be at Author's sole expense. Author shall make any claim, or initiate any suit thereon, within two years after the receipt of each statement of account hereunder; thereafter, Author shall be deemed to have accepted such statement.

A model audit clause reads:

Author may examine Publisher's books and records having to do with this agreement once a year, on three days' written notice to Publisher. The examination shall take place at Publisher's offices, during normal business hours, and may be conducted by Author or his qualified representative. If the examination reveals discrepancies in Publisher's favor exceeding 5 percent of the payments due on the statements subject to examination, Publisher shall bear the cost of the examination.

The audit provision of most contracts is never exercised, at least in part because, sadly, most books—and authors—don't earn enough to make an audit worthwhile. The fundamental honesty of most publishers is, of course, also an important factor.

Competing Works

An author might be tempted to rework material in a book published by one house and sell it to another, while the first book remains in print. The first publisher resents this sort of competition, for good reason. The publisher's solution is a clause prohibiting an author from publishing a second work, on the same or a similar subject, that interferes with sales of the first work during the term of the contract. If the book has a long life, the contract may last for the duration of the copyright of the book, as much as the life of the author plus fifty years, so this clause is worth some attention. It will resemble this one:

Author shall not publish, or arrange to publish, during the term of this agreement, any competing work based on or derived from the Work, or on the same subject, that is likely to diminish sales of the Work.

This clause, as written, can be a serious problem for a college or university professor, or anyone else whose career depends on publication of works in a narrowly defined field.

The competing-works clause should be as limited as possible. It should permit you to publish other works in the same general field which are not directly competitive. It should exclude works, such as magazine articles, that won't compete with your book. It should require the publisher to prove that the newer work actually impaired sales of the older. It should look like this:

> Author shall not publish or arrange to publish any book-length work on the same subject as the Work that will diminish sales of the Work.

If you plan to write another book on the same general subject, you may be able to convince your publisher to exclude it from the noncompetition clause:

> Publisher agrees that Author may publish a book dealing with civil strife in South Africa, and that such a book shall not be considered a competing work under this agreement.

One writer, an academic who not atypically depends on publication to keep from perishing, spent over two months negotiating the competing-works clause in her publishing contract for a book about the ability of divorced people to get along. The clause originally prohibited her from publishing or arranging for the publication of "any work likely to compete with the Work, directly or indirectly." That clause could have been interpreted to prevent her from publishing anything else in her field. The obvious consequences to her ability to survive need no elaboration. With a conviction born of necessity, she went to work on her publisher to get the clause modified. She threatened, cajoled, even begged a little, and finally persuaded her publisher (not a textbook publisher) to allow her to publish scholarly works on the same subject and popular works on any subject "other than the relationship between formerly married persons." The language was made so specific to allow her a broad range of other publication opportunities. At the same time, she was not permitted to do another book that would adversely affect her publisher's chance for future sales of the work in question.

Collaborators may be able to negotiate a noncompetiton clause that applies only to their joint work, not to work either writes independently. See page 64 and Chapter 3.

Both authors and publishers occasionally misunderstand the effect of a first-refusal or option clause and its relationship with a competing-works clause. The two clauses cover different issues and don't overlap. The first-refusal clause allows the publisher the opportunity to acquire the author's next work. If the publisher rejects it, the author may submit it elsewhere (it can get more complicated; see page 62). But the competing-works clause may prevent the author from selling the book to another house, even though the first house didn't want it.

The Remainder/Overstock Clause

Aside from hearing low sales reports and reading bad reviews, an author's most painful moment comes when he discovers his work on the remainder table. This means the publisher has given up on the book and is selling off some or all remaining stock at huge discounts that do little more than recover manufacturing costs. To the publisher, no matter how strong the commitment to the printed word, books are a commodity—if they sell, great, print more; if they don't, too bad, cut your losses. But no publisher will remainder a book if it can be sold any other way, because the remainder industry pays a pittance for the books it buys.

The publishing contract affects remainders in three ways: it sets a reduced royalty, or none at all, for books sold as remainders; it may prevent a book from being remaindered until a certain time has passed after first publication; and it may allow the author a chance to buy copies of the book at remainder price. A remainder clause that protects the author's interest looks like this one:

> If, at least two years after first publication of the Work, the Publisher, in its sole discretion, believes that it has on hand stock of the Work that could not be sold at usual terms, it may sell the same at the best obtainable price. Publisher shall, however, first offer copies of the Work to Author at that price, and Author shall have thirty days within which to notify the Publisher in writing of his desire to purchase some or all such copies, after which the Publisher may dispose of them elsewhere. No royalties shall be payable on such sales made at or below Publisher's cost of manufacture. A royalty of 10 percent of Publisher's actual cash receipts shall be made on such sales above Publisher's cost of manufacture.

The Out-of-Print Clause

Every author—and publisher—hopes all books will remain economically viable forever. Most don't. Publishing agreements in general let the publisher decide when to toll the bells for a given title. That unrestricted, unilateral right to decide when a book's time is up is not in the author's best interest. The publisher's usual out-of-print clause reads something like this:

> If the Work has been out-of-print in all editions for a period of six months, and the Author demands in writing that the Publisher reissue the Work, the Publisher shall have six months after receiving such notice to return the Work to print or enter into a contract to do so. If the Publisher fails to do, the Author may terminate this agreement, and all rights granted herein shall

revert to the Author, subject to all licenses or options previously granted by the Publisher. The Work shall be deemed out-of-print when it is not available in any edition in any language throughout the world. The Publisher may dispose of any remaining copies of the Work, and the plates and negatives used in its manufacture, without further liability to the Author.

A good out-of-print clause is quite different. First, *out-of-print* should be defined against an objective standard, not left to the publisher's unfettered discretion. The best standard is the book's sales or its earnings:

The Work shall be considered out-of-print when its sales fail to reach 1,000 copies in any twelve-month period.

The Work shall be considered in print so long as the Author earns at least $1,000 in any two consecutive accounting periods.

Many publishers resist such numerical tests. The next best standard is one that requires the publisher to maintain an inventory of books for sale through normal retail outlets:

The Work shall be deemed in print so long as Publisher makes it available for sale in a regular English-language edition in reasonable quantity through normal retail outlets.

Second, as with the remainder clause, the out-of-print clause should give the author the right to purchase unsold copies, plates, and negatives. If the author sells publication rights to a second publisher, the deal will be better if the publisher can use existing production material instead of resetting and reshooting the entire book. Leftover inventory may also have some value. So you should aim for a provision like this:

Publisher shall offer Author the opportunity to purchase the existing inventory of the Work, if any, at its cost of manufacture, and mechanicals, plates, and negatives at their scrap value. Author shall have thirty days after receiving notice of such opportunity to exercise his rights hereunder. If he does not do so, Publisher may dispose of all such material without further liability to Author.

About once a year, an author calls to ask what can be done about the publisher who destroyed inventory, plates, and negatives without notifying him. If the publishing agreement obligated the publisher to give the author the chance to buy them, the publisher owes the author the value of the lost opportunity, which may mean the publisher must print as many copies as were pulped. But most clauses contain an out for the publisher:

Publisher's failure to notify Author shall not be deemed breach of this agreement.

You won't find these more favorable out-of-print provisions in any "standard" publishing contract. You'll have to bargain for them. The book business is full of sad stories of publishers who have lost interest in a book but prefer to keep it (although sales have all but dried up) and won't return the rights to the frustrated author. The book is not technically out of print, because the publisher still has a few dusty boxes in its warehouse, but viewed practically, the book is dead. If you have a clause stating your book is automatically out-of-print if it sells less than 500, 1,000, or even 2,000 copies in a year, you are obviously in a much stronger position to insist on a marketing push or the reversion of rights. The repeated resale of rights to a book published over and over again can be a profitable cottage industry.

The normal out-of-print clause doesn't work automatically. It requires that you notify the publisher, and demand, in writing, that the publisher put your book back in print. The letter on page 61 is an author's formal notice to his publisher that the author's book is out of print, coupled with the demand that the publisher reprint the book. It includes a demand that the publisher not pulp or remainder unsold copies of the book without first giving the author the chance to buy them. The form is an example. Its contents must be modified to match the terms of the publishing contract.

The Agency Clause

Some contracts contain a provision allowing the publisher to pay royalties directly to the author's agent, if he has one. It looks like this:

> Publisher is hereby directed by Author to pay all sums due hereunder to the Author's literary agent: MegaWorld Associates, and said agent's receipt of such payment shall constitute full compliance with Publisher's obligations hereunder.

This provision is to protect the publisher against competing claims, one by the author and one by the agent, for payment of royalties. It matters only if you have an agent who insists, as most do, on handling your royalty payments. See Chapter 4.

Another provision that sometimes appears in the agency clause may be far more objectionable. It allows the agent to act for you in dealing with the publisher and bind you by his actions.

> Publisher may rely on the agent in respect of all matters under this agreement, including settlement of any controversies arising out of it, in full discharge of Publisher's obligations hereunder.

Peter Penman
28 West Twelfth Street
New York, NY 10000

May31, 20___

The Sluggard Press
1010 South 50th Street
San Francisco, CA 94100

Gentlemen:

I believe that my book, entitled *The Angry Author*, which you published in accordance with the contract between us dated December 15, 19__, is out-of-print. Section 15 of that contract provides:

If the work goes out of print, as defined in this agreement, and if within six months after receipt of Author's written demand, Publisher fails to reprint it, then this agreement shall terminate and all rights granted herein to Publisher shall revert to Author subject to any license or licenses previously granted hereunder.

This letter is my formal notice to you and demand on you that you reprint the work. Please let me know as soon as possible if you do not intend to reprint it. Please, too, refrain from remaindering or pulping unsold copies of the work without first giving me the chance to buy them in accordance with Section 16 of our contract.

Very truly yours,

Peter Penman

The clause may read as follows:

> Author hereby appoints Agent his attorney in fact, to act for him in all matters arising out of this agreement.

If you sign a contract containing a clause like either of these, you've given your agent a power of attorney to bind you in dealing with your publisher. Unless you trust your agent as you do your mother, you probably shouldn't agree to such a provision. The agent may argue that the publisher must be able to get a decision about a subsidiary rights deal, for example, and that to reach the author may be impractical. That argument works only if the author lives where there are no telephones.

The Option and Right-of-First-Refusal Clauses

Every book is a gamble for the publisher. It may earn back its investment; it may not. Books by established authors sometimes seem to be a sure thing. Just the same, gamblers in all fields have gone broke betting their whole pile on heavy favorites that end up losers. Publishing—where all too often even the hottest project turns out to be a financial bomb—is no different. One way the publisher can hedge its bet on a particular project is to tie a successful author to the house for future projects. That way, if your last book is a big success, your publisher can capitalize on your fame by publishing and profiting from your next. But how can a publisher require you to keep publishing with it, given that indentured servitude is no longer an acceptable American social practice? Publishers have invented two contract clauses that, so far, have passed legal muster. One is known in the trade as the option clause and the other the right-of-first-refusal clause.

Please understand that neither the option nor the right-of-first-refusal clause does you—the author—any good. They buy you nothing; at the same time, they restrict your freedom to seek the best market for your next book. If you've had a happy experience with your publisher, you're likely to want to submit your next manuscript to that publisher anyway. If not, no contractual provision should force you to do so. Therefore, it's best to sign a contract that contains neither of these clauses, although if the publisher insists on one, a right-of-first-refusal clause with a short response time is obviously more palatable than a true option.

Let's look at the worst clause first.

The Option Clause

The option clause often requires the author to sell his next work to the publisher on the same terms as those contained in the current publishing contract. In a sense, the publisher buys not only the right to publish the first book but the enforceable right to publish the next. The option prevents the author from submitting the book to any other publisher unless the original publisher decides not to take the book on the pre-established terms. This sort of option must usually be exercised within a relatively short time after the author submits his second book.

> Author grants Publisher the option to publish Author's next work, on the same terms and conditions contained in this agreement. Publisher shall exercise its option within ninety days after receipt of the complete manuscript of that work. If Publisher declines to exercise the option, Author shall be free to publish the work elsewhere.

The Right-of-First-Refusal Clause

The right-of-first-refusal clause gives the publisher first chance at the author's next book. The terms of a first-refusal clause aren't fixed as they are by an option clause; they are usually left to negotiation. The clause isn't nearly as powerful a weapon for the publisher as is the option clause.

The fact that a first-refusal clause is better than a true option clause doesn't mean that you have nothing to worry about. First, you should be able to trigger the clause by submitting a proposal, not an entire manuscript. You'll probably need an advance to live in even moderate comfort while you're writing; it'll do no good to get one after your book is done. Next, the publisher should have a limited time—perhaps thirty days—within which to exercise the right of first refusal. The typical clause allows ninety days, but you can negotiate a shorter time. Third, you should delete language that forces you to offer the book to your first publisher after its initial rejection under the right of first refusal. You should also avoid a clause that bars you from accepting an offer for less money than your first publisher offered. If the publisher insists on restricting your right to sell your work where you please, the restriction should at worst require a comparison of all the material terms (lawyer's talk for what's important), financial and otherwise.

IMPORTANT • Don't neglect to establish a time in which the publisher must act. Without one, you may be kept dangling for month after frustrating month while your publisher decides not to publish your manuscript.

EQUALLY IMPORTANT • Make sure the clause may be exercised only if the publisher is not in breach of the publishing contract. A provision of this kind may assure you of timely royalty payments. And note that the clause is enforceable even if the author's first book has gone out of print, unless the clause says otherwise: ". . . unless this agreement has terminated."

A good clause will resemble this one:

> Providing it is not in material breach of any provision of this agreement, and unless this agreement has terminated, Publisher shall have the right of first refusal to acquire the rights to publish Author's next book-length work. Publisher shall notify Author within thirty days after receiving a proposal for that work, containing an outline and at least one sample chapter, whether Publisher wishes to negotiate for its acquisition. If Author and Publisher cannot reach agreement on the terms of acquisition within thirty days after Author's receipt of such notice, Author shall be free to publish the work elsewhere.

Last refusal and matching provisions look like this:

> Author shall not dispose of rights in the Work to any other publisher on terms equal to or less favorable than those offered by Publisher hereunder.

> Author shall offer Publisher the opportunity to match the financial terms of any offer received from any other person or entity before entering into an agreement to publish with that person or entity.

Co-Author Clauses

If your book involves your collaboration with one or more other authors, each term of your contract will apply to each author, "jointly and severally." This quaint legal expression means that the publisher can look to each author to fulfill all the obligations of the contract as if the others didn't exist. For example, if there is an adverse judgment in a copyright infringement suit, all authors are independently liable to repay the publisher. The publisher doesn't care about any arrangements the authors make among themselves; the publisher's only concern, in this context, is that each author be wholly and individually responsible. We discuss the rights of one author vis-à-vis the other in Chapter 3.

The Boilerplate Clauses

Boilerplate is legal jargon for all that incomprehensible, apparently unimportant stuff at the back of the contract. The language of boilerplate dates back to the time of Charles Dickens and the English chancery courts. These clauses cover the publisher's bankruptcy, contract assignment, amendments or modifications, the law governing contract disputes, how notices are given, and how disputes are to be resolved. Let's briefly review them.

Bankruptcy

Almost every publishing contract appears to terminate, and to revert rights to the author; if the publisher becomes insolvent or goes bankrupt. But the federal bankruptcy law overrides the provisions of the contract and prevents automatic reversion of the publication rights your contract grants the publisher. Those rights are valuable to the publisher—and its creditors. Under bankruptcy law, those valuable rights belong to the bankrupt estate, administered by the bankruptcy court. You can't get them back until the court says you can, and the wait can be a long one.

Nevertheless, the clause is of some use. After the bankruptcy procedure ends, you may be able to recover your rights.

Assignment

Assignments typically occur when a publisher sells out to a conglomerate, or the conglomerate sells off the publisher, or when an author must assign his income to a creditor. Almost every publishing contract contains an assignment clause. A typical one looks like this:

> This agreement shall be binding upon and inure to the benefit of the assignees and successors of the parties, but neither party may assign this agreement except in writing with the other's prior written consent, provided that Publisher may assign this agreement to a person or entity acquiring all or substantially all of the Publisher's business or assets.

That clause is intended to protect both publisher and author if either wants to transfer rights under the contract to a third party. The assignment clause describes what must happen for an assignment to be valid. Often the nonassigning party must agree in writing to the assignment for it to be valid, although some assignments, especially those made by the publisher, can typically be made unilaterally. The requirement that both assignment and consent to assignment be in writing is a way to protect against misunderstanding and confusion. This is especially important when a third party is involved. The publisher is concerned that you, the author, not assign your royalty income to an unknown third party who sues the publisher when you fail to make sure royalties are paid to the assignee. You should be concerned about the identity of your publisher and your publisher's commitment to your work. A new publisher, assigned your original publisher's rights, may not like you or your book. The consequences are obvious.

Assignment clauses usually permit the publisher to dispose of his entire business without your permission. Otherwise, your one-book tail could wag a very large dog.

Amendments and Waivers

Just as assignments and consents must be in writing to prevent confusion, the provision covering amendments to the contract and waivers of breached provisions should provide that they are enforceable only if in writing, signed by the parties.

> This is the entire agreement between the parties, and supersedes any prior agreement or understanding between them. No waiver or modification of any provision shall be valid unless it is in writing, signed by the party to be charged. The waiver of any breach or default hereunder shall not be deemed a breach of any later breach or default.

Publishers have been known to forgive an author's trespasses—late delivery, excessive author's alterations, unseemly displays of temperament. Authors can't contractually count on the publisher's continuing generosity, because one act of forgiveness doesn't mean all future failures will also be overlooked.

Notice

Pay particular attention to the provision telling how notice must be given. It requires the author to let the publisher's designated representative know where he can be reached in case he's needed by keeping the publisher apprised of the author's current address. Do this in writing.

Notices shall be sent to the parties as follows, until written notice of a change of address is received:

PUBLISHER:	**AUTHOR:**
Fran Lee	Barbara Buch
Executive Editor	333 W. Oaklawn St
Superior Publishers	Berkeley, CA 94777
45 E. 23d Street	
New York, NY 10000	

Make sure the contract accounts for mail delays, by considering notice to be received only after three to five days after mailing.

Governing Law

The governing-law provision burdens an author who lives at one end of the country and whose publisher's principal office is 3,000 miles away. The clause always says that the law of the state where the publisher has its headquarters applies. Often that state is New York, Massachusetts, or California. The clause may go on to say that jurisdiction and venue over any dispute shall be in the publisher's home state. This means the author gives up any right to insist on being sued where he lives and agrees to fight legal battles on the publisher's home ground. There is usually not much an author can do about this provision except to understand it.

> This agreement shall be governed by the laws of the State of New York, regardless of where it is entered into or is to be performed. Author shall be deemed to have consented to personal service of process in the State of New York.

Arbitration and Mediation

More and more publishing contracts contain arbitration clauses. These take the resolution of disputes out of the judicial system and put it in a system of private conflict resolution called mediation or arbitration.

Mediation is less formal than arbitration and doesn't bind the conflicting parties. Mediators, who should be trained in techniques of fact-finding and conflict resolution, help the parties to resolve their problem themselves. Few major publishers will agree to mediate a contract dispute, but a number of small ones will.

Arbitration is a binding substitute for a lawsuit, effective even if one of the parties resists it. There are several organizations of arbitrators, each with its own rules. The most commonly used is the American Arbitration Association. Arbitration usually takes less time than court litigation, is less technical, and is commonly less expensive. In this sense it is beneficial to authors. But be warned: arbitration is not a perfect way to settle disputes. It is still fairly costly, and there is no guarantee that the arbitrator will be more fair, knowledgeable, or competent than a judge will be. The big advantages of arbitration are its relatively lower cost and its speed compared to courtroom litigation, which may drag on for three years before you ever get to trial. On the whole, you should prefer a contract with an arbitration clause:

> Any dispute arising out of this agreement shall be resolved by arbitration in New York, New York, under the rules then in effect of the American Arbitration Association. The parties shall jointly choose an arbitrator. If they cannot agree, each party shall appoint a representative who in turn shall choose the arbitrator. The arbitrator shall possess expertise in the field of publishing. The arbitrator may award costs, including reasonable attorney's fees, to the prevailing party. The arbitration award may be enforced in any court having jurisdiction.

IN CONCLUSION: A LITTLE GENERAL ADVICE

If you have read this chapter carefully, you've been inoculated against the disease called ignorance—perhaps the worst malaise that afflicts writers when they first examine the formidable document known as the publishing contract. But heed the cliché: a little knowledge is a dangerous thing. The contract you are about to sign will have a major impact on your artistic and financial future. It's wise to check your conclusions with someone who knows more than you do (see Chapter 11).

SAMPLES • There are sample publishing contracts in Appendix C:

- A trade book contract from a major publisher
- A contract used by an independent West Coast house
- A textbook contract

None of these contracts is perfect; none fits every need, whether yours or your publisher's. They are included to show you what a real publishing contract looks like. Try comparing clauses among the several contracts intended to cover the same issues, and see for yourself which seems best suited to you and your work.

2 PUBLISHING IN MAGAZINES

INTRODUCTION

The golden days of the great general circulation magazines—*Collier's, Look, The Saturday Evening Post,* the weekly *Life*—are gone, probably forever. Gone with them, unfortunately, are large writer's fees and expense accounts. Today the newsstands are inundated with a bewildering variety of special interest magazines. Most of these depend largely on work by freelance writers. A few pay well, but most are downright miserly. Nevertheless, many writers remain interested in magazine work. Beginners often find it much easier to sell a piece to a magazine than to interest a publisher in a book-length work. Experienced writers rely on magazines and journals to provide supplementary income and exposure between books. And all sorts of writers find magazines a useful test bed for ideas they hope will later grow into longer works.

Whatever your reason for writing for magazines, it's important that you understand the legal relationships between you and your publisher. The legal issues you must understand and the decisions you will have to make are very much like those you encounter in book publishing. Generally, though, you will be pleased to know their number is fewer and they tend to be less complex.

There are two main avenues to magazine sales. Each has very different legal implications. First, you may be a staff writer or contributing editor. If you are, you probably have a contractual relationship with the magazine that employs you. You receive a salary or a negotiated fee for your work. You're on the payroll. The most significant advantage of a staff position is the supposedly reliable paycheck that accompanies it.

The more common approach to magazine writing is through the free-lance contract. As a freelancer, you are an independent contractor. You don't appear on the magazine's payroll. No payroll taxes are withheld, nor, as a rule, are any fringe benefits available to you. Instead you are paid for the specific job you do or, more properly, for the product of your labor.

NOTE ON "WORK MADE FOR HIRE" • Don't confuse the copyright law concept of "work made for hire" or "employee for hire" with the question of whether you are a freelancer or a staffer. Freelance writers, who aren't employees at all for labor law purposes, may be employees for hire when it comes to deciding the extremely important question of who owns their work product. A comprehensive description of work made for hire appears in Chapter 7, on copyright law. In summary, the Copyright Act of 1976 says a work made for hire either is one written in the course of employment or is a commissioned work, the idea for which originated with the employer and the contract for which specifies in writing that it is a work made for hire. Thus, whether you are a staffer or a freelancer, your work may be a work made for hire. If it is, it belongs to the magazine, not to you.

THE FREELANCE CONTRACT

Typically, the process leading to publication in a magazine begins with a writer's inquiry, to ask for an assignment or to establish interest before submitting a completed article or story. Either way, if the writer and the publisher agree that the work will be published, they have entered into a contract. This sort of contract usually need not be in writing to be enforceable, but if it isn't, its contents may be difficult to prove. It's almost always much easier to decide what the parties intend if they write down their understanding. This needn't be a burdensome task. As we learned in Chapter 1, an exchange of letters can be as binding as a formal document.

You'll find illustrative contracts and a discussion of key terms for freelance magazine work in the next section of this chapter, but before you read them, let's cover some necessary background and generalities.

Whether you work on commission, after submitting an inquiry, or whether you send prospective publishers a finished article, the contract terms you will have to consider and negotiate are essentially the same.

And, although your negotiating position is somewhat stronger if you've already completed a piece someone wants to buy, never forget that if an editor wants to publish your work in her magazine, you have some bargaining power.

Remember, too, that your copyright in an article consists of a number of separate rights, each of which can be exploited separately. As owner of the copyright, you possess a unique monopoly over your work. You can sell all your rights, or some of them, or none of them. In the last case, of course, your work won't be published. When you negotiate with a magazine, find out what rights the publisher must have and what rights she can do without. Your contract should clearly delineate the rights you are selling and reserve all others. It's a good idea to include this statement in your contract: "I reserve all rights in my work that I don't grant you by this contract."

For example, a magazine's editor may care nothing about the movie rights to your article and may not care about whether it ever appears in a book. Of course, before you get too carried away with clever schemes to hold onto these, or any other rights, your first job is to analyze what, if any, value your work is likely to have beyond a one-time appearance in a magazine. Be sure you concentrate on protecting the subsidiary rights likely to have real value and don't waste your energy on pie-in-the-sky possibilities. For example, if you are convinced that your article can be sold to television as the basis for a docudrama, you should be particularly careful to reserve your dramatic rights.

In the magazine business, rights normally are divided into a number of functional categories. After we review them, we'll have more to say about how you actually reserve as many of your rights as possible. Remember, you own the entire copyright to start, and you can sell all or any part of it.

The Number of Times the Work May Be Published

Most often, a publisher will only want the right to publish your work one time. Some publishers may want the right to repeat publication of a particularly popular piece, however, or to publish it in different places if they own more than one magazine. You, as the author, probably want to grant the minimum rights the publisher will accept, unless your main goal is simply to get published. If you don't expressly transfer more, all the publisher gets is the right to publish your work as part of the initial collective work (the magazine) and revisions of it, and in future collective works in the same series. See Chapter 7 for more about collective works.

The Length of Time the Right to Publish May Be Exercised

One of the most important issues in a freelance magazine publishing contract is the length of time the publisher has to publish your work. It's almost always in your interest to be sure the publisher's right to publish your story doesn't go on forever. The publisher will almost surely ask you to sign a contract prohibiting you from arranging for publication in another medium until a stated time after the original publication; usually one to three months is considered reasonable. Obviously, if you are going to be prevented from selling your work to another until after the first publication runs it, you want to be sure this happens reasonably promptly. Unless a magazine pays you well for lost opportunities to publish elsewhere, never sell the right to pigeonhole your work for a long period of time.

Geographical Territory

Playboy publishes editions in several European countries and languages; so does *PC World*. *The Reader's Digest*, *Cosmopolitan*, and a number of other American magazines are also international publications. If you are dealing with a magazine with editions outside the United States, ask whether it plans to publish your work in other countries or in languages other than English. The publisher may or may not be willing to pay you more for the right to publish elsewhere, but you won't know until you ask. If the publisher equivocates or refuses to pay more, make sure you sell only the right to publish in the United States. You may be able to sell the foreign rights yourself to another publication. Or, if initial publication of your work brings critical acclaim, you may even be paid again to adapt it for the international edition of the same magazine.

More typically, you will be dealing with a publisher who publishes only in the United States and in English. In this situation, the publisher is unlikely to care about overseas and non-English-language rights. Be sure you reserve them. Pay particular attention to those countries likely to be interested. (Japan, for example, is an excellent market for materials about computers—and American film stars.)

The Right to Allow Others to Publish

Normally, you'll want to reserve all nonmagazine rights except the minimum the publisher needs for her own purposes. This is because you and your agent, if you have one, are likely to be the most knowledgeable and energetic when it comes to finding other places to publish your work. The amount your work will fetch in the marketplace is also a factor. If your article is unlikely to sell for more than a few hundred dollars, no one except you will be particularly interested in marketing it.

Does this mean you should never let a magazine become involved in the ownership of your piece more than is necessary for its one-time publication of your article? Not always. There are a few circumstances when you may want a publication, especially a prestigious one, to sell non-magazine rights for you. Doesn't this mean you must give the magazine a cut? Sure, but why not? If the magazine's general know-how and contacts with book publishers are what make the sale, the magazine has earned its share. For example, we know a writer who established his reputation with an *Esquire* article and parlayed that article into a book contract—with help from his *Esquire* editor.

The Right to Allow Others to Adapt Your Work

Motion picture and television producers are always looking for what they refer to, without intending an insult, as "properties." With the advent of cable and pay television, this search has intensified and there are now more potential buyers than in the days when the networks ruled the entertainment roost. When a producer finds a desirable property—whether a novel, a short story, or a nonfiction work—he buys film rights, either outright or by purchasing an option to purchase them later. This is serious business because, generally speaking, film rights are worth far more than print rights. Sometimes they can even be valuable beyond the imagination of the author (not an easy trick). Who, for example, would have thought that Bruce Jay Friedman's *Lonely Guy's Book of Life* would be worth six figures? The lesson is clear: hang on to the right to adapt your work for other media—especially film.

And who had foresight enough to imagine, a few years ago, that electronic publishing of nontechnical works (video games, daily news reports, and the like) would be of any great commercial significance? It's now obvious that these electronic communication forms will fundamentally change how Americans receive information, and, incidentally, provide considerable income to creative people. So protect your rights to share income from exploitation in this new form of publishing by thinking hard about its potential for your work and negotiating a fair share for yourself. Consider, too, whether you or your publisher is better able to sell those rights.

The Right to Republish in an Anthology

Some anthologists have an unfortunate habit. They ask for permission to print work written by others without offering to pay for it. A staff writer for a major magazine told us about the anthologist who blandly assumed our friend would be honored to give him rights—gratis—to a 20,000-word profile previously published in a national magazine. Our friend makes his living as a writer. He responded with a demand for a substantial fee. In his letter, he explained that he understood the economics of the publishing business well enough to know the anthologist and the publisher planned to make money from the anthology or they wouldn't be publishing it. He suggested, politely but firmly, that those who wrote the work reprinted in the anthology should share the bounty. The response: a check for $1,000. If our friend hadn't reserved anthology rights when he signed his original magazine contract, he'd have had nothing to say about the terms of inclusion, and he'd likely have received little or no pay from the anthologist.

The Right to Condense, Abridge, or Change

Face the unpleasant fact that magazine publishers and editors must fit your writing into their overall presentation. For most types of material (poetry is usually an exception), they demand and need the right to modify your words. This means when you sell the right to publish in a periodical, you'll likely be asked to sell the right to alter those words, both for length and content. If you feel strongly about the sanctity of your words, you should probably try another business. It is reasonable, however, for you to negotiate for the right to see and discuss changes in your work before publication. It's also reasonable to limit changes to those that don't alter the overall sense of your work. Often your only chance to do this occurs when the work is in galleys, so your response must be quick.

Fact-Checking and Other Expenses

Your magazine editor will sometimes insist that you do extensive fact-checking before publication. The editor wants to be sure that the contents of the article are accurate, to avoid embarrassment or, worse, a libel suit. Preliminary research and fact-checking can sometimes require significant out-of-pocket expenses. If you expect to be asked to spend substantial time doing either of these, negotiate for expense reimbursement or an additional fee.

Kill Fees

You may be lucky enough to get an assignment to write an article either because your inquiry catches an editor's attention or because the editor needs a piece and knows you can write it. But the magazine may change its mind before publication. If the piece is never published, you can't expect to be paid as if it were. On the other hand, you've devoted time and effort to the writing of it, and you deserve compensation, in addition to retaining all rights to sell your work to others.

The kill fee is the mechanism magazine publishers and freelance writers have evolved to deal with this problem. You get the kill fee—usually no more than 30 percent of the price for the published article—if you do your job but the magazine doesn't publish your work. The kill fee should be part of the written contract, in order to avoid disagreements about the amount of the fee and whether you're entitled to it.

The Right to the Use of Characters

Suppose you invent a colorful or memorable character or characters who you think may come to have literary lives of their own. Perhaps the characters will even prove to have substantial value outside the original worth in your story (consider Mickey Mouse and Yogi Bear). Someone else may even want to write a whole series of stories or perhaps do a film treatment based on these characters. If you think you may be in this situation and want to be the one to develop your characters in other media, don't grant that right to the publisher. Reserve it. (See the sample magazine contracts on pages 77–79.)

Illustrations

If you provide illustrations for your article, you should be compensated separately for them. For an idea of what they may be worth, consult *Ethical Guidelines and Pricing Handbook*, published by the Graphic Artists Guild.

If you value your original art, do your best to negotiate for its return in the same condition it was in when you delivered it to your publisher.

Most agreements instead provide that the publisher is not "the insurer" of the material;' that means the publisher isn't responsible for it.

Miscellaneous Terms

Magazine publishing contracts contain other terms, although not nearly as many as book publishing contracts. In addition to the terms dealing with rights we've covered above, you'll probably see provisions covering delivery of the manuscript, payment, forfeiture of payment if you don't deliver on time, a cancellation clause, a limited promise not to compete, warranties and indemnities, and copyright. Most of these terms have been covered in some detail in our discussion of the publishing contract, and we suggest you refer to that material.

SAMPLE MAGAZINE PUBLISHING CONTRACTS AND WHAT TO DO ABOUT THEM

The language in magazine publishing contracts tends to be simpler than that in book contracts. We include a couple of samples here. You'll note that they differ dramatically. One is a comprehensive letter agreement that covers the terms we just discussed in some detail. The other is squeezed onto the back of the publisher's payment check. It's not nearly as thorough as the detailed agreement, but, in most situations, it does the job.

Let's now assume you've done some negotiating for the sale of an article, and the publisher wants it. You'll likely receive either a letter or a check, depending on the publisher. A typical publisher's letter appears on the following page.

And here's another approach, a typical back-of-the-check contract:

> Received from Prurient Publications, Inc., as payment in full for all right, title, and interest, including copyright, in the contribution entitled "Love with the Improper Stranger." The endorser warrants the originality, authorship, and ownership of that contribution and further warrants that the contribution has not been published before and that its publication will not infringe on any copyright, proprietary right, or other right and that it does not defame or invade the privacy of any person.

When you endorse the check, you've agreed to the terms of the contract.

Each of these is a contract binding on you and the publisher. Obviously, however, they present you with different problems. The problem with the contract-on-the-back-of-the-check is that it covers so

Prurient Publications, Inc.
Times Square
New York, NY 10001

February 12, 20_____

Walter Wary
444 North Street
Anchorage, AK 99500

Dear Sir:

We would like to publish the following contribution: Your story entitled "Love with the Improper Stranger." We are prepared to pay $500, as payment in full, upon receipt of the copy of this letter enclosed, signed by you to indicate your agreement with the terms and conditions set forth below.

1. You hereby grant Prurient Publications, Inc., all magazine rights of every kind in the contribution and all reprint and anthology rights in the contribution, all for the period of the copyright, including all extensions thereof, in all languages throughout the world.

2. You represent and warrant to us that you are the author of the contribution; that it is original and has not been published before; that it does not infringe upon any copyright, proprietary right, or any other right of any kind; that it contains nothing which violates any law; and that you have the unimpaired right to convey the rights you have granted us in this agreement.

3. We shall have the right in our sole and exclusive discretion, to edit, rewrite, condense, abridge, or otherwise change the contribution as we may require.

4. You grant us the right to use your name, biographical information, and likeness, to promote, publicize, or advertise our publications.

5. We shall obtain copyright for the contribution separately in your name and agree to affix the required copyright notice.

6. If we do not publish the contribution within one year of the date of this contract, or if we cease publication before publishing, the contribution shall revert to you and you shall have no obligation to return any payment made to you for said contribution.

7. You shall not write and allow the publication of any article, story, or book dealing with the subject matter of the contribution by any publisher other than us within six months after publication of the contribution by us.

Prurient Publications, Inc.

By Perry Publisher

Agreed and accepted:

Walter Wary
Dated:

Walter Wary
444 North Street
Anchorage, AK 99500

February 29, 20____

Prurient Publications, Inc.
Times Square
New York, NY 10001

Re: "Love with the Improper Stranger"

Gentlepeople:

I'm pleased that you want to publish my story entitled "Love with the Improper Stranger." Here are the terms on which I am willing to allow you to do so:

1. I grant you one-time North American publication rights in the English language in your magazine called *Prurience.* You must publish the story no later than December 31, 20____. If you do not, your right to publish it shall end, but I may keep any money you have paid me.

2. I reserve all rights I do not grant you specifically in this letter.

3. You acknowledge that you have received my manuscript of the story and that you find it acceptable for publication.

4. You agree to pay me $500 for the rights I grant you in this letter immediately upon accepting this letter as a contract between us.

5. I agree not to publish the story in any other magazine before you publish it or within ninety days after you publish it.

If you agree with the terms I have stated in this contract, please sign the enclosed copy where I've indicated and return it to me, along with a check for $500. When signed, the letter will be a contract between us.

Very truly yours,

Walter Wary

Agreed and accepted:
Prurient Publications, Inc.

By: _____

few of the terms that may be important to you. The problem with the longer contract is not that it covers too little ground—in fact, it's fairly comprehensive. Rather, the difficulty is how it handles a number of important issues, often negatively as far as you're concerned.

How should you respond to what you have received from the publisher, assuming you do want it to publish your work? You have a number of choices. Let's look at them.

1. If you've received a contract-on-the-back-of-a-check and you don't care about anything but getting your work published and being paid for it, endorse the check and deposit it. Similarly, you can sign and return the detailed contract and ask for your money. In either situation, don't expect comfort, legal or otherwise, if you become unhappy with the way the publisher has dealt with your work.
2. Don't cash the check or sign the proffered contract. Instead, negotiate what's important to you and insist the terms be in writing, signed by both you and your publisher. You needn't be as formal as the lawyer who drafted the letter agreement above. An illustration of how you might respond to Prurient appears on page 79.

MAGAZINE SERIALIZATION OF BOOKS

Serialization is what happens when an excerpt or several excerpts from a book-length work appear in a serial publication, such as a magazine, that is published in successive issues. If serialization takes place before a book is published, it's called "first serialization." If the excerpt appears in a magazine after your book is published, that's "second serialization." Sometimes an entire book first appears in installments in a magazine, as in *The New Yorker*. At other times, material is serialized in a magazine before any book contract is negotiated.

First serialization rights to a book can be lucrative. They are almost always more valuable than second serialization rights. First serialization may also be of great benefit to you in other ways. The appearance of a part of your book in a magazine should attract readers who will want to buy it when it appears.

As a general rule, the book's publisher will want to arrange for first serialization. The publisher will share the income from first serialization with you, usually fifty-fifty, although other splits are routinely negotiated. If the book is likely to be a bestseller, the price tag on first serialization rights may be surprisingly high, whereas serialization of an average "how to" book may return only a few hundred dollars.

Now let's assume you have held onto all your serialization rights, or, at least, required your book publisher to obtain your consent to its grant of serialization rights. In this situation, you have something to say about the serialization contract. Here are the things to watch out for:

1. Limit the magazine rights to the minimum the serialization publisher needs. Reserve all others, especially the rights to publish the material later in book form if those rights haven't already been sold.

2. If you sell your work in installments, make sure you can deliver the balance on the schedule the publisher puts in the contract. If you can't, you may find yourself unable to collect your fee. What's worse, if you've delivered some installments, and they've actually appeared in print, you may be required to repay money already received if you fail to deliver the last installment.

3. Be sure both you and your publisher agree with the magazine about the time period within which your material must be serialized. First serialization should be carefully coordinated with your book publication date. What's more, some first serialization contracts bar you from publishing the book until some months after the excerpt has appeared. Thus, if you haven't nailed down the publication date exactly, the magazine publisher has a great deal of control over your book's publication date! This is a distressing example of the tail wagging the dog.

4. Be aware that the serialization publisher will probably want the right to extend the time for publication if your manuscript is late. This can create unpleasant problems if your material has already been sold to a book publisher. If you have magazine deadlines as well as a deadline with your publisher, you have that much more reason to deliver your work on time.

5. Your exposure to possible liability for defamation, obscenity, and copyright infringement is essentially the same whether your piece appears in a magazine or book (see Chapters 5 through 9).

6. Make sure the magazine serialization publisher is required by contract to print the proper copyright notice for your work. Yes, you'll probably be protected by the magazine's copyright even if the right notice is omitted, but why take a chance? Make the publisher assume responsibility for printing your notice. And, because you should own the copyright, your name should appear as the copyright owner in the notice, like this: © 1988 by Walter Wary. For more about copyright, see Chapters 7, 8, and 9.

7. If your material is scheduled for book publication, insist that the magazine publisher print the name of your book, your name as its

author, its publisher, its date of publication, and its cover price. After all, one important reason for first serialization is to sell your book. Give the potential buyer all the help you can. If your book is being released by a small publisher, it is essential that the article contain full information on how to order by mail. Otherwise, potential customers are likely to be unable to find it.

8. Normally, when you're dealing with a magazine, you're not selling the right to serialize an entire book, only an excerpt. Sometimes the serialization contract will state the magazine publisher's right to choose an excerpt of a stated maximum number of words. Other times you will be selling the right to serialize a specific portion of your work. Be very precise about what you're selling if you plan to sell different excerpts to different magazines.

A SAMPLE FIRST SERIALIZATION MAGAZINE CONTRACT

A typical first serialization contract with an author who has retained serialization rights looks like the sample on the following page. Our sample is for the right to publish an entire book-length work in a magazine in several installments. It's easy to modify this contract to cover the publication of several excerpts (but less than the whole work) or the purchase of the right to publish a single excerpt.

If this contract were for installment excerpts of less than the entire work, it would probably contain a provision allowing the magazine publisher to choose selections totaling up to a specific number of words. If the agreement covered one publication of a single excerpt, the agreement would specify publication in a single issue. In some situations, it's also important to define which part of the work may be excerpted because of a possibility of selling other excerpts elsewhere.

If the author were concerned about coordinating publication of the excerpt with publication of the book, he would specify that the magazine publication date is firm ("of the essence," in legal language) and that the magazine publisher loses all rights (except to pay the agreed fee) if the deadline isn't met.

A clause reserving to the author all rights not specifically granted to the magazine publisher isn't strictly necessary. Why? Because the author owns all rights not granted to another. Nevertheless, an explicit reservation-of-rights clause is a wise precaution.

Slick Magazine, Inc.
25 Boulder Dam Highway
Las Vegas, NV 50000

January 10, 20___

William Wary
Algonquin Hotel
New York, NY 10000

Dear Mr. Wary:

We understand you are writing a novel of approximately 100,000 words, dealing with the hardships of being rich, successful, and famous (called "the Work"). We have received the first installment of the Work, of about 30,000 words. We have also received a complete outline of the Work, and we have approved it for publication in *The Easy Life* ("our Magazine"). A copy of the outline is attached to this letter contract and is hereby made a part of it.

You and we desire that the Work be published in our Magazine when the Work is completed.

You and we agree:

1. You grant us the exclusive rights to publish the first installment of the Work in the English language in our Magazine in North America, and you shall grant us the same rights in the remainder of the Work when it is completed.

2. You undertake to deliver two additional installments of the Work of about 35,000 words each on March 31 and June 30, 20___. You shall deliver the completed manuscript to us on June 30, 20___, or sooner.

3. If you deliver the Work as Section 2 of this agreement provides, we shall complete serial publication of the Work no later than December 31, 20___. We may determine, in our sole discretion, the number of installments, the intervals between installments, and the time of publication of the Work. If you delay delivery of the Work, we may extend the completion of our publication of the Work for a time equal to the delay.

4. You represent and warrant to us that the Work is your original work; that it will not violate any copyright or other proprietary right or invade the privacy of or defame any person; that you have the unimpaired right to enter into this agreement with us and to grant the rights you have granted us in the agreement; and that you have entered into no agreement concerning the Work which is inconsistent with any of the provisions of this agreement.

5. We shall obtain copyright for the Work in your name upon publication and shall affix proper notice of copyright to the Work as it is published.

6. You agree that the Work shall not be published in any form, in whole or in part, before we complete its publication and for three months after publication of the last installment in our magazine.

7. In consideration of your grant of rights to us, we shall pay you $3,000 as follows:
   a. $1,000 upon your and our execution of this agreement.
   b. $1,000 when you deliver the second installment of approximately 35,000 words.
   c. $1,000 when you have delivered the third installment of approximately 35,000 words.

   Each installment shall be satisfactory in form and content to us, or we shall not be obligated to pay any sum than otherwise due you. We hereby acknowledge that the first installment is satisfactory in form and content.

8. If you fail to deliver the entire Work to us in form and content acceptable to us, we may cancel our agreement with you by giving you thirty days' written notice. Upon cancellation, you shall refund all money we have advanced you under this agreement and, when we have received that money, we shall return all copies of your manuscript then in our possession.

9. We shall include a footnote to the title of each excerpt stating the title of the Work, and its title, its publisher and date of publication, and its cover price.

If this letter contract accurately states our agreement, please indicate by dating and signing the enclosed copy and returning it to us.

Very truly yours,
Slick Magazines, Inc.

By: _____

Agreed and accepted:
Dated:

Author: _____

Social Security Number:

3   COLLABORATION

INTRODUCTION

If you have an idea for a book but don't have enough time or energy to complete your work alone, you may consider working with someone else. It may even be essential that you collaborate because you lack particular skills or knowledge. But before you begin any joint project, consider the risks. Two heads may often be better than one, but all too often they result in double the work load and half the efficiency.

A writing partnership conceived in a romantic glow, its goals and methods left to chance, is apt to produce very little but anger and bitterness. If you've decided to work with another writer, or with a photographer or illustrator, you can minimize later frustration both by discussing the details of your proposed collaboration openly and honestly, and by writing down your agreement as clearly as possible. To leave the details of a collaboration hanging in the air makes as little sense as letting a publisher publish your manuscript with the details to be worked out later.

JOINT PROJECTS: THE MAIN PROBLEM AREAS

When you analyze the elements of any joint writing venture, you'll find the potential problem areas fall into about half a dozen categories. For example, there are problems of creative and artistic control, business problems, arrangements to be made between the collaborators, and arrangements to be made with the outside world. You need contractual structures to rely on when things are going well and devices to fall back on to solve problems should they develop.

Let's start our discussion by introducing a pair of collaborators who are about to embark on a new writing venture. Susan Sternstuff is both experienced and highly disciplined. She has produced five book-length manuscripts, three of them published. She's also done several dozen magazine pieces. She knows a lot about working against deadlines.

Norman Novicio is an accomplished rock climber who has little patience with the world below 14,000 feet. He's been working at writing for three years, first penning secret poems and then graduating to serious, if somewhat rhapsodic, prose about mountaineering. Norman has yet to score a victory in the marketplace, but Susan, who has read his unpublished work, believes he has great potential.

Susan bases her belief in Norman on his talent for describing the natural world. She wants to work with him not only because of his descriptive skill but because he's an expert in several challenging and popular outdoor activities. Susan believes there is a strong market for material of this kind. Norman, on the other hand, believes he can learn a great deal about writing from Susan, and he recognizes the difference between what he has done (writing for himself alone) and what he wants to do (writing for a paying audience). The two resolve to write a book on rock climbing.

Now let's join Susan and Norman as they sit down to plan their collaboration. What should they think about? What should they include in their written agreement? (On pages 97–100, we present Norman and Susan's completed contract. As you read the material on how they arrived at it, you may want to jump ahead now and then.)

Dividing the Work

First, Norman and Susan should recognize that although a collaboration is a joint effort, there's no such thing as an equal division of work. Even if they try to devise a scheme in which each is responsible for precisely half the page count of their work, they are almost sure to fail. Of course, most experienced writers know better than to attempt such artificial schemes.

Second, our two friends should recognize that a successful collaboration almost always demands a successful initial negotiation. The two of them must be prepared to discuss, disagree, and perhaps argue until they reach an honest consensus. This is necessary even if they agree in advance that one of them will have final editorial and creative control. The other still needs to know the limits and obligations the agreement imposes on both. One usual method to assure relative equality between collaborators is to develop an outline of the proposed project and then assign responsibility for the work.

Norman and Susan should also agree on a completion schedule or timetable. To mean anything, the schedule must be realistic, and both writers must be committed to it. Each collaborator should be aware of the other's working habits and personality, as well as the demands on their time. Neither should promise the impossible nor allow the other to promise more than seems reasonable. One successful formula for avoiding the bad feelings associated with a missed deadline, used by a successful writer friend, goes like this: first, estimate your completion date absolutely honestly. Then double it. Finally, add three months.

Norman and Susan will have to develop their own approach to working together. In doing so, they should pay close attention to the several common patterns that have worked well for others. Perhaps the most common involves each writer working independently to produce a manuscript (or part of it). The other member of the team then comments on it. The original author then does a rewrite, again subject to review and comment. Another approach involves working together, bouncing ideas back and forth, until one or the other writer feels inspired to turn the material into text. This latter method is slower, but it usually results in a much closer collaboration and identity of style. If one member of the team is to have final say (artistic control) over the entire project, or part of it, this should be clearly provided for in the contract.

Making Decisions

Once Susan and Norman have agreed on their working methods, they should move on to the other important issues. One of those, of course, is business. For example, this book counsels you to seek professional advice from a lawyer, agent, or accountant when you recognize the need for it. But who should make the decision that help is needed and hire the advisor? Your answer may be that each collaborator should have an equal say in the choice of agent, lawyer, and accountant. It's quite possible, though, that one of the collaborators will have no desire to negotiate with anyone. Norman, for example, has never dealt with an agent, mistrusts lawyers, and has little taste for doing any business. Even after reading this book, while hanging from chocks on Half Dome, he's not sure it makes sense to try. Susan, after all, has already negotiated several book contracts, apparently with some skill and success.

Given this background, these two might well decide that Susan should represent both collaborators in dealing with third parties, reserving to Norman the right to veto decisions affecting both. As part of this agreement, Norman should also insist that any agreement between the collaborators and anyone else must be signed by both writers.[1]

Susan would be wise to agree to this, both because it makes good sense and because it's for her own protection. If she gets the power to contract for the two of them without Norman's signature, she puts herself in the position of trustee for Norman, a role that can be legally uncomfortable (and expensive) for her if things go badly.

What a Collaboration Is—and Isn't

When two or more persons get together to conduct business for profit, the law considers them to have formed a partnership. Each partner is completely responsible for all the debts and obligations of the partnership, not just half of them, and each partner has the power to bind the partnership to those debts and obligations. The hazards are obvious. Your partner can make promises on your behalf about which you know nothing and to which you would strenuously object if you were aware of them.

A collaboration between writers should normally not be a partnership. (One possible exception occurs when two writers intend to produce a series of books on related topics and publish them themselves. If that's your intention, you need a good deal of information about small business organization.)[2] Your written collaboration agreement is the place to make it clear that you and your collaborators are not partners.[3]

If a collaboration is not a partnership, then what is it? Legally, it's a device for deciding who owns the product of creative work by two or

---

1.   An "innocent" third party—one who doesn't know about the collaborators' agreement that both must sign contracts affecting them—can legally hold the nonsigning collaborator to a contract signed by the other collaborator.

2.   For help in making decisions about small-business structure, see Kamoroff, *Small Time Operator,* and Clifford, *The Partnership Book.* Full information about the former can be found in the Resource Directory, Appendix A.

3.   Each partner is liable for all the debts and obligations of the partnership—including those one partner incurs without the other's consent.

more people. Each collaborator is what the law calls a "tenant-in-common" of the work. Unless their agreement says otherwise (which, of course, yours should), this means each collaborator has the legal right to treat the work as if he or she owns it. Each collaborator can independently copyright the work. Each collaborator can independently allow others to use the work (by the license or assignment of nonexclusive rights in the work to others). This can occur even though the other collaborator knows nothing about the license or assignment and would not agree to it if she did.

Each collaborator, as a tenant-in-common, owes the other certain obligations of trust. Unless there is a contrary agreement, any income either collaborator receives for the work belongs to all the collaborators in equal shares. Similarly, one collaborator can't take advantage of an opportunity to earn money through the product of the collaboration without sharing the proceeds with the others.

It's possible for the collaborators to agree between themselves—in writing—that only one of them can exercise some or all of the legal rights described above. Unfortunately, if a third party who knows nothing about the agreement between the collaborators is misled by the collaborator who doesn't have legal control into some business transaction—say, buying rights in the work—the other collaborator is stuck. Why? Because an innocent third party is legally entitled to rely on the promises made by the errant collaborator. If this occurs, the injured collaborator's only recourse is to rely on the agreement to claim her proper share of the proceeds from the errant collaborator.

Money and Authors' Credit

After Norman and Susan agree as to the division of work and the business details described above, they must decide two issues that have ruined many potentially profitable collaborations—authors' credit (billing) and money.

"Billing" means whose name should appear on the title page, and in what form (e.g., "Susan Sternstuff and Norman Novicio," "Susan Sternstuff with Norman Novicio," or "Norman Novicio as told to Susan Sternstuff"). "Money" means who gets how much if the book succeeds.

The best advice about both of these issues is to talk them over candidly. If your ego—or your collaborator's—is going to cause a problem, it's better to find out before you sink a year of your life into a project. Once you've made your decisions, reduce your agreement to writing.

What are the most practical ways to deal with billing? Start by asking yourself whether any good reason exists not to list the authors in traditional alphabetical order. Sometimes, of course, there is. If your collaborator is James A. Michener, there's obvious market value in letting Michener's name appear before yours. You can also approach this problem by weighing the value of each co-author's contributions. If one of you will work harder, longer, or more productively than the other, perhaps the order of billing should reflect it. If all else fails, toss a coin.

If Susan and Norman contribute equal amounts of work to their project, they will probably decide to share income equally. They need not, of course; Susan's superior skill and connections with the publishing world may mean she's entitled to a larger share. The agreement is the place to set this out. (Incidentally, never doubt that money and billing are closely connected. We even know an author who traded a 5 percent share of project income to get his name listed first.) The collaborators' respective needs may also determine how money is divided. For example, a collaborator who has immediate financial needs may give up potential royalty or subsidiary rights income for a larger share of the advance.

Probably the ugliest problem confronting collaborators occurs when one writer spends her share of the advance without producing her share of the work. Obviously, you will want your written agreement to reflect what happens if one person doesn't perform as expected. We discuss this unfortunate problem on page 94.

Money Management

Whatever the division of income, the collaborators must also decide how to handle the money. They may put it in a joint bank account, split it, or work out some other arrangement, such as releasing the money to themselves over time as work on their joint project progresses. Or they may arrange for each to receive their shares directly, according to the division of total income they have agreed to.

Income is only half the writer's financial equation, however. The other half is how to deal with expenses. If the collaborators anticipate the need to spend money to produce the work, they should agree in advance not only to put aside the money but also how the decision to spend will be made. Again, the normal way is by joint control over spending decisions. At the very least, Norman and Susan should each have the right to say no to any proposed major expenditure.

Duration

From the author's point of view, a written work has a finite economic life, measured by the duration of the copyright.[4] When Susan and Norman write their collaboration agreement, they should normally make it last for the life of the copyright plus any extension and renewals. See Chapter 7.

The Next Book

What happens if one co-author wants to reserve the right to solo on his next work, and that work may be on the same subject as the collaborative work? Suppose, for example, Norman expects to gain courage and confidence from his project with Susan and wants to write his next mountain-climbing book alone. And suppose this second book is an elaboration of some of the themes discussed in the first book. If the collaboration agreement says nothing about the subject, Norman is free to proceed. He can even produce a book directly competitive with the joint work (unless the agreement with its publisher bars him from doing so. See Chapter 1, page 56). He might even legally base portions of his go-it-alone project on material Susan collected for the first book.

Even if legal, is this fair? Probably not. Norman shouldn't be able to trade on Susan's contribution to the first work and grab all the profits of a second for himself. But there is another side to this issue. While it may not be fair to allow Norman alone to reap the benefits from a second work that takes off from his joint success with Susan, he should not be prevented from fairly trading on his skill and experience in his field. Put another way, it's obviously not fair to bar Norman forever from writing other books about what he knows best.

How can Norman and Susan compromise their conflicting needs and ideas of what is fair? We can provide no pat answer or formula, but here is one approach that should help:

The contract should provide that Norman is free to write a second book about mountaineering so long as it's not a sequel to the first book. Whether or not it is a sequel can be defined in the agreement. Normally, if the second book deals with the same subject matter and is an exten-

---

4.   When the copyright ends, the work falls into the public domain, which means anyone may publish it, without the copyright owner's permission. See Chapter 7.

sion of the same approach to the subject matter as the first, it would be considered a sequel. If it takes a different approach (technical, not travelogue, say, or is fiction instead of "how-to"), it would not. Norman should probably not be free to write a sequel within a stated time after the first book is published (say, three years) unless Susan agrees, in writing, in advance. An alternative would be to let Norman go ahead, reserving to Susan a small share of Norman's income.

Warranties and Indemnities

Norman's the expert. Susan's the skilled researcher. Each will be doing some work on their book independently. What if one or the other improperly uses the work of some third party without letting the co-author know, or includes libelous material in his contribution? Unfortunately for the innocent collaborator, neither the plaintiff in a lawsuit nor the publisher who insisted on a warranties-and-indemnities clause in the publishing contract will be moved by protestations of innocence. The law is clear—when both authors claim credit for a work, both are responsible for its contents.

The best way to avoid problems of this kind is to know your collaborator. Even so, the same warranties-and-indemnities clause that the publisher insists each writer sign should also be a part of the collaboration agreement. Each collaborator should promise the other that all material contributed to the work is original and doesn't invade anyone else's rights. Each collaborator should promise to take care of losses or damages, including the costs of defense, if a third party successfully asserts a claim based on violation of those rights.[5]

Assignment

The actual work of writing a book with another is an intensely personal business. It should be obvious, then, that neither collaborator should be free to substitute someone else on the job without the other's consent. To forestall this possibility, it's reasonable to include what lawyers call an assignment clause in the contract, which requires one party's consent before the other party can assign his rights and obligations. Thus, unless

---

5. For a full discussion of the warranties-and-indemnities clause, see Chapter 1, page 49.

Norman agrees, Susan should not be able to substitute her friend Sarah if she gets a better offer halfway through the book and wants to quit.

If Susan merely wants to assign her right to income from the book to her creditors, however, there is little or no danger to Norman, so long as the agreement requires notice of the assignment.

Resolving Disputes—Mediation and Arbitration

Despite their best intentions, collaborators sometimes disagree. They may differ on editorial choices, on business decisions, or on interpretation of their collaboration agreement. As in any business relationship, opportunities for disagreement are infinite.

But differences of opinion need not kill a worthwhile project. The existence of a collaboration agreement—which imposes obligations on the collaborators—and the investment of time and energy in a collaborative work provide a practical incentive to discuss and resolve disagreements.

What if the collaborators can't work out their differences by themselves? As a last resort, they may wind up in court. But the collaboration agreement can provide a quicker, cheaper, generally more satisfying way to resolve their dispute, by submitting it to an objective third party.

If the collaborators want to reserve final control over the outcome, they can agree to submit the dispute to a mediator. A mediator listens to both parties, asks questions, and helps the collaborators arrive at their own decision, often a compromise for both. Usually, a skilled mediator will lead the parties to a rational settlement of their differences that both find acceptable. But since mediation does not impose a solution, there is no assurance people using it will resolve their problem once and for all.

Arbitration, on the other hand, is very much like a private court. The parties agree in advance to abide by the arbitrator's decision. Like the mediator, the arbitrator listens to the parties and analyzes their evidence; unlike the mediator, the arbitrator renders a binding decision. Either party may present the arbitrator's decision to a court for enforcement if the other party is unwilling to do what it requires.

The collaboration agreement can contain a simple provision requiring the parties to submit a dispute to mediation, arbitration, or both (mediation first; if it doesn't take, then arbitration). The clause should spell out in some detail how the process of resolving disputes will work. In addition, it should set time limits, discuss how to choose a mediator or arbitrator, and allocate costs. For example, an arbitration clause may first encourage the parties to agree on one arbitrator. If they can't, each may have the right to choose one arbitrator, who, in turn, chooses a third. (The idea is, of course, that two people a little removed from the dispute should be able to agree on the choice of the swing voter more readily than the angry collaborators.)

When Collaborations Don't Work

Quitting the Collaboration

The most common problem between collaborators occurs when one co-author is unwilling to complete work or falls far behind schedule. Another predictable problem occurs when a collaborator is unable to work because of death or disability. These events can also take place after the work is completed but before publication, which raises somewhat different issues. Finally, the peaches-and-cream relationship with which our erstwhile collaborators began their project may begin to curdle as they discover the special strains of joint creative work. To bring this rather generalized discussion down to earth, let's see how Susan and Norman cope with some of these strains.

Susan is startled late one afternoon to hear Norman's voice on her telephone-answering machine. After a couple of false starts, Norman confides to the machine that he is unhappy with Susan's work and her personality, and that he wants to complete the book himself.

Will our model couple face a showdown over ownership of the manuscript and the ideas supporting it, or will they find a compromise that will save their joint project? If Norman and Susan anticipated the possibility of problems, their collaboration agreement can help them resolve their difficulty. Their agreement should provide who gets control of the incomplete manuscript and supporting research material in case of serious disagreement; who gets what share of advances and royalties, and on what basis; and who pays for getting the work finished. Even if all this has been done, however, it will probably be necessary to discuss a number of issues that weren't (and realistically could not have been) foreseen in the original agreement. In other words, Norman and Susan will probably need to arrive at a separation agreement. When this is done, it, too, should be reduced to writing.

In our current hypothesis, it's Norman, the expert in subject matter, but not the professional writer, who wants to continue on his own. But what about Susan, the professional writer, who has invested time in the project? She may not agree with Norman's proposed solution and, at the very least, will want to be compensated for her efforts.

Of course, the possibility the authors will have disagreements should be covered in the original contract. One way is to provide that if the joint project falls apart, neither author may continue to work independently. While this sort of solution may have a certain emotional attraction, it normally makes little economic sense, unless, of course, the work product of the collaboration isn't worth saving.

A second possible solution allows both authors to continue, independently, splitting the manuscript, the advance money, and the right to write a book based on their joint work. This solution may be even worse than the first one, because it makes Susan and Norman competitors who will likely face serious problems of infringing each other's copyright unless they are able to agree to a sensible division of the existing manuscript. Even if they can work out who owns what, this sort of arrangement would also have to be approved by their publisher, who might very well refuse to go along with it.

The most realistic solution normally allows one author to complete the work and requires him to compensate the other fairly and give credit for the other's contribution. This approach has obvious advantages: the issues are simplified and the book may actually get written.

If you're left with the feeling that undoing a collaboration presents a series of dramatic dilemmas, you're right. There is no formula solution that will always satisfy all the needs and desires of the parties. Often the best you can do is establish a framework for settling this sort of dispute in advance, and then try to arrive at an imperfect, but workable, compromise. Because it's not always easy to achieve compromise yourself, the collaboration should provide for help through mediation or arbitration by a third party. You may leave standards or issues for the third party to develop, or you may prefer to establish general criteria for mediation in advance. But keep in mind that the collaboration agreement itself, no matter how detailed its provisions, is unlikely to satisfy anyone if a serious dispute arises, so a simple clause, coupled with mediation or arbitration, may be preferred. Here's an example of what this sort of contract clause might look like:

> In case of a major dispute where one or both parties find it impossible to continue the project jointly, the work will be continued by the person best able to bring it to a successful completion.

If Susan and Norman submit Norman's request to continue the project alone to mediation or arbitration, what might happen? If they can't arrive at a mediated compromise, the impartial decision-maker will surely consider the amount of time Susan devoted to the project, her earning history, the subjective nature of her contribution to the project and to the development of Norman's skills as a writer, and the value of her lost opportunity to work on other projects. Again, the factors to be considered may be spelled out in the original collaboration agreement, or in a special arbitration or mediation agreement arrived at by the parties with the help of the mediator or arbitrator, or both.

The same principles apply to the use of collected research materials that haven't yet been incorporated into a manuscript. These materials have value that, ideally, shouldn't be lost because collaborators can no longer work together.

Death or Disability

When a collaborator dies or becomes disabled before the joint work is complete, the issues are different, although the immediate impact on the survivor is approximately the same as if one person refused to continue for other reasons. The main difference, of course, is that the dead or disabled collaborator has no choice about completing the work.

In cases of death or disability, the agreement should allow the survivor complete control over the unfinished work. The survivor should be free to finish it or arrange for another author to join him to complete it. And the survivor should have control over arrangements for publication. But the absent collaborator should receive credit as co-author. As for income from the work, the dead author's estate or the disabled author should receive his fair share.

One good way to calculate that share is to figure out the reasonable cost of getting the deceased person's share of the remaining work done and then subtract this amount from his future income. It's also possible to adjust the basic share to match the contribution made by the deceased or disabled collaborator. If he did 10 percent of the work he'd promised to do, his share should be 10 percent of what he would otherwise get.

Boilerplate

The same kind of boilerplate most publishing contracts contain should also appear in the collaboration agreement. Susan and Norman live and work in California, so California law will almost certainly apply unless they say otherwise in their agreement. If Susan lives in Chicago, though, and Norman in Denver, they should decide where disputes will be resolved and specify the place in their agreement.

The agreement should also contain a clause requiring amendments to be made in writing, signed by both parties, for the same reasons—certainty and clarity—that applied to their original agreement.

A SAMPLE COLLABORATION AGREEMENT

Here's the collaboration agreement Susan and Norman worked out.[6]

COLLABORATION AGREEMENT

This agreement is between Norman Novicio and Susan Sternstuff, as of November 21, 20__, at San Francisco, California.

1. The parties undertake to collaborate in the writing of a nonfiction book ("the Book") about rock climbing for the general reader, tentatively entitled *The Hard Place*. An outline of the book is attached to this agreement and made part of it by this reference.

2. Each party shall work cooperatively with the other to provide and develop ideas and text for the Book. They shall also cooperate in efforts to secure publication of the Book and to market other rights in it to the maximum extent possible.

3. All decisions of all kinds affecting the Book and its commercial use and value shall be jointly made. Specifically, no decision about the employment of professional advisors and representatives, or about the style and content of the Book (except as Paragraph 4 provides), or about agreements and contracts concerned with the Book, shall be made unless both parties agree.

4. The parties shall work together in the following way: Novicio shall provide a detailed outline of information about rock climbing, including technical information, experiences and anecdotes, and descriptions of equipment and locales. He shall also provide taped statements and descriptions of the characters. Sternstuff shall incorporate the outline and taped material into a manuscript. Novicio shall then review and make suggestions for the revision of the manuscript. Novicio shall have final authority over the technical contents of the manuscript, and Sternstuff shall have final authority over the style and manner of presentation of the material in the manuscript.

5. The parties intend to complete the Book by December 21, 20__. If they do not, they may mutually agree to extend the deadline for completion. If they do not mutually extend the deadline, they shall decide which of them, if either, may complete the Book. If they agree, they shall write out and sign the terms of their agreement at that time. If they cannot agree, they shall attempt to mediate their dispute, jointly agreeing on a mediator. If no mediation takes place within forty-five days from the deadline, or if one or more

---

6. Don't use this agreement as it is. It's an example and an illustration, not a model. Collaborations are unique and delicate ventures, and their creation deserves the most careful analysis.

mediation sessions are held but do not result in agreement, the dispute shall be decided by arbitration following the rules and procedures of the American Arbitration Association. The settlement agreement, if any, or the arbitrator's award, shall determine all rights either may have arising out of this collaboration agreement.

6.   If the Book is completed, the parties shall hold joint copyright in it.

7.   If the Book is completed, the parties shall work together to find a publisher for it. Neither may enter into an agreement for publication of the Book without first obtaining the other's consent and signature on the publication agreement.[7]

8.   All payments, of whatever kind, resulting from publication of the Book and the license, sale, or other disposition of subsidiary rights in the Book shall be divided equally between the parties. If possible, each party's share shall be paid directly to that party.

9.   Authorship credit for the Book shall be equal for the parties, and their names shall appear in alphabetical order.

10.   Neither party may make changes in the Book after its completion without the written consent of the other. That consent shall not be unreasonably withheld.

11.   Either party may assign his or her rights to income from publication of the Book or the disposition of subsidiary rights to a third party, but that third party shall have no other rights in or to the Book, and the assignment shall be effective only if the assigning party notifies the other party in writing. Neither party may assign any other rights or obligations of this agreement without first obtaining the other party's written consent.

12.   The parties must agree before incurring any expenses in connection with the Book. Those expenses shall be shared equally by the parties.

13.   Nothing in this agreement shall be deemed to create a partnership or a joint venture between the parties, who are collaborators on this single work.

14.   Unless this agreement is first terminated by a settlement agreement or arbitration award, or by the death or disability of one or both of the parties, its term shall equal the copyright in the Book, including all extensions.

15.   If either party is unable to complete his or her work on the manuscript, for any reason, the survivor may complete it, alone or with another, as if the survivor were the sole author. The party who is unable to complete his or her work shall nevertheless receive credit as a co-author of the Book and that party, or his or her estate, shall receive that party's prorated share in the

---

7.   Remember, either collaborator has the power (but not the right) to mislead a publisher into thinking that just one signature is enough to make a deal.

income from publication of the Book and disposition of subsidiary rights in it, taking into account the parties' respective contributions to the completed Book, after deducting expenses incurred in completing the Book, including any salaries, fees, or royalties paid to another to complete the Book. The surviving party shall have sole authority to make all decisions otherwise required to be made jointly under this agreement if the other party is disabled or deceased.

16. During the three years after first publication of the Book, or until November 19, 20__, whichever occurs sooner, neither party may publish or allow the publication of a sequel to the Book without the prior written consent of the other. A work is a "sequel" if it is substantially based on the material in the Book, deals with the same subject, is similar in style, development, and presentation to the Book, and is pointed toward the same market as that for the Book.

17. Material collected by either party in preparation for the Book (e.g., tapes, reference books, equipment) shall belong to that party if acquired at his or her expense. If acquired at the expense of both parties, that material shall belong to both parties and shall be disposed of only by the parties' agreement.

18. Each party represents and warrants that he or she has full power to enter into this agreement and that any material provided for the Book does not infringe or violate the rights of any other person, including but not limited to copyright, and is original. Each party shall hold the other harmless from, and indemnify the other against, all damages and costs, including reasonable attorneys' fees, from any breach of these warranties and representations.

19. Any dispute or claim arising out of or relating to this agreement or any breach of this agreement may be submitted to mediation under terms to be agreed on by the parties at the time. Should the parties fail to agree on a mediation procedure or should a mediation session be held and fail to produce agreement, the dispute or claim shall be submitted to arbitration in accordance with the Rules of the American Arbitration Association; judgment on the award rendered may be entered in any court having jurisdiction thereof.

20. This agreement constitutes the entire understanding of the parties and may be modified only by a written statement signed by both of them.

21. This agreement shall benefit and bind the successors, personal representatives, and assigns of the parties, but neither party may assign his or her rights, except the right to royalties or other income from the Book, without first obtaining the other party's written consent, and the assignment of royalties or other income shall be effective only if the assigning party first notifies the other party of the assignment in writing.

22. The parties agree to perform all acts and execute all documents necessary or desirable to carry out this agreement.

23.   This agreement is executed in and shall be subject to the laws of the State of California.

Dated:
Norman Novicio
Susan Sternstuff

ALTERNATIVES TO COLLABORATION

There are alternatives to collaboration for the writer who wants to work with someone else. One is to write on commission. The commissioned writer may legally be almost a collaborator or may more closely resemble a ghostwriter. If the commissioned writer is clever about negotiating her agreement, she will be paid a set amount on a pay-as-you-go basis. A writer who is being paid for her work doesn't usually share in the copyright, and generally she won't receive editorial control over the work.

Now let's suppose that instead of collaborating with Susan, Norman has decided to commission her, or to hire her as a ghostwriter for all or part of the book. What issues should concern them?

Payment

Susan should make sure that she gets paid on a specified schedule, so that even if Norman is unhappy with the results of her efforts, she'll be paid for her time.

Expenses

Susan should be certain Norman will reimburse her for agreed out-of-pocket expenses she incurs while researching and writing the book. Often an expense allowance is agreed on in advance. The writer has the freedom to spend it as she sees fit as long as the total isn't exceeded.

Percentage Participation

If Susan thinks the book will be a great success, she would be wise to negotiate for a small percentage of Norman's royalty income. If Norman is willing, Susan might also negotiate for partial credit, such as "by Norman Novicio, with the assistance of Susan Sternstuff."

Cooperation

Norman should cooperate with Susan to make her work as efficient as possible. For example, Susan should be sure Norman agrees, in writing, to give her access to all research material he's gathered. The agreement should provide some penalty if Norman refuses to cooperate. The penalty can be money, paid to Susan if Norman fires her without justification or unjustifiably withholds his cooperation.

Submission and Approval

Susan will want to insist that Norman review each section or chapter of the work as she completes it, and Norman should insist that Susan turn in work to him regularly, on an agreed schedule. Neither person wants surprises. The two should agree in advance whether Norman has the right to dictate changes of substance, style, or both, if Susan's work doesn't please him. If Norman is dissatisfied, he should be obligated to give Susan one reasonable chance to cure any problems. If she can't, or won't, Norman should have an absolute right to remove her from the project. If this occurs, Susan should keep any money Norman has already paid her, but she should be entitled to nothing more (remember the schedule of payments?).

Indemnity

If Norman is providing the background information for the book, he should indemnify Susan against liability for injuries done others, for defamation, for copyright infringement, and the like. The converse is true. Susan should indemnify Norman for her direct, specific contributions (see page 92 in this chapter and page 49 in Chapter 1 for more on this subject).

Death and Disability

The death and disability problem exists for both Susan and Norman. If Susan is unable to complete her work, Norman's obligation to continue compensating her should be adjusted. If Norman is unable to cooperate with Susan, she should have the choice whether to complete the book on her own or end the assignment.

Authority to Deal with Others

Even though a ghostwriter's name doesn't appear on the title page, a ghostwriter may be better equipped to deal with agents and publishers than the nominal author. If that's the case, the parties should spell out the ghostwriter's authority in their agreement.

Ownership

Editors and ghost writers sometimes feel that they've done so much work on a book that they've become co-authors. Whether they have is in part a matter of the parties' intent, which isn't always easy to determine. So Norman should make absolutely sure that the agreement states that he owns the copyright in the work. Susan may perform editorial miracles but should only become a co-author if she and Norman agree that she should.

4 THE LEGAL RELATIONSHIP BETWEEN WRITER AND AGENT

INTRODUCTION

Long before you whip the last page of your novel out of your typewriter (or your printer), you'll begin to plan your search for an appropriate publisher. You might scout out suitable publishing houses and submit your work directly. Many people have done so successfully, but your work is likely to sit on the slush pile until an overworked editorial assistant finally samples a few pages.

One way to improve the odds is to ask around until you find someone who knows your target publishing houses and who is willing to introduce you to an editor. This networking technique can be a very effective way to get a good book idea to an interested editor.

Many writers decide against representing themselves, concluding that it makes more sense to engage an agent to try to sell their work. Obviously, writers who abhor selling things, and all the business negotiations and interactions that commonly accompany sales, will be particularly interested in arranging for help with this part of their literary lives. Others who are more comfortable with business decisions may feel differently, asking what, exactly, an agent can do for them that they can't do for themselves.

There is, of course, no easy answer to whether you need an agent. Your decision should very properly be influenced by all sorts of subjective factors peculiar to your situation. However, we can give you some general insights about what a good agent can do for you.

First, an agent probably understands the marketplace much better than you do. The agent should know which editors at what publishing houses want books like yours, and what sort of contract terms similar works have produced. In addition, a good agent will have established a reputation as a judge of books and can usually get an editor to pay attention to a particular manuscript.

After the agent finds a publisher who expresses an interest in your book, the agent's knowledge and negotiating skills become most important. A good agent, armed with a first-rate manuscript, will know how to test the market among several publishers to obtain the most advantageous contract. And because the agent has been involved in many more publishing transactions than you have, she should be able to help you separate the possible from the pipe dream.

No agent can afford to search for a buyer forever. It sometimes happens that an agent becomes impatient after several months of unsuccessful efforts to find a publisher for a book and advises the author to sell for less than it's worth, for the sake of a deal (and the agent's commission). After all, the agent earns only 10 or 15 percent of the amount you get, so she has a relatively small stake in your project. For example, we recently talked to an author about a proposed sale where the agent begged the author to take a $10,000 advance, claiming it was absolutely top dollar. At first, the author—who had little experience with publishing contracts—was ready to go along. Finally, though, she relied on her instincts, screwed up her courage, and said, "I'm sure you can do better." A few weeks later she signed for a $30,000 advance.

Money isn't all an agent can help you get, however. Part of her responsibility is to put you in touch with the best editor and the best house. We've worked with clients who turned down a larger advance in favor of what appeared to be better editorial and marketing support.

Agents also perform other unique, valuable services. Some give parties to introduce their author clients to key editors and publishers (sometimes they even sober up the authors afterward). More important, they often encourage authors when they are down, demand better work when they are lazy, and even (occasionally) lend them money when they are broke. In short, a good agent can be an invaluable friend, confidante, and counselor.

FINDING A GOOD AGENT

Finding an agent who believes in your work, has successfully dealt with similar work, and will diligently work to enhance your best interests is a lot like finding a good doctor or lawyer. Your best approach is to talk to established writers and get their recommendations. Failing this, you can consult agents' professional groups, such as the Society of Authors' Representatives or the Independent Literary Agents Association (see the Resource Directory, Appendix A, for addresses). You can also consult recent back issues of *Publishers Weekly*, paying particular heed to the "Rights and Permissions" column. Here you will find lots of useful industry gossip, including which agents sold what to whom and for how much.

After you develop a list of agents you think might be suitable, it's time to approach them. Your submission strategy is very much the same as when you're submitting a manuscript or a proposal to a publisher: send a query first, describing your professional self and your work. If you have an established writer friend, perhaps a writing instructor who is willing to recommend you, take full advantage of the relationship. Don't be discouraged if you encounter some rejections. Successful agents are often fully occupied with their existing clients. If you're a beginning professional writer, you may find yourself working with a relatively inexperienced agent. That's not necessarily bad; you'll probably get more attention than you would from an established agent, and the hunger for success may drive your agent to extremes of activity on your behalf. Just make sure the agent knows what a publishing contract is really about, by engaging in a little cross-examination after reading Chapter 1.

Once you've found an agent who wants to represent you, your next task is to be sure the two of you are comfortable together. This is crucial. Never trust your literary future to a supposedly "hot" agent who you feel is too slick, or too restrained, or too different from you for your comfort. Chances are you'll regret it if you do.

At this point, you can—and should—check your prospective agent's references. Ask the agent for a list of clients, and call two or three to seek an honest appraisal of the agent's work. Don't be shy. It's your literary future that may be at stake.

When you're comfortable with an agent, and satisfied that objective facts support her sterling reputation, it's time to reduce your relationship to writing. Traditionally, many agents have avoided written agreements, preferring to proceed on a warm grin and a handshake. This is bad business for both of you. The issue is not whether you trust each other, but whether your agreement is clear. An unwritten agreement is unclear by definition, because it exists only in the memories of the parties. When a dispute arises, memories are notoriously unreliable.

THE AGENCY CONTRACT

The contract with your agent can be a simple letter signed by the agent and yourself. The form is not important; the contents are. On page 113, we include a sample agency agreement. The sample won't be suitable for everyone. Without some modification, it may not be suitable for anyone. But if you analyze it in light of the following discussion, it should help you identify the issues you will want to cover, as well as giving you guidance as to how to cover them.

The Grant of Authority and Its Limits

The single most important feature of the agency agreement is the grant of authority. This is where you define the scope of the agent's work on your behalf and set the limits on her power to act for you.

Remember that your agent is dealing with your rights, and that you, not your agent, have ultimate control over the sale of these rights. Your agent proposes; you dispose. Your agent can't sign a contract for you and bind you unless you authorize it. Our advice: never grant anyone any broad or open-ended authorization to act on your behalf. See Chapter 1, page 60.

Your Agent's Obligation to You

The agency agreement should also define the agent's obligation to you—normally, that she will use her best efforts, or commercially reasonable efforts, to place your work. "Best efforts" and "commercially reasonable" are legal expressions that have meaning in the publishing business. While the phrases aren't precise, they both mean the agent must act in good faith on your behalf, use reasonable methods and techniques to promote your interests, and make a conscientious effort to sell your work. "Best efforts" and "commercially reasonable efforts" don't imply that the agent must pull out all the stops, use every wile, and devote all her attention to you. If an agent falls seriously short of what's considered to be reasonable in a particular circumstance, however, the efforts clause will enable you to cancel your contract, even if you ignore the advice on page 109 and omit a termination clause.

Your agency agreement should state that your agent must submit all offers to you, whether or not the agent thinks they are good. Naturally, you'll get a recommendation along with the offer. Take this advice seriously; but don't be intimidated into accepting an offer that, for one reason or another, doesn't suit you. You have no obligation to do so.

Your Obligation to Your Agent

If yours is an "exclusive agency" relationship, you must compensate your agent even if another agent represents you and obtains a deal for you. In this situation, you would have to pay two commissions. If you succeed in selling your work yourself, however, you would owe your agent no commission. Although authors should prefer exclusive agency relationships with their agents, agents generally insist on a clause that gives them the right to a commission even if the author sells the work without the agent's help. They usually ask for what is called an "exclusive sale" arrangement. Under an exclusive sale arrangement, you are obligated to pay the agent's commission even if you sell the work yourself. Many agents won't represent an author on any other terms.

An exclusive sale arrangement for a particular work is probably reasonable in many circumstances, but authors should beware of broader agreements. For example, if the agreement you are asked to sign gives your agent the right to represent all your work, whenever you wrote it, you may find yourself paying a commission on the sale of books and articles you completed years before you even met the agent. There's nothing inherently unfair about this arrangement; your agent will argue that particular works didn't sell until she took over your representation. The point is to know what you're signing and its implications.

If you write a work during the term of an agency agreement and the work doesn't sell before the agency relationship ends, your obligation to pay a commission should really depend on whether the agent was involved in initiating or negotiating the deal you ultimately make. If so, you should be required to pay up. If not, you shouldn't have to. The agency agreement should make this clear.

Some agents go further, insisting on a clause that allows them a commission on all sales that take place within a stated time after termination of the agency agreement, whether or not the agent had anything to do with the sale. If the period isn't more than ninety days, a clause of this kind is fair. It inhibits the author from quitting an agent specifically to make a separate deal and save the commission, and, at the same time, it doesn't tie her to the agent forever.

Warranties and Indemnities

The warranties-and-indemnities clause states that you have the legal right to sell your manuscript. Obviously, your agent wants to be sure that you have the right to deal with the particular work and to enter into the agency agreement with her. If you don't, you should pay the price, not your agent. For example, if you foolishly sign two exclusive sale agreements, the second agreement may be void as far as your first agent is concerned, but the warranties-and-indemnities clause still gives your second agent the right to be compensated if she succeeds in placing your work. She also needs this provision to be sure you will stand behind her if she winds up liable to a publisher for a sale she unknowingly lacked the authority to make. In this situation, you, not either of your agents, should bear the burden of your stupidity or cupidity.

The Length of the Agency Relationship

A particular agency relationship should last as long as it remains mutually beneficial to you and your agent. Often an agent wants to bind you to the longest possible term because it may take many years for an author to begin earning significant income. The author, on the other hand, wants the contract to act as an incentive for the agent to work hard and sell manuscripts promptly. One successful mechanism for moving the agent to action is a provision that gives the agent a definite time in which to succeed in selling your work (say, a year). If she does, her right to represent you automatically continues for the balance of the contract term. Your contract can even require that the agent produce income for you in a stated minimum amount each year. But most agents will almost certainly reject an obligation like this one. Be aware, too, that an agent may make a real investment in you and your career which deserves a reasonable period of time to pay off.

NOTE ON NOVICE AGENTS • Although no agent was born an agent, and every agent had to land that initial sale for that first client, you shouldn't tie yourself to a novice for a long term without an escape clause of the kind we've just described. There are all sorts of people who call themselves agents but who don't have much of a track record.

Terminating the Agreement

A good agency agreement has a termination clause that sets forth the mechanism for ending the business relationship. Pay attention to this provision. You might want to be able to terminate the agency at any time. Or you, and your agent, might be more comfortable with a provision that requires each of you to give notice a substantial period, perhaps thirty, sixty, or ninety days, in advance of actual termination. This notice period allows for an orderly transition, especially important if the agent has a number of submissions in the hands of publishers. And be sure you understand any provision that allows your agent to collect commissions for sales of your work made after your agreement has terminated.

To illustrate why all of these details can be important, suppose your agent has worked hard for almost a year, with no luck. The publishing business is as tight as a drum, she says. You believe her but also feel someone else can represent you more effectively. As a result, you write a letter, certified mail, return receipt requested, in which you bid her a fond farewell and terminate the agency. You also notify the publishers that your soon-to-be-former agent was talking with about your book, also by certified mail. Two weeks later, the acquisitions editor your agent had been cultivating for eleven months finally comes through with a contract offer. You sign the contract and deposit your $10,000 advance check in the bank.

Don't spend all that money just yet. Chances are you will have to subtract your agent's commission. Why? Because many agency agreements state that contracts signed within ninety days after termination are deemed signed during the term of the agency agreement. Of course, this sort of clause, like any other, is negotiable, and you may want to try to shorten or eliminate the post-termination period.

The Agent's Right to Assign Your Agreement

The relationship between agent and writer is a personal one, sometimes intensely so. You should insist, therefore, that the agreement you sign with your agent can't be transferred to another agent without your permission. If your agent is an employee of an agency, or has partners, you may well want to reserve the right to terminate the agency relationship if she leaves or isn't able to work with you. On the other hand, you may not want or need so close a dependency, in which case it won't matter to you which agent represents you.

Representing the Competition

Your agent may also represent other authors who write similar, competing work. Don't be surprised, then, if the agency agreement includes a provision specifically allowing her to represent competing authors. If that sort of conflict bothers you, you should probably find another agent. But remember, it's to your advantage to have a successful agent, and successful agents have many—often competing—clients.

Commissions and Payments

When dealing with unpublished authors, some agents require a reading fee before they will read the author's work for the first time. There is nothing unethical about the reading fee, particularly if the agent is prepared to give the author a critique and discuss marketing strategies. The agent, after all, can't pursue other business if she's reading your manuscript. Another reason for the reading fee is to discourage casual submissions. If the author has to pay before an agent will read his work, he'll likely be more selective and more committed in dealing with the agent. But this is only an apologia for, not an endorsement of, reading fees. Surveys have shown that the reading fee doesn't always buy useful editorial advice.

The traditional agent's commission has been 10 percent of the author's gross income from the sale of rights to a particular literary work. In recent years, most agents have increased their commission to 15 percent. You should certainly discuss the commission rate, and it's acceptable to ask for a reduced commission if you have an argument for it, such as your own extensive contacts with publishers.

The commission on foreign sales ranges up to 20 percent, justifiable only if that commission is to be split with a subagent or corresponding agent abroad.

Some agents expect their authors to pay for out-of-pocket expenses, such as long-distance telephone calls, photocopying, and postage, at least up to a stated limit of, say, $100. Others are willing to absorb those expenses.

Your agency agreement may well provide that your publisher make payments directly to your agent, and that your agent can withhold commissions from the check. This is generally reasonable, assuming you trust your agent. (If you don't, find another.) Your publisher would rather write one check than two, and your agent would like to be sure her commission is paid before your landlord grabs your royalty check.

In addition, your agent can probably read a royalty statement with greater insight than you.

But make sure the agreement requires the agent to pay you your share promptly and allows you to examine her books at any time. Be sure, too, that the agreement requires your agent to keep your money separate from her own, in a client trust account. An agent is a trustee, holding money that doesn't belong to her. Most are scrupulous about maintaining separate bank accounts, but a newcomer to the business may need the added incentive of a provision in your contract.

Multiple Agents

You may want to retain one agent for publishing and arrange for another to represent you in dealing with film and television sales. Or you may not. If your agent has significant experience in Hollywood, or with film rights agents, you may be much better off allowing her to handle or supervise the sale of the film rights. Be realistic, though. If you've just sold your first novel, you probably won't need—or even be able to get—a first-rate film rights agent. Your literary agent will test the waters; if there's interest in film rights, that's the time to pursue a specialized agent. Discuss this possibility before the fact and include your arrangements in your written agency agreement.

You or your agent may also want to use separate agents for domestic and foreign rights deals. A number of agents do nothing but market rights on the international market. This is big business for many types of books, and you may well want to work with a specialist, directly or through your agent. Of course, if the agent you have chosen to represent you is well connected abroad, it makes sense to build foreign representation into your agreement. When thinking about foreign rights, you should keep in mind that your domestic publisher may demand the authority to market these rights, or to share in the take even if you sell the rights yourself (see Chapter 1, page 19).

If you employ multiple agents, be sure that the agency commission structure doesn't penalize you. In general, the combined commissions of the multiple agents shouldn't exceed 5 percent more than the basic commission: 15 percent for a 10 percent agent, 20 percent for a 15 percent agent. Be sure, too, that each agent knows about the other's role and that their authority doesn't overlap. A lawyer can help you sort things out—and should if you find yourself in this sort of mess.

EXAMPLE • One writer we've worked with called to boast about the interest a Hollywood film agent had shown in his work. He'd even been offered an agency agreement, handsomely printed. Our friend seemed a little chagrined when we asked him to compare the commission clauses in his literary agency agreement and the offered film rights agency agreement. The two agreements, together, would have obligated him to a total commission of 30 percent for a movie sale! We were able to negotiate a combined commission of 20 percent—to his evident relief.

Do You Need an Arbitration or Mediation Clause?

The same considerations that apply to disputes between you and your publisher (see Chapter 1, page 67) or your collaborator (see Chapter 3, page 93) apply to those between you and your agent. The nature of the author-agent relationship probably makes mediation a good first alternative, but since arriving at a mediated solution is essentially voluntary, your mediation clause should be backed up by an enforceable arbitration clause.

A SAMPLE AGENCY AGREEMENT

Agency agreements may be written in lawyer's language and format or in the form of a letter, either from author to agent or from agent to author. In any case, the agent prepares the agreement, and its legal effect is the same.

No two agents use the same agreement, although most agreements resemble each other. The agreement that follows is a composite, neither the best nor the worst of the breed. It's included to show you what an agency agreement looks like and to illustrate the points covered in this chapter. The author accepts the agreement by signing a copy of it and returning the signed copy to the agent.

AGENCY AGREEMENT

Dear_____:

This letter will confirm your appointment of me as your sole and exclusive agent throughout the world pursuant to the following agreements and understandings:

1. (a) I shall counsel and advise you professionally and shall market all your literary rights, including, but not limited to, publishing, motion picture, stage, radio, and television rights, in all the literary material that you submit to me during the term of the agency, and the preexisting literary material listed on Schedule A, attached to and made a part of this agreement.

   (b) The term *literary material* includes any material that you may now, or at any time during the term of this agreement, own or to which you have any right, title, interest, or control, including, but not limited to, literary, dramatic, and musical material, books, plays, dramas, stories, episodes, scripts, recordings, motion pictures and radio and/or television programs, formats, and outlines.

2. I agree to exercise reasonable commercial efforts in marketing your literary material and promoting your professional standing. I retain the right to render my services to anyone else in any capacity, even if their work may compete with yours, and to appoint others to assist me in fulfilling this agreement, including subagents.

3. I agree to submit to you any offers received. No agreement shall bind you without your consent and signature.

4. I agree to collect and receive for you all money due you from marketing your literary rights, to hold that money while it is in my possession and control, and to remit it to you promptly after I receive it. I shall be entitled to retain as my full agency commission 15 percent of all such money collected, but if I appoint a subagent, or if another agent represents your literary material, the combined commission for all such co-agents shall not exceed 20 percent. I will also be entitled to deduct and retain from such money the full amount of direct out-of-pocket expenses I incur on your behalf, such as telephone, telegraph, postage, and reproduction expenses. I may deduct travel expenses I incur on your behalf only if you approve them in advance.

5. I shall maintain accurate books and records of your account, and shall submit complete and accurate statements to you quarterly. You shall have the right to inspect and audit those books twice a year, during normal business hours and after giving me reasonable written notice, at your own expense, but if the audit uncovers an error in my favor greater than 10 percent, I will bear the expense.

6. Our agreement shall have an initial term of two years, beginning on the date of this letter. The agreement shall review automatically for additional terms of one year each unless terminated by thirty days' prior written notice by either party to the other. If within six months

after the date of termination you, or an agent representing you, enters into a contract for the sale of literary rights with respect to which I had been negotiating before the termination, and the terms obtained in the contract are no more favorable than the terms that I could have obtained, then that contract shall be deemed entered into during the term of this agreement.

7. Each of us represents and warrants that we are free to enter into and fully perform this agreement and that we do not have nor shall have any contract or obligations which conflict with any of its provisions.

8. Any claim or dispute arising out of this agreement shall be determined by arbitration, conducted under the then-prevailing rules of the American Arbitration Association, in New York, New York. The award of the arbitrator may be entered for judgment in any court having jurisdiction. The arbitrator may award reasonable attorney's fees to the prevailing party.

9. This agreement constitutes the entire agreement between us and may be changed only by a written instrument signed by both of us. This agreement shall be governed by the laws of the State of New York pertaining to contracts entered into and to be performed within that state.

Sincerely,

Agency, Inc.

By: _____

Agreed and accepted:

_____

Dated:

5 WATCH YOUR WORDS: THE CONFUSING LAW OF DEFAMATION

INTRODUCTION

When you were little, did your mother ever warn you, "Open your mouth again and you'll be in big trouble!"? You, being an embryonic writer, probably kept right on talking and, as a result, served time in solitary confinement.

Now that you're a writer with adult responsibilities, you risk much greater penalties if you open your mouth at the wrong time. Just a few thoughtless or unguarded words may well result in expensive, agonizing litigation, and the prospect of a large court judgment against you.

Your dilemma, of course, is that you can't take your mother's advice to heart, because you make your living by opening your big mouth. Your task, then, is to learn to discriminate between situations where it's legally safe to mouth off and those where it isn't. In this chapter, and the next, we will alert you to the broad rules of libel, invasion of privacy, and misappropriation of a person's right of publicity. Does this mean we will provide you with definitive, absolutely reliable guidelines or rules of thumb? No. They simply don't exist.

We shall lay out the general principles governing the protection of "personality." But you should realize that while common sense will help you solve most problems identified in the other chapters of this book, the law of defamation and privacy is both so complex and so dynamic that you can't always rely on it to guide you. Put more directly, common sense is sometimes a stranger to these areas of law. So if you have any doubts about how they affect your work, talk to a competent advisor.

DEFAMATION DEFINED—OR, WHAT HAPPENS IF YOUR WORDS AREN'T TRUE?

If you express untrue facts about a person that injure his reputation, you have "defamed" that person. Traditionally, defamation has either taken the form of "slander," accomplished by speaking, or "libel," accomplished by writing or broadcast. Historically, the difference between the two mostly had to do with how large an audience the defamer reached. Gradually, however, the term *libel* has come to be used in many circumstances to describe both libel and slander. We'll use it to include both here, although slander is technically a separate form of defamation.

Congress has never enacted a federal libel law. Rather, each state has developed its own law of libel. As a writer whose work may well be distributed in all fifty states and the District of Columbia, you must therefore be concerned with fifty-one variations on a common theme. There's an added complication, however. Although no federal statutory law covers defamation, the federal courts—most notably the U.S. Supreme Court—have created considerable defamation law by virtue of their power to interpret the Constitution, in this instance, the freedom of speech and freedom of press protections of the First Amendment. Because all state and federal courts are bound by the pronouncements of the U.S. Supreme Court, the Court has become very important in deciding what is libel and what is not. We discuss this in more detail later in this chapter.

A WORKING DEFINITION OF LIBEL

Fortunately, although some differences exist among the fifty states' definitions of libel, most are very similar. A basic working definition looks like this:

> Libel is a false statement of fact made about an identifiable living person in print or through broadcast that tends to bring the subject into public hatred, ridicule, or contempt, or to injure him or her in his or her business or occupation.

If you'd like to see how your state incorporates this general definition into law, go to the nearest library and get a copy of your state's statutes.

Look in the index under "libel" or "defamation."[1] If you want to do further research in the area, a comprehensive place to start is Sack, *Libel, Slander, and Related Problems,* Practicing Law Institute, New York, 1980.

Now let's pause a moment and look at what a law professor would call the "elements," or prerequisites, of a successful lawsuit based on defamation. How would he analyze a particular set of facts to determine whether it amounts to defamation? He'd surely search for the following factors:

1. Falsity: A statement may cause overwhelming harm to another. But if the statement is true, it's not defamatory,[2] and the injured party can't win an action for libel against the statement's author or publisher.

2. Statement of Fact: If a statement is one of opinion, not fact, it's protected under the First Amendment of the United States Constitution, and it can't be libelous.[3]

3. Publication: Was the statement "published" by communicating it to a third party? Until you publish a false, injurious statement, you haven't committed a libel. It isn't enough to communicate the false statement to the person about whom you're making it. You must share it with someone else. You can deliver all the scurrilous, lying letters you want about your obnoxious next-door neighbor to the nasty creature himself; as long as you don't give the letter to the milkperson or anyone else, you haven't committed a libel.

4. Identification: Are there enough clues in your statement to identify the plaintiff? For you to libel someone, you don't have to name names, but a reasonable reader or listener must be able to figure out whom you're talking about. For example, if Santa Claus were alive and real and you wrote a piece just before Christmas about "that obese, red-suited figure who was seen chasing an elf through the gift-wrapping department," you couldn't successfully defend yourself by claiming that because you didn't mention any names, no one knew whom you meant. (You could, of course, defend yourself successfully if you were able to prove your statements were true.)

5. Injury: Did your false statement cause actual injury, such as loss of reputation, a job, a spouse, or the like? Here the law stretches a bit to

---

1. In Texas, for example, you'll find a reference to "Texas Revised Civil Statutes, Article 5430." In California, the reference is to "California Civil Code Section 45."

2. Other grounds for suit may exist, though; see Chapter 6, "The Right to Be Left Alone."

3. *Baker v. Los Angeles Herald Examiner,* 42 Cal. 3d 254 (1986).

help the person who claims to be defamed. For example, if the publisher of the libel knew that the statement was false or can be proved to have had serious doubts about its truth, actual injury is often presumed without having to be proved. The same is true for some kinds of libelous statements, such as those attacking a woman's chastity or accusing one of being a criminal. And even if it's not possible to prove the person making the false statement knew it was wrong, mental anguish, despite the absence of external evidence such as loss of a job or spouse or business, can often support a court judgment of actual injury.

WHO IS LIBELED IS IMPORTANT

Throughout most of its history, in England and the United States, the law of libel has imposed strict liability for false, injurious statements. "Strict liability" means that the defamer's intentions and state of mind are legally irrelevant. No matter how hard the defamer may have tried to determine the truth, and no matter whether the defamer acted in good faith, the only defense to a charge of libel was, traditionally, the truth of the damaging statement. Thus, even an innocent mistake, based on conscientious research, would cost the writer a libel judgment.

More recently, however, the U.S. Supreme Court has broadened fundamental First Amendment protection for free speech and press by changing this strict liability rule to give writers and publishers more protection when they write or publish material about public officials and public figures. In short, since the famous *New York Times v. Sullivan* case,[4] decided in 1964, the defamation rules applied to public officials and public figures have differed from those for private individuals. As we shall see, strict standards of liability still generally apply when writing or speaking about purely private individuals, even in this area where the Supreme Court has relaxed the legal standards.

Because the special requirements for public figures are extremely important, let's examine what has come to be known as the *New York Times* Rule in more detail. At the height of the civil rights movement, an ad appeared in the *New York Times* attacking the actions of certain southerners, including the police of Montgomery, Alabama. L. B. Sullivan, then the commissioner of public affairs in Montgomery, sued the paper. The case finally reached the U.S. Supreme Court.

The court recognized the special requirements of the First Amendment, guaranteeing the press freedom to comment on the conduct of public officials. In balancing the right to publish damaging statements

---

4.   376 U.S. 254.

that turned out to be untrue against the right of the public official to be free from libel, the court established a special rule that prohibits a public official from recovering damages as a result of a defamatory falsehood relating to his official conduct, unless he proves that the statement was made with "actual malice." In this context, "actual malice" means that a statement was spoken or printed with knowledge that it was false or with reckless disregard of whether or not it was false.

Another son of Dixie, Wally Butts, was responsible for the extension of this *New York Times* rule. Butts was accused in a *Saturday Evening Post* article of giving inside information about University of Georgia football strategies to Bear Bryant, Alabama's coach. Butts sued the publisher and won when he was able to establish that the *Post* had shown a "reckless disregard of the truth" in publishing the story. When the Supreme Court rendered its decision, it added public figures to the category of people who must show "actual malice" before they can recover for defamatory statements. Because this public figure category gives writers a great deal of trouble, we'll examine it in more detail in the next section of this chapter.

As noted above, the rules have also been changed somewhat when it comes to purely private individuals. The U.S. Supreme Court, while encouraging the states to maintain their own law of libel for private persons, has used its First Amendment interpretive power to require that these laws include some element of fault on the part of the writer or other person making the defamatory statement.[5] Where does that leave us when it comes to libeling private persons? Unfortunately, no uniform standard exists among the states in the wake of the *Gertz* decision. Some states insist that the person claiming to be libeled must prove the defendant was negligent in determining the truth of the defamatory statement; others require that the author or publisher show reckless disregard for the truth of the libelous material. In effect, this limits the old rule that any false statement, no matter how innocently made, could form the basis of a lawsuit. Now a writer or broadcaster has at least to have been careless, or inattentive, if not badly motivated, before he can be successfully sued for an injurious lie.

MORE ABOUT THE DIFFERENCE BETWEEN PUBLIC AND PRIVATE PEOPLE

Why bother to distinguish between public and private figures? There are two accepted theoretical answers. First, by entering the public arena, an individual chooses to subject himself to closer scrutiny of his activi-

---

5.   *Gertz v. Robert Welch, Inc.*, 418 U.S. 323 (1974).

ties. As a society, we place importance on the public right to know what's happening, and the concomitant right of the press and publishing industry to report it. Indeed, these ideas are part of our most basic law, the First Amendment to the U.S. Constitution.

The second reason to treat the defamation of public and private persons differently has to do with fairness. A well-known person normally has much greater access to the media to rebut an unfair attack than does an ordinary citizen.

Once we understand the reasons why the law treats public and private figures differently, the next and more difficult question is "How do we tell one from the other?" What distinguishes a public figure from a private person? Or, to put it another way, what must an ordinary person do to lose the protection of his private status?

The answer is all too often imprecise and confusing. To begin with, it's clear that "public officials" are in the category of people who are entitled to a lower standard of protection. All people who hold important elective or appointive office fall into this category whether they like it or not. But is every public employee a public official? No. Only those employees who have substantial responsibility for the conduct of government affairs are sure to qualify. For example, a person who runs for or wins a public office, such as a seat in Congress or on a school board, or someone like a sheriff or a member of a utilities commission, would be considered a public official who has lost the cloak of privacy. But a secretary in the auditor's office or an accountant at the library would still be viewed as a private person, unless there is something extraordinary in his duties that routinely catapults him into the limelight.

Although it's usually not hard to tell who's a public official, it's an exercise in medieval logic to determine who's a public figure. Remember, the standard of defamation that requires a showing of "actual malice" before a recovery can occur has been extended to public figures. The categories of people classified as public figures in court decisions include the following:

1. Those who wield "pervasive power and influence and are public figures for all purposes";
2. Those who thrust themselves or their views into public controversy or use methods that bring them into the public eye to influence others (known as "limited public figures" or "vortex public figures," because they thrust their ideas into the vortex of public opinion);[6] and
3. Those who have regular and continuing access to the media.

---

6.   See *Webber v. Telegram-Tribune Company*, 194 Cal. App. 3d 265, and 194 Cal. App. 3d 974b.

All of these standards are vague and subject to conflicting interpretation when applied to specific people and fact situations. In trying to understand them, especially when you write about the controversial activities of a particular person and you can't absolutely guarantee the technical accuracy of every one of your facts, it will help if you ask the following questions:

- Is there really a major public controversy, or am I inventing or exaggerating one to justify my work?
- Is the subject of my story really thrusting himself into the controversy, or am I dragging him in?
- Does the subject really have public status sufficient to guarantee he can fight back through the media?
- Is the subject a public figure for all purposes (because he's powerful and influential), or only for the purposes of the particular public controversy I'm covering in my work?

Remember, your analysis is designed to tell you how careful you must be. So if you err, err on the side of conservatism. If there is a question in your mind about whether a person is a public figure or a public official, it's probably because you want to write something unpleasant or damaging. Be tough-minded and self-critical, and above all, document your facts every way you can. If you have doubts, ask an expert.

MORE ABOUT ACTUAL MALICE

So much for the difference between public and private citizens. Let's now assume you are dealing with a public figure. Despite your fact-checking, you've written certain things that turn out not to be true. The public figure threatens to sue. You know that he has to prove you were guilty of actual malice, but you're not sure just what that means.

Here's a lawyer's definition:

> Actual malice is either a corrupt or wrongful motive of personal spite, ill will, or hurtful intent, or reckless disregard of the truth or falsity of the statement made. It may be based on the defamer's hatred or dislike of the person defamed, or it may express itself in culpable negligence.

Let's get at a more practical understanding through a series of illustrations:

You're a newswriter. Your neighbor repairs cars in his front yard, and you don't like it. You've had words with your neighbor, but when he threatened to let a torque wrench do his talking, you beat a hasty retreat.

It occurs to you that your neighbor is violating your town's zoning ordinance by fixing cars at home, and that he hasn't been cited because the city administration is looking the other way. So you write a story about your neighbor's nasty habits of home auto repair and state there must be payoffs to City Hall to keep the zoning officials at bay. You haven't the slightest idea whether your neighbor actually made a payoff, but you get your story published anyway. You've libeled your neighbor unless, perchance, you discover after your story's been published that he did make a payoff. (Actual malice doesn't even come into the picture yet, because your neighbor is pretty clearly neither a public official nor a public figure.)

Suppose someone told you there was, indeed, a payoff. This particular source has proven himself of questionable reliability in the past, and a couple of your questions reveal he has no access to inside information about your neighbor or any possible payoff. Despite all this, when the source tells you that the payoff probably went straight to the mayor, you proceed to write the story and get it published. It turns out your source was, as usual, unreliable. Libel? Yes, as to your statements about both your neighbor and the mayor. True, the mayor, who is a public official, would have to prove both that the story was false and that it was malicious, but this won't be difficult under the circumstances. You didn't care enough to check the facts, even though you had reason to doubt the veracity of your source. At the very least, you had an obligation to investigate your information thoroughly before printing your story. You've demonstrated actual malice because you've shown a reckless disregard for the truth or falsity of your statement.

Let's change our story a little. This time your information comes from a person of impeccable reputation who has always been accurate in the past. She tells you of dirty dealing in City Hall, names names, and describes secret meetings in detail. You begin a thorough investigation. You talk to the mayor, who denies that any bribery having to do with zoning enforcement took place but admits meeting with your neighbor. Your neighbor is evasive, contradicts himself during your interview, and appears visibly shaken when you ask about the payoff, but he says the car in question was owned by a friend. In addition, a friend who knows the mayor states that he has seen your neighbor working on the mayor's car on several occasions. You have a deadline, so you don't verify ownership of the car before you go to print. In your state, verification merely takes a phone call to the Motor Vehicles Registry.

It turns out there never was a payoff and that while the car your neighbor worked on looked like the mayor's and even had a similar license number, it did belong to someone else. You promptly print a retraction. Is your story libelous?

The mayor probably wasn't libeled. You did a reasonably good job of checking for the truth, although you made an honest mistake. But your neighbor may succeed in making his case stick. Why? Your statements about him were untrue, damaging, and published. And because he is neither a public official nor a public figure, he need not prove actual malice (in most states), just negligence. You were negligent when you failed to check ownership of the car.

HOW MUCH FACT-CHECKING IS ENOUGH?

We've learned that if you check your facts carefully, you are much less likely to be successfully accused of libel for your erroneous, damaging statement. This is particularly true if you are commenting on a public official or public figure. How much fact-checking must you do before you can conclude that you haven't violated the *New York Times* Rule by showing "a reckless disregard for the truth or falsity" of your statements? The easy answer is "The more, the better." But there is no standard for determining how much fact-checking is enough. Courts look at the peculiar facts of each situation.

If you work for a daily, and there's a fast-breaking story, you need not be as thorough and as careful as a historian, with time for deep research to verify facts. Similarly, if you're an investigative reporter, taking the time to run down what appears to be a major municipal scandal, you must be more careful than a news reporter working on a tight deadline.[7] The general rule is that the more lead time you have before publication, the greater your duty to check and recheck your facts.

TIPS ON AVOIDING DEFAMATORY STATEMENTS

Although there is no advice we can offer that will tell you for certain how to avoid all defamatory statements, let's flag some likely trouble areas where extreme care is warranted.

1. Don't accuse someone of a criminal act or a crime unless you are absolutely sure he has confessed or been convicted. Even then it's wise to cite the record that backs up your statement.

---

7. Have a look at *Wolston v. Reader's Digest Assoc., Inc.*, 443 U.S. 157 (1979), where the U.S. Supreme Court discusses this doctrine in more detail than we can here.

2. Don't attribute a physical or mental disease to someone without the absolute conviction, based on hard evidence, that you can prove your assertion.
3. Be particularly careful when associating someone with a group or a cause held in disrepute. Thus, if you say someone is a member of a disreputable religious cult in a story criticizing the cult, you'd better be able to document your assertion of membership. The fact that the person attended a meeting or two is not enough.
4. Don't accuse someone of being dishonest or incompetent in his occupation. Instead you may want to describe what happened in a particular situation.
5. Don't impute unchastity to someone, particularly if that someone is a woman. While this taboo may not be as strong as it once was, and there are undoubtedly people who would be insulted if you claimed they didn't have an active sex life, judges are very likely to base their actions on old-fashioned notions of morality.

Here are several illustrations of statements that would be libelous if not true:

- "Mr. Smith's theft of the painting can only be explained as a criminal act or the act of a demented man."
- "Brown's failure to take the minimum precautions required of a competent mechanic caused the steering gear to collapse."
- "Mrs. Al Truistic was released from County Jail today to receive treatment for a social disease she contracted while plying her trade on Main Street last month."

DEFENDING AGAINST A CHARGE OF LIBEL

The best defense is a good offense—provable truth. A true statement, no matter how damaging, can't be libelous. Truth is often a matter of perception, however, and hard to pin down. Legal "truth"—as a defense to a libel suit—is doubly so, because it doesn't count unless it's proven to the satisfaction of a judge or jury. Davy Crockett—or was it Walt Disney?—said, "Be sure you're right, then go ahead." We can't improve on that.

Experienced writers have developed several journalistic habits they rely on to keep them out of trouble. Many imagine that these are complete substitutes for telling the truth and will serve as a complete defense in any potential libel lawsuit. This is just plain wrong. Although some of these devices offer the writer some protection, some of the time, they are never a complete shield. Let's take a quick look at the common ones:

THE ATTRIBUTION DEFENSE • Can you avoid a successful libel claim by attributing your assertions to others? Attributing a fact or statement to a usually reliable source is of some help, but you are still responsible for what you publish. Check and cross-check your source's assertions of facts, especially if you have any reason to doubt them. The more damaging the story, the more certain you'd better be before you quote or paraphrase someone's harmful words about another.

THE "IT IS ALLEGED" DEFENSE • Some writers believe that if they precede a damaging statement with "It is alleged that . . . ,"or similar qualifying language, they are protected because they haven't really said that the charge or statement was true. Not so. Blind and unquestioning use of this common journalistic technique won't protect you if the allegation turns out to be untrue and injurious.

THE "OPINION" DEFENSE • If you can figure out the difference between fact and opinion, and clearly categorize your statements as your opinion only, you won't lose a libel suit based on those statements, even if they turn out to be untrue. Why? Quite simply, the First Amendment protects your right to express an opinion, even if it's odd or weird or damaging.[8] If, however, you confuse fact with opinion—that is, call something an opinion that is both objectively verifiable and wrong—the consequences can be expensive.

Here's an illustration: You're a restaurant reviewer. You have a terrible meal at a restaurant. The main course was an undistinguishable mass of stringy, overdone meat and other objects. Your review says, "The main course was the worst single dish I've ever encountered in a restaurant." You have clearly stated an opinion. No libel. If you say, "I couldn't tell what Chef Louis served me, except that I found it to be inedible," again, you've uttered no libel. You've stated your opinion about the quality of the food (although your statement looks like a fact). But if you assert, "The main course, billed as lamb, developed its tough, stringy texture on the track at Santa Anita," you'd better be able to prove that Chef Louis served horsemeat. If you can't, the fact that the meat was truly awful won't help you.

8.	See *Baker v. Los Angeles Herald Examiner,* 42 Cal. 3d 254 (1986).

THE FAIR-COMMENT DEFENSE • Another traditional defense to libel is known as "fair comment." This is similar to the constitutionally based opinion defense, with some important differences.

Fair comment is not a national legal doctrine based on the First Amendment. Rather, the details of the defense vary from state to state. In general, to qualify as fair comment, a statement must be a criticism, not an allegation of fact. The writer must state the facts on which his criticism is based. The statement must deal with a matter of public interest. The writer must believe the facts to be true. Finally, the statement must not be malicious.

This defense may be obsolete, because the opinion defense has replaced it. If it still has vitality, it's most useful for critics of goods or services offered to the public, or for political commentators publishing criticism of public figures.

THE DEFENSE OF PRIVILEGE • In some very few instances, you can publish a libelous statement without paying the legal price because the public's right to be informed outweighs the libeled person's individual rights. A libelous statement that fits this category is said to be "privileged."

The privilege defense occurs most often when a reporter accurately reports public statements made during a public proceeding, such as a trial or a legislative session, which later turn out to be wrong. For example, suppose a reporter writes a story, quoting Judge Howard Smith as saying, "The defendant was a real criminal." The quote, which the reporter copied directly from the official court transcript, turned out to be in error because the court stenographer had not heard what the judge said. In fact, Judge Smith said, "The defense was real critical." The defendant could not recover against the reporter, who reported an (erroneous) official record faithfully.

But be careful. Under the law of most states, to be privileged, your statement must meet the following criteria:

- The statement you're reporting must be made by a public official or a participant in a public proceeding, as part of the speaker's participation. The rules on who is covered vary somewhat from state to state.
- You must report what happened fully. You cannot omit other statements or events that take place during the proceeding that would tend to offset the effect of the libelous, privileged statement.
- You must be scrupulously accurate. If you make a mistake in the way you report the record or transcript, the privilege defense no longer applies.
- You must be fair and evenhanded in your writing.

• You must not know in some independent way that the statement is false, or have reason to believe it is false, or even seriously doubt its truth. For instance, to return to the above example, if you knew that the court reporter who works in Judge Smith's courtroom is about to retire because he is hard of hearing, that Judge Smith is well known for being polite, and that the defendant is a prominent civic leader, you would probably have a duty to check further before running the "criminal" quote.

THE DEFENSES OF CONSENT AND REPLY • Another relatively rare defense is available if the libeled person consents to publication of the libelous statement. It's rare that a person agrees to allow a libelous statement to be published about himself and then sues, but it does sometimes happen. For example, if a person has been libeled by a third person and agrees with you to respond to the libelous charges, you may print both sides of the story. The problem here, of course, is to make sure you can prove consent. A tape recording with an explicit conversation about consent is probably your best evidence.

Suppose a candidate is attacked in the heat of a political campaign. He's permitted to defend himself with a false statement about the attack. Even if his false statement turns out to be libelous, the defense of "reply" will protect those who publish it, so long as the statement was made in good faith, without malice, and pertains to a story about the attack without exceeding the scope of the attack.

MISTAKES

If your libelous statement reasonably creates an impression in the reader that John A. Doe is a thief, even though you meant to write John B. Doe, you've got problems. Your mistake may have been innocent, but the burden is entirely on you to prove it. Just claiming that you made a mistake is not enough to relieve you of liability for defamation. You must prove that you weren't negligent, that you did what a reasonable person would have done under the circumstances.

It's impossible to define what is negligent and what isn't with any certainty. Generally, the test of negligence is whether a reasonable person, of reasonable prudence, would have acted as the defendant did. The law builds the concept of the "reasonable person" into the definition of negligence to allow flexibility in dealing with the infinite variety of actions that may harm another. Use your common sense. Find a way to check facts before you allow them to be published. Make sure you (or your publisher) has a means to verify the truth of your assertions, and use it.

RETRACTING A LIBELOUS STATEMENT

Even if you don't have a complete defense to a charge of libel, you may be able to reduce its potential financial impact substantially by using a legal doctrine known as "mitigation of damages." But the doctrine of mitigation is not a complete defense. It can reduce the costliness of publishing a defamatory writing, but it can't stop a lawsuit.

The most common—and frequently misunderstood—way to mitigate is by use of a retraction. The effect of a retraction is defined by statute and varies from state to state. Generally, however, if a retraction is demanded by the defamed person and the publisher does retract within the time limit set by the statute, the person claiming to be defamed can recover only actual, compensatory damages in court, not punitive damages.[9] This can be extremely important, because juries seem eager to punish writers and publishers for libel with million-dollar judgments. A prompt, honest retraction will often stave off such ruinous results. It may even convince the libeled person not to sue.

Traditionally, retraction has been available to the publishers of newspapers and magazines and to broadcasters, but not to book writers, because once a book was distributed it was impossible to recall. But today, with shorter print runs and changing technology, books are produced more like magazines, so it is often possible to run a retraction in a subsequent printing. If the potential libel problem is bad enough, it is even possible to destroy copies in the offending print run or to sticker them with corrected material.

HOW LIBEL LAW APPLIES SPECIFICALLY TO FICTION

Once upon a time, a fiction writer who carefully disguised his characters, even though they were based on living persons, could ignore the libel laws. Even not-so-carefully disguised characters seemed safe as

---

9. "Compensatory damages," as these words imply, compensate the injured party for the damage he's suffered; lost earnings from a lost job and doctor's bills from treatment for emotional upset are examples. "Punitive damages" punish the wrongdoer for his wrongful act and don't depend on the cost of the injured party's losses.

long as the fictional character bore a different name and description from the real person's. Indeed, a genre of fiction, the roman à clef, depended on a knowledgeable audience's recognition that Senator A was really Jack Kennedy, President B was Dwight Eisenhower, and so on.

This section began with the words, "Once upon a time" because in 1979 the California Supreme Court issued a ruling that may force every novelist in the country to add layers of disguise to her characters. Indeed, *Bindrim v. Mitchell*[10] has probably resulted in more goatees, hair transplants, and sex change operations in the American novel than any legal decision in history.

The case that gave rise to all this creativity involved author Gwen Davis Mitchell and Dr. Paul Bindrim, a psychotherapist who conducted nude therapy sessions in southern California. Ms. Mitchell, who attended a nude marathon therapy session conducted by Dr. Bindrim, wrote a novel, *Touching*, in which a main character also conducted nude therapy sessions.

The novel's psychotherapist character was quite different from Dr. Bindrim in most physical ways, and the chief dramatic incident in the novel—a patient's suicide—had no relationship whatsoever to any event in Dr. Bindrim's life. Nevertheless, Dr. Bindrim won a substantial judgment against Ms. Mitchell and her publisher because the court accepted his contention that the novel's character was based on him; that the similarity was recognizable by members of the public; that the character's personality and behavior cast aspersions on Dr. Bindrim's professional competence; and that he was injured in his profession.

Most states haven't followed the *Bindrim* principle. A New York case has rejected a claim much like Dr. Bindrim's made by a young woman who found an unpleasant coincidence between herself and a fictional character whose first name, physical appearance, and neighborhood were similar to hers.[11] The character's sexual activities were wholly different. The court (in a split decision, two judges to one) found the similarities "superficial" and the differences "so profound that it is virtually impossible" to equate the claimant and the fictional character. It's worth noting that the author, who was sued along with his publisher, had known the plaintiff for several years. Where does this leave you?

• To the extent that the nature and the activities of fictional characters are similar to those of persons who can be identified, there is possible

---

10.   12 Cal. App. 3d 61(1979).

11.   *Springer v. Viking Press*, 457 N.Y.S.2d 246, aff'd 60 N.Y.2d 916, 458 N.E.2d 1256 (1983).

legal risk if the actions of the fictional character portray the real person in a damaging and untrue way. While other state courts may not follow the California Supreme Court in piercing an author's disguise, the risk is there.

- To the extent that the characters in a fictional work are truly fictional, there is no problem.
- An author of a fictional work who bases a character on a real person who is recognizable, but sticks to the objective facts of the real person's life and doesn't embellish them with unflattering material, is also on firm legal ground.

Now consider the roman à clef. Suppose you want to write a novel about contemporary Washington, D.C., and you make your central character a Pentagon bureaucrat. You know a lot about a real-life Department of Defense employee and model your fictional character on this very recognizable person, who is extraordinarily competent and monogamous. As your story develops, this character makes a silly, unprofessional mistake because he was preoccupied by a love affair with an admiral's secretary. World War III results. Would you have a chance of beating a libel suit? Not likely. But if you change the character's job, age, appearance, and personal history, you may succeed in defending yourself by establishing that your book isn't about the defense department employee.

Now let's look at some of these same issues from a different angle. Suppose you want to base a character who is mentally ill, or sexually active, or an unsuccessful businessman, on a living person. If you do, how can you be sure you're safe? The answer, sadly, is that in an area as confusing and changing as libel, it's difficult to be positive of anything, but you can certainly take steps to reduce the risk, such as the following:

1. Restrict the use of living models to minor characters only, who are not likely to be recognized.
2. Be sure real people used as models are public officials or public figures. In this area, however, there is a second problem. An author must be careful not to appropriate the public figure's commercial value and thus invade his "right of publicity." See Chapter 6.
3. Do the obvious things, such as changing the name of the character and as many other details as possible—such as locale, profession, physical appearance, perhaps even sex. Obviously, the more different a character looks and acts from the person used as a model, the less likely he or she will be recognized and, therefore, the weaker the basis for a successful lawsuit.

4. Base your character on a dead person. A dead person can't be libeled in most states.[12]

NOTE • Nuisance suits by people whose names are similar to names used in fictional works are on the rise. To avoid this sort of problem, do some checking. If you invent an obnoxious captain named O'Leary and place him in the New York Police Department, it makes sense to check to see if there is a real person of that rank with that name. If so, you'll just have to get along with O'Malley or Schwartz.

WHO'S LIABLE FOR LIBEL?

All those directly involved in the chain of publication of a libelous statement can in theory be held responsible. The writer, publisher, broadcaster, and distributor are all potential defendants in a libel action. This is why publishing contracts almost always contain a clause among the author's warranties, representations, and indemnities, in which the author in essence tells the publisher, "I haven't libeled anyone or invaded anyone's privacy, and if I have, I'll pay for it." (See Chapter 1, page 49.)

The risks to you are obvious if you sign a publishing contract containing such a clause. Because you are in a better position than anyone else to know the facts that underlie your statements, it makes sense to place ultimate responsibility for reliability on your shoulders. But the analysis of whether those facts are potentially libelous is probably best made by your publisher's lawyer or by your own experienced legal advisor. Unless you want to face big, expensive trouble later, it's wise to level with your publisher if you have any doubts about the truth of the potentially defamatory statements you make in your work. In this situation, you and the publisher have the same interest—not to be sued—and the lawyer will very likely be able to help you avoid potential problems.

LIBEL INSURANCE

There's always the risk that someone will be offended by your published work enough to sue you and your publisher. One way to protect against risk is insurance. Publishers can—and do—buy insurance against losses from defamation claims.

---

12. Except, perhaps, in New Jersey and a few other states. See *Weller v. Home News Publication Co.*, 112 N.J. Super. 502, 271 A.2d 738 (1970), which held that invasion of privacy and libel actions survive the injured person's death.

Several enlightened publishers now include their authors under their insurance umbrella. Some exposure remains, because the insurance company almost always insists on a deductible, similar to your automobile collision insurance deductible; but the impact of a losing defense can be reduced to tolerable levels by insurance. See Chapter 1, page 51, for a discussion of insurance.

6

THE RIGHT TO BE LEFT ALONE: PROTECTING PRIVACY AND PUBLICITY

INTRODUCTION

You know something about the law of defamation if you've read Chapter 5. (If you haven't, do it now, so you'll have some background for what's to come.) You know it's dangerous to publish untruths about a person that injure that person's reputation for chastity, good health, business competence, honesty, and the like. Unfortunately, however, even though your words are true, they may leave you open to a lawsuit if they create a damaging false impression about another. Worse, your truthful words may cause you problems if they seriously invade the privacy of a person out of the public eye, or if they discuss a famous individual who wants to trade on his own fame without your help. And even if your reporting is impeccable, in the sense that it meets all ethical and legal standards, the way you go about obtaining your facts may cost you dearly if you illegally violate the privacy of another.

These fact situations give rise to several challenging legal doctrines that commentators often lump together under the heading "invasion of privacy." A better label for them is "protection of personality rights." Under either name, however, the important thing to understand is that several distinct rights, which differ from one another dramatically, are involved.

THE RIGHT TO BE LEFT ALONE

The origin of the differing protection of personality rights is a famous law review article by Louis B. Brandeis and Samuel D. Warren, called "The Right to Privacy."[1] Brandeis, later to sit on the U.S. Supreme Court, and his law partner and collaborator identified a "right to be left alone" that had not existed before their article appeared. Warren and Brandeis complained, "Gossip is no longer the resource of the idle and of the vicious, but has become a trade, which is pursued with industry as well as effrontery."[2]

In the hundred-odd years since that germinal article, state courts and legislatures have developed several broad approaches to protect people's right to be left alone. In addition, the federal courts have added a national overlay to the somewhat varying state laws. We can't hope to set forth every nuance of every state law here, but we can alert you generally to the dangers you face. If, after reading what follows, you sense a problem, seek the help of a competent publishing lawyer.

With that warning firmly in mind, let's look at the right to be left alone in more detail.

THE TROUBLE WITH TELLING THE TRUTH

If you publish embarrassing or unpleasant facts, offensive to ordinary sensibility, about a private person whose activities are not matters of public interest, you've invaded that person's privacy. To understand this concept fully, let's examine each of the elements that might get you into trouble.

PUBLICATION • First, you must publish, which means you must share the facts with an audience. Conveying questionable facts to a small number of people isn't usually enough to get you in trouble. But you, as a writer, are almost certain to spread the word sufficiently to get yourself in trouble if you allow it to be published in a book, magazine, newspaper, or journal, even if circulation is fairly limited.

---

1. 4 ***Harvard Law Review*** 193 (1890).
2. Id. at 196.

PRIVATE FACTS • The facts you write about must be private. If you disclose disagreeable facts already widely known, you haven't invaded the subject's privacy, because privacy didn't exist. For example, if you write about a person's attendance at an event open to the public, you've revealed nothing secret. And if the facts you've published are a matter of public record, your right to publish them is even further protected.[3]

OFFENSIVE ACTS • The published facts must be offensive to give rise to a successful lawsuit. Again, there is little guidance in court cases to help you decide what is and what is not offensive. The answer to that question probably depends on the standards of the community where the case is tried and, certainly, on the nature of the embarrassing facts. Southern courts, for example, seem far more likely to find offense than those in the North. Again, the general rule is that if you believe certain statements might be offensive about a private person, you had better think twice before you publish.

IDENTIFIABLE PERSON • The facts you publish must make it reasonably possible to identify the subject for you to be in legal jeopardy. In response to this sort of problem you are likely to disguise the subject with a change of name, occupation, and physical characteristics. If you do this well enough, you will have no problem. The danger, of course, lies in creating a disguise people can see through. For the most part, courts have respected an author's good faith attempt to avoid embarrassment through disguise.[4]

---

3. There are, however, a few "public facts" cases where there has been a successful legal action. Most of these deal with photographs, frequently of people in embarrassing situations. An Alabama woman successfully sued a newspaper for a front-page picture showing her exiting a fun house, skirts about her ears. *Daily Times Democrat v. Graham*, 162 S.2d 474 (1964). A football fan, photographed at a game with his fly open, didn't recover, although the court seems to have been sympathetic. *Neff v. Time, Inc.*, 406 F. Supp. 858 (W.D.Pa. 1976). The Alabama woman won because the court found the newspaper had selected a particularly embarrassing photograph because it was embarrassing.

4. See *Wojtoicz v. Delacorte Press*, 43 N.Y.2d 858, 374 N.F.2d 129 (1978). The case, decided by New York's high court, involved the motion picture *Dog Day Afternoon*. In this decision, the wife and children of the man on whose misadventures the film was based sued for libel and invasion of privacy. Because neither their names nor their likenesses were used in the film, the Wojtoicz family lost their claim that their privacy had been invaded. But the case of *Bindrim v. Mitchell*, discussed both in Chapter 5 and later in this chapter, has cast doubt on the fiction writer's safe use of a living person as the model for a character in a work of fiction if that person is even remotely recognizable.

The General Interest Defense

Even though you publish private facts about an identifiable person, you may be legally safe if the embarrassing or unpleasant material you disclose is of general interest. No matter how offensive to ordinary sensibilities, if the facts are sufficiently connected with a "newsworthy event," their publication is constitutionally protected.[5] A daredevil surfer named Virgil found this out when he sued Time, Inc., for publishing a description of his bizarre habits, involving, among other things, eating bugs. These revelations were published in the context of Virgil's willingness to take risks as a surfer. The court held that Virgil's unusual behavior, coupled with his extraordinary athletic exploits, made his story newsworthy.

Is an author always on shaky legal ground if he discloses embarrassing or unpleasant facts about a purely private person? No. People who are neither public figures nor public officials legally face disclosure of particular facts about their lives (embarrassing or not) that are themselves in the public interest. A private person's life becomes a matter of public interest in any number of ways, and no easy definition is possible. Courts have recognized the public interest inherent in all phases of life, from birth through death, in criminal behavior and the procedures of the court, in odd behavior (like Virgil's), and in the whole range of stories considered "newsworthy."

If you're a journalist, the likelihood is that everything you write will be newsworthy, and that's the attitude most courts have taken. (If you write book-length works, this related defense of fair comment is somewhat less valuable. See Chapter 5, page 126.)

Public Officials and Figures Have Little Legal Privacy

Virtually by definition, public officials and public figures have no right of privacy for any acts that relate to their public life. This means facts about them may be published without much concern for liability, unless the area touched on has no remote relationship to their public status.[6] Who is a public figure? We discussed this in some detail in Chapter 5, pages 118–121.

---

5.   *Virgil v. Time, Inc.*, 527 F.2d 1122 (9th Cir. 1975), cert. denied 425 U.S. 998 (1976); *Neff v. Time, Inc.*, 406 F. Supp. 858 (W.D.Pa 1976).

6.   See *Kapellas v. Kofman*, 1 Cal. 3d 20, 459 P.2d 912 (1969).

The Passage of Time Can Create a Right of Privacy

There can be legal problems if you write about painful or embarrassing events that took place years ago, even though they were widely reported at the time. Put another way, the passage of time may well erase the public's interest in a particular story, at least as far as invasion of privacy law is concerned, and leave you vulnerable to a successful lawsuit. Be particularly careful about writing the "Where are they now?" sort of story of the "call-girl-becomes- a-school-teacher," "murderer-promoted-to-choir-director" genre. The courts have been far from uniform in dealing with this problem, but enough adverse law exists to warn you of the potential danger of digging up once-public but long-forgotten scandals. The general rule is that a news story, no matter how old, may be republished without danger to the writer. But the writer must distinguish between the facts of the story and the identity of the subject. Unless that identity is, of itself, a matter of public interest, the writer should avoid identifying the subject.[7]

In 1975, the U.S. Supreme Court strengthened writers' rights by establishing a constitutional privilege to publish accurate facts contained in public judicial records as long as the facts are believed to be true.[8] Again, the general rule is that if you believe certain statements about a private person might be offensive, you'd better think twice before you publish, even after you have carefully checked your facts.

INTRUSIVE FACT-GATHERING

We live in an age crowded with public figures (and even more people who aspire to that status). As a people, we seem to have an insatiable curiosity about all sorts of "celebrities," even the self-proclaimed. Not surprisingly, an industry has grown up pandering to this cult of fame, and some over-zealous writers have gone further than the courts allow.

If you ask photographer Ron Galella, he can tell you some of the legal perils of over-zealous fact-gathering. Jacqueline Kennedy Onassis, tired

---

7. *Briscoe v. Reader's Digest Assn.*, 4 Cal. 3d 529, 483 P.2d 34 (1971); *Melvin v. Reid*, 112 Cal. App. 285, 297 P.91 (1931). The *Melvin* case involved a former prostitute who had successfully defended herself in a notorious murder trial years before. In the *Briscoe* case, a man had been convicted of hijacking. In both cases, the subjects had lived quietly for many years and had avoided disclosure of the unpleasant facts about themselves. In both cases, the court respected the rehabilitated subject's right not to be identified with past transgressions.

8. *Cox Broadcasting Corp. v. Cohn*, 420 U.S. 469 (1975).

of seeing Galella with his camera thrust in her face and weary of his dogging her on the streets of New York, sued to keep him at bay. She won. Despite the First Amendment's guarantee of freedom of the press, Galella was permanently barred from approaching the Onassis family to photograph them; from communicating with the family, or attempting to; from conducting surveillance of the family; and from using photographs of Jackie O. for advertising or trade without her consent. The court recognized that even a person as well known as Jacqueline Onassis, who, in other circumstances, obviously didn't shrink from having her picture in the paper, should still be free from harassment.[9]

In other lawsuits, it has been established that a fact-gatherer can't legally lie to gain access to a home, climb a wall and trespass, break and enter, or plant an electronic listening device.[10]

What are the implications for the working journalist? You're trained to be aggressive when you're after the facts. You have a limited right to be intrusive, but you have no right to harass, to trespass, to rely on electronic aids, or to gain access through lies.

INVASION OF PRIVACY BY PORTRAYING A PERSON IN A FALSE LIGHT

We've learned that in certain extreme circumstances it can be dangerous to tell the truth about the private life of someone who doesn't want the truth told. Now let's look at a somewhat different question. What if you present a person in a false light by publishing statements that are, strictly speaking, true, but that create an untrue impression? Suppose, for example, you publish a photograph of a young woman holding a baby, and you caption the photograph with the woman's wedding announcement? Or suppose you write that a well-known businessman was seen standing in line at an unemployment insurance office? In the first situation, the implication may well be that the baby was born out of wedlock and in the second that the executive is out of a job. Assuming neither of these implied scenarios is true, this sort of reporting can obviously get you in trouble, especially if done deliberately. If, when you wrote your story, you knew the baby belonged to the young woman's sister, or the businessman was observing the operations of the unemployment insurance agency as part of a government commission, no court is likely to

---

9.   *Galella v. Onassis*, 487 F.2d 986 (2d Cir. 1973).

10.   See *Nader v. General Motors Corp.*, 25 N.Y. 2d 560, 255 N.E. 2d 765 (1970); *Pearson v. Dodd*, 410 F.2d 701 (D.C. Cir.), cert. denied, 395 U.S. 947 (1969).

sympathize with your claim that the pictures were not in themselves false. If you publish material that creates a deliberately false impression about a person and injures his feelings as a consequence, and if a reasonable person or a person of ordinary sensibilities would have suffered the same hurt feelings, you may pay a stiff price.

But what if you make an innocent mistake? Suppose you didn't realize that the well-dressed businessman on the unemployment line was really carrying out an assignment from the governor? Can the businessman successfully sue even though the report obviously wasn't malicious? There is no good answer. It's far from clear whether the injured party must prove "actual malice" to sue successfully. The Supreme Court has created this confusion in two cases that treat the issue differently. In the first, *Time, Inc. v. Hill*,[11] the court denied recovery to a family that complained that its ordeal as hostages in a kidnapping was worse than it had actually been portrayed in *Time* magazine.

The Supreme Court applied a legal test virtually the same as that in *New York Times Co. v. Sullivan*,[12] (see Chapter 5, page 118, for a discussion of the *New York Times* Rule), saying the Hills could recover only if the story maliciously cast them in a false light. The court defined actual malice as publication "with knowledge of its falsity or in reckless disregard of the truth."[13]

Seven years later, however, in *Gertz v. Robert Welch, Inc.*,[14] the court either narrowed or overruled the earlier *Hill* decision (it's not clear which) by holding that a person whose reputation is injured must prove actual malice only if he is a public figure or public official. The logical implication of this decision is that people out of the public eye, who are cast in a false light, don't have to show malice. Unfortunately, however, given the earlier *Hill* case, which was not directly overruled, this issue is so unclear that lower courts have made a number of conflicting rulings.

"FACTION" AND "DOCUDRAMA"

These terms have been coined to describe the genre of writing that purposefully combines fact and fiction. Truman Capote's *In Cold Blood* is one well-known example, Norman Mailer's *The Executioner's Song* another.

---

11. 385 U.S. 374 (1967).
12. 376 U.S. 254 (1964).
13. 385 U.S. at 387–388.
14. 418 U.S. 323 (1974).

It should be obvious that a work of "faction," or a "docudrama," leaves the writer wide open to a lawsuit for invasion of privacy. If you are accurate in depicting intimate facts about the subject and the subject is a private person, the legal doctrine we call the "right to be left alone" may flatten you. If, on the other hand, you invent material, or embroider what you know about a real subject with fictional details, you run the real risk of showing him in a false light, unless you disguise him beyond any possible recognition.

Until the case of *Bindrim v. Mitchell*,[15] a writer could protect herself from charges of false light and invasion of privacy by simply changing the name and recognizable characteristics of her subjects, a technique still useful except, perhaps, in California, where the Bindrim decision may have changed this easy rule of thumb. In California, a person's privacy may be invaded even if an author changes his name and physical characteristics, if the person can prove he was reasonably recognizable. A New York case, decided after *Bindrim v. Mitchell*, seems to have rejected the California approach.[16] See Chapter 5 for a detailed discussion.

The writer who chooses to write potentially damaging material about real living people in fiction form thus faces a genuine dilemma: should the writer be thoroughly truthful and publish facts as she knows them, or should she attempt to disguise her characters? Until Bindrim is amplified by more decisions, it's impossible to be sure, but the best (perhaps not reliable) advice we can offer is to make your disguise impenetrable.

CHECKLIST: WHERE DOES ALL THIS LEAVE US?

At this point, you should be confused. The courts, including the U.S. Supreme Court, certainly are, so if you think you understand this area perfectly, you may well be vulnerable to making a dangerous mistake. Lawyers and judges have tried to make rules covering a number of troubling ethical issues by rationalizing a number of individual fact situations. Unfortunately, these rationalizations do very little to help you when you have to make a decision whether to publish words that might injure another person. In this context, the best advice we can offer is a

---

15.   92 Cal. App. 3d 61(1980).

16.   *Springer v. Viking Press* 457 N.Y.S.2d 246, aff'd 60 N.Y.2d 916, 458 N.E.2d 1256 (1983).

series of questions designed to help you determine what is likely to cause you problems:

1. Would my mother or brother or neighbor be offended by the facts I want to publish?
2. If so, is the person I want to write about a public official? A public figure? Just an ordinary person?
3. If he's just an ordinary person, are his activities—the ones I want to write about—of general interest to the public now? If they were once of public interest, do they genuinely remain so?
4. Have I done a thorough a job of checking my facts?

If you can answer these questions with ease, the answers will probably dictate your actions. If you can't, or if for some other reason you have any doubts whatsoever, talk to an expert. The consequence of guessing wrong can be a financial disaster.

7 WHAT IS COPYRIGHT?

THE CONSTITUTIONAL FOUNDATION

Our most basic law recognizes that a writer's work product deserves legal protection. Article I, Section 8, Clause 8, of the United States Constitution gives Congress the power "to promote the progress of science and the useful arts," by securing to authors and inventors for a limited time the exclusive right to their respective writings and discoveries. If you analyze these few words, you'll find several concepts still crucial to you today.

To begin with, they establish that the power to regulate copyrights rests with Congress. Under other legal doctrines derived from the Constitution's Supremacy Clause, any copyright law enacted by Congress preempts the states from enacting competing copyright laws of their own. Since January 1, 1978, when the Copyright Act of 1976 took effect, we have in fact enjoyed one national copyright law. Before that, as we'll see, two sets of copyright laws existed: one federal and one the collection of state copyright laws. Until 1978 the federal government hadn't preempted the entire field.

In addition, it's important to note that while the Copyright Clause of the Constitution protects you, as an author, it does so only incidentally. The underlying purpose of the clause is "to promote the progress of science and the useful arts," not the wealth or fame of writers. Thus you are the beneficiary of laws designed for the common good, not specifically to make you rich.

The "Useful Art" of Writing

According to the Constitution, you practice a "useful art." That's what entitles your work to copyright protection. Fortunately for you, *useful* has always been interpreted broadly over the years to mean, among other things, useful enough for someone to want to plagiarize.

Securing Rights to the Author

The copyright laws passed by Congress under the Copyright Clause "secure" certain rights to the author. This means others can't use them without your permission. If they do, you may sue either to compel them to pay you damages, or to stop them from infringing on your copyright, or both.

Exclusive Rights

Your rights, as the author of a copyrighted work, are "exclusive." This means you have a monopoly over their use. "Copyright," even though it's a singular noun, is really a collection of rights. The collection includes the right to reproduce the copyrighted work, to prepare derivative works based on it, to sell copies of it, to perform it publicly, and to display it publicly. You can grant some or all of these rights to people or businesses, to exploit on your behalf, or you can deny everyone in the world the right to deal with your work.[1]

Here is a place where copyright law and the publishing contract meet. If you examine the discussion of "subsidiary rights" in Chapter 1, page 17, you'll see that these rights are the constituent parts of your copyright. It's up to you whether or not you wish to sell the copyright in your work in one piece, or in lots of smaller pieces (called subsidiary rights), or not at all.

---

1.   There are limited exceptions, mostly having to do with classroom use, public broadcasting, and the second and later phonograph recordings of music. These exceptions may be important if you write songs but are not relevant for this book. Again, the general rule is that no one can compel you to publish your literary work if you don't wish to.

The Length of Copyright

Your monopoly—the exclusive copyright—can be a destructive thing. The only reason the Constitution gives you this power is to encourage you to spend the time (and take the risk of failure) inherent in creating or inventing something new and useful. To prevent the monopoly from impeding the progress of the useful arts indefinitely, the Constitution requires the monopoly to be for a limited time. It's up to Congress to decide how long, which it has done in each Copyright Act. See page 150.

The "Author"

Although the constitutional Copyright Clause uses the word *authors*, this has come to mean "originators." Congress, through legislation, and the courts, through interpretation of that legislation, have defined and redefined *author* to build in the requirement that a writer produce original work through intellectual labor. This means anyone who first expresses an idea in tangible form, whether through the medium of words or painting or sculpture or photographs or music, is an author for copyright purposes. Who isn't included in the broad definition of *author?* Copyists aren't. The missing element is originality. Thus, when an author sues to deal with an infringer, the author must establish that the infringed work was original.

NOTE ON "WORK FOR HIRE" • Sometimes, the person who actually creates an original work is not the author, as far as the Copyright Act is concerned. This occurs, for example, when a writer is on the staff of a publication and is paid a salary or set fee to write, implicitly giving the employer the right to obtain copyright in the employer's name. It also occurs when a freelancer is commissioned to write—under certain very specific circumstances. This concept of work for hire is important and confusing. We'll discuss it fully later in this chapter.

"Writings"

Copyright applies to "writings," according to the Copyright Clause. Just as the word *author* has been given a broadened meaning, so has *writings*. Writings now include works of art, photographs, motion pictures, recorded television programs, and all other expressions of original ideas, tangibly embodied, containing some independent intellectual labor, and perceivable to any human sense. Any of those works is a writing and can be copyrighted.

So much for analysis of the Constitution's Copyright Clause. Today, practical application of copyright law stems primarily from copyright legislation enacted by Congress and, before January 1, 1978, from certain principles of state law.

THE GREAT COPYRIGHT DIVIDE: THE LAW BEFORE JANUARY 1, 1978, COMPARED WITH CURRENT LAW

From 1909 until December 31, 1977, the Copyright Act of 1909 governed the copyright of published works. State copyright protection—what lawyers call "common law copyright"—applied to unpublished works, because publication was a necessary condition to protection under the 1909 act. In general, as soon as a work was published, the 1909 act took over.

The Copyright Office's detailed comparative summary of the 1909 act and the Copyright Act of 1976 is set out in Appendix D. There are, however, only a small number of key differences between the old law and the new which are likely to be of concern to authors whose work appeared during 1977, or before. For example, if you're interested in finding out whether a work published before January 1, 1978, is still subject to copyright or has fallen into the public domain, you've got to consider the effect of the 1909 act. You must, therefore, become familiar with the provisions of the 1909 act governing the duration of copyright.

A fairly comprehensive summary of the 1909 act and the 1976 act appears in Appendix D. Here are the major differences between the two acts:

	1909 Act	*1976 Act*
Protection of unpublished work	No protection in general	Full protection through registration and deposit
Omission of or serious error in copyright notice	Loss of copyright	May be cured, but may reduce copyright protection
Duration	28 years	Life of author + 50 years or, in certain cases, a single term of 75 years after publication

	1909 Act	*1976 Act*
Renewal	Additional 28 years if application filed on time	No renewal; one term only
Work made for hire	Not defined by Act	Defined in detail by the Act
Failure to deposit copy	Forfeits copyright	May lead to a fine

NOTE • It's impossible to provide all the information you need in a table. Use it to identify possible problems. Then find the appropriate material elsewhere in this chapter.

ESTABLISHING YOUR COPYRIGHT

The law allows you to copyright your work only if it meets a few important criteria. The work must be original, in fixed and tangible form (not merely a good idea residing in your fertile but undisciplined imagination), and it must eventually be registered as the Copyright Office regulations and forms require. We'll examine the general principle in this chapter and the formalities of copyright registration in the next.

The "Original Work" Requirement

Only "original works" are eligible for copyright. To be original, a work does not have to be entirely new. The work can be substantially similar to another work, so long as it originated with its author and was not copied from someone else's work. Some difference is required, but not much. Because of the volume of applications for copyright registration, the Register of Copyrights can't possibly compare each newly submitted work with all others to see if the new work is original enough to qualify. Thus, in effect, the Copyright Act is enforced by other authors who discover what seem to be works that infringe on theirs and do something about it.

Defining the difference between an original work and one that isn't original, in copyright terms, is a challenge. In the abstract, originality means the author of the work didn't copy it from another's work. To illustrate, consider the difference between copying the local telephone directory, which is clearly not original, and using the names, addresses, and telephone numbers to create a categorized listing in some entirely new way. This would be copyrightable.

The "Fixed and Tangible Form" Requirement

To qualify for copyright registration, a work may not be ephemeral. It must be perceptible by the human senses, directly or with the aid of a device such as a tape recorder. A song, sung nightly to an audience but never recorded or written down, can't be copyrighted until it is written or recorded.

The work is not the physical embodiment but the content embodied. If that concept sounds metaphysical, it is. But its application is much easier than its definition. For example, that sung melody, notes hanging in the air for a moment, can't be copyrighted. Once its composer writes down the melody, it can be copyrighted. Once it's copyrighted, the composer has the exclusive right to all the other manifestations of the melody: performing it, arranging it, adapting it to opera or to rock 'n' roll. The concept also explains how the author of a work embodied as a novel has the right to control reproduction of the work as a film or a television miniseries or a play adapted from the book or a magazine excerpt. To borrow a notion from every lawyer's first year of law school, copyright is a bundle of rights, not a single right. Each of those rights may have value and can be protected.

Registration and Notice

The strict copyright requirements of the Act of 1909 were relaxed by the Act of 1976, and relaxed further on March 1, 1989, when amendments to the 1976 Act brought us into conformity with the Berne Convention, a major copyright treaty. See page 165 of this book for details.

Although the Act no longer requires either notice or registration to obtain copyright, it encourages both by providing certain procedural benefits to a notice-giving, registered copyright owner, including easier proof of ownership in an infringement action and the chance for an improved award of costs and damages.

Failure to comply with the formal requirements for copyright nearly always led to forfeit of copyright under the 1909 act. The 1976 act is more forgiving. Many serious errors or omissions—fatal to copyright under the 1909 act—are curable under the new law. One, however—untimely renewal under the 1976 act of a copyright obtained under the 1909 act—remains fatal. See page 151, later in this chapter. And see

Chapter 8 for a more complete discussion of copyright registration and other formalities.

NOTE ON PUBLIC DOMAIN • Once a work loses its copyright protection, either because the author failed to obtain it or because the term of copyright has expired, it becomes part of the public domain. Public domain material may be copied by anyone, without infringing its creator's copyright. When we consider derivative and collective works later in this chapter, we'll see that works already in the public domain or otherwise ineligible for copyright protection may be assembled into an anthology or other work for which copyright protection may be obtained. But a work that has entered the public domain can't itself ever again be subject to a valid copyright.

CATEGORIES OF COPYRIGHTABLE WORKS

The 1976 act establishes seven categories of works of authorship: literary works, musical works, dramatic works, pantomime and choreographic works, pictorial, graphic, and sculptural works, motion pictures and other audiovisual works, and sound recordings. The list, found in Section 102(a) of the act, is an aid in registration but is not exclusive. If you invent a new means of expression, and it's an analogue of any of the list of seven in the act, your work will be eligible for copyright.

Literary works possess a common factor: "verbal or numerical symbols or indicia." This category is a catchall for works expressed by means of symbols or indicia. To be "literary" for copyright purposes, "works" need not have real literary merit. The Copyright Office won't reject a badly written, incomprehensible, or silly work. What's more, even a compilation of individually uncopyrightable items, such as a business directory or a catalog, is copyrightable. Few critics would find much about the *Physicians Reference Directory* for Minneapolis that's literary, but the Copyright Act doesn't care.

For writers, the main concern with the category of musical works is song lyrics. If the lyrics are integrated with music, then the entire work is a musical work. If the lyrics are just "adaptable" to music, then the lyrics may be separately copyrighted as a literary work.

Dramatic works are those with a story an audience can see or hear performed before it, a story that can be represented to an audience as actually occurring and not just narrated. The means of performance is not critical to the definition of this category. Performance may be live or on film or on tape. The crucial factor is that the story is written to be played to an audience.

The category including pictorial, graphic, and sculptural works is important to writers because it includes photographs, illustrations, and prints. Each work of this kind is eligible for copyright, whether or not used to illustrate a text. Each is entitled to copyright separate from the text it illustrates.

Pantomime and choreographic works, motion pictures and other audiovisual works, and sound recordings are outside the scope of this book, even though all three may be based on written works. If a written work exists, it's entitled to copyright under one of the other categories of the Copyright Act, and the embodied performance of the work can be copyrighted separately from the underlying text.

The copyright category to which your work belongs determines which copyright application form you should use. Chapter 8 contains a description of the forms of the most use to writers, along with filled-in samples.

HOW LONG IS A COPYRIGHT VALID?

The Original Copyright Term

Once you've complied with registration requirements, either under the 1909 act or the 1976 act, your protection extends for the number of years the law provides. Under the old 1909 law, the term of copyright protection began on the day the work was published, or, for a few categories of work that could be registered in unpublished form, on the date of registration. Either way, the initial term of copyright protection extended for twenty-eight years. The copyright owner could apply for renewal of copyright during the last year of the initial copyright term, the renewal to last another twenty-eight years.

The 1976 act avoids the need to renew copyright for works copyrighted after December 31, 1977, by offering protection for one long period. The basic rule is that copyright protection extends for the life of the author plus fifty years. If the work is a joint work, prepared by two authors or more who are not employees for hire, the copyright term lasts fifty years after the last surviving author's death. Works made for hire, and anonymous and pseudonymous works (unless the author reveals his or her identity in the files of the Copyright Office), are entitled to copyright protection for seventy-five years from the year of publication or one hundred years from creation, whichever comes first. If an anonymous author, or one using a pseudonym, wants the benefits of the basic, "life-plus-fifty" copyright term, it's available, but the author must be willing to reveal his identity in Copyright Office records.

Renewal of Copyright

The 1976 act has changed the rules for renewing the copyright in works copyrighted under the 1909 act. The second term of copyright is now forty-seven years, not twenty-eight. This means that a work copyrighted under the 1909 act is eligible for total copyright protection of seventy-five years. If the copyright was renewed before 1978, when the new act took effect, then the term of the renewed copyright is automatically extended to allow a total seventy-five years of copyright protection. If, however, the work was still in its first twenty-eight-year copyright term on January 1, 1978, when the 1976 act took effect, then the copyright owner must apply for renewal. The second term will be forty-seven years, not twenty-eight years as under the 1909 act. Three Copyright Office Circulars, R15, R15a, and R15t, explain these duration rules in detail.

But remember, there is no automatic renewal for these works. A special form for renewal, Form RE, should be used. A filled-in sample copy appears in Chapter 8.

WARNING • The initial term of copyright protection ends on December 31 of the last year of the term. The copyright owner must apply for renewal of works subject to the 1909 act during the last year of the copyright term.[2] The Copyright Office must receive the application and fee before the deadline. If it doesn't, copyright is lost and the work enters the public domain. There is no grace period, and copyright renewal applications are not like income tax returns, which are dated from the postmark. The Copyright Office will accept a number of renewals on the same form, but only for works originally copyrighted during the same year. The current renewal fee is $6.

HOW TO GET HELP FROM THE COPYRIGHT OFFICE

A number of copyright complications exist, particularly for works written by authors no longer living. If you have questions, the Copyright Office is equipped to answer them. Our experience with the people who run the Copyright Office has been good; they know what they're doing and they're happy to help. The Copyright Office also publishes a number of reasonably understandable free publications. To get a list, ask for Circular R2. A package of application forms and circulars is contained

---

2. Copyright Act, Section 304(a).

in the Copyright Office Information Kit. To get any of these publications, write to the Copyright Office, Library of Congress, Washington, DC 20559, or use the order form reproduced in Appendix D. You may also call the Copyright Office twenty-four hours a day, at (202) 707-9100, and leave a message asking for forms.

WHAT CAN'T BE COPYRIGHTED?

Even though compilations of facts and the particular expression a writer uses to describe facts are protectable under the Copyright Act, the general rule is that the fact itself is not entitled to copyright protection.[3] If facts were copyrightable, then the first author who wrote that John F. Kennedy died on November 22, 1963, would be the last author legally entitled to write that during the term of copyright. During the copyright period, all other books referring to the date of Kennedy's death would infringe on its copyright.

Even though facts themselves are not protectable, the form of expression of these facts is. Thus no one may copy the way the facts are presented or embodied in a copyrighted work. Fictional elements contained in a factual work are also protected.[4] This means a hazard faces the author who relies on secondary sources of factual material in a subsequent work. If that author rewrites someone else's material only slightly, he may be an infringer. The more he copies, of course, the more likely he is to infringe.

EXAMPLE • The facts are that Marilyn Monroe was born, grew up, married several times, made a number of films, and died. Those facts are available to anyone who wishes to use them. Arthur Miller used them in his play *After the Fall,* and Norman Mailer used them in a long reminiscence about her. Other biographies of Marilyn Monroe exist which treat the same facts in entirely different ways. All may be independently copyrighted. As long as no one copies the way the facts are expressed by the others, none is a copyright infringer. If another writer borrows sentences from either Mailer or Miller, however, even though they are directly descriptive of facts in Monroe's life, they are infringers.

---

3.   See *Landsberg v. Scrabble Crossword Game Players, Inc.* (9th Cir 1984) 736 F.2d 485. Unavoidable similarity in expressing the facts about Scrabble strategy doesn't amount to infringement.

4.   There's a danger in mixing fact and fiction. If the result libels someone, the author may find himself unable to rely on truth as a defense. See Chapters 5 (on libel) and 6 (on invasion of privacy) for more on this serious problem.

Because news stories (not feature stories) are supposed to be factual, all the facts contained in them can be put to use in your work so long as you avoid copying the language used to express them in the story. Even if some of the purported facts later turn out to be fictional, your copyright is protected so long as you acted in good faith. "Good faith" means that you didn't know or have reason to know the "facts" were actually fiction.

Occasionally, an author will claim his work is factual until a later writer uses those facts in another work, whereupon the first writer changes his ground and claims his work was really fiction all the time. Courts have protected the rights of the second writer in those circumstances, holding that an author who says he has related facts can't pull the legal rug out from under someone who's relied on that assertion.

Although facts themselves are not protected, the way an author selects and arranges them may be. That's why directories are entitled to protection. No individual entry in the directory is copyrightable, but the choices of entries and the way they're put together provide enough originality to warrant overall protection.

When a fiction writer creates a character, and gives that character life and meaning by a description in words, that character may be protected by copyright. The test is whether the character is well developed and delineated. A second author who uses the same character type won't be an infringer. But if the second author steals a full word portrait, disguising only a few superficial characteristics of the second character, infringement has occurred. It's impossible to provide a formula that guarantees no problem in borrowing from a character in a previously copyrighted work. It's useful, though, to list common characteristics and to look for similar descriptive words, to see if the two characters under analysis are so similar that the later infringes on the earlier.

Titles Can't Be Copyrighted

Titles can be extremely valuable. Sometimes their value is as unexpected as lightning from blue sky. For example, Dr. David Reuben's book *Everything You Always Wanted to Know About Sex and Were Afraid to Ask* didn't seem a likely candidate for a motion picture sale. Indeed, the contents of the book were not useful to the film producer. But the title, the enormous publicity surrounding the book, and its identity with a reading public measured in the millions made the title a commodity in and of itself.

Valuable as they may be, titles can't be copyrighted. But the law isn't as stupid as Charles Dickens would have us believe,[5] and it does offer ways to protect the value of a literary title. Perhaps the most useful is the legal doctrine called "passing off" or "palming off," which simply means one person can't legally use a title created by another in hopes of fooling the public into thinking that the second work was created by the author of the first.

Palming off occurs only when the first title has been published, when it's achieved "secondary meaning," and when the second title creates a likelihood of confusion of authorship with the first. Thus a title is fair game, unless it's attached to a successful published work. Even publication is probably not enough to protect a title from being used by another. The title must also have associations in the public's mind that link it to the work and its author. If you find a title on an obscure book few have heard of, you may be safe in using it. Finally, in situations where a title is changed a little, the palming off doctrine applies only if the first title and the second are so similar as to lead a reasonable person to conclude that both belong to the same author or work.

The mass market paperback publisher of *Peyton Place* discovered the limits of the passing off doctrine when it sued the publisher of a book called *The Girl from Peyton Place*. The court decided that the inclusion of "Peyton Place" in the second book was not an infringing use because it was the title of a legitimate biography of the first book's author. The court concluded that the title of the biography was not an attempt to fool the public.[6]

Obscene Work Can't Be Copyrighted (Or Can It?)

There was a time when the Copyright Office rejected material it considered obscene out of hand. Officials of the Copyright Office decided what was obscene more or less arbitrarily. Today, however, although the Copyright Office may still deny copyright registration to obscene works, it must apply the standards developed by the courts to determine what is obscene. And although courts have been anything but clear in announcing standards of obscenity, it's safe to say these standards are much narrower than those that used to be applied by the Copyright Office. Today, because of the confusion as to what is and isn't obscene,

---

5. "The law is a ass—a idiot," spoken by Mr. Bumble. Dickens, Charles: *Oliver Twist* (The American News Co., New York), p. 197.

6. *Pocket Books, Inc. v. Dell Pub.* Co., 49 Misc.2d 252, 267 NYS2d 269 (Sup. Ct. 1966).

the Copyright Office is unlikely to reject an application for any but the most patently hard-core material.

NOTE ON LIBEL AND SEDITION • If a work submitted for copyright contains material that appears libelous or seditious,[7] it will still be accepted for copyright, because the material is legally protected by the First Amendment until its libelous or seditious character is established in court, and because it would be almost impossible for the Copyright Office to decide whether the contents are libelous or seditious.

COPYRIGHT LAW AS IT APPLIES TO DERIVATIVE AND COLLECTIVE WORKS

The 1976 Copyright Act defines a "compilation" as "a work formed by the collection and assembling of preexisting materials or of data that are selected, coordinated, or arranged in such a way that the resulting work as a whole constitutes an original work of authorship."[8] In other words, a compilation is what results when an author takes material or information that already exists (and which may not be copyrighted or even copyrightable in its original form) and puts it together in a new way. For the purposes of copyright registration, it doesn't matter whether the preexisting materials or the data are themselves original or were already copyrighted (although it matters to the authors, of course). What counts for copyright purposes is the way the materials are collected and assembled, or the data selected, coordinated, or arranged. If the preexisting materials or data are themselves copyrightable, but have not been copyrighted, then the compilation is a "collective work." If they are already copyrighted, it's a "derivative work."

The Act defines a "derivative work" to be "a work based upon one or more preexisting works, such as a translation, musical arrangement, dramatization, fictionalization, motion picture version, sound recording, art reproduction, abridgment, condensation, or another form in which a work may be recast, transformed, or adapted." The Act goes on:

> A work consisting of editorial revisions, annotations, elaborations, or other modifications which, as a whole, represent an original work of authorship, is a "derivative work."

---

7.   Seditious material is that which advocates the overthrow of the government by violent or unlawful means.

8.   Copyright Act, Section 101.

Both compilations and derivative works may be copyrighted. But the new Copyright Act protects only materials contributed by the author of the work—not the preexisting material. In other words, what the compiler or deriver copyrights is only his contribution, separate from the material he has compiled or based his derived work on. The compiler's originality consists in selecting and organizing the material or data. The author of a derivative work finds originality in changing an earlier work. Assuming these changes result in a distinguishable version, different from the earlier work, they are copyrightable.

The fact that the author of a derivative or compiled work can copyright his work doesn't, of course, rob the original copyright holders of their rights. Unless the material is already in the public domain (i.e., has lost or outlasted its copyright, or was never copyrighted), the compiler or derivative work author may legally use the material only with the permission of the original copyright owner. The author of the derivative work gets only what the owner of the original copyright grants. The new copyright, in the derivative work, doesn't give the derivative author any additional rights.

EXAMPLE • Suppose a novelist sells dramatic adaptation rights in her novel to a playwright. The dramatic adaptation rights sold refer specifically to an English-language dramatization, to be performed in the United States and Canada. The playwright, who authors the derivative work based on the novel, holds a copyright only on his particular theatrical version in the English language in the United States and Canada. He has neither the right to the original novel, nor the right to translate, nor to license the translation, of his theatrical version into another language.

If, however, a work enters the public domain (say, it was never copyrighted, or the copyright has run out), then anyone can base a derivative work on it without getting permission. Even if the author of the original work gave the author of a particular derivative work an exclusive right to create the derivative work in a certain language and area, as in the example just above, the underlying work is fair game for anyone who wants to use it for any purpose once it is in the public domain. You may write a musical play about Don Quixote, even though *Man of La Mancha* already exists.

WHO OWNS A COPYRIGHT?

The 1976 Copyright Act vests copyright ownership in the author or authors of the work. "Author," however, is not defined in the act. Implicit in the structure of the act is the idea that the author is the creator of a work, the person who brings originality to it. While this seems simple and straightforward enough, copyright ownership is often anything but that. As we shall see, copyrights (and parts of copyrights) are commonly bought, sold, assigned, and traded so that figuring out who owns what can be harder than deciphering the plot of a clever whodunit. Let's look at the most common copyright ownership issues under separate headings:

Works "Made for Hire"

The big exception to the general rule that the creator of a work is its author for copyright purposes occurs when the work is "made for hire."

Under the 1909 act, it was sometimes difficult to tell whether or not a work was made for hire. The 1976 Copyright Act attempts to clarify old ambiguities and protect the writer in the process. It defines a work made for hire as one prepared by an employee within the scope of her employment or one specially ordered or commissioned.[9] Does the definition mean that whenever a writer works for someone else and produces a piece of writing, it belongs to the employer? Does the definition mean that when a freelance writer agrees to produce a job by prior arrangement, not on speculation, the freelancer has become an employee for hire? The answer to both questions is "Not necessarily." The apparently simple and straightforward definition of work made for hire under the 1976 act turns out not to be so simple and straightforward after all.

Within the Scope of Employment

When trying to establish whether a work is made for hire, it's important to understand if the writer has prepared it "within the scope of his or her employment." The law says an employee is someone whose employer has the right to direct and supervise the manner in which the employee does her job. Being on the employer's payroll isn't the test. Assuming the writer is an employee, however, the work produced must still be within the scope of employment—that is, done pursuant to the writer's duties as an employee. If not, it's not a work for hire. For example, if Joan Smith, who was hired to repair exotic automobiles, wrote a repair manual for obscure British electrical systems that turned out to be a classic, her employer would have no rights to that work merely because Joan was on the payroll. She would become an employee for

---

9. Copyright Act, Section 101.

hire, and the manual would become a work made for hire, only if she was hired to write such books, or the book project was specifically developed and approved as part of the continuing employment relationship.

Working on Commission—The Freelancer for Hire

It's possible for a writer who isn't an employee to create a work made for hire. A freelancer may be asked to produce a work on special order or commission. Even under these circumstances, the Copyright Act makes the writer the copyright holder unless the work is performed under a written contract, signed by both the writer and whoever commissions the work, which states that the work is for hire. To repeat, if no such agreement dealing with rights as an author is signed by both parties, then the work is not made for hire even though that work is done on commission or special order.

To become a work made for hire, a commissioned work must meet two further tests:

First, it must be produced at the "instance" and "expense" of the employer. This means, at least in theory, that the employer must ask the writer to do the work and pay for it. If the writer approaches the employer with the story idea, then the resulting work is technically not one made for hire, although in the real world the technicality is often ignored and the commissioned author willingly signs a work-for-hire agreement.

It's possible that a writer who thought up a story idea did preliminary work before approaching a publisher (say, a magazine) and was then forced to sign a work-for-hire agreement as a condition of publication. In this case, she might be able to have the agreement voided by a court on the grounds that it wasn't a legitimate work-for-hire agreement. As of this writing, however, there are no appellate court cases that say so.

Second, to be a work made for hire, the commissioned work must be specially ordered or commissioned for use as a contribution to a collective work, as a part of a motion picture or other audiovisual work, as a translation, as a supplementary work, as a compilation, as an instructional text, as a test, as answer material for a test, or as an atlas. "Supplementary work" is a secondary adjunct to a work by another author that introduces, concludes, illustrates, explains, revises, comments on, or assists in the use of the other work. Front and back matter in a book and illustrations commissioned to enhance a book are good examples.

Does Work-for-Hire Matter?

Often a writer would rather not create a work made for hire, to keep ownership of the copyright in the work, so it's important to understand how to avoid that consequence. The easy way is to make sure that no written contract includes a clause explicitly saying you are one. If you sign a written agreement, however, and the other tests are met, your work will be made for hire. This means you aren't the "author," for copyright purposes, and your work no longer belongs to you. Your only compensation is the payment set out in the contract.

Creating a work made for hire has its advantages, of course. You work on a specific assignment, for an agreed fee. You don't have to worry about marketing your writing. If your ego doesn't need the gratification that ownership of copyright sometimes provides, writing as an employee for hire offers its own satisfactions. In certain fields of technical and advertising writing, almost all writing is done for hire. Screenwriters, too, are employees for hire, more often than not. They get credit as writers, but they don't own the copyright on the screenplays they write. Finally, the California legislature has adopted a law that mandates unemployment insurance, disability insurance, and workers' compensation coverage for those who create works made for hire, under certain circumstances.

If the employer in an employment-for-hire situation breaches the agreement with the writer (by using it for a purpose completely outside the scope of the agreement, for example, or by failing to pay the employee), the writer may have good legal cause for retrieving the copyright but is probably not entitled to take copies of the work already made by the employer. There is also a good chance the employee for hire can recover money damages for the value of the work done and not paid for. If the commissioning party fails to pay your compensation, you may be able to establish that you own the copyright, because of what the law calls "failure of consideration." This doctrine can be extremely useful, because the commissioning party would then breach your copyright by publishing the work. Remedies for breach of copyright are potent. See Chapter 9.

Collective Works

You'll recall that a collective work is called a "compilation," for copyright purposes. This means it's an assemblage of separate and distinct works, each of which may be eligible for copyright on its own by its author. However, the Copyright Act also provides that the person who assembles the separate works can copyright the collection, if the holders of the individual copyrights allow. The collective copyright allows the author to reproduce and distribute each contribution (but only as part of the collective work), as well as to revise the collective work. An allowable revision would be to add or drop short stories to or from an anthology. But the copyright in the collective work does not give the collective author the right to modify the contributed work in any way, unless its author allows it. If the collective author wants the power to edit or revise, she must get it from the original author by contract.[10]

If you are the author of a contribution to a collective work, you should consider how much authority over your work you're willing to give the collective author. You may, for example, wish to allow the collective author to edit your work—or you may not. You may want to permit her to offer your contribution as a reprint—or you may not. Normally, you will want to restrict the rights granted to the collective authors to the right to reprint your work. If the collective author wants more rights, you should deal with her request on a case by case basis.

Joint Copyright Ownership

So far, we have discussed situations in which the copyright in a given work is owned by one person. It's also possible for two or more people to own a single copyright in a single work. There are three ways in which joint copyright ownership commonly occurs. Let's look at them one at a time.

Co-authors

If a work is created by two or more authors in either inseparable or interdependent parts, the authors are co-owners of the copyright in that work. Does this mean every work put together by more than one creator leads to one jointly owned copyright? No. The spectrum of jointly created works runs from the obviously separable or independent collaborative efforts of a writer and a photo illustrator to that rare and miraculous collaboration between two writers who honestly can't identify who wrote what. The narrative/photo example would not lead to joint copyright ownership, no matter how closely the writer and the artist worked

---

10.   Copyright Act, Section 201(c).

together. But the example of the closely interwoven prose work obviously would, if the two writers so intended.

Joint authors need not actually write together, nor is it necessary for one joint author to contribute actual writing for joint ownership to result. If one co-author contributes plot ideas and the other turns the ideas into prose, the two are probably joint authors and joint copyright owners, unless they agree on some other arrangement.

The difference between this example and the narrative/photo example lies in the ability to separate photographs from text. Separating the contributed plot from the words on paper expressing it is impossible.

NOTE ON COLLABORATION AGREEMENTS • Chapter 3, on collaboration and collaboration agreements, appears in this book because people who work together all too often wind up bitter enemies over misunderstandings about duties and responsibilities, ownership and control, and money. Joint authorship adds its own significant perils to the hazards of writing for a living. Before you do any significant work with a co-author, please understand your copyright rights discussed here, but also pay close attention to Chapter 3, and reduce your entire agreement to writing.

Transfer of Copyright

Joint ownership can also result when the sole author of a work transfers part ownership of a copyright to one or more people or corporations, or transfers the entire copyright to others. It can occur, too, if the author assigns her copyright to another—for example to her publisher, and the publisher then arranges for a second author to contribute to the work. If the second author is not an employee for hire, then the copyright becomes a joint one.

Community Property Law

A copyright also commonly ends up owned jointly if the author is married and resides in a community property state, such as California, unless there is a written agreement to the contrary.[11] In some states, if a

---

11. For an excellent discussion of community property law and how to change the legal status of property by agreement among spouses, see *California Marriage and Divorce Law,* Ihara and Warner, Nolo Press. Readers who live in separate property states that follow "equitable distribution" rules should be aware that copyrights are property subject to division like any other. The owners of valuable copyrights who face divorce should see a lawyer.

couple live together, their property, including copyrights, may be treated as jointly owned if a court finds they have made an oral agreement to do so. Written agreements to share copyright ownership are routinely recognized.

Complications of Joint Ownership

Now let's look at some of the legal complications of joint copyright ownership. Perhaps the most important thing to understand is that each joint author has the right to deal with the whole work, including those parts contributed by others. Any joint author can grant a nonexclusive license without obtaining the consent of the other authors.[12] There is a big exception to this rule, however. The joint author who grants a license to a third party can't destroy the value of the work in the process. And the joint author who authorizes use of the work must account to the other joint authors for their share of any proceeds. This is true whether the exploiting joint author makes money by licensing rights to others or by exploiting the work herself.

One joint author can transfer only what he owns—his share of ownership. If there are three joint authors, and each owns an undivided one-third financial interest in the work, then the most an author can transfer is a one-third financial interest.[13] The nonexclusive license, however, entitles the licensee to publish the entire work. The licensee is obligated only to compensate the joint author who gave him the license.

Joint authors should be clear among themselves about who may deal with their rights. To avoid confusion, one practical approach is for the joint authors to agree in writing that they will make decisions unanimously, or by majority vote, before any of them may authorize the exploiting of any jointly owned rights. Another approach is to make one joint author the business agent for the others. If any agreement along these lines is made, it's a good idea to record it in the Copyright Office so that third parties are put on notice of the arrangement. If the joint authors keep their arrangements to themselves, an unknowing third party could deal with one of the joint authors, obtain rights, and then successfully defend against any claim by the other joint authors based on the theory that the transferring joint author had no right to make the transfer. Two general principles of law apply in this situation: First,

---

12.   If the joint author could grant an exclusive license, she could prevent the other joint authors from exercising their right to license the work.

13.   An "undivided interest" entitles each owner to act as if she owned the whole work, but her share of the proceeds equals the fraction she owns.

innocent third parties should not be held responsible for knowledge of agreements between others they know nothing about. Second, if an official source of information exists, such as the records of the Copyright Office, a third party can't ignore the existence of the information and still claim to be innocently misled.

Terminating the Grant of Copyright

The owner of a copyright who has conveyed it to someone else may recapture the copyright by complying with some detailed notification and recordation provisions of Sections 203 and 304(C) of the Copyright Act of 1976. Oversimplified, the law allows the owner to cause copyright to revert after thirty-five or forty or fifty-six years.

CONCLUSION AND TRANSITION

We've laid out the basic concepts of copyright here, along with an introduction to the copyright law that's been in effect in this country for most of this century. The next two chapters tell you how to obtain copyright in your work and what to do about copyright infringement.

8 COPYRIGHT FORMALITIES

INTRODUCTION

Obtaining federal copyright protection is easy. You must simply express your work in fixed and tangible form. Since March 1, 1989, when the United States finally signed the Berne Convention, a treaty establishing international protection for copyright owners, copyright claimants need no longer include a copyright notice on copies of the work nor register the work with the Copyright Office. But it still makes sense to include the notice and to register, and it's still necessary to deposit one copy (of an unpublished work) or two copies (of a published work).

Now let's explore copyright formalities—and the consequences of ignoring them—in detail.

COPYRIGHT NOTICE IS ESSENTIAL FOR FULL PROTECTION

The copyright notice, also called the copyright legend, is extremely important even if it's no longer required. If you publish your work without it, a defendant in an infringement action can claim to be an innocent infringer who in good faith believed that a work wasn't subject to copyright.[1] Innocent infringers can reduce the amount of damages they must pay to the copyright owner (see Chapter 9).

---

1. Copyright Act, Section 405(a)(1).

A copyright claimant must seek registration of copyright with the Copyright Office (whether the copyright is granted or not) in order to sue for infringement. Seeking registration also lets you sue for statutory damages and show the court evidence of your copyright.

In fact, including the copyright legend on every published copy of your work is so important that if you license use of the copyright to others, your written license agreement should require the licensee to include the copyright notice on all copies of the work. If the licensee fails to do so, that failure can jeopardize your copyright, even though you had no direct control over the licensee's action.

The Copyright Act of 1976 defines "publication" for copyright purposes as "the distribution of copies to the public by sale or transfer of ownership, or rental, lease, or lending . . . , or the offer to do any of those things. Performing the work in public, or displaying it in public, doesn't constitute publication. Neither does sending a manuscript to a publisher who does not print the work. But sending the work to a retailer for sale does constitute publication. So does offering it for sale through the mail.

WHAT A PROPER COPYRIGHT NOTICE LOOKS LIKE

The form of the copyright notice is simple. Unfortunately, many authors and publishers commonly and needlessly complicate it. All the Copyright Act requires is a legend in any one of the three following forms:

Copyright 1999 Gloria Grimes
Copr. 1999 Gloria Grimes
© 1999 Gloria Grimes

Any one of these forms satisfies U.S. law. However, to comply with the Universal Copyright Convention, which protects your copyright in other countries that have agreed to be bound by it, you should include the ©. And because some Latin American countries also require the words "All Rights Reserved," you might as well include them, too. The following form is good in the United States and all countries recognizing the Universal Copyright Convention:

© 1999 Gloria Grimes. All rights reserved.

Let's now look at these requirements in detail.

The Author's Name

The name in the copyright notice must be the name of the "author," as the Copyright Act defines "author." Chapter 7, pages 145, 157, and 160, should be reviewed if you have questions about what the act means by "author."

If you've written a work made for hire, you won't have to worry about copyright, because it belongs to your employer (if you're a staffer) or the publisher who commissioned the work (if you're a freelancer).

How multiple authors handle their copyright notice—or notices—depends on their working relationship and the nature of their product. Collaborators should include their names in the notice:

© 1993 Susan Sternstuff and Norman Novicio. All rights reserved.

A writer who is responsible for text, and the photographer whose photographs are separate from the text, will prefer individual copyright notices:

Text copyright 1981 Christopher Marlowe
Photographs copyright 1979, 1981, Nicephore Niepce[2]

The copyright notice for a collective work may show the collector's name. The better practice is to show the name of each contributor (and the date of publication of the contributed work) separately:

© 1990 Albert Able
© 1994 Brenda Bell
© 1995 Zuleika Dobson

If you use a pen name, that's the name to appear in the copyright notice; otherwise, why bother? The same principle applies to the anonymous author:

© 1992 Noma Feather

Copr. 1991 Anonymous[3]

Publishing contracts frequently state that the publisher will obtain copyright for the work. Sometimes the contract allows the publisher to

---

2.   We've assumed the photos include some previously published and some first published in the year the book is first published.

3.   The length of copyright for a pseudonymous or anonymous author depends on that author's willingness to reveal her identity to the Copyright Office. If she is willing, she obtains copyright for her life, plus fifty years. If not, copyright lasts seventy-five years from date of publication.

obtain copyright in the publisher's name, not the author's. We've discussed the implications in Chapter 1, page 16, which you should reread if this issue concerns you. Our position is that the author, not the publisher, should own the copyright, and most publishers, if pressed, will agree.

The Year of Publication

The year to include in the copyright notice is the year of publication. Under the 1909 act, the term of copyright protection began in "the year of publication." The publication year was also used to calculate when "common law" copyright protection (for unpublished works) was lost. So before 1978 it was crucial to know when publication occurred.

Under the 1976 act, publication remains an important concept, even though the term of copyright for a single author is measured by the author's life plus fifty years. The publication date is still important because certain types of copyright notice defects and failure to register can be cured for five years after publication. Also, for joint works, works written by an author who uses a pseudonym or wants to be anonymous, and works made for hire, the term of copyright protection begins with the year of first publication and lasts seventy-five years.

If you revise a work already copyrighted, you should register the revised work and obtain a fresh copyright. The year in which the revision is published should then appear in the copyright notice, after the year copyright was first obtained.

Remember, when you create or complete a work isn't relevant to the date that appears in the copyright notice. What counts is when you first publish it.

WHAT HAPPENS IF YOU OMIT THE COPYRIGHT NOTICE?

What if your copyright notice is either omitted or defective for works published before March 1989 (which were required to include a proper notice and to be registered)? You can preserve some rights *if you act promptly,* but you won't be able to obtain a full recovery against an innocent infringer (see Chapter 9).

The 1976 act excuses copyright notice omission for "a relatively small number of copies," or, if the work is registered within five years after publication without the notice, if the copyright owner cures the defect promptly after discovering it. Otherwise, the work may fall into the public domain. If you've omitted the copyright notice from your published work, make sure all subsequent copies contain the proper notice. If it's practical to provide stickers with the copyright notice to all distributors of your work, do so.

The uncertainties about how to cure the omission of the copyright notice for work published before March 1989 make it extremely important for you to be sure the notice appears on your published work.

THE EFFECT OF A DEFECTIVE COPYRIGHT NOTICE

What if one or two of these essential elements of the copyright notice are omitted? All three elements of the notice—the word copyright (or the abbreviation copr. or the ©), the year of publication, and the author's name—must appear in the notice. An invalid notice is treated and cured as if it were omitted for work published before March 1989.

Names

If the notice leaves out the author's name, the author had five years to protect his copyright by registering with the Copyright Office (if the work wasn't already registered) and using reasonable efforts to affix the corrected legend to copies of the work in the process of being distributed. This includes those in the hands of distributors and retailers, but not those already in the hands of the public.

If the notice contains the wrong author's name, or a misspelled version of the name, the real author suffers no loss of protection unless an infringer was innocently misled by the mistaken legend. If, for example, the infringer asks the person named in the notice for permission to publish the work—and gets it—the infringer was misled. The infringer must make a reasonable, good faith effort to check the facts, however. If the author's name and the name in the copyright notice are different, anyone wishing to use the material should contact both.

Authors are entitled to use pseudonyms or to remain anonymous without sacrificing copyright protection. This means the copyright legend can include the author's nickname or a trade name, or even the author's last name only, unless the public might be confused by the absence of the author's full, correct name.

The Year of Copyright

If your copyright notice states any year previous to the actual year of publication, your notice is valid, but the year stated in the notice is treated as if it were the year of publication. This won't ordinarily matter at all unless you are an anonymous or pseudonymous author, or in another of the relatively rare situations where your copyright depends on the year of publication, in which case it shortens the duration of your copyright.

If the mistaken year is just one year later than the actual year of publication, the notice is valid, and needn't be corrected.

If the year stated in the copyright notice is more than one year after the actual year of publication, the notice is invalid, which is the same as no notice at all. See page 168 for advice on how to cure the error.

HOW TO REGISTER YOUR COPYRIGHT

Registration is the second necessary step to obtain full copyright protection. You can't bring a copyright infringement lawsuit unless you've registered.[4] Proper registration also enables the court to award you both statutory damages for infringement of your copyright and attorneys' fees.[5] These are reasons enough to complete an application form, prepare it, deposit copies, and write a check for $20.

Copyright Application Forms

Copyright forms are prescribed and printed by the Copyright Office, and you can obtain as many copies as you need, free, by writing to:

Information and Publication
Section LM-455
Copyright Office
Library of Congress
Washington, DC 20559

or by calling (202) 707-9100.

The Copyright Office recognizes that all works aren't alike, so different forms must be used for different kinds of work. (See Chapter 7, page

---

4.   Copyright Act, Section 411(a).
5.   Copyright Act, Section 412.

149, for the details and definitions. The instructions for the forms will also help.) Each form has been assigned a code. Here are the forms most likely to be used by a writer:

- *Form TX:* For "nondramatic literary works"
- *Form PA:* For "works of the performing arts," including, among others, dramatic works
- *Form VA:* For "works of visual art," such as photographs or illustrative drawings
- *Form GR/CP:* For a group of works contributed to periodicals, used as an adjunct to a basic form (TX, VA, or PA)
- Form SE: For serials, such as magazines and newspapers
- *Form RE:* For renewal of copyright granted under the 1909 Act
- *Form CA:* For supplementing or correcting a form previously filed

All these forms include instructions. Sample copies of the forms are reprinted on pages 173–194, filled in to illustrate several common ways forms are used.

NOTE TO MAGAZINE WRITERS • As Form GR/CP implies, it's possible to save money by including several works on one application. If one author has written a number of pieces for various periodicals, the author may group them under one copyright application.[6] Also, a group of related works by the same author may be copyrighted under the same application.[7]

Filing the Copyright Application Form

Along with the application form and fee, you must submit one complete copy of an unpublished work or two complete copies of the best edition of a published work. Once the unpublished work is published, you have three months from the date of publication to make the deposit. You won't sacrifice copyright protection by failing to do so, but your failure may result in a fine of up to $250 for each work and, if you fail to respond to a demand for registration from the Copyright Office, you may be liable for a fine of $2,500 as well.[8]

---

6. Copyright Act, Section 408(C)(2).

7. Copyright Act, Section 408(C)(1). But the Copyright Office hasn't yet implemented this provision with regulations and forms, so you may not be able to take advantage of it.

8. Copyright Act, Section 407.

The "best edition" is the one most suitable for the Library of Congress, which keeps deposited works.[9] As a general rule, the hardcover edition of a book is "better" than a paperbound edition, and a trade paperback is better than a mass market paperback. (For definitions of these publishing terms, see the Glossary.)

The Copyright Act requires that the three elements for registration of a copyright claim be delivered to the Copyright Office together. When you consider the volume of mail the Copyright Office receives each day, there's good reason to comply with this reasonable requirement.

Mistake and Omissions in Registration

The Copyright Office recognizes the possibility that even intelligent, well-meaning authors may err in completing copyright registration forms. So the Register of Copyrights provides a form to use for corrections—Form CA. You'll find a completed form in the next section of this chapter.

Sample Copyright Forms

The completed samples illustrate how to use copyright forms for a variety of circumstances:

1. Form TX: a single book by a single author, not yet published
2. Form TX: a single book by joint authors
3. Form TX: a work made for hire
4. Form PA: a single dramatic work by a single author, adapted from a novel
5. Form TX and GR/CP: a group of works by an author using a pseudonym
6. Form TX and Form VA: a single book with text by one author and photographs, separately copyrighted
7. Form RE: renewal of copyright for a work copyrighted under the 1909 act
8. Form CA: a corrected registration to cure an error in the wrong title of a book
9. Form SE: a periodical

---

9. Copyright Act, Section 101.

- 1 • A single work, unpublished
  - • A single author

FORM TX
For a Nondramatic Literary Work
UNITED STATES COPYRIGHT OFFICE

REGISTRATION NUMBER

_____

TX _____ TXU _____

EFFECTIVE DATE OF REGISTRATION

_____

Month _____ Day _____ Year _____

[Leave this space blank. The Copyright Office fills it in and returns it to you as evidence of your registered copyright.]

DO NOT WRITE ABOVE THIS LINE. IF YOU NEED MORE SPACE, USE A SEPARATE CONTINUATION SHEET.

1

TITLE OF THIS WORK ▼   **GOING HOME**

PREVIOUS OR ALTERNATIVE TITLES ▼   **NONE**

PUBLICATION AS A CONTRIBUTION If this work was published as a contribution to a periodical, serial, or collection, give information about the collective work in which the contribution appeared.   Title of Collective Work ▼   **N/A**

If published in a periodical or serial give: Volume ▼   Number ▼   Issue Date ▼   On Pages ▼

2

a

NAME OF AUTHOR ▼   **THOMAS WOLFRAM**

DATES OF BIRTH AND DEATH
Year Born ▼ **1939**   Year Died ▼

Was this contribution to the work a "work made for hire"?
☐ Yes
☐ No

AUTHOR'S NATIONALITY OR DOMICILE
Name of Country
OR { Citizen of ▶ **U.S.**
Domiciled in ▶

WAS THIS AUTHOR'S CONTRIBUTION TO THE WORK
Anonymous?   ☐ Yes ☒ No
Pseudonymous? ☐ Yes ☒ No
If the answer to either of these questions is "Yes," see detailed instructions.

NATURE OF AUTHORSHIP Briefly describe nature of material created by this author in which copyright is claimed. ▼

NOTE
Under the law, the "author" of a "work made for hire" is generally the employer, not the employee (see instructions). For any part of this work that was "made for hire" check "Yes" in the space provided, give the employer (or other person for whom the work was prepared) as "Author" of that part, and leave the space for dates of birth and death blank.

b

NAME OF AUTHOR ▼

DATES OF BIRTH AND DEATH
Year Born ▼   Year Died ▼

Was this contribution to the work a "work made for hire"?
☐ Yes
☐ No

AUTHOR'S NATIONALITY OR DOMICILE
Name of Country
OR { Citizen of ▶
Domiciled in ▶

WAS THIS AUTHOR'S CONTRIBUTION TO THE WORK
Anonymous?   ☐ Yes ☐ No
Pseudonymous? ☐ Yes ☐ No
If the answer to either of these questions is "Yes," see detailed instructions.

NATURE OF AUTHORSHIP Briefly describe nature of material created by this author in which copyright is claimed. ▼

c

NAME OF AUTHOR ▼

DATES OF BIRTH AND DEATH
Year Born ▼   Year Died ▼

Was this contribution to the work a "work made for hire"?
☐ Yes
☐ No

AUTHOR'S NATIONALITY OR DOMICILE
Name of Country
OR { Citizen of ▶
Domiciled in ▶

WAS THIS AUTHOR'S CONTRIBUTION TO THE WORK
Anonymous?   ☐ Yes ☐ No
Pseudonymous? ☐ Yes ☐ No
If the answer to either of these questions is "Yes," see detailed instructions.

NATURE OF AUTHORSHIP Briefly describe nature of material created by this author in which copyright is claimed. ▼

3

a YEAR IN WHICH CREATION OF THIS WORK WAS COMPLETED **1998** ◀ Year
This information must be given in all cases.

b DATE AND NATION OF FIRST PUBLICATION OF THIS PARTICULAR WORK
Complete this information ONLY if this work has been published.
Month ▶ _____ Day ▶ _____ Year ▶ _____ ◀ Nation

4

See instructions before completing this space.

COPYRIGHT CLAIMANT(S) Name and address must be given even if the claimant is the same as the author given in space 2. ▼

**THOMAS WOLFRAM
10 ELM ST.
ASHVILLE, CA 90001**

TRANSFER If the claimant(s) named here in space 4 is (are) different from the author(s) named in space 2, give a brief statement of how the claimant(s) obtained ownership of the copyright. ▼

DO NOT WRITE HERE OFFICE USE ONLY

APPLICATION RECEIVED

ONE DEPOSIT RECEIVED

TWO DEPOSITS RECEIVED

FUNDS RECEIVED

MORE ON BACK ▶ • Complete all applicable spaces (numbers 5-9) on the reverse side of this page.
• See detailed instructions.   • Sign the form at line 8.

DO NOT WRITE HERE

Page 1 of _____ pages

173

EXAMINED BY

CHECKED BY

☐ CORRESPONDENCE
  Yes

FORM TX

FOR
COPYRIGHT
OFFICE
USE
ONLY

DO NOT WRITE ABOVE THIS LINE. IF YOU NEED MORE SPACE, USE A SEPARATE CONTINUATION SHEET.

PREVIOUS REGISTRATION Has registration for this work, or for an earlier version of this work, already been made in the Copyright Office?

☐ Yes ☒ No If your answer is "Yes," why is another registration being sought? (Check appropriate box) ▼

a. ☐ This is the first published edition of a work previously registered in unpublished form.

b. ☐ This is the first application submitted by this author as copyright claimant.

c. ☐ This is a changed version of the work, as shown by space 6 on this application.

If your answer is "Yes," give: **Previous Registration Number** ▼   **Year of Registration** ▼

5

DERIVATIVE WORK OR COMPILATION
Preexisting Material Identify any preexisting work or works that this work is based on or incorporates. ▼

a   N/A

b   **Material Added to This Work** Give a brief, general statement of the material that has been added to this work and in which copyright is claimed. ▼

    N/A

6

See instructions
before completing
this space.

DEPOSIT ACCOUNT If the registration fee is to be charged to a Deposit Account established in the Copyright Office, give name and number of Account.
Name ▼   **Account Number** ▼

a

7

b   **CORRESPONDENCE** Give name and address to which correspondence about this application should be sent.   Name/Address/Apt/City/State/ZIP ▼

    THOMAS WOLFRAM
    10 ELM ST.
    ASHVILLE, CA 90001

    Area code and daytime telephone number ▶ 213-999-9999   Fax number ▶ 213-998-9999
    Email ▶ twolfram@math.com

CERTIFICATION* I, the undersigned, hereby certify that I am the

Check only one ▶
☒ author
☐ other copyright claimant
☐ owner of exclusive right(s)
☐ authorized agent of _____

of the work identified in this application and that the statements made
by me in this application are correct to the best of my knowledge.

Name of author or other copyright claimant, or owner of exclusive right(s) ▲

8

Typed or printed name and date ▼ If this application gives a date of publication in space 3, do not sign and submit it before that date.

    THOMAS WOLFRAM   Date ▶ JAN. 28, 1998

Handwritten signature (X) ▼

☞   X _____ *Thomas Wolfram* _____

**The filing fee of $20.00 is effective through June 30, 1999. After that date, please write the Copyright Office,
check the Copyright Office Website at http://www.loc.gov/copyright, or call (202) 707-3000 for the latest fee information.**

**Mail
certificate
to:**

Name ▼

    THOMAS WOLFRAM

**Certificate
will be
mailed in
window
envelope**

Number/Street/Apt ▼

    10 ELM ST.

City/State/ZIP ▼

    ASHVILLE, CA 90001

9

2 • A single book, published
 • Joint authors
 • Previously published under another title
   and revised: a "derivative work"

[Leave blank]

FORM TX
For a Nondramatic Literary Work
UNITED STATES COPYRIGHT OFFICE

REGISTRATION NUMBER

_____

TX _____ TXU _____
EFFECTIVE DATE OF REGISTRATION

_____

Month   Day   Year

DO NOT WRITE ABOVE THIS LINE. IF YOU NEED MORE SPACE, USE A SEPARATE CONTINUATION SHEET.

1

TITLE OF THIS WORK ▼
GONE HOME

PREVIOUS OR ALTERNATIVE TITLES ▼ **THE OPEN ROAD**

PUBLICATION AS A CONTRIBUTION If this work was published as a contribution to a periodical, serial, or collection, give information about the collective work in which the contribution appeared.   **Title of Collective Work ▼**
N/A

If published in a periodical or serial give: **Volume ▼**   **Number ▼**   **Issue Date ▼**   **On Pages ▼**

2 **a**

NAME OF AUTHOR ▼
JANE A. FOX

DATES OF BIRTH AND DEATH
Year Born ▼   Year Died ▼
1950

Was this contribution to the work a "work made for hire"?
☐ Yes
☐ No

AUTHOR'S NATIONALITY OR DOMICILE
Name of Country
OR { Citizen of ▶ **U.S.**
{ Domiciled in ▶

WAS THIS AUTHOR'S CONTRIBUTION TO THE WORK
Anonymous?   Yes **X** No
Pseudonymous?   ☐ Yes **X** No
If the answer to either of these questions is "Yes," see detailed instructions.

NOTE

Under the law, the "author" of a "work made for hire" is generally the employer, not the employee (see instructions). For any part of this work that was "made for hire" check "Yes" in the space provided, give the employer (or other person for whom the work was prepared) as "Author" of that part, and leave the space for dates of birth and death blank.

NATURE OF AUTHORSHIP Briefly describe nature of material created by this author in which copyright is claimed. ▼
CO-AUTHOR OF ENTIRE TEXT AND AUTHOR OF ILLUSTRATIONS

b

NAME OF AUTHOR ▼
THOMAS L. BIRD

DATES OF BIRTH AND DEATH
Year Born ▼   Year Died ▼
1947

Was this contribution to the work a "work made for hire"?
☐ Yes
X No

AUTHOR'S NATIONALITY OR DOMICILE
Name of Country
OR { Citizen of ▶ **U.S.**
{ Domiciled in ▶

WAS THIS AUTHOR'S CONTRIBUTION TO THE WORK
Anonymous?   ☐ Yes **X** No
Pseudonymous?   ☐ Yes **X** No
If the answer to either of these questions is "Yes," see detailed instructions.

NATURE OF AUTHORSHIP Briefly describe nature of material created by this author in which copyright is claimed. ▼
CO-AUTHOR OF ENTIRE TEXT

c

NAME OF AUTHOR ▼

DATES OF BIRTH AND DEATH
Year Born ▼   Year Died ▼

Was this contribution to the work a "work made for hire"?
☐ Yes
☐ No

AUTHOR'S NATIONALITY OR DOMICILE
Name of Country
OR { Citizen of ▶
{ Domiciled in ▶

WAS THIS AUTHOR'S CONTRIBUTION TO THE WORK
Anonymous?   ☐ Yes ☐ No
Pseudonymous?   ☐ Yes ☐ No
If the answer to either of these questions is "Yes," see detailed instructions.

NATURE OF AUTHORSHIP Briefly describe nature of material created by this author in which copyright is claimed. ▼

3 **a**

YEAR IN WHICH CREATION OF THIS WORK WAS COMPLETED   This information must be given **◀** Year in all cases.
1998

b DATE AND NATION OF FIRST PUBLICATION OF THIS PARTICULAR WORK
Complete this information ONLY if this work has been published.   Month ▶ **4**   Day ▶ **1**   Year ▶ **98**
U.S.   **◀** Nation

4

See instructions before completing this space.

COPYRIGHT CLAIMANT(S) Name and address must be given even if the claimant is the same as the author given in space 2. ▼
JANE A. FOX
654 - 24TH ST.
SAN FRANCISCO, CA 94114

THOMAS L. BIRD
323 W. 53RD ST.
N.Y., NY 11111

TRANSFER If the claimant(s) named here in space 4 is (are) different from the author(s) named in space 2, give a brief statement of how the claimant(s) obtained ownership of the copyright. ▼

DO NOT WRITE HERE   OFFICE USE ONLY

APPLICATION RECEIVED

ONE DEPOSIT RECEIVED

TWO DEPOSITS RECEIVED

FUNDS RECEIVED

MORE ON BACK ▶ • Complete all applicable spaces (numbers 5-9) on the reverse side of this page.
                    • See detailed instructions.   • Sign the form at line 8.

DO NOT WRITE HERE
Page 1 of _____ pages

EXAMINED BY

CHECKED BY

☐ CORRESPONDENCE
  Yes

FORM TX

FOR
COPYRIGHT
OFFICE
USE
ONLY

DO NOT WRITE ABOVE THIS LINE. IF YOU NEED MORE SPACE, USE A SEPARATE CONTINUATION SHEET.

PREVIOUS REGISTRATION Has registration for this work, or for an earlier version of this work, already been made in the Copyright Office?

☒ Yes ☐ No If your answer is "Yes," why is another registration being sought? (Check appropriate box) ▼

a. ☐ This is the first published edition of a work previously registered in unpublished form.

b. ☐ This is the first application submitted by this author as copyright claimant.

c. ☒ This is a changed version of the work, as shown by space 6 on this application.

If your answer is "Yes," give: **Previous Registration Number ▼** X111111 **Year of Registration ▼** 1989

5

DERIVATIVE WORK OR COMPILATION

a Preexisting Material Identify any preexisting work or works that this work is based on or incorporates. ▼

A NONFICTION BOOKLENGTH REMINISCENCE ON THE 1960S

b Material Added to This Work Give a brief, general statement of the material that has been added to this work and in which copyright is claimed. ▼

THREE NEW CHAPTERS AND SUBSTANTIAL CHANGES IN SEVEN PRE-EXISTING CHAPTERS

6

See instructions
before completing
this space.

DEPOSIT ACCOUNT If the registration fee is to be charged to a Deposit Account established in the Copyright Office, give name and number of Account.

a Name ▼   Account Number ▼

7

CORRESPONDENCE Give name and address to which correspondence about this application should be sent.   Name/Address/Apt/City/State/ZIP ▼

b JANE A. FOX AND T. L. BIRD
654 - 24TH ST.
SAN FRANCISCO, CA 94114

Area code and daytime telephone number ▶ 415-666-6666   Fax number ▶ 415-555-5555

Email ▶ jafox@henhse.com

CERTIFICATION* I, the undersigned, hereby certify that I am the

Check only one ▼
☐ author
☐ other copyright claimant
☐ owner of exclusive right(s)
☐ authorized agent of _____

of the work identified in this application and that the statements made
by me in this application are correct to the best of my knowledge.

Name of author or other copyright claimant, or owner of exclusive right(s)) ▲

8

Typed or printed name and date ▼ If this application gives a date of publication in space 3, do not sign and submit it before that date.

JANE A. FOX   THOMAS L. BIRD   Date ▶ 4/15/98

☞ Handwritten signature (X) ▼

X _____ Jane A Fox   Thomas L. Bird _____

The filing fee of $20.00 is effective through June 30, 1999. After that date, please write the Copyright Office,
check the Copyright Office Website at http://www.loc.gov/copyright, or call (202) 707-3000 for the latest fee information.

Mail
certificate
to:

Certificate
will be
mailed in
window
envelope

Name ▼
JANE A. FOX

Number/Street/Apt ▼
654 - 24TH ST.

City/State/ZIP ▼
SAN FRANCISCO, CA 94114

YOU MUST:
• Complete all necessary spaces
• Sign your application in space 8
**SEND ALL 3 ELEMENTS
IN THE SAME PACKAGE:**
1. Application form
2. Nonrefundable filing fee in check or money order
   payable to   Register of Copyrights
3. Deposit material
MAIL TO:
Library of Congress
Copyright Office
101 Independence Avenue, S.E.
Washington, D.C. 20559-6000

9

3 • A single work made for hire
  • Published as a contribution to a periodical

FORM TX
For a Nondramatic Literary Work
UNITED STATES COPYRIGHT OFFICE

REGISTRATION NUMBER

_____

TX _____ TXU _____

EFFECTIVE DATE OF REGISTRATION

_____

Month   Day   Year

[Leave blank]

DO NOT WRITE ABOVE THIS LINE. IF YOU NEED MORE SPACE, USE A SEPARATE CONTINUATION SHEET.

1

TITLE OF THIS WORK ▼
HOMEWARD BOUND

PREVIOUS OR ALTERNATIVE TITLES ▼ **N/A**

PUBLICATION AS A CONTRIBUTION If this work was published as a contribution to a periodical, serial, or collection, give information about the collective work in which the contribution appeared.   Title of Collective Work ▼
AIRWAYS MAGAZINE

If published in a periodical or serial give: Volume ▼ **12**   Number ▼ **4**   Issue Date ▼ **JUNE 1998**   On Pages ▼ **4–6,16**

2 **a**

NAME OF AUTHOR ▼
UNION AIRELATIONS, INC.

DATES OF BIRTH AND DEATH
Year Born ▼   Year Died ▼

Was this contribution to the work a "work made for hire"?
X Yes
☐ No

AUTHOR'S NATIONALITY OR DOMICILE
Name of Country
OR { Citizen of ▶ **U.S.**
     Domiciled in ▶ _____

WAS THIS AUTHOR'S CONTRIBUTION TO THE WORK
Anonymous?   ☐ Yes **X** No
Pseudonymous? ☐ Yes **X** No
If the answer to either of these questions is "Yes," see detailed instructions.

NATURE OF AUTHORSHIP Briefly describe nature of material created by this author in which copyright is claimed. ▼
ENTIRE TEXT

NOTE

Under the law, the "author" of a "work made for hire" is generally the employer, not the employee (see instructions). For any part of this work that was "made for hire" check "Yes" in the space provided, give the employer (or other person for whom the work was prepared) as "Author" of that part, and leave the space for dates of birth and death blank.

b

NAME OF AUTHOR ▼

DATES OF BIRTH AND DEATH
Year Born ▼   Year Died ▼

Was this contribution to the work a "work made for hire"?
☐ Yes
☐ No

AUTHOR'S NATIONALITY OR DOMICILE
Name of Country
OR { Citizen of ▶ _____
     Domiciled in ▶ _____

WAS THIS AUTHOR'S CONTRIBUTION TO THE WORK
Anonymous?   ☐ Yes ☐ No
Pseudonymous? ☐ Yes ☐ No
If the answer to either of these questions is "Yes," see detailed instructions.

NATURE OF AUTHORSHIP Briefly describe nature of material created by this author in which copyright is claimed. ▼

c

NAME OF AUTHOR ▼

DATES OF BIRTH AND DEATH
Year Born ▼   Year Died ▼

Was this contribution to the work a "work made for hire"?
☐ Yes
☐ No

AUTHOR'S NATIONALITY OR DOMICILE
Name of Country
OR { Citizen of ▶ _____
     Domiciled in ▶ _____

WAS THIS AUTHOR'S CONTRIBUTION TO THE WORK
Anonymous?   ☐ Yes ☐ No
Pseudonymous? ☐ Yes ☐ No
If the answer to either of these questions is "Yes," see detailed instructions.

NATURE OF AUTHORSHIP Briefly describe nature of material created by this author in which copyright is claimed. ▼

3 **a**

YEAR IN WHICH CREATION OF THIS WORK WAS COMPLETED This information must be given in all cases.
1998 ◀ Year

b DATE AND NATION OF FIRST PUBLICATION OF THIS PARTICULAR WORK
Complete this information ONLY if this work has been published.
Month ▶ **JUNE** Day ▶ **1** Year ▶ **1998**
U.S. ◀ Nation

4

COPYRIGHT CLAIMANT(S) Name and address must be given even if the claimant is the same as the author given in space 2. ▼
UNION AIRELATIONS, INC.
P.O. BOX 414
LOS ANGELES, CA 90002

See instructions before completing this space.

TRANSFER If the claimant(s) named here in space 4 is (are) different from the author(s) named in space 2, give a brief statement of how the claimant(s) obtained ownership of the copyright. ▼

APPLICATION RECEIVED

ONE DEPOSIT RECEIVED

TWO DEPOSITS RECEIVED

FUNDS RECEIVED

DO NOT WRITE HERE
OFFICE USE ONLY

MORE ON BACK ▶ • Complete all applicable spaces (numbers 5-9) on the reverse side of this page.
• See detailed instructions.   • Sign the form at line 8.

DO NOT WRITE HERE
Page 1 of _____ pages

DO NOT WRITE ABOVE THIS LINE. IF YOU NEED MORE SPACE, USE A SEPARATE CONTINUATION SHEET.

PREVIOUS REGISTRATION Has registration for this work, or for an earlier version of this work, already been made in the Copyright Office?

☐ Yes ☒ No If your answer is "Yes," why is another registration being sought? (Check appropriate box) ▼

a. ☐ This is the first published edition of a work previously registered in unpublished form.

b. ☐ This is the first application submitted by this author as copyright claimant.

c. ☐ This is a changed version of the work, as shown by space 6 on this application.

If your answer is "Yes," give: **Previous Registration Number** ▼ _____ **Year of Registration** ▼ _____

5

DERIVATIVE WORK OR COMPILATION

a Preexisting Material Identify any preexisting work or works that this work is based on or incorporates. ▼ _____

b Material Added to This Work Give a brief, general statement of the material that has been added to this work and in which copyright is claimed. ▼ _____

6

See instructions
before completing
this space.

DEPOSIT ACCOUNT If the registration fee is to be charged to a Deposit Account established in the Copyright Office, give name and number of Account.

a Name ▼ _____ Account Number ▼ _____

b **CORRESPONDENCE** Give name and address to which correspondence about this application should be sent. Name/Address/Apt/City/State/ZIP ▼

SARA SMITH, V-P PUBLICATIONS
UNION AIRELATIONS
P.O. BOX 414, LOS ANGELES, CA 90002

Area code and daytime telephone number ▶ **213-555-9999** Fax number ▶ **213-555-9995**

Email ▶ **ssmith@uaire.com**

7

CERTIFICATION* I, the undersigned, hereby certify that I am the

Check only one ▶
☒ author
☐ other copyright claimant
☐ owner of exclusive right(s)
☐ authorized agent of _____
Name of author or other copyright claimant, or owner of exclusive right(s) ▲

of the work identified in this application and that the statements made
by me in this application are correct to the best of my knowledge.

8

Typed or printed name and date ▼ If this application gives a date of publication in space 3, do not sign and submit it before that date.

UNION AIRELATIONS, BY SARA SMITH _____ Date ▶ **JULY 7, 1998**

Handwritten signature (X) ▼

X _ _ _ _ _ _ _ _ _ _ _ _ _ _ _ _ _ _ _

The filing fee of $20.00 is effective through June 30, 1999. After that date, please write the Copyright Office,
check the Copyright Office Website at http://www.loc.gov/copyright, or call (202) 707-3000 for the latest fee information.

9

Mail
certificate
to:

Name ▼
UNION AIRELATIONS, ATTN: SARA SMITH, V-P

Number/Street/Apt ▼
P.O. BOX 414

Certificate
will be
mailed in
window
envelope

City/State/ZIP ▼
LOS ANGELES, CA 90002

YOU MUST:
• Complete all necessary spaces
• Sign your application in space 8
SEND ALL 3 ELEMENTS
IN THE SAME PACKAGE:
1. Application form
2. Nonrefundable filing fee in check or money order
   payable to Register of Copyrights
3. Deposit material
MAIL TO:
Library of Congress
Copyright Office
101 Independence Avenue, S.E.
Washington, D.C. 20559-6000

*17 U.S.C. § 506(e): Any person who knowingly makes a false representation of a material fact in the application for copyright registration provided for by section 409, or in any written statement filed in connection
with the application, shall be fined not more than $2,500.
September 1997—300,000   ♻ PRINTED ON RECYCLED PAPER   ☆U.S. COPYRIGHT OFFICE WWW: March 1998

4 • A single, dramatic work, adapted from another's German novel
• A single author

For a Work of the Performing Arts
UNITED STATES COPYRIGHT OFFICE

REGISTRATION NUMBER

_____

PA _____ PAU _____

EFFECTIVE DATE OF REGISTRATION

_____

Month _____ Day _____ Year _____

[Leave blank]

DO NOT WRITE ABOVE THIS LINE. IF YOU NEED MORE SPACE, USE A SEPARATE CONTINUATION SHEET.

1

TITLE OF THIS WORK ▼
BOUND FOR HOME

PREVIOUS OR ALTERNATIVE TITLES ▼

NATURE OF THIS WORK ▼ See instructions
DRAMA

2

a NAME OF AUTHOR ▼
HAROLD ALAN HAWKE

DATES OF BIRTH AND DEATH
Year Born ▼ **1929** Year Died ▼

Was this contribution to the work a "work made for hire"?
☐ Yes
☐ No

AUTHOR'S NATIONALITY OR DOMICILE
Name of Country
OR { Citizen of ▶ **U.S.**
{ Domiciled in ▶

WAS THIS AUTHOR'S CONTRIBUTION TO THE WORK
Anonymous? ☐ Yes ☒ No
Pseudonymous? ☐ Yes ☒ No
If the answer to either of these questions is "Yes," see detailed instructions.

NATURE OF AUTHORSHIP Briefly describe nature of material created by this author in which copyright is claimed. ▼
ENGLISH TRANSLATION AND DRAMATIZATION

NOTE
Under the law, the "author" of a "work made for hire" is generally the employer, not the employee (see instructions). For any part of this work that was "made for hire" check "Yes" in the space provided, give the employer (or other person for whom the work was prepared) as "Author" of that part, and leave the space for dates of birth and death blank.

b NAME OF AUTHOR ▼

DATES OF BIRTH AND DEATH
Year Born ▼ Year Died ▼

Was this contribution to the work a "work made for hire"?
☐ Yes
☐ No

AUTHOR'S NATIONALITY OR DOMICILE
Name of Country
OR { Citizen of ▶
{ Domiciled in ▶

WAS THIS AUTHOR'S CONTRIBUTION TO THE WORK
Anonymous? ☐ Yes ☐ No
Pseudonymous? ☐ Yes ☐ No
If the answer to either of these questions is "Yes," see detailed instructions.

NATURE OF AUTHORSHIP Briefly describe nature of material created by this author in which copyright is claimed. ▼

c NAME OF AUTHOR ▼

DATES OF BIRTH AND DEATH
Year Born ▼ Year Died ▼

Was this contribution to the work a "work made for hire"?
☐ Yes
☐ No

AUTHOR'S NATIONALITY OR DOMICILE
Name of Country
OR { Citizen of ▶
{ Domiciled in ▶

WAS THIS AUTHOR'S CONTRIBUTION TO THE WORK
Anonymous? ☐ Yes ☐ No
Pseudonymous? ☐ Yes ☐ No
If the answer to either of these questions is "Yes," see detailed instructions.

NATURE OF AUTHORSHIP Briefly describe nature of material created by this author in which copyright is claimed. ▼

3

a YEAR IN WHICH CREATION OF THIS WORK WAS COMPLETED **1998** ◀ Year
This information must be given in all cases.

b DATE AND NATION OF FIRST PUBLICATION OF THIS PARTICULAR WORK
Complete this information ONLY if this work has been published.
Month ▶ _____ Day ▶ _____ Year ▶ _____ ◀ Nation

4

COPYRIGHT CLAIMANT(S) Name and address must be given even if the claimant is the same as the author given in space 2. ▼
HAROLD A. HAWKE
1500 BROADWAY #104
NEW YORK, NY 10000

TRANSFER If the claimant(s) named here in space 4 is (are) different from the author(s) named in space 2, give a brief statement of how the claimant(s) obtained ownership of the copyright. ▼

See instructions before completing this space.

APPLICATION RECEIVED

ONE DEPOSIT RECEIVED

TWO DEPOSITS RECEIVED

FUNDS RECEIVED

DO NOT WRITE HERE OFFICE USE ONLY

MORE ON BACK ▶ • Complete all applicable spaces (numbers 5-9) on the reverse side of this page.
• See detailed instructions. • Sign the form at line 8.

DO NOT WRITE HERE
Page 1 of _____ pages

EXAMINED BY

CHECKED BY

CORRESPONDENCE
Yes

FORM PA

FOR
COPYRIGHT
OFFICE
USE
ONLY

DO NOT WRITE ABOVE THIS LINE. IF YOU NEED MORE SPACE, USE A SEPARATE CONTINUATION SHEET.

PREVIOUS REGISTRATION Has registration for this work, or for an earlier version of this work, already been made in the Copyright Office?

X Yes ☐ No If your answer is "Yes," why is another registration being sought? (Check appropriate box) ▼

a. ☐ This is the first published edition of a work previously registered in unpublished form.

b. ☐ This is the first application submitted by this author as copyright claimant.

c. **X** This is a changed version of the work, as shown by space 6 on this application.

If your answer is "Yes," give: **Previous Registration Number** ▼ **C111111**   **Year of Registration** ▼ **1982**

5

DERIVATIVE WORK OR COMPILATION Complete both space 6a and 6b for a derivative work; complete only 6b for a compilation.

a. Preexisting Material Identify any preexisting work or works that this work is based on or incorporates. ▼

GERMAN NOVEL—"DER HEIMAT," BY LUDWIG SCHIMMEL

b. Material Added to This Work Give a brief, general statement of the material that has been added to this work and in which copyright is claimed. ▼

ENGLISH TRANSLATION AND DRAMATIZATION FOR THE STAGE

6

See instructions
before completing
this space.

DEPOSIT ACCOUNT If the registration fee is to be charged to a Deposit Account established in the Copyright Office, give name and number of Account.

Name ▼   Account Number ▼

7

CORRESPONDENCE Give name and address to which correspondence about this application should be sent.   Name/Address/Apt/City/State/ZIP ▼

HAROLD A. HAWKE
1500 BROADWAY #104
NEW YORK, NY 10000

Area Code and Telephone Number   ▶ **212-222-9999**

Be sure to
give your
daytime phone
◀ number

CERTIFICATION* I, the undersigned, hereby certify that I am the

Check only one ▼

X author

☐ other copyright claimant

☐ owner of exclusive right(s)

☐ authorized agent of _____
          Name of author or other copyright claimant, or owner of exclusive right(s) ▲

of the work identified in this application and that the statements made
by me in this application are correct to the best of my knowledge.

Typed or printed name and date ▼ If this application gives a date of publication in space 3, do not sign and submit it before that date.

HOWARD A. HAWKE   Date ▶ **MARCH 12, 1998**

☞ Handwritten signature (X) ▼

Howard A. Hawke

8

MAIL CERTIFI-CATE TO

Name ▼
HAROLD A. HAWKE

Number/Street/Apt ▼
1500 BROADWAY #104

City/State/ZIP ▼
NEW YORK, NY 10000

Certificate will be mailed in window envelope

YOU MUST:
• Complete all necessary spaces
• Sign your application in space 8

SEND ALL 3 ELEMENTS
IN THE SAME PACKAGE:
1. Application form
2. Nonrefundable $20 filing fee
   in check or money order
   payable to *Register of Copyrights*
3. Deposit material

MAIL TO:
Register of Copyrights
Library of Congress
Washington, D.C. 20559-6000

9

---

*17 U.S.C. § 506(e): Any person who knowingly makes a false representation of a material fact in the application for copyright registration provided for by section 409, or in any written statement filed in connection with the application, shall be fined not more than $2,500.

May 1995—300,000   ♻ PRINTED ON RECYCLED PAPER   ☆U.S. COPYRIGHT OFFICE WWW: February 1998

5 • A group of related works contributed to periodicals within a 12-month period
• A single pseudonymous author

Note: A separate Form TX is required for *each* work—only one is reproduced here.

[Leave blank]

FORM TX
For a Nondramatic Literary Work
UNITED STATES COPYRIGHT OFFICE

REGISTRATION NUMBER

_____

TX _____ TXU _____

EFFECTIVE DATE OF REGISTRATION

_____

Month _____ Day _____ Year _____

DO NOT WRITE ABOVE THIS LINE. IF YOU NEED MORE SPACE, USE A SEPARATE CONTINUATION SHEET.

1

TITLE OF THIS WORK ▼

SEE FORM GR/CP, ATTACHED

PREVIOUS OR ALTERNATIVE TITLES ▼

PUBLICATION AS A CONTRIBUTION If this work was published as a contribution to a periodical, serial, or collection, give information about the collective work in which the contribution appeared.   **Title of Collective Work ▼**

If published in a periodical or serial give: Volume ▼   Number ▼   Issue Date ▼   On Pages ▼

2

a NAME OF AUTHOR ▼

WALTER WARY, WHOSE PSEUDONYM IS WALTER WEARY

DATES OF BIRTH AND DEATH
Year Born ▼ **1956**   Year Died ▼

Was this contribution to the work a "work made for hire"?
☐ Yes
☐ No

AUTHOR'S NATIONALITY OR DOMICILE
Name of Country
OR { Citizen of ▶ **U.S.**
     { Domiciled in ▶

WAS THIS AUTHOR'S CONTRIBUTION TO THE WORK
Anonymous?   Yes **X** No
Pseudonymous? **X** Yes ☐ No
If the answer to either of these questions is "Yes," see detailed instructions.

NOTE

Under the law, the "author" of a "work made for hire" is generally the employer, not the employee (see instructions). For any part of this work that was "made for hire" check "Yes" in the space provided, give the employer (or other person for whom the work was prepared) as "Author" of that part, and leave the space for dates of birth and death blank.

NATURE OF AUTHORSHIP Briefly describe nature of material created by this author in which copyright is claimed. ▼
ENTIRE TEXT

b NAME OF AUTHOR ▼

DATES OF BIRTH AND DEATH
Year Born ▼   Year Died ▼

Was this contribution to the work a "work made for hire"?
☐ Yes
☐ No

AUTHOR'S NATIONALITY OR DOMICILE
Name of Country
OR { Citizen of ▶
     { Domiciled in ▶

WAS THIS AUTHOR'S CONTRIBUTION TO THE WORK
Anonymous?   ☐ Yes ☐ No
Pseudonymous? ☐ Yes ☐ No
If the answer to either of these questions is "Yes," see detailed instructions.

NATURE OF AUTHORSHIP Briefly describe nature of material created by this author in which copyright is claimed. ▼

c NAME OF AUTHOR ▼

DATES OF BIRTH AND DEATH
Year Born ▼   Year Died ▼

Was this contribution to the work a "work made for hire"?
☐ Yes
☐ No

AUTHOR'S NATIONALITY OR DOMICILE
Name of Country
OR { Citizen of ▶
     { Domiciled in ▶

WAS THIS AUTHOR'S CONTRIBUTION TO THE WORK
Anonymous?   ☐ Yes ☐ No
Pseudonymous? ☐ Yes ☐ No
If the answer to either of these questions is "Yes," see detailed instructions.

NATURE OF AUTHORSHIP Briefly describe nature of material created by this author in which copyright is claimed. ▼

3

a YEAR IN WHICH CREATION OF THIS WORK WAS COMPLETED This information must be given in all cases.
_____ **1998** _____ ◀ Year

b DATE AND NATION OF FIRST PUBLICATION OF THIS PARTICULAR WORK
Complete this information ONLY if this work has been published.
Month ▶ _____ Day ▶ _____ Year ▶ _____   ◀ Nation

4

See instructions before completing this space.

COPYRIGHT CLAIMANT(S) Name and address must be given even if the claimant is the same as the author given in space 2. ▼
WALTER WARY
444 NORTH ST.
ANCHORAGE, ALASKA

TRANSFER If the claimant(s) named here in space 4 is (are) different from the author(s) named in space 2, give a brief statement of how the claimant(s) obtained ownership of the copyright. ▼

DO NOT WRITE HERE
OFFICE USE ONLY

APPLICATION RECEIVED

ONE DEPOSIT RECEIVED

TWO DEPOSITS RECEIVED

FUNDS RECEIVED

MORE ON BACK ▶ • Complete all applicable spaces (numbers 5-9) on the reverse side of this page.
• See detailed instructions.   • Sign the form at line 8.

DO NOT WRITE HERE
Page 1 of _____ pages

CORRESPONDENCE
Yes

FOR
COPYRIGHT
OFFICE
USE
ONLY

DO NOT WRITE ABOVE THIS LINE. IF YOU NEED MORE SPACE, USE A SEPARATE CONTINUATION SHEET.

PREVIOUS REGISTRATION Has registration for this work, or for an earlier version of this work, already been made in the Copyright Office?

☐ Yes ☒ No If your answer is "Yes," why is another registration being sought? (Check appropriate box) ▼

a. ☐ This is the first published edition of a work previously registered in unpublished form.

b. ☐ This is the first application submitted by this author as copyright claimant.

c. ☐ This is a changed version of the work, as shown by space 6 on this application.

If your answer is "Yes," give: **Previous Registration Number** ▼   **Year of Registration** ▼

5

DERIVATIVE WORK OR COMPILATION

Preexisting Material Identify any preexisting work or works that this work is based on or incorporates. ▼

a N/A

b **Material Added to This Work** Give a brief, general statement of the material that has been added to this work and in which copyright is claimed. ▼

N/A

6

See instructions
before completing
this space.

DEPOSIT ACCOUNT If the registration fee is to be charged to a Deposit Account established in the Copyright Office, give name and number of Account.

Name ▼   **Account Number** ▼

a

7

b **CORRESPONDENCE** Give name and address to which correspondence about this application should be sent.   Name/Address/Apt/City/State/ZIP ▼

WALTER WARY
444 NORTH ST.
ANCHORAGE, ALASKA

Area code and daytime telephone number   ▶ 907-112-2111   Fax number   ▶ 907-112-2112

Email ▶ walter@wweary.com

CERTIFICATION* I, the undersigned, hereby certify that I am the

Check only one ▶ {
☐ author
☐ other copyright claimant
☐ owner of exclusive right(s)
☐ authorized agent of _____

of the work identified in this application and that the statements made
by me in this application are correct to the best of my knowledge.

Name of author or other copyright claimant, or owner of exclusive right(s)) ▲

8

Typed or printed name and date ▼ If this application gives a date of publication in space 3, do not sign and submit it before that date.

WALTER A. WARY   Date▶ MAY 4, 1998

☞   Handwritten signature (X) ▼

X _____ Walter Wary _____

**The filing fee of $20.00 is effective through June 30, 1999. After that date, please write the Copyright Office,
check the Copyright Office Website at http://www.loc.gov/copyright, or call (202) 707-3000 for the latest fee information.**

Mail
certificate
to:

Certificate
will be
mailed in
window
envelope

Name ▼
WALTER WARY

Number/Street/Apt ▼
444 NORTH ST.

City/State/ZIP ▼
ANCHORAGE, ALASKA

YOU MUST:
• Complete all necessary spaces
• Sign your application in space 8
**SEND ALL 3 ELEMENTS
IN THE SAME PACKAGE:**
1. Application form
2. Nonrefundable filing fee in check or money order
payable to *Register of Copyrights*
3. Deposit material
MAIL TO:
Library of Congress
Copyright Office
101 Independence Avenue, S.E.
Washington, D.C. 20559-6000

9

*17 U.S.C. § 506(e): Any person who knowingly makes a false representation of a material fact in the application for copyright registration provided for by section 409, or in any written statement filed in connection
with the application, shall be fined not more than $2,500.

September 1997—300,000   ♻ PRINTED ON RECYCLED PAPER   ☆U.S. COPYRIGHT OFFICE WWW: March 1998

ADJUNCT APPLICATION
for Copyright Registration for a
Group of Contributions to Periodicals

- Use this adjunct form only if you are making a single registration for a group of contributions to periodicals, and you are also filing a basic application on Form TX, Form PA, or Form VA. Follow the instructions, attached.

- Number each line in Part B consecutively. Use additional Forms GR/CP if you need more space.

- Submit this adjunct form with the basic application form. Clip (do not tape or staple) and fold all sheets together before submitting them.

[Leave blank]

FORM GR/CP
For a Group of Contributions to Periodicals
UNITED STATES COPYRIGHT OFFICE

| TX | PA | VA |

EFFECTIVE DATE OF REGISTRATION

_____
(Month)   (Day)   (Year)

FORM GR/CP RECEIVED

_____

Page _____ of _____ pages

DO NOT WRITE ABOVE THIS LINE. FOR COPYRIGHT OFFICE USE ONLY

A

Identification of Application

IDENTIFICATION OF BASIC APPLICATION:
• This application for copyright registration for a group of contributions to periodicals is submitted as an adjunct to an application filed on: (Check which)

[X] Form TX   [ ] Form PA   [ ] Form VA

IDENTIFICATION OF AUTHOR AND CLAIMANT: (Give the name of the author and the name of the copyright claimant in all of the contributions listed in Part B of this form. The names should be the same as the names given in spaces 2 and 4 of the basic application.)

Name of Author **WALTER WARY, WHOSE PSEUDONYM IS WALTER WEARY**

Name of Copyright Claimant **WALTER WARY**

B

Registration for Group of Contributions

COPYRIGHT REGISTRATION FOR A GROUP OF CONTRIBUTIONS TO PERIODICALS: (To make a single registration for a group of works by the same individual author, all first published as contributions to periodicals within a 12-month period (see instructions), give full information about each contribution. If more space is needed, use additional Forms GR/CP.)

[X] Title of Contribution **"LOVE WITH THE IMPROPER STRANGER"**
Title of Periodical **PRURIENCE**   Vol. **7** No. **11** Issue Date **DEC. '97** Pages **16–18**
Date of First Publication **OCT.   22   1997**   Nation of First Publication **U.S.**
       (Month)   (Day)   (Year)   (Country)

[X] Title of Contribution **"TIMING IS EVERYTHING"**
Title of Periodical **PRURIENCE**   Vol. **7** No. **12** Issue Date **NOV. '97** Pages **4–5,22**
Date of First Publication **NOV.   17   1997**   Nation of First Publication **U.S.**
       (Month)   (Day)   (Year)   (Country)

[X] Title of Contribution **"HOPE SPRINGS"**
Title of Periodical **PLAYPERSON**   Vol. **27** No. **4** Issue Date **APR. '98** Pages **86, 94–96**
Date of First Publication **MAR.   20   1998**   Nation of First Publication **U.S.**
       (Month)   (Day)   (Year)   (Country)

[ ] Title of Contribution _____
Title of Periodical _____   Vol. ___ No. ___ Issue Date ___ Pages ___
Date of First Publication _____   Nation of First Publication _____
       (Month)   (Day)   (Year)   (Country)

[ ] Title of Contribution _____
Title of Periodical _____   Vol. ___ No. ___ Issue Date ___ Pages ___
Date of First Publication _____   Nation of First Publication _____
       (Month)   (Day)   (Year)   (Country)

[ ] Title of Contribution _____
Title of Periodical _____   Vol. ___ No. ___ Issue Date ___ Pages ___
Date of First Publication _____   Nation of First Publication _____
       (Month)   (Day)   (Year).   (Country)

[ ] Title of Contribution _____
Title of Periodical _____   Vol. ___ No. ___ Issue Date ___ Pages ___
Date of First Publication _____   Nation of First Publication _____
       (Month)   (Day)   (Year)   (Country)

DO NOT WRITE ABOVE THIS LINE. FOR COPYRIGHT OFFICE USE ONLY.

B

Continued

Title of Contribution _____
Title of Periodical _____ Vol.____ No._____ Issue Date _____ Pages _____
Date of First Publication _____ Nation of First Publication _____
          (Month)   (Day)   (Year)   (Country)

Title of Contribution _____
Title of Periodical _____ Vol.____ No._____ Issue Date _____ Pages _____
Date of First Publication _____ Nation of First Publication _____
          (Month)   (Day)   (Year)   (Country)

Title of Contribution _____
Title of Periodical _____ Vol.____ No._____ Issue Date _____ Pages _____
Date of First Publication _____ Nation of First Publication _____
          (Month)   (Day)   (Year)   (Country)

Title of Contribution _____
Title of Periodical _____ Vol.____ No._____ Issue Date _____ Pages _____
Date of First Publication _____ Nation of First Publication _____
          (Month)   (Day)   (Year)   (Country)

Title of Contribution _____
Title of Periodical _____ Vol.____ No._____ Issue Date _____ Pages _____
Date of First Publication _____ Nation of First Publication _____
          (Month)   (Day)   (Year)   (Country)

Title of Contribution _____
Title of Periodical _____ Vol.____ No._____ Issue Date _____ Pages _____
Date of First Publication _____ Nation of First Publication _____
          (Month)   (Day)   (Year)   (Country)

Title of Contribution _____
Title of Periodical _____ Vol.____ No._____ Issue Date _____ Pages _____
Date of First Publication _____ Nation of First Publication _____
          (Month)   (Day)   (Year)   (Country)

Title of Contribution _____
Title of Periodical _____ Vol.____ No._____ Issue Date _____ Pages _____
Date of First Publication _____ Nation of First Publication _____
          (Month)   (Day)   (Year)   (Country)

Title of Contribution _____
Title of Periodical _____ Vol.____ No._____ Issue Date _____ Pages _____
Date of First Publication _____ Nation of First Publication _____
          (Month)   (Day)   (Year)   (Country)

Title of Contribution _____
Title of Periodical _____ Vol.____ No._____ Issue Date _____ Pages _____
Date of First Publication _____ Nation of First Publication _____
          (Month)   (Day)   (Year)   (Country)

Title of Contribution _____
Title of Periodical _____ Vol.____ No._____ Issue Date _____ Pages _____
Date of First Publication _____ Nation of First Publication _____
          (Month)   (Day)   (Year)   (Country)

Title of Contribution _____
Title of Periodical _____ Vol.____ No._____ Issue Date _____ Pages _____
Date of First Publication _____ Nation of First Publication _____
          (Month)   (Day)   (Year)   (Country)

May 1995–50,000

☆U.S. COPYRIGHT OFFICE WWW FORM: 1995: 387-237/44

6a• **A single work, published**
  • **Two authors, one the writer of the text, the other the photographer**
  • **Separate copyrights, one applied for on Form TX (text), the other on Form VA (Visual Arts)**

FORM TX
For a Nondramatic Literary Work
UNITED STATES COPYRIGHT OFFICE

REGISTRATION NUMBER

[Leave blank]

TX _____ TXU _____
EFFECTIVE DATE OF REGISTRATION

Month _____ Day _____ Year _____

DO NOT WRITE ABOVE THIS LINE. IF YOU NEED MORE SPACE, USE A SEPARATE CONTINUATION SHEET.

1

TITLE OF THIS WORK ▼
BOUNDING HOME

PREVIOUS OR ALTERNATIVE TITLES ▼

PUBLICATION AS A CONTRIBUTION If this work was published as a contribution to a periodical, serial, or collection, give information about the collective work in which the contribution appeared.   **Title of Collective Work ▼**

If published in a periodical or serial give: Volume ▼   Number ▼   Issue Date ▼   On Pages ▼

---

2 a

NAME OF AUTHOR ▼
THERESA CATT

DATES OF BIRTH AND DEATH
Year Born ▼ **1954**   Year Died ▼

Was this contribution to the work a "work made for hire"?
☐ Yes
☒ No

AUTHOR'S NATIONALITY OR DOMICILE
Name of Country
OR { Citizen of ▶ **U.S.**
      Domiciled in ▶

WAS THIS AUTHOR'S CONTRIBUTION TO THE WORK
Anonymous?   Yes ☒ No
Pseudonymous? ☐ Yes ☒ No

If the answer to either of these questions is "Yes," see detailed instructions.

NATURE OF AUTHORSHIP Briefly describe nature of material created by this author in which copyright is claimed. ▼
ENTIRE TEXT

NOTE

Under the law, the "author" of a "work made for hire" is generally the employer, not the employee (see instructions). For any part of this work that was "made for hire" check "Yes" in the space provided, give the employer (or other person for whom the work was prepared) as "Author" of that part, and leave the space for dates of birth and death blank.

b

NAME OF AUTHOR ▼

DATES OF BIRTH AND DEATH
Year Born ▼   Year Died ▼

Was this contribution to the work a "work made for hire"?
☐ Yes
☐ No

AUTHOR'S NATIONALITY OR DOMICILE
Name of Country
OR { Citizen of ▶
      Domiciled in ▶

WAS THIS AUTHOR'S CONTRIBUTION TO THE WORK
Anonymous?   ☐ Yes ☐ No
Pseudonymous? ☐ Yes ☐ No

If the answer to either of these questions is "Yes," see detailed instructions.

NATURE OF AUTHORSHIP Briefly describe nature of material created by this author in which copyright is claimed. ▼

c

NAME OF AUTHOR ▼

DATES OF BIRTH AND DEATH
Year Born ▼   Year Died ▼

Was this contribution to the work a "work made for hire"?
☐ Yes
☐ No

AUTHOR'S NATIONALITY OR DOMICILE
Name of Country
OR { Citizen of ▶
      Domiciled in ▶

WAS THIS AUTHOR'S CONTRIBUTION TO THE WORK
Anonymous?   ☐ Yes ☐ No
Pseudonymous? ☐ Yes ☐ No

If the answer to either of these questions is "Yes," see detailed instructions.

NATURE OF AUTHORSHIP Briefly describe nature of material created by this author in which copyright is claimed. ▼

---

3 a

YEAR IN WHICH CREATION OF THIS WORK WAS COMPLETED **1998**
◀ Year in all cases.
This information must be given

b DATE AND NATION OF FIRST PUBLICATION OF THIS PARTICULAR WORK
Complete this information ONLY if this work has been published.
Month ▶ **AUG.** Day ▶ **30** Year ▶ **1998**
U.S. ◀ Nation

4

See instructions before completing this space.

COPYRIGHT CLAIMANT(S) Name and address must be given even if the claimant is the same as the author given in space 2. ▼
THERESA CATT
6714 MACARTHUR BLVD.
OAKLAND, CA 94600

TRANSFER If the claimant(s) named here in space 4 is (are) different from the author(s) named in space 2, give a brief statement of how the claimant(s) obtained ownership of the copyright. ▼

DO NOT WRITE HERE
OFFICE USE ONLY

APPLICATION RECEIVED

ONE DEPOSIT RECEIVED

TWO DEPOSITS RECEIVED

FUNDS RECEIVED

MORE ON BACK ▶ • Complete all applicable spaces (numbers 5-9) on the reverse side of this page.
• See detailed instructions.   • Sign the form at line 8.

DO NOT WRITE HERE
Page 1 of _____ pages

DO NOT WRITE ABOVE THIS LINE. IF YOU NEED MORE SPACE, USE A SEPARATE CONTINUATION SHEET.

PREVIOUS REGISTRATION Has registration for this work, or for an earlier version of this work, already been made in the Copyright Office?

☐ Yes ☒ No If your answer is "Yes," why is another registration being sought? (Check appropriate box) ▼

a. ☐ This is the first published edition of a work previously registered in unpublished form.

b. ☐ This is the first application submitted by this author as copyright claimant.

c. ☐ This is a changed version of the work, as shown by space 6 on this application.

If your answer is "Yes," give: **Previous Registration Number** ▼   **Year of Registration** ▼

5

DERIVATIVE WORK OR COMPILATION

Preexisting Material Identify any preexisting work or works that this work is based on or incorporates. ▼

a   N/A

b **Material Added to This Work** Give a brief, general statement of the material that has been added to this work and in which copyright is claimed. ▼

    N/A

6

See instructions
before completing
this space.

DEPOSIT ACCOUNT If the registration fee is to be charged to a Deposit Account established in the Copyright Office, give name and number of Account.

a **Name** ▼   **Account Number** ▼

7

b **CORRESPONDENCE** Give name and address to which correspondence about this application should be sent.   Name/Address/Apt/City/State/ZIP ▼

   THERESA CATT
   6714 MACARTHUR BLVD.
   OAKLAND, CA 94600

Area code and daytime telephone number ▶ 415-555-6789   Fax number ▶ 415-555-8789

Email ▶ tcatt@mouser.com

CERTIFICATION* I, the undersigned, hereby certify that I am the

Check only one ▶

☐ author
☐ other copyright claimant
☐ owner of exclusive right(s)
☐ authorized agent of _____

of the work identified in this application and that the statements made
by me in this application are correct to the best of my knowledge.

Name of author or other copyright claimant, or owner of exclusive right(s   ) ▲

8

Typed or printed name and date ▼ If this application gives a date of publication in space 3, do not sign and submit it before that date.

   THERESA CATT   Date ▶ SEPT. 12, 1998

☞ Handwritten signature (X) ▼

   X _

The filing fee of $20.00 is effective through June 30, 1999. After that date, please write the Copyright Office, check the Copyright Office Website at http://www.loc.gov/copyright, or call (202) 707-3000 for the latest fee information.

Mail certificate to:	**Name** ▼ THERESA CATT	**YOU MUST:** • Complete all necessary spaces • Sign your application in space 8
Certificate will be mailed in window envelope	**Number/Street/Apt** ▼ 6714 MACARTHUR BLVD.	**SEND ALL 3 ELEMENTS IN THE SAME PACKAGE:** 1. Application form 2. Nonrefundable filing fee in check or money order payable to *Register of Copyrights* 3. Deposit material
	City/State/ZIP ▼ OAKLAND, CA 94600	**MAIL TO:** Library of Congress Copyright Office 101 Independence Avenue, S.E. Washington, D.C. 20559-6000

9

186

6b • **The application for photographs illustrating the book in sample 6a**

FORM VA
For a Work of the Visual Arts
UNITED STATES COPYRIGHT OFFICE

REGISTRATION NUMBER

[Leave blank]

VA   VAU

EFFECTIVE DATE OF REGISTRATION

Month   Day   Year

DO NOT WRITE ABOVE THIS LINE. IF YOU NEED MORE SPACE, USE A SEPARATE CONTINUATION SHEET.

1

TITLE OF THIS WORK ▼

BOUNDING HOME

NATURE OF THIS WORK ▼ See instructions

PREVIOUS OR ALTERNATIVE TITLES ▼

PUBLICATION AS A CONTRIBUTION If this work was published as a contribution to a periodical, serial, or collection, give information about the collective work in which the contribution appeared.   **Title of Collective Work ▼**

If published in a periodical or serial give: **Volume ▼**   **Number ▼**   **Issue Date ▼**   **On Pages ▼**

2
a

NAME OF AUTHOR ▼

ELISSA LYON

DATES OF BIRTH AND DEATH
Year Born ▼   Year Died ▼
1960

Was this contribution to the work a "work made for hire"?
☐ Yes
☒ No

AUTHOR'S NATIONALITY OR DOMICILE
Name of Country
OR { Citizen of ▶   **U.S.**
    Domiciled in ▶

WAS THIS AUTHOR'S CONTRIBUTION TO THE WORK
Anonymous? ☐ Yes ☒ No
Pseudonymous? ☐ Yes ☒ No

If the answer to either of these questions is "Yes," see detailed instructions.

NATURE OF AUTHORSHIP Check appropriate box(es). **See instructions**
☐ 3-Dimensional sculpture   ☐ Map   ☐ Technical drawing
☐ 2-Dimensional artwork   ☒ Photograph   ☐ Text
☐ Reproduction of work of art   ☐ Jewelry design   ☐ Architectural work
☐ Design on sheetlike material

b

NAME OF AUTHOR ▼

DATES OF BIRTH AND DEATH
Year Born ▼   Year Died ▼

Was this contribution to the work a "work made for hire"?
☐ Yes
☐ No

AUTHOR'S NATIONALITY OR DOMICILE
Name of Country
OR { Citizen of ▶
    Domiciled in ▶

WAS THIS AUTHOR'S CONTRIBUTION TO THE WORK
Anonymous? ☐ Yes ☐ No
Pseudonymous? ☐ Yes ☐ No

If the answer to either of these questions is "Yes," see detailed instructions.

NATURE OF AUTHORSHIP Check appropriate box(es). **See instructions**
☐ 3-Dimensional sculpture   ☐ Map   ☐ Technical drawing
☐ 2-Dimensional artwork   ☐ Photograph   ☐ Text
☐ Reproduction of work of art   ☐ Jewelry design   ☐ Architectural work
☐ Design on sheetlike material

NOTE
Under the law, the "author" of a "work made for hire" is generally the employer, not the employee (see instructions). For any part of this work that was "made for hire" check "Yes" in the space provided, give the employer (or other person for whom the work was prepared) as "Author" of that part, and leave the space for dates of birth and death blank.

3
a

YEAR IN WHICH CREATION OF THIS WORK WAS COMPLETED This information **1998** ◀ Year must be given in all cases.

b DATE AND NATION OF FIRST PUBLICATION OF THIS PARTICULAR WORK
Complete this information ONLY if this work has been published. Month ▶ **AUG.** Day ▶ **30** Year ▶ **1998**
U.S. ◀ Nation

4

COPYRIGHT CLAIMANT(S) Name and address must be given even if the claimant is the same as the author given in space 2. ▼

ELISSA LYON
104 HOLLIS ST.
EMERYVILLE, CA 94602

See instructions before completing this space.

TRANSFER If the claimant(s) named here in space 4 is (are) different from the author(s) named in space 2, give a brief statement of how the claimant(s) obtained ownership of the copyright. ▼

APPLICATION RECEIVED

ONE DEPOSIT RECEIVED

TWO DEPOSITS RECEIVED

FUNDS RECEIVED

DO NOT WRITE HERE OFFICE USE ONLY

MORE ON BACK ▶ • Complete all applicable spaces (numbers 5-9) on the reverse side of this page.
• See detailed instructions.   • Sign the form at line 8.

DO NOT WRITE HERE
Page 1 of _____ pages

DO NOT WRITE ABOVE THIS LINE. IF YOU NEED MORE SPACE, USE A SEPARATE CONTINUATION SHEET.

PREVIOUS REGISTRATION Has registration for this work, or for an earlier version of this work, already been made in the Copyright Office?

☐ Yes ☐ No If your answer is "Yes," why is another registration being sought? (Check appropriate box) ▼

a. ☐ This is the first published edition of a work previously registered in unpublished form.

b. ☐ This is the first application submitted by this author as copyright claimant.

c. ☐ This is a changed version of the work, as shown by space 6 on this application.

If your answer is "Yes," give: **Previous Registration Number** ▼   **Year of Registration** ▼

5

DERIVATIVE WORK OR COMPILATION Complete both space 6a and 6b for a derivative work; complete only 6b for a compilation.

a. Preexisting Material Identify any preexisting work or works that this work is based on or incorporates. ▼

N/A

6

See instructions before completing this space.

b. Material Added to This Work Give a brief, general statement of the material that has been added to this work and in which copyright is claimed. ▼

N/A

DEPOSIT ACCOUNT If the registration fee is to be charged to a Deposit Account established in the Copyright Office, give name and number of Account.

Name ▼   **Account Number** ▼

7

CORRESPONDENCE Give name and address to which correspondence about this application should be sent. Name/Address/Apt/City/State/ZIP ▼

ELISSA LYON
104 HOLLIS ST.
EMERYVILLE, CA 94602

Be sure to give your daytime phone ◄ number

Area Code and Telephone Number ► 415-555-0011

CERTIFICATION* I, the undersigned, hereby certify that I am the

check only one ▼

☒ author

☐ other copyright claimant

☐ owner of exclusive right(s)

☐ authorized agent of _____

    Name of author or other copyright claimant, or owner of exclusive right(s) ▲

8

of the work identified in this application and that the statements made by me in this application are correct to the best of my knowledge.

Typed or printed name and date ▼ If this application gives a date of publication in space 3, do not sign and submit it before that date.

ELISSA LYON   Date► SEPT. 15, 1998

☞ Handwritten signature (X) ▼ _Elissa Lyon_

Mail certificate to:

Name ▼

ELISSA LYON

Certificate will be mailed in window envelope

Number/Street/Apt ▼

104 HOLLIS ST.

City/State/ZIP ▼

EMERYVILLE, CA 94602

9

*17 U.S.C. § 506(e): Any person who knowingly makes a false representation of a material fact in the application for copyright registration provided for by section 409, or in any written statement filed in connection with the application, shall be fined not more than $2,500.

March 1995—300,000   ☆U.S. COPYRIGHT OFFICE WWW FORM: 1995

7• **Renewal of copyright for a work copyrighted under the 1909 Act**

Warning: You *must* file the renewal application *at the right time.* See the instructions for Form RE. If you miss the applicable dates, the work loses its copyright and falls into the public domain. See Chapter 7.

FORM RE
For Renewal of a Work
UNITED STATES COPYRIGHT OFFICE

REGISTRATION NUMBER

[Leave blank]

_____

EFFECTIVE DATE OF RENEWAL REGISTRATION

_____

| Month | Day | Year |

DO NOT WRITE ABOVE THIS LINE. IF YOU NEED MORE SPACE, USE A SEPARATE CONTINUATION SHEET(RE/CON).

1

RENEWAL CLAIMANT(S), ADDRESS(ES), AND STATEMENT OF CLAIM ▼ (See Instructions)

1
Name ...... **RONALD REDUX**
Address ... **24 OAKLAWN AVE., SAN FRANCISCO, CA 94000**
Claiming as **THE AUTHOR**
(Use appropriate statement from instructions)

2
Name ......
Address ...
Claiming as

3
Name ......
Address ...
Claiming as

2

TITLE OF WORK IN WHICH RENEWAL IS CLAIMED ▼
HOMEBOUND

RENEWABLE MATTER ▼ **ORIGINAL WORK**

PUBLICATION AS A CONTRIBUTION If this work was published as a contribution to a periodical, serial, or other composite work, give information about the collective work in which the contribution appeared. **Title of Collective Work ▼**

If published in a periodical or serial give: Volume ▼   Number ▼   Issue Date ▼

3

AUTHOR(S) OF RENEWABLE MATTER ▼
RONALD REDUX

4

ORIGINAL REGISTRATION NUMBER ▼ ORIGINAL COPYRIGHT CLAIMANT ▼
XX111111   **RONALD REDUX**

ORIGINAL DATE OF COPYRIGHT

If the original registration for this work was made in published form, give:
DATE OF PUBLICATION: **6**   **20**   **1970**
(Month)   (Day)   (Year)

OR

If the original registration for this work was made in unpublished form, give:
DATE OF REGISTRATION: _____
(Month)   (Day)   (Year)

MORE ON BACK ▶ • Complete all applicable spaces (numbers 5-8) on the reverse side of this page.
• See detailed instructions.   • Sign the form at space 7.

DO NOT WRITE HERE
Page 1 of _____ pages

RENEWAL APPLICATION RECEIVED   FORM RE

CORRESPONDENCE ☐ YES

EXAMINED BY _____   FOR
                                                 COPYRIGHT
CHECKED BY _____   OFFICE
                                                 USE
                                                 ONLY

DO NOT WRITE ABOVE THIS LINE. IF YOU NEED MORE SPACE, USE A SEPARATE CONTINUATION SHEET (RE/CON).

RENEWAL FOR GROUP OF WORKS BY SAME AUTHOR: To make a single registration for a group of works by the same individual author published as contributions to periodicals (see instructions), give full information about each contribution. If more space is needed, request continuation sheet (Form RE/CON).

5

1
Title of Contribution: ....

Title of Periodical: .... Vol: .... No: .... Issue Date: ....

Date of Publication: .... Registration Number: ....
     (Month)   (Day)   (Year)

2
Title of Contribution: ....

Title of Periodical: .... Vol: .... No: .... Issue Date: ....

Date of Publication: .... Registration Number: ....
     (Month)   (Day)   (Year)

3
Title of Contribution: ....

Title of Periodical: .... Vol: .... No: .... Issue Date: ....

Date of Publication: .... Registration Number: ....
     (Month)   (Day)   (Year)

4
Title of Contribution: ....

Title of Periodical: .... Vol: .... No: .... Issue Date: ....

Date of Publication: .... Registration Number: ....
     (Month)   (Day)   (Year)

DEPOSIT ACCOUNT: If the registration fee is to be charged to a Deposit Account established in the Copyright Office, give name and number of Account.

Name _____

_____

Account Number _____

CORRESPONDENCE: Give name and address to which correspondence about this application should be sent.

Name **RONALD REDUX**

Address **24 OAKLAWN AVE.**

SAN FRANCISCO,   **CA**   **94000** (Apt)
(City)   (State)   (ZIP)

Area Code and Telephone Number ▶ **415-222-2222**

Be sure to give your daytime phone number

6

CERTIFICATION* I, the undersigned, hereby certify that I am the: (Check one)
☐ renewal claimant   ☐ duly authorized agent of _____
     (Name of renewal claimant) ▲
of the work identified in this application and that the statements made by me in this application are correct to the best of my knowledge.

Typed or printed name ▼   **RONALD REDUX**   Date ▼ **JULY 1, 1998**

👉   Handwritten signature (X) ▼   *Ronald Redux*

7

MAIL CERTIFI-CATE TO

Name ▼ **RONALD REDUX**

Number/Street/Apt ▼ **24 OAKLAWN AVE.**

City/State/ZIP ▼ **SAN FRANCISCO, CA 94000**

Certificate will be mailed in window envelope

YOU MUST:
• Complete all necessary spaces
• Sign your application in space 7

SEND ALL ELEMENTS IN THE SAME PACKAGE:
1. Application form
2. Nonrefundable $20 filing fee in check or money order payable to *Register of Copyrights*

MAIL TO:
Register of Copyrights
Library of Congress
Washington, D.C. 20559

8

⊘FORM CA
For Supplementary Registration
UNITED STATES COPYRIGHT OFFICE

REGISTRATION NUMBER

[Leave blank]

| TX | TXU | PA | PAU | VA | VAU | SR | SRU | RE |

EFFECTIVE DATE OF SUPPLEMENTARY REGISTRATION

Month   Day   Year

DO NOT WRITE ABOVE THIS LINE. IF YOU NEED MORE SPACE, USE A SEPARATE CONTINUATION SHEET.

A

TITLE OF WORK ▼ **GOING HOME**

REGISTRATION NUMBER OF THE BASIC REGISTRATION ▼
XX111111

YEAR OF BASIC REGISTRATION ▼
1998

NAME(S) OF AUTHOR(S) ▼
THOMAS WOLFRAM

NAME(S) OF COPYRIGHT CLAIMANT(S) ▼
THOMAS WOLFRAM

B

LOCATION AND NATURE OF INCORRECT INFORMATION IN BASIC REGISTRATION ▼

Line Number . . . . Line Heading or Description . . . .

INCORRECT INFORMATION AS IT APPEARS IN BASIC REGISTRATION ▼
1998

CORRECTED INFORMATION ▼
1997

EXPLANATION OF CORRECTION ▼
TYPOGRAPHICAL ERROR

C

LOCATION AND NATURE OF INFORMATION IN BASIC REGISTRATION TO BE AMPLIFIED ▼

Line Number **4, 9, 10** . . . . . . Line Heading or Description **CLAIMANT'S ADDRESS** . . . .

AMPLIFIED INFORMATION ▼

CLAIMANT'S ADDRESS IS:

SUITE 1010

THE ALGONQUIN HOTEL

NEW YORK, NY 10000

EXPLANATION OF AMPLIFIED INFORMATION ▼

MORE ON BACK ▶ • Complete all applicable spaces (D -G) on the reverse side of this page.
• See detailed instructions.   • Sign the form at space F.

DO NOT WRITE HERE

Page 1 of _____ pages

DO NOT WRITE ABOVE THIS LINE. IF YOU NEED MORE SPACE, USE A SEPARATE CONTINUATION SHEET.

CONTINUATION OF: (Check which) ☐ PART B OR ☐ PART C

D

DEPOSIT ACCOUNT: If the registration fee is to be charged to a Deposit Account established in the Copyright Office, give name and number of Account.

Name _____

Account Number _____

CORRESPONDENCE: Give name and address to which correspondence about this application should be sent.

Name   **THOMAS WOLFRAM**

Address   **SUITE 1010, THE ALGONQUIN HOTEL**

NEW YORK,   NY   10000 (Apt)

(City)   (State)   (ZIP)

Area Code and Telephone Number ▶ _____

Be sure to
give your
daytime phone
◀ number

E

CERTIFICATION* I, the undersigned, hereby certify that I am the: (Check one)

☐ author ☐ other copyright claimant ☐ owner of exclusive right(s) ☐ duly authorized agent of _____

(Name of author or other copyright claimant, or owner of exclusive right(s) ▲

of the work identified in this application and that the statements made by me in this application are correct to the best of my knowledge.

Typed or printed name ▼   **THOMAS WOLFRAM**

Date ▼ **MARCH 30, 1999**

☞ Handwritten signature (X) ▼   *Thomas Wolfram*

F

**MAIL
TO**

**Certificate
will be
mailed in
window
envelope**

Name ▼

THOMAS WOLFRAM

Number/Street/Apt ▼

SUITE 1010, THE ALGONQUIN HOTEL

City/State/ZIP ▼

NEW YORK, NY 10000

G

---

*17 U.S.C. § 506(e): Any person who knowingly makes a false representation of a material fact in the application for copyright registration provided for by section 409, or in any written statement filed in connection with the application, shall be fined not more than $2,500.

October 1994

☆U.S. COPYRIGHT OFFICE WWW FORM: 1996

192

9• A serial (magazine, journal, etc.)

FORM SE
For a Serial
UNITED STATES COPYRIGHT OFFICE

REGISTRATION NUMBER

[Leave blank]

_____ U

EFFECTIVE DATE OF REGISTRATION

_____

| Month | Day | Year |

DO NOT WRITE ABOVE THIS LINE. IF YOU NEED MORE SPACE, USE A SEPARATE CONTINUATION SHEET.

1

TITLE OF THIS SERIAL ▼

PRURIENCE

Volume ▼	Number ▼	Date on Copies ▼	Frequency of Publication ▼
7	11	**NOV. 1998**	monthly

PREVIOUS OR ALTERNATIVE TITLES ▼

2

a NAME OF AUTHOR ▼
PRURIENT PUBLICATIONS

DATES OF BIRTH AND DEATH
Year Born ▼   Year Died ▼

Was this contribution to the work a "work made for hire"?
☐ Yes
☐ No

AUTHOR'S NATIONALITY OR DOMICILE
Name of Country
OR { Citizen of ▶ **U.S.**
{ Domiciled in▶

WAS THIS AUTHOR'S CONTRIBUTION TO THE WORK
Anonymous?   ☐ Yes ☒ No
Pseudonymous? ☐ Yes ☒ No
If the answer to either of these questions is "Yes," see detailed instructions.

NATURE OF AUTHORSHIP Briefly describe nature of material created by this author in which copyright is claimed. ▼
☒ Collective Work   Other:

NOTE

Under the law, the "author" of a "work made for hire" is generally the employer, not the employee (see instructions). For any part of this work that was "made for hire" check "Yes" in the space provided, give the employer (or other person for whom the work was prepared) as "Author" of that part, and leave the space for dates of birth and death blank.

b NAME OF AUTHOR ▼

DATES OF BIRTH AND DEATH
Year Born ▼   Year Died ▼

Was this contribution to the work a "work made for hire"?
☐ Yes
☐ No

AUTHOR'S NATIONALITY OR DOMICILE
Name of Country
OR { Citizen of ▶
{ Domiciled in▶

WAS THIS AUTHOR'S CONTRIBUTION TO THE WORK
Anonymous?   ☐ Yes ☐ No
Pseudonymous? ☐ Yes ☐ No
If the answer to either of these questions is "Yes," see detailed instructions.

NATURE OF AUTHORSHIP Briefly describe nature of material created by this author in which copyright is claimed. ▼
☐ Collective Work   Other:

c NAME OF AUTHOR ▼

DATES OF BIRTH AND DEATH
Year Born ▼   Year Died ▼

Was this contribution to the work a "work made for hire"?
☐ Yes
☐No

AUTHOR'S NATIONALITY OR DOMICILE
Name of Country
OR { Citizen of ▶
{ Domiciled in▶

WAS THIS AUTHOR'S CONTRIBUTION TO THE WORK
Anonymous?   ☐ Yes ☐ No
Pseudonymous? ☐ Yes ☐ No
If the answer to either of these questions is "Yes," see detailed instructions.

NATURE OF AUTHORSHIP Briefly describe nature of material created by this author in which copyright is claimed. ▼
☐ Collective Work   Other:

3

a YEAR IN WHICH CREATION OF THIS ISSUE WAS COMPLETED
1998 ◀Year
This information must be given in all cases.

b DATE AND NATION OF FIRST PUBLICATION OF THIS PARTICULAR ISSUE
Complete this information ONLY if this work has been published.
Month ▶ **OCT.** Day▶ **20** Year ▶ **1998**
U.S. ◀ Nation

4

See instructions before completing this space.

COPYRIGHT CLAIMANT(S) Name and address must be given even if the claimant is the same as the author given in space 2. ▼
PRURIENT PUBLICATIONS
TIMES SQUARE
NEW YORK, NY 10001

TRANSFER If the claimant(s) named here in space 4 is (are) different from the author(s) named in space 2, give a brief statement of how the claimant(s) obtained ownership of the copyright. ▼

APPLICATION RECEIVED

ONE DEPOSIT RECEIVED

TWO DEPOSITS RECEIVED

REMITTANCE NUMBER AND DATE

DO NOT WRITE HERE
OFFICE USE ONLY

MORE ON BACK ▶
• Complete all applicable spaces (numbers 5-11) on the reverse side of this page.
• See detailed instructions.
• Sign the form at line 10.

DO NOT WRITE HERE
Page 1 of _____ pages

193

DO NOT WRITE ABOVE THIS LINE. IF YOU NEED MORE SPACE, USE A SEPARATE CONTINUATION SHEET.

PREVIOUS REGISTRATION Has registration for this issue, or for an earlier version of this particular issue, already been made in the Copyright Office?
☐ Yes ☒ No If your answer is "Yes," why is another registration being sought? (Check appropriate box) ▼

a. ☐ This is the first published edition of an issue previously registered in unpublished form.

b. ☐ This is the first application submitted by this author as copyright claimant.

c. ☐ This is a changed version of this issue, as shown by space 6 on this application.

If your answer is "Yes," give: **Previous Registration Number** ▼　　　　　**Year of Registration** ▼

5

DERIVATIVE WORK OR COMPILATION Complete both space 6a and 6b for a derivative work; complete only 6b for a compilation.
a. Preexisting Material Identify any preexisting work or works that this work is based on or incorporates. ▼

b. Material Added to This Work Give a brief, general statement of the material that has been added to this work and in which copyright is claimed. ▼

6

See instructions
before completing
this space.

—space deleted—

7

REPRODUCTION FOR USE OF BLIND OR PHYSICALLY HANDICAPPED INDIVIDUALS A signature on this form at space 10 and a check in one of the boxes here in space 8 constitutes a non-exclusive grant of permission to the Library of Congress to reproduce and distribute solely for the blind and physically handicapped and under the conditions and limitations prescribed by the regulations of the Copyright Office: (1) copies of the work identified in space 1 of this application in Braille (or similar tactile symbols); or (2) phonorecords embodying a fixation of a reading of that work; or (3) both.

a ☐ Copies and Phonorecords　　　b ☐ Copies Only　　　c ☐ Phonorecords Only

8

See instructions.

DEPOSIT ACCOUNT If the registration fee is to be charged to a Deposit Account established in the Copyright Office, give name and number of Account.
Name ▼　　　　　**Account Number** ▼

9

CORRESPONDENCE Give name and address to which correspondence about this application should be sent.　Name/Address/Apt/City/State/ZIP ▼

PRURIENT PUBLICATIONS
TIMES SQUARE
NEW YORK, NY 10001

Area Code and Telephone Number ▶ 212-111-11111

Be sure to
give your
daytime phone
◀ number

CERTIFICATION* I, the undersigned, hereby certify that I am the
Check only one {
☐ author
☐ other copyright claimant
☐ owner of exclusive right(s)
☐ authorized agent of _____

of the work identified in this application and that the statements made
by me in this application are correct to the best of my knowledge.

Name of author or other copyright claimant, or owner of exclusive right(s) ▲

10

Typed or printed name and date ▼ If this application gives a date of publication in space 3, do not sign and submit it before that date.

PRURIENT PUBLICATIONS, INC. BY HUNTLEY HAVERSTOCK, PRES.　　　date ▶ NOV. 11, 1998

☞　Handwritten signature (X) ▼

Huntley Haverstock

11

*17 U.S.C. § 506(e): Any person who knowingly makes a false representation of a material fact in the application for copyright registration provided for by section 409, or in any written statement filed in connection with the application, shall be fined not more than $2,500.

April 1993—100,000　　　　　　　　　　　　　　　　　　　　　☆U.S. COPYRIGHT OFFICE WWW FORM: 1993

9 HOW TO PROTECT YOUR COPYRIGHT

INTRODUCTION

The owner of a copyright has many valuable rights. These include the right

1. To reproduce the copyrighted work in copies . . . ;
2. To prepare derivative works based upon the copyrighted work;
3. To distribute copies . . . of the copyrighted work to the public by sale or other transfer of ownership, or by rental, lease, or lending;
4. In the case of literary, musical, dramatic, and choreographic works, pantomimes, and motion pictures and other audiovisual works, to perform the copyrighted work publicly; and
5. In the case of literary, musical, dramatic, and choreographic works, pantomimes, and pictorial, graphic, or sculptural works . . . to display the copyrighted work publicly.[1]

These rights are exclusively the property of the copyright owner, and anyone who invades them has infringed the owner's copyright.

The 1976 act contains page after page of exceptions to the exclusive rights of the copyright owner. Many of the exceptions have to do with library and educational use of materials subject to copyright. Other

---

1. Copyright Act, Section 106.

exceptions cover performance on various broadcasting systems and reproduction of music on phonograph record. We won't cover all these exceptions, because most aren't significant to many writers. One exception, though, for "fair use," is of great importance. It's best understood in the context of lawsuits for infringement and defenses against infringement claims. We discuss fair use later in this chapter.

INFRINGEMENT

How does copyright protection help you to foil those characters so unspeakably unscrupulous as to steal your work? In several ways, but principally by allowing you to file suit and get a court to order the plagiarist to stop infringing (the order is called an injunction). The court can also award you money damages and attorney's fees.

NOTE ON COPYING PROTECTED WORK • Making and distributing copies of copyrighted work is blatant infringement, a fact ignored by many teachers who persist in turning copying machines into small presses.[2] A limited exception for educational copying does exist, allowing copying of copyrighted work that isn't readily available and can't be obtained in time for its intended use, but abuses abound. Litigation against Kinko's Copy Centers in New York established that the common practice of assembling "course readers" that are barely disguised anthologies without obtaining permission or payment is infringement.

WHAT DOES IT TAKE TO PROVE INFRINGEMENT?

To win an infringement action, the person who brings the lawsuit (called the plaintiff) must prove two things: first, that the plaintiff owns the copyright, and second, that the party being sued (the defendant) has copied the copyrighted work, or a portion of it, in a way that violates the list of exclusive rights granted by the Copyright Act.

---

2.   This practice may become less attractive as authors' and publishers' organizations get courts to punish college faculties and administrators and copy services—an encouraging trend.

Ownership

Proving ownership is usually easy. Under the law, certain people can qualify as owners of copyright and, if the owner or owners properly registered their claim to copyright, the evidence to prove ownership is easy to find.

Copying

Proving copying, on the other hand, can sometimes be difficult. Occasionally, it's possible to prove by direct evidence that infringement took place. For example, if you claim a work infringes your copyright and can show it contains the same words as your copyrighted work, a reasonable juror will almost surely conclude that your copyright has been violated.

Sometimes, though, as in a situation where one author has paraphrased another or has followed the structure and organization of his work, it's more difficult to prove that copying took place. In this situation, you must use indirect evidence to prove that the defendant copied your protected work. That evidence must establish both that your work and the work you claim infringes are "substantially similar" and that the defendant had access to the protected work. "Access" simply means reasonable opportunity to view your work. It can sometimes be hard to prove this if your work is unpublished. But if the similarity between the two works is striking, the court can infer that access must have existed.

The tough issue in an infringement case is that of "substantial similarity." Again, the law complicates matters by recognizing two kinds of substantial similarity. If the similarity is "literal," that is, word-for-word, then the copying constitutes infringement, if there's enough of it. Two stolen lines from an eight-line poem are enough to prove substantial similarity. Two lines from an 800-page book, on the other hand, may not be.

If no literal similarity exists, then the court will look for comprehensive similarity, meaning similarity of structure and abundant use of paraphrase. If the work that's claimed to infringe follows a similar sequence of events or establishes a similar interplay of characters, there is evidence of structural similarity. Once a pattern of structural similarity is found to exist, the court will look for similarity of expression. The combination is strong evidence of substantial similarity and, therefore, that infringement may have occurred.

DEFENDING AGAINST A CLAIM OF COPYRIGHT INFRINGEMENT

Even if the copyright owner proves all the required legal elements of an infringement case, the defendant may still win by showing that the use of the plaintiff's work falls within one of the several copyright exceptions that allow for the use of copyrighted material without permission. The most important exception, contained in Section 107 of the Copyright Act, is that for "fair use." Here's what Section 107 says:

> Notwithstanding the provisions of Section 106, the fair use of a copyrighted work, including such use by reproduction in copies . . . or by any other means specified by that section, for purposes such as criticism, comment, news reporting, teaching (including multiple copies for classroom use), scholarship, or research, is not an infringement of copyright. In determining whether the use made of a work in any particular case is a fair use, the factors to be considered shall include
>
> (1) the purpose and character of the use, including whether such use is of a commercial nature or is for nonprofit educational purposes;
> (2) the nature of the copyrighted work;
> (3) the amount and substantiality of the portion used in relation to the copyrighted work as a whole; and
> (4) the effect of the use upon the potential market for or value of the copyrighted work.

The fair use doctrine is an attempt to balance the needs of third parties with the rights of the author. This balancing act normally requires a comparison of the author's use of his material with that of the person who would otherwise infringe. It permits at least some copying of a protected work in some circumstances even though the copyright owner has not given permission to the copier.

Section 107 may look like a definition. It isn't. Rather, it's a codification of a set of general principles developed over the years under the old Copyright Act. The basic purpose is to balance competing interests and do what's right and equitable. Here are some general rules courts have developed over time:

- If the copier is competing with the originator in the same market, for the same customers, fair use will likely not save him.

- If the copying user is a critic or commentator, discussing the concepts contained in the original work, the fair use defense is very valuable.[3]

- The more the copying user takes from the original work, the less likely fair use will help him.

HINT • An author wishing to quote from portions of a copyrighted work by relying on the fair use doctrine and without getting formal permission should be very careful to give the copyright owner full credit. Supply the author's and publisher's names, and include the price of the copyrighted work and detailed instructions on how to order it. By turning what might be considered a rip-off into a plug, much potential trouble may be avoided, although giving credit does not protect against a claim of infringement.

THE RESULTS OF WINNING A COPYRIGHT INFRINGEMENT ACTION

What does the copyright owner get if he wins an infringement action? The court will probably issue an injunction telling the infringer to stop using the material. The court may impound existing infringing copies or order them destroyed. Money damages are also available to the successful plaintiff in any of several forms. The plaintiff is entitled to actual damages for all the copies of his work sold by the infringer. This is frequently measured by the royalties that similar owners and licensees would receive for similar material. The plaintiff may be able to force the defendant to turn over profits made from the defendant's infringing exploitation of the work. Or the plaintiff may choose "statutory damages" instead. This means he gives up his right to actual damages or the recovery of the defendant's profits. In return, the court may award him from $200 (for an innocent infringement) to $100,000 (for a willful infringement). It's up to the judge to consider the facts, decide the issues, and determine the amount of damages to award the successful plaintiff.

---

3. See *Maxtone-Graham v. Burtchaell* (2d Cir 1986) 803 F.2d 1253, in which the verbatim copying of 7,000 words was held to be fair use. But compare *Salinger v. Random House* (2d Cir 1987) 811 F.2d 90, in which far fewer copied words were an unfair taking—because they were highly expressive and original.

WHAT TO DO IF YOU'RE THE VICTIM OF INFRINGEMENT

As you should now know, questions about a copyright owner's rights, whether or not infringement has occurred, and if it has, what sort of legal action should be taken, can be confusing and legally complicated. This is as true if you feel you may be an infringer (innocent or not) as it is if you believe your copyrighted work has been stolen. If a considerable amount of money or serious questions of professional standing are involved, as they often are, the advice of a lawyer experienced in the field will prove invaluable. Your publisher should be knowledgeable in this area. See the Resource Directory, Appendix A, for assistance in locating an attorney. However, if the infringement is less serious, but still annoying (and you have not licensed your work to a publisher), you will probably want to deal with it yourself. For example, suppose a small weekly newspaper prints a portion of one of your works without permission and without asking to pay. You might start by writing a letter pointing out what happened and asking for reasonable remuneration. If this doesn't work, and the publication is located in the same state you are, you might consider suing in small claims court. Depending on the state, you can sue for from $500 to $5,000. In court, be ready to prove both that the infringement occurred and the reasonable value of the infringed work.

10 TAX AND THE FREELANCE WRITER

WHAT THIS CHAPTER COVERS

All of us who earn an income must deal with taxation. But freelance writers encounter special problems, because, typically, they work at home, can't easily predict their income from month to month (much less year to year), are forced to work at writing part-time, and may not have corporate retirement plans to provide for their future. This book would be incomplete without some useful information about taxes; but we can't cover the tax laws in general, or this chapter would be at least as big as the rest of the book. So we'll limit our discussion to federal tax issues that affect freelance writers in special ways. People who are employed as writers and sometimes work at home are subject to tax rules that deal with "employee business expense." We won't cover those rules.

THE WRITER AS TAXPAYER

The American tax system is more than a way for the federal government to collect money; it's also a tool of social policy. When it was good for the country to encourage oil exploration, companies that did so got a tax break—called the "oil depletion allowance"—big enough to fund many small nations. But the tax laws offer no such break to writers, which speaks volumes about the place of the writer in our polity.

Instead, recent tax "simplification" has left us wounded in its wake. Rates have, of course, come down. But we've lost important deductions, face complicated and confusing forms, and will almost certainly see tax increases that will undo the benefit of reductions.

What have we lost? Well, it's common for writers to see their income ride a roller coaster from year to year. A technique called "income averaging," which permitted bad years to offset good, often reduced taxes substantially. But income averaging is gone. Those of us who use personal computers in our work must keep extensive records or run the risk of losing the deduction for their cost. And the qualifications for the home office deduction are harder to meet.

A few islands of solace remain, but before we explore them, we must consider the effects of the threshold "hobby-loss limitation rule."

The Hobby-Loss Limitation Rule

Deductions, which reduce the amount of your income subject to tax, are a privilege granted by the government. Personal deductions, such as those for charitable contributions, medical expenses, and state taxes, are available to all of us.

Deductions for business expenses, however, may be claimed only by those who can establish that they are, in fact, for business purposes. A writer who earns little from writing may have to prove that writing is a business, not a hobby, before deducting all the costs of writing. If the Internal Revenue Service (IRS) believes that your writing career is a hobby, your deductions are limited to the amount of your hobby income. Let's see how the hobby-loss limitation rule works:

You earned $800 last year from the sale of several travel articles. But you bought a new computer, used only for writing, that cost $1,400.[1] It appears that your loss for the year was $600. But the hobby-loss limitation rule allows you to take only an $800 deduction for the cost of the computer, because that's the amount of income your hobby writing produced. You can offset your hobby income, but you lose the excess. The tax code adds a little insult to the injury, by requiring you to treat the deduction as a "miscellaneous itemized deduction" on Schedule A of your return and to subtract 2 percent of your adjusted gross income from the total of those deductions before subtracting them, in turn, from your income.

---

1.   It's important to note that for the purpose of this example, you're deducting the entire cost of the computer in one year (called "expensing"), instead of spreading the cost over the useful life of the computer (called "capitalizing"). See below for more.

The tax law offers two ways to prove that your writing work is a business, not a hobby. If you've made a profit from writing in any three of the last five consecutive years, you win, although this year was a fiscal disaster. But even if you can't pass the three-out-of-five-year test, you may still be able to convince the IRS that writing is your business, *if:*

- You run your little business like a business, with financial records, letterhead, business cards, and other evidence that you're serious;
- You don't operate at a dead loss, or with a string of high-expense, low-income years stretching back unbroken in history;
- Your claimed expenses don't include the frivolous, the outrageous, or the mostly pleasurable; and
- You're good enough at writing to be taken seriously.

This test is called the "facts-and-circumstances" test.

If you're allowed to treat these expenses as ordinary and necessary business expenses, you may deduct them from your writing income on Schedule C of your return and the total of the deductions may exceed your income. That means you can reduce your other (nonwriting) income by the loss from your writing business.

The Write-off

The costs of doing business as a freelance writer, as we've just seen, can reduce your taxable income from writing and from other sources. Taking these deductions is known as "writing off." There are two ways to write off business expenditures. One is called "expensing," the other "depreciating."

When you write off an expenditure in a single tax year, you're "expensing" the expenditure. That is, you're treating it as an expense against your income in the year you spend the money and earn the income. The effect of the expense on your taxable income is dramatic: it happens all at once.

The alternative, depreciation, spreads the deduction over several years. Each year, you deduct a portion of the total expenditure. The theory of depreciation is that you'll get years of service out of the property you purchased, so you should recover a part of the property's cost each year of its useful life. If, for example, you bought a desk and three chairs for your writing office, at a cost of $560, you would find that the IRS presumes the useful life of the furniture to be seven years. It appears that you could deduct one-seventh of the furniture's cost, or $80, in each of the seven years, beginning with the year you bought it.

Oh, if it were that simple! The complications arise immediately. First, it's the "basis" you may depreciate, not the purchase price. The two are usually the same, but sometimes they differ. For real property (land and buildings), the purchase price may have to be adjusted up or down before you know what the basis is.

Second, you're allowed to deduct only half the depreciation you'd otherwise be entitled to for the first year, because of a rule called the "half-year convention." No matter when you actually bought the furniture, it's assumed that you had the use of it for business purposes for half the year, so you may take half the first-year depreciation, or $40.[2]

Third, you may choose to speed up the rate at which you depreciate by taking advantage of "accelerated depreciation."[3] Normal depreciation is called "straight-line" depreciation because a graph of the depreciation you take each year would show a straight line. Accelerated depreciation lets you deduct a multiple of the straight-line depreciation each year. Under the tax law current for this edition of the book, you may use the "200 percent declining balance method" to accelerate depreciation for most property.[4] You must subtract each year's depreciation from your basis and use what's left of the basis to calculate the next year's depreciation. When you finally reach the year in which your accelerated depreciation would be less than straight-line depreciation, you may switch back to the straight line method until the property is "fully depreciated."[5] Here's how the system works for the desk and chairs:

Your basis is $560. The useful life is seven years. Straight-line depreciation would be $80 a year for seven years.

Accelerated depreciation allows you to deduct twice the straight-line depreciation the first year. First-year depreciation would be $80, except for the half-year convention, which reduces it to $40. But you may double the first-year straight-line depreciation by accelerating it, so you can claim $80 after all. To figure the depreciation for the second year, you

---

2.   Actually, it's even more complicated. If you acquire 40 percent or more of your assets during the last quarter of the year, you must apply something called the "midquarter convention" to *all* the property you want to depreciate that year. The midquarter convention assumes that you put each item of depreciable property into service in the middle of the quarter in which you acquired it. The effect is to reduce your allowable first-year depreciation.

3.   Internal Revenue Code §168(b).

4.   Internal Revenue Code §168(b)(1)(A).

5.   Internal Revenue Code §168(b)(1)(B).

must subtract that $80 from your $560 basis, leaving $480 left to depreciate over the seven-year useful life. For the second year, then, you divide $480 by seven, which is $69, and double it. So your depreciation for the second year is $138. If you subtract $138 from $480, you have $342 left to depreciate.

The third year, you divide $342 by seven, and double it, for depreciation of $98. In the fourth year, your accelerated depreciation would be $70, calculated by subtracting $98 from $342, leaving $244; dividing that by seven, leaving $35; and doubling it. But your straight-line depreciation that year would exceed accelerated depreciation, so you'd switch to that method. It works like this: Take what's left of the basis ($244) and divide it by the remaining years of useful life (two and a half years, because the half-year convention allowed you to take half a year's depreciation the first year). The fourth-year depreciation is, therefore, $98. Finally, for the fifth year, your depreciation will also be $98. After the fifth year, your furniture will be fully depreciated, and you'll get no more deductions for it.

Depreciation is confusing. The rules for depreciation change from time to time, so if you depreciate, you may be applying different rates to property you acquired at different times. The Internal Revenue Code offers an alternative: you may expense (write off in one year) up to $10,000 worth of depreciable property.[6] This is a blessing for most writers, especially if they can time the purchase of expensive equipment and furniture to occur during a year of heavy income.

Allocation

Many writers use business property partly for business use and partly for personal use. If you do, you must allocate your depreciation or expense so that you don't deduct as a business expense the costs of personal use. Freelance writers who don't work at home simply apply the percentage of business use to determine how much to deduct. Writers who have an office at home face more challenging calculations.

The Home Office Deduction

Because the opportunity for abuse is so great, the Internal Revenue Service sought and won tough requirements for the home office deduction in the Tax Reform Act of 1986. This is what the rules require of you:

---

6. Internal Revenue Code §179(a).

First, you must designate space within your home as your home office and use it "exclusively," "on a regular basis," as your "principal place of business" or to meet or deal with your clients in the ordinary course of your business.[7] If you're lucky enough to have a separate structure on your property that you use as an office, it needn't be your principal place of business, as long as you use it in connection with your writing business.[8]

The first test means that you must make no other use of the space you designate as your home office. It doesn't mean, however, that you can claim the deduction only if you set aside a whole room as your office. A corner of the den will do, if you use it regularly and exclusively as your principal place of business or as the place you meet or deal with clients.

The kinds of expenditures you may deduct for your home office include water, heat, and electricity costs; repairs; maintenance; and depreciation. But you can't claim a deduction for your total household costs. You must allocate them by space. If your apartment measures 1,200 square feet, and your office corner measures 100 square feet, you may deduct only one-twelfth of your costs. If you've set aside a whole room for your office, and the room measures 300 square feet, you may deduct one quarter of your costs. If you own your house, you may depreciate a portion of your basis in it, calculated by comparing the size of the office with the size of the whole house.

Finally, once you determine the allocated expenses, your deduction is limited to what's left after you add the deductions allocable to your home office and all your other deductions for your writing business, and subtract that sum from your gross income from writing for the year. Confusing? You bet. Here's an example to make it clearer:

You earned $4,000 from writing last year. Your home office deductions totaled $1,200, and all your other writing business deductions amounted to $1,900. So your total deductions were $3,100. If you subtract $3,100 from $4,000, you're left with $900. That's all the home office deduction you can take for the year. The excess—$300 must be carried forward to use as a deduction against your writing income next year.[9]

If you're a homeowner, you may know that you can defer taxes on your gain when you sell a home and buy or build another within two years. But if you're entitled to depreciation as part of your home office

---

7.   Internal Revenue Code §280A(c)(1)(a)-(b).
8.   Internal Revenue Code §280A(c)(1)(c).
9.   Internal Revenue Code §280A(c)(5).

deduction the year you sell your house, you'll lose a portion of that deferred-tax benefit. When you sell your home, you calculate gain by subtracting your *basis* from the selling price. Basis—greatly simplified—is what you paid for your house, plus the cost of improvements, minus any depreciation you've taken. Your home office depreciation, therefore, will increase the amount of your gain. You can avoid this result by making sure you're *not entitled* to the home office deduction the year you sell your house, by using the space for something other than your home office.

Because tax returns for self-employed taxpayers are more likely to be audited, and because home office deductions are rigorously examined by the IRS, it pays to keep full, complete records of all home office expenses. Keep utility bills, phone bills, and (if you use the home office to see clients) a log or diary of client visits.

The Cost of Writing

Many writers spend a lot of time and money preparing to write. They spend money in the process of writing. They hope they'll earn back these expenses when their work is published. Sometimes they do; often they don't.

The IRS has attempted to treat these expenses to the writers' disadvantage in the past. It took the position that writers must "capitalize"—that is, amortize their expenses over the life of the project for which the money was spent, treating writing much like the construction of a building or the production of a motion picture. A writer would have to keep separate records of expenses for each writing project, guess about the useful life of each project, and risk penalties if the guess was wrong. And the IRS went further, asserting that a writer could deduct expenses only if the related project earned income! That meant a writer (not a hobby-loss writer, but a real, productive, sole-source-of-income writer) could spend a lot of money on a book no one wanted and be refused the deduction for the expenses of creating it, a double blow.

The courts told the IRS that this approach is not what the law required or allowed. Organized writers groups, such as the National Writers Union, the Authors Guild, and most category fiction groups, are fighting the IRS. The price of deductibility is eternal vigilance. But a footnote to Section 263A of the Internal Revenue Code as amended by the 1986 Tax Reform Act gave the IRS another shot at inflicting this cruel and unusual punishment. Efforts to overcome the effects of the infamous footnote were under way at the time of this writing.

Retirement Plans: The Last Tax Shelter?

As a self-employed person, you'll find a number of opportunities available to help you save tax dollars. We've discussed a number of them above. Now we'll talk about the best of them: retirement plans for the self-employed.

Self-employed writers may choose among the following:

- Individual retirement accounts (IRA)
- Keogh Plans, also called HR–10 Plans
- Simplified employee plans (SEPs)

This smorgasbord of choices can be tailored to fit almost any budget, as long as there's a little left to invest when all the year's expenses are paid.

Try your hardest to park some money in one or more retirement plans, because that money will then be excluded when you calculate your gross income. In short, you won't pay taxes on it when you earn it, although you will when you draw money out of the retirement plan, at age 59½ and later, when your years of heavy earnings are behind you. (Well, that's the theory.) In effect you earn your tax rate on the money you invest in a self-employed retirement plan the year you contribute it, and your earnings on the contribution also earn not only their nominal rate of return but also the amount of income tax you'd otherwise pay on those earnings. It's an unbeatable deal.

IRAs were the retirement vehicle of choice for most of us until the Tax Reform and Simplification Act of 1986 complicated them beyond reach. For example, if you (or your spouse) work for an employer, even part-time, you may be eligible for inclusion in your *employer's* retirement plan. That's good: But if it's a qualified plan (as the Internal Revenue Code defines it—ask your boss or the personnel department to verify qualification), and if your income reaches certain threshold levels, you won't be able to take a deduction for the IRA.[10] The formulas for the limitation on your deduction are complicated, and they may change with the next Congress and administration, so we won't set them out here. If you're eligible for the IRA deduction, however, you can keep up to $2,000 out of your taxable income.[11]

Keogh Plans are available to any self-employed person, regardless of participation in the qualified plan of his or her employer. Set-up costs and annual reporting requirements can be burdensome if you choose

---

10. Internal Revenue Code §§219,408.
11. Internal Revenue Code §219.

investment options other than those offered by savings and loan associations and banks, but if you're willing to accept relatively low interest, the Keogh approach can be useful.

Simplified employee plans, on the other hand, live up to their name. The SEP is a means for employers to make contributions to their employees' IRAs. But if you're self-employed, whether full-time or part-time, you are your own employer, and you can make those contributions to yourself![12] The deduction is limited to $30,000 or 15 percent of your net earnings for the year, whichever is less. A number of other rules, somewhat complex, apply to SEPs, but they remain an underused way to reduce taxes and save for the future.

CONCLUSION

We've only skimmed the surface of the tax law as it applies specially to writers. Many good sources of tax information exist, including the annual editions of books written by J. K. Lasser, several major accounting firms, and H & R Block. If you think you may have a tax problem (or opportunity), by all means seek expert help. The risk of being wrong is great, the cost of losing a benefit easily avoided.

---

12.   Internal Revenue Code §408(k).

11 LEGAL RESOURCES FOR THE WRITER

INTRODUCTION

Many writers don't seek legal help because they don't know where to look for it, or because they fear they can't afford competent advice. The purpose of this chapter is to convince you that there are ways to understand the laws and legal procedures that affect you, and to work with a lawyer without ending up in the poorhouse.

The place to start is with your own education. A multitude of resources exist, designed to help you better understand the law and how it may affect you. Those resources include self-help books such as this one, the programs and publications of writer's organizations, informal networks of writers, and numerous workshops, seminars, and periodicals. Even the federal government provides potentially valuable help if you know where to look. Appendix A contains an annotated list of books, periodicals, and organizations to assist you.

Once you've used these resources to take your legal education to its practical limit, this chapter will help you decide whether you need a lawyer and, if you do, how to find one and get the most legal help for the least legal expense.

WHEN DO YOU NEED A LAWYER?

The first step in deciding what legal help you need is to recognize and define the problems you face. If you look back through this book, you'll see that the substance of each chapter deals with decisions that may require the help of a lawyer. This isn't the same as saying they always do. There is, of course, a great deal an informed writer can do for herself.

What can a good lawyer do for you that you—or your agent—can't do for yourself? An experienced literary lawyer has a much broader base of information about publishing than any one writer is likely to have, and the lawyer should be familiar with problems that most agents aren't, such as libel and the hazards of collaboration. These problems crop up long before you need to worry about a publishing contract.

What's more, a lawyer is trained—and paid—to be objective. Your lawyer should not say yes to your every request. Rather, the two of you should explore possibilities, consequences, and alternatives to be as sure as you can that you've chosen a course that makes sense. You'll recall from our discussion on agents in Chapter 4 that because an agent is self-interested in any negotiation, he is by definition not in a position to be completely objective. A good agent knows the literary marketplace better than most lawyers, enough to appraise your chances of improving on an offer. A lawyer, on the other hand, may offer additional insights, because his fee, unlike an agent's commission, doesn't depend on the deal being made.

When you are offered a deal, hiring a lawyer to comment on the contract and help you structure it to your maximum advantage need not cost a fortune. If you have a sound basic understanding of how a publishing deal is put together and what sorts of changes are possible, two or three hours of legal help are likely to be all you need.

If you're offered a major deal, perhaps for film rights or mass market paperback rights, you should certainly seek the advice of a lawyer. Not only will you want to be absolutely sure the terms of the contract are the best you can get, you'll also need tax advice! Guessing wrong with a lot of money at stake can be catastrophic, and proper planning can quite literally save you a fortune. Again, though, it's up to you to inform yourself of the basic rules of the area that concerns you. As you surely must know by now, only an informed consumer is likely to receive good service in this hurry-up world, whether provided by carpenter, surgeon—or lawyer.

WHERE CAN YOU FIND LEGAL HELP?

Legal help is available from all sorts of people and places. Lawyers are trained to provide it. But no lawyer was born with the Copyright Act clenched between his baby gums. To learn the law, lawyers take courses, talk to experts, read lots of books, and learn from experience. You can do the same thing, we hope with more focus and more enjoyment. You will be particularly effective at this if you remember that although lawyers are a good source of legal information, they are not the only source.

Friends

If you have friends who write professionally, find out all you can about their legal problems and triumphs. If they're willing to talk about the terms of their publishing contracts, listen. In short, take advantage of any and all information you can gather from others whose problems are similar to yours.

But while you're exercising your curiosity, don't lock up your caution. Unless you know a lot of writers willing to talk about the business of writing, your sample of friends is likely to be small. In addition, as you should now realize, publishing is a business in which different literary subcategories commonly follow surprisingly different rules. For example, the business experiences of a novelist and a textbook writer will have only a passing similarity, and a screenwriter works in an environment almost totally different from that of a popular historian. Further, dealing with a small or mid-size regional publisher may be only remotely similar to dealing with Viking-Penguin or Random House. And even within the same house, the contracts and underlying financial assumptions differ significantly; Addison-Wesley's general trade contract only generally resembles its Health Sciences Division contract.

In addition, when you talk to writer friends, be aware that your friends probably have their own axes to grind. Their experiences are sure to have colored their feelings toward a particular publisher, or toward publishers in general. Again, keep an open mind and try to separate the sensible from the silly.

Writers' Organizations Offering Legal Help

Writers' organizations already have programs sure to be relevant to at least some of your needs. Organizations—listed in the Resource Directory, Appendix A—offer a wealth of general advice to writers about their professional activities. The Authors Guild, for example, has prepared a set of sample publishing contracts much fairer to authors than the ones usually proffered by most publishers. It's not likely you'll persuade your potential publisher to adopt the entire Authors Guild contract, but you'll be better equipped to bargain if you know what your organized colleagues feel is advantageous. The Authors Guild surveys of financial terms, published in its bulletin, are also useful reading.

Check the list of organizations in the Resource Directory to find one or more that suits you. When you join, be sure to get a list of all the services the organization provides, and don't be bashful about using them. Among the most efficient ways to further your professional education are workshops, courses, and seminars sponsored by these writers' organizations. The range of legally oriented workshops for writers is extensive, covering everything from how to organize a profit-making or tax-exempt business entity to the intricacies of copyright law. Usually taught by experts, these sponsored educational gatherings are a source of reliable general information, an opportunity for you to ask questions about your specific needs, and a place to test your ideas against other people's experience. Such organizations as California Lawyers for the Arts (San Francisco and Los Angeles), the Media Alliance (San Francisco), Volunteer Lawyers for the Arts (New York), and the Mystery Writers of America (chapters in several cities) sponsor instructive gatherings for working writers. So do other organizations, such as the Writers Connection (Cupertino, California) and romance writers' groups.

Because workshops usually cost something, come prepared to get your money's worth. Take time to research the workshop subject and, once you have some background, make a list of questions you want answered. Don't expect the workshop leader to conduct a legal clinic for your benefit, but do be politely assertive so that you get answers to your main questions. Most workshops and seminars are designed to convey a great deal of information to many people in a relatively short time, so extensive discussion of every point isn't possible.

Legal Help from the Government

It is impossible to list all the free and low-cost material relating to the legal problems of writers available from the U.S. Government. The Government Printing Office catalogs thousands of items, some suitable only for writers who do research in a particular field, some specifically designed to answer general business questions, and many published by government agencies with which you'll frequently be doing regular business. The Internal Revenue Service, for example, publishes a number of guides to help you avoid tax problems. Check the Resource Directory for some titles.

One area of particular interest to writers is copyright. The Copyright Office issues "Publications of the Copyright Office," Circular R2, which describes most Copyright Office material in enough detail for you to decide you want it. A sample order form used by the Copyright Office is included in Appendix D.

In addition, the Government Printing Office will send you a general catalog upon request. This will allow you to better determine the subject areas in which information is available. Most departments, agencies, and bureaus of the government will also happily send you a list of their publications.

Legal Information from Books and Periodicals

A writer should have a good working knowledge of how the law interacts with publishing before entering into any legally binding relationship. While this book provides a useful framework for your thinking, it doesn't pretend to be able to answer all your questions. Published materials are only tools, useful in the hands of a skilled craftsperson, dangerous in the hands of one who uses them thoughtlessly. For a professional writer without legal training to take a complex form or contract out of the book and adopt it as her own, without analysis, all but guarantees trouble before the contract term ends. We say this to remind you once again to check what you read here with experts when you face significant decisions about your rights or your earnings.

HOW TO CHOOSE A LAWYER

Now let's assume you have a good grounding in literary law, but you quite sensibly want to establish a relationship with a lawyer who will be available to review contracts, answer questions, and generally provide expert support.

Choosing a good lawyer is not a task to be taken lightly. A poor choice may hurt your writing business until you admit your mistake and choose again. A compatible and knowledgeable lawyer can do much to enhance your literary career.

You can find a lawyer in any of a number of ways. No one method guarantees a successful choice, but some improve the odds considerably.

Relying on word-of-mouth referrals is wise only if you know the person making the referral well enough to evaluate her judgment and experience. Talk with other writers you know, particularly those who have already been through whatever it is you're facing. For example, if you're about to negotiate and sign a textbook publishing contract, why not seek out the local author of a successful text? Find out if she used a lawyer and, if so, whether she was happy with his services. Organizations of fellow writers may also be good sources of information about competent, experienced lawyers. Many organizations don't have formal referral services, but they do know people. In California, Illinois, and New York, special purpose lawyers' referral services exist, designed to help writers, artists, and other creative people (see the Resource Directory).

Make sure the lawyer you choose is not a general practitioner, or even a business or contract lawyer, with little or no background in the book business. Because malpractice suits against lawyers are more common than they were a few years ago, most sensible lawyers are reluctant to practice law in unfamiliar terrain, but such a surplus of lawyers exists that some will grab any client who can pay. The whole area of writers' rights, copyright, libel, publishing contracts, and the like is too specialized for a lawyer to handle optimally if he only practices literary law once in a while. If you have or know a lawyer in general practice, however, he should be able to suggest the name of at least one lawyer who does represent writers.

Unfortunately, anyone may claim to be a literary law specialist. The organized bar has no procedure to certify that a person is really an expert in literary law, and no private groups provide this service as physicians' specialty boards do in medicine. If you are referred to a literary "specialist," it's up to you to probe to find out whether the claimed specialty is based on experience or wishful thinking. If you despair of finding experienced legal help near your home (this will be a real problem in many areas of the country), you should consider establishing a long-distance relationship with a lawyer who practices where enough literary business exists to support him. Much can be accomplished by telephone and through correspondence, although for many clients it's a comfort to work with a lawyer face to face. Again, see the Resource Directory, Appendix A.

HOW TO CHECK UP ON A LAWYER

The starting point in checking up on a prospective legal representative is to talk with those who made the referral. Ask specifically about the nature of the work the lawyer did for the person giving you the recommendation. If another lawyer is making the referral, find out if there is financial consideration involved between the two lawyers. Despite the fact that ethical rules limit the nature of such a financial relationship, it is still all too common for an attorney to pay for a referral with some of the money he collects from a referred client. A financial arrangement of this kind can impair objectivity.

If your initial inquiries prove satisfactory, your next step is to call the lawyer to explain what you need. If possible, talk to the lawyer directly. Your purpose is both to find out if this person has the experience and inclination to counsel you, and to see if you get a positive feeling from the conversation. Don't expect to get a definitive answer to specific legal questions, or unlimited time, during this initial (usually free) conversation.

Your first question should focus on the lawyer's recent, relevant experience. It's fair for you to ask about representative clients. Some lawyers will name their clients; others will not. Be suspicious of one who won't tell you anything about other writer-clients. If the lawyer does have experience representing writers, make sure that the work the lawyer has done is similar to the work you need accomplished. Writing a will for a novelist isn't the same as analyzing a publishing deal for her.

Probably the single greatest cause of client dissatisfaction with lawyers is unresponsiveness. Many capable lawyers are overextended and must set priorities simply to survive. Often what you consider urgent may be mere routine to your lawyer. Be forthright. Ask the candidate if he has time to handle your problems and if he can respond promptly if you have an emergency. There is nothing more frustrating than a lawyer, no matter how competent, who doesn't return calls for a week. In this regard, it's wise to ask if there is a backup lawyer to handle your affairs when he is not available.

It's tempting to call a couple of representative clients to verify the glowing report the lawyer has given herself. Many clients may be willing to share their experiences with you; others may not want to be bothered. If you plan to check references, by all means let the lawyer know in advance.

THE INITIAL CONSULTATION

Your next step is to meet your prospective counselor. Some lawyers will give one exploratory consultation free, if you ask. It's probably better to pay a reasonable amount for the lawyer's time, to establish yourself as a person who expects good service and to pay fairly for it. Establish the fee in advance. If you're still exploring to satisfy yourself that this lawyer is the one for you, plan for a brief meeting. Come prepared with a succinct statement of your needs and your resources and copies of any documents that define your position; but unless a particular problem is reasonably small or routine, don't expect the legal answers to all your problems in half an hour.

If, after your initial consultation, you have any doubts about the lawyer, trust your instincts. It's worth considerable effort to find someone you are comfortable working with.

FEES AND BILLS

How Much Will It Cost?

Distasteful as you may find it, a discussion of fees and billing practices should take place before you begin work with a lawyer. Most lawyers charge an hourly rate. The rate varies with geography and experience. It pays to be forthright and determine in advance what you are being charged for the services you need.

There is no way to tell you, definitively, how much a lawyer will cost. Fees vary widely. If you're dealing with a sole practitioner working out of an office in his home, you will obviously expect to pay less than if your lawyer is a senior partner whose corner office benignly overlooks the world below. Typical fees range from $75 to $250 an hour. The members of lawyer referral services offer a free half-hour consultation to those who pay the service a relatively small fee. California Lawyers for the Arts currently charges $20, none of which goes to the lawyer. Additional lawyer's time is billed at a rate negotiated with the client, often lower than what the lawyer usually charges.

What Am I Paying For?

Lawyers normally bill by the hour, unless some other fee arrangement is made. You should be charged for smaller increments than a full hour at the appropriate fraction of the lawyer's hourly rate. Many clients are angry when they learn that each phone call, even for a "quick question," is billed for a minimum quarter-hour or tenth-hour. Lawyers present interesting (and largely valid) rationalizations for this practice. Each phone call, they say, interrupts some other project. Time is lost directly because of the interruption and indirectly because it takes at least a few minutes to pick up what was laid aside to take the call. Many lawyers have developed the wise habit of making notes of every phone call. If you add up the time spent answering the quick question, dictating a memo to the file, and returning to the interrupted work, you'll readily see how the lawyer can devote fifteen minutes to your five-minute telephone call. Besides, it's not just your lawyer's time, it's his wisdom and experience (and overhead) you're paying for.

There's an easy way to be sure you and your lawyer understand his billing policy. Ask for a fee agreement, which explains it and obligates both you and the firm to abide by it. California recently began requiring a lawyer who expects a client's fees to exceed $1,000 to provide such an agreement to the client or risk not getting paid.

An example of a rather stiff, formal fee letter from a good-sized firm appears on the next page. A fee letter, much more friendly in tone, follows.

The Billing Cycle

Law office accounting and billing systems often grind exceedingly slowly. You may not be billed for a telephone conversation, a meeting, or time to draft a contract until several weeks have passed.

These days many lawyers' bills are quite detailed and descriptive, the consequence of computerized billing systems; just the same, you have every right to question a bill. Question your own memory first. If you're sure you've spotted a mistake, don't hesitate to point it out. Call the office at once to ask for an explanation. An honest lawyer will provide you with one.

There's another side to this problem, however, which is the lawyer's reasonable assumption that you'll remember the valuable work he did for you, even if it happened early last month, and pay for it promptly. Lawyers, being human despite evidence to the contrary, will work harder for those clients who pay on time.

Contingency Fees, or "A Piece of the Action"

What if you need a lawyer, but you don't have any money? What if you have a great book idea that you're convinced will make you a fortune? Will a lawyer take a percentage of your prospective income from the project in return for legal work?

Lawyers who represent creative clients in the entertainment business sometimes do take "points," or "a piece of the action," and the same may be true for lawyers who represent writers. In general, though, a lawyer will rarely represent a writer of books on a contingency basis. The uncertainties are simply too great.

An ethical question also exists. If your lawyer's compensation depends on whether you make a deal, he may be subject to subtle pressure to say yes to you, when the appropriate answer is no.

Law Offices
AVOCADO AND JURIS
A Professional Corporation
One Montgomery Street
San Francisco, CA 94104

January 3, 20_____

Dolores Ottero
10105 Folsom Street
San Francisco, CA 94111

Dear Ms. Ottero:

The purpose of this letter is to confirm our discussion concerning fees.

The services we perform for you will be billed at our hourly rate (except for matters such as estate planning and pension planning, in which there is a relatively standard fee).

Our hourly charges currently are as follows: The time of partners is charged at the rate of $150–$250 per hour. Au other attorney time is charged at the rate of $100–$125 per hour. My billing rate is $175 per hour. Paralegal time, if any, is charged at the rate of $50 per hour. Accumulated time will be billed for payment on a monthly basis, as the work progresses. Costs and disbursements paid by us will also be billed for payment on a monthly basis. Rates are subject to change, but you will be notified of any such change.

With respect to what constitutes billable time, it is our policy to bill in minimum units of one-quarter hour. This includes any phone calls, even ones that take a very few minutes. Our principal "product" is our time. Even a brief phone call requires the attorney to interrupt the project he or she is then working on, prepare a note or memorandum regarding the phone conversation, and then attempt to regain his or her train of thought on the project that he or she had been working on. A similar rationale applies to our minimum charge of one-half hour for all correspondence.

Also, the standards with respect to billable time apply to calls and letters on your behalf with other people, especially including our own professional advisors.

Just as we are pleased to discuss our work, we are pleased to discuss fees, and encourage you to speak with us at any time you might have a question concerning our work or fees.

If you accept the terms and conditions stated in this letter, please date, sign, and return the enclosed copy. Should you have any questions, please do not hesitate to call me. We are looking forward to working with you.

Very truly yours,

Aviva Avocado
AVOCADO AND JURIS

Agreed and accepted:

_____

Dated:

DA:aw

Law Offices
AVOCADO AND JURIS
A Professional Corporation
One Montgomery Street
San Francisco, CA 94104

January 3, 20____

Dear Dolores:

I think it a good idea for us to agree in advance about my fees. I charge $125 an hour, and I bill in minimum increments of a quarter-hour, even for brief phone conversations, if they're substantive. I'll also bill you for any costs I incur on your behalf, such as postage, document production, and long-distance telephone charges.

I'll bill you once a month, and I'd like for you to pay me within thirty days of the billing date, because I'll have cash flow problems if you don't.

Please let me know if you ever have any questions about my bills. I'm always ready to discuss them.

Sincerely,

Aviva Avocado

HOW TO BE A GOOD CLIENT

Don't be fooled for a minute; your lawyer's affable pleasantries during working hours are billed at the usual rate. Business is business, fun is fun. Keep the two separate. When you call or visit your lawyer, be ready, be brief, and be organized. In short, spend as little time in your lawyer's company as possible, at least during those billable working hours.

When you call for an appointment, give your lawyer some advance warning of what you're after. It pays to find out what information or documents you should send him or bring with you to a meeting. Organize the materials you're to provide and list the questions you want answered.

Be as honest as possible when you're discussing a problem with your lawyer. We all want to appear to be clever, hard-headed business people, but at times we all do things, or make commitments that, in hindsight, turn out to be foolish. Don't compound your problems by hiding them from the person you've hired to give you workable legal advice. He can't guess what's happened to you; and facts withheld, or half-revealed, will almost surely return to haunt you.

Pay attention, take notes, and ask questions until you are satisfied you understand what your lawyer is telling you. It's easy and not uncommon for a lawyer to hide behind obfuscating language to escape confronting a difficult problem, especially one with which he isn't completely familiar. Your penetrating questions can help your lawyer admit he doesn't know everything so that the two of you can deal with your problem honestly.

Finally, inform yourself. As a professional writer, you're conducting a business. You have an obligation to understand the nature of your business. Use the resources listed in this book to find out as much as you can about your business. If you become a pretty good amateur literary lawyer on your own, you should only have to rely on your lawyer for more complicated help.

The writer who receives a publishing contract and wants legal advice about it should analyze the agreement first. He should use his research and analytical tools in his own behalf. Only then should he seek legal advice. If he is reluctant to negotiate on his own behalf, a lawyer can do it for him. But if he's willing to be his own champion, he can ask for help in deciding what's possible and how to achieve it. His lawyer should be able to provide him with effective arguments for achieving his goals. The result: a better contract and more money in the writer's pocket.

Be Not Fearful

This chapter should prepare you to deal effectively and efficiently with a lawyer, whose workings should no longer seem mysterious to you. By planning, learning, organizing, and expressing your requirements, you will remain in charge of the relationship with your lawyer. The same approach will also work when you must deal with your agent or your editor.

12

THE AUTHOR AND THE BUSINESS OF PUBLISHING*

INTRODUCTION

Every piece of work involved in moving a completed manuscript into a reader's hands takes place within a framework of future considerations. A book signed today will be positioned on a publication list for its formal launch anywhere from nine months to two years (or more) later. During this period, events take place which influence the book and its commercial life, including the design of its cover, what stores order it, how it is promoted, where on the shelf it is placed, how long it stays on the shelf, and, often, whether it ends up in the hands of a reader or forgotten on a remainder table. A crucial irony of the publishing business is that the decisions that contribute so much to the success or failure of a book often have little to do with its quality. Many good books never have a reasonable chance to succeed because of decisions made by an ill-informed publisher. And occasionally, the most unlikely suspect enjoys an immense success in spite of a publisher's complete lack of attention.

In spite of the direct relationship between a book's performance and its publisher's support, the lore of the publishing industry is full of unexpected success and unanticipated failure. Every season, certain books succeed or fail despite the efforts (or lack thereof) of their publishers.

---

* As we mentioned in the introduction, the author of this chapter is Peter Beren, whose professional publishing experience is both broad and longstanding.

Unfortunately, publishers too often use an unexpected success story to justify not promoting other books. It's as if they believe that they don't have to make much of an effort to market all sorts of other books because one totally obscure book occasionally turns into a bestseller without any promotional effort.

To ensure the best possible chance for success, every author should acquire a working knowledge of the business side of publishing. We don't exaggerate when we say it's equally important to write with passion, turn a good phrase, and sign an advantageous publishing contract. If you understand how a book is published, it stands to reason you'll be able to communicate more effectively with key publishing people during the publishing process. And your improved ability to communicate will have a positive effect on the success of your book. As author and former publishing executive Leonard Felder put it in *Publishers Weekly*, an author's understanding of the publishing environment is a key to success: "I would estimate that 40 percent of the tension and disagreements between writers and book industry people could be alleviated if authors knew when to suggest good ideas and when it's too late."

It may be an exaggeration to say that Hemingway or Faulkner would have sold more books if they had better understood the needs of their publishers' promotion department; it's no exaggeration at all to say that most writers are unaware of the extent to which they can influence the fate of their books. Unfortunately, instead of learning how to contribute positively to a book's success, many writers adopt the posture of passive victim. Complaints of this type proliferate. Indeed, if you spend any time at all around other authors, you've probably heard many horror stories about publishers. Sadly, because so few publishing companies put a high priority on maintaining good communications with their authors, the complaints of writers are all too often justified. At other times, grievances are the result of the author's misunderstanding of the way the publishing business works. Lachlan MacDonald offers a telling satire of typical publishing relationships:

> *BOOK FABLE: EXCUSES, EXCUSES*
> by Lachlan P. MacDonald
>
> *The Author's Tale* • "The editor was so enthusiastic and supportive, I never thought there would be so many problems with getting the book out and getting it into the stores. Before it ever came out, she quit the publishing house and opened her own literary agency. I wrote her and called long distance, but she never calls back. I feel I was romanced."
>
> *The Editor's Story* • "It was a good idea, with some fresh scenes, but the line editing took forever and the author didn't follow some suggestions that were crucial. Nevertheless, we went to press on schedule, and I'm sorry the house

didn't follow through after I left. They're so disorganized. I still love the book and if X ever does anything more, I want to see it, but . . ."

The Publisher's Story • "She was recommended by one of our investors, you know, and she was good at grammar and spelling and punctuation, even if she didn't have the editorial background. But she made these crazy deals. I think she was having a breakdown. We didn't let her go; it was her decision. And the book was one of a half-dozen we were left with. We put it out and gave it a push, but nothing happened. Have you seen the new book on running we have out?"

The Production Manager's Story • "It was a great design and seemed like an interesting subject, but the manufacturer made a last-minute switch in the text stock, and there were bindery errors, and the shipment was two days late. You can't be looking over the vendor's shoulder every minute . . ."

The Printer • "If the book was selling well, you wouldn't hear a murmur. But when it bombs in the bookstores, they look around for someone else to sell the books to, and the first person they think of is the printer. So they want credit for 23 cases of books because it was two days late and one page was out of order in two dozen copies. This happens every day . . ."

The Promotion Director • "The ads and the reviews and the promo were right on schedule, but we didn't have books in the stores because of the late delivery. And the author didn't proof it right, so there was a glaring error on page 93, and one page was out of order. That killed us for TV."

The Reviewer • "I never heard of the book before. Do you know how many books come in here in one day? I'll look for it, but why not send me another copy; it may be too late to write anything, but at least I'll look at it."

The Chain Buyer • "We'll fill any orders that come in, but we can't stock new titles just now. Things are just too tight. Try after the ABA, after Christmas, after you get a book club sale, after you get on the Tonight Show, etc. etc."

The TV Show Talent Coordinator • "If it isn't in all the stores, we can't touch it."

The Mom & Pop Stores • "Is it a local author? Will you leave, uh, one, on consignment? Can I have a reading copy?"

The Author's Mother • "It looks nice. I put it on the coffee table. You were always so good with words. Not like your brother, but it seems all he can do is make money, no matter what he touches it turns to . . ."[1]

Experienced writers eventually learn how to navigate the shoals of the publishing process, gaining wisdom from past mistakes. Publishers

---

1.   © 1980 Lachlan P. MacDonald. From his newsletter, *Publishing in the Output Mode,* San Luis Obispo, California. All rights reserved. Used by permission of author.

could—and should—speed this process by educating writers, especially novices, in the publishing process. But because most publishers don't, we think it important to review it in detail, with emphasis on the areas where an author's input can be creative and helpful.

Our job is to help you learn enough about the way the book business works so you can avoid becoming its victim. You are the single person with the most to gain if your book does well. To the publisher, yours is only one book among many. You must learn to invest yourself in the publishing process to give your book its greatest chance of success.

Let's now take a look at the publishing process, especially the critical places where you can influence the success of your book.

THE EDITOR'S ROLE

Before the production stage, authors work closely with the editorial department. Traditionally, the editor who acquires the book and sees it through the long and exhausting publishing process is the author's advocate to the publisher and the publisher's advocate to the author. We can't overemphasize the importance of a good relationship with your editor.

In most publishing houses, it's the editor who transmits the author's enthusiasm, desires, knowledge, and reactions to the other departments. The general feeling (often not true) is that the production and marketing departments would be besieged by authors demanding special attention if there were no editor to serve as a buffer.

The author-editor relationship is full of potential strain. If you feel estranged from your editor, you should take prompt action to talk out the difficulties. It's crucial that you concentrate on your common goal, a successful publishing outcome. Don't waste energy on concerns not central to this purpose.

If, despite your best efforts, the relationship between you and your editor is beyond repair, you may want to request another editor. View this as a last resort, however, because if your publisher can't accommodate your request (because of work schedules, for example), you may lose additional goodwill.

It's also important that you build relationships with people at your publisher other than your editor, because editors in today's "revolving door" publishing business are often either coming or going. Good editors get hired away or laid off; bad ones get fired.

If your editor should suddenly leave the scene just as your book is being published, you'll want other in-house advocates to continue the support of your book. This person could be a senior editor, an assistant to the publisher, or the marketing director. The important thing is to have some friendly allies in your corner. Your first step is to find out immediately who has inherited the project. Move quickly to develop a strong rapport with your new advocate. Use your phone, the mail, and, if you can afford the time and money, make a personal visit.

In some cases, an assistant takes over for an interim period and may appear to lack the organizational influence of your original editor. In others, the new editor may not seem very interested in you or your book. If you face either of these situations, don't become discouraged or angry. Above all, don't give up. Enthusiasm often carries the day in publishing houses. Try to light a fire under the new editor. If this seems impossible, use the other relationships you've established to try to move your book to an editor with more enthusiasm.

BOOK PRODUCTION AND PRICING

An Overview

A first-time author may assume that once a publisher gets a manuscript, it's sent directly to the printer. Before the book is manufactured, "preproduction" must occur, a process concerned with a lot more than getting type straight on a page. Preproduction involves the final preparation and editing of the manuscript and preparation of any ancillary materials, including front matter and back matter. This process goes on to include typesetting, illustration, and book and cover design. All of these steps involve nonrecurring costs that are known as "plant costs." When this is all done, your book will probably be sent on disk to an independent printer who will use the files to produce film and then plates. Film can be reused for subsequent printings with little added cost.

Manufacturing involves the actual printing and binding of the book. Often referred to as PP&B (paper, printing, and binding), manufacturing costs will also include such miscellaneous costs as the freight bill for shipping the books to the publisher's warehouse from the printer. The manufacturing process involves a galaxy of options—from the weight of the paper to the type of lamination (coating) to be used on the cover or jacket. The use of color and the design of the jacket or cover are particularly significant parts of this process. The choice of color and graphics work together to affect both the cost and the marketing of the book. Because of this, cover or jacket meetings often involve editors, marketing people, and many others besides production department personnel.

The list price of a book is directly influenced by preproduction, manufacturing (PP&B), and royalty costs. Publishers can multiply some portion of these costs by anywhere from four to ten when pricing books. (Industry averages are in the range of five or eight to one.) Thus, if a book's unit manufacturing cost and some measure of preproduction or "plant" costs (exclusive of royalties) is $1, it will commonly bear a retail price from $4 to $10, depending on the formula pricing policy of the publishing house. Some houses include royalty costs or a measure of overhead; some do not. Of course, this formula approach is mitigated by the realities of the marketplace (the prices of competing books, hardcover or softcover format, the income of the people likely to buy it, and so on), but this formula approach is a general practice. Generally, publishers aim at a gross profit margin of between 40 percent and 60 percent of their investment for first printings. Thus, if we take the suggested list price of a book and apply the average discount to wholesalers, retailers, libraries, and so on, we should arrive at a figure that is roughly twice the difference between that figure (sales receipts) and the total of paper, printing, and binding costs, the author's royalty, and an amortization of the plant costs (cost of goods sold). Here is an example:

EXAMPLE • The list price of our hypothetical book is $12.95. It costs $10,000 to design, typeset, lay out, paste-up, and produce a camera ready mechanical for the cover. Let's assume we are printing 10,000 copies and it costs $10,000 to print them (paper, printing, binding). This includes miscellaneous costs, such as transportation to our warehouse. The author's royalty is 8 percent of list. The average sales discount is 47 percent off list price.

$$\begin{aligned}
\text{Plant (per copy) costs} &= \$1.00 \text{ (10,000 books at \$10,000)} \\
\text{PP\&B} &= \$1.00 \text{ (10,000 books at \$10,000)} \\
\text{Royalty} &= \underline{\$1.04} \text{ (8 percent of 12.95)} \\
&\ \$3.04
\end{aligned}$$

Sales receipts
(53 percent of list: $12.95) = $6.86

$$\text{Gross margin} = \frac{\text{Net income}^2}{\text{Sales receipts}}$$

$$\begin{array}{l}
6.86 \quad \text{(sales receipts)} \\
\underline{-3.04 \ \text{(cost of goods)}} \\
3.82 \quad \text{(net income)}
\end{array} \qquad \frac{3.82 \ \text{(net income)}}{6.86 \ \text{(sales receipts)}} = 55.7\% = \text{gross margin}$$

2.　[Net income = sales receipts − cost of goods]

The amortization of the plant costs is an important issue and the object of continuing controversy in the publishing world. The conventional wisdom holds that because 75 percent of all books published will not go into a second printing, the price of the books in the first printing must absorb all of the plant costs. Of course, this may become a self-fulfilling prophecy, since such an amortization procedure may drive the price of the first printing to an unsaleable level. Some publishers are experimenting with pricing formulas that assume subsequent printings and thus amortize print costs over a longer time. This is probably a favorable trend from the author's point of view.

Creating a Castoff

The book's editor generally produces the preliminary "castoff." The castoff estimates the number of pages the finished book will have, as well as the format (such issues as paper or cloth, trim size), number of illustrations, and so on. The production department assumes responsibility for the final castoff and the manufacturing costs estimate ("quote").

Publishers take into account all of the preproduction costs in their pricing formulas. As noted above, they either levy them entirely on the first printing, or amortize them over the anticipated life of the book. So, if you, as an author, neglect to include a part of a bibliography in your manuscript and a publisher must hire a researcher to complete it, this cost gets added to the preproduction tally. It is definitely in your interest to minimize any problems or delays within the final stages of the editorial process. This generally means being as responsive to the publisher's reasonable requests as possible. If, with a little extra effort, you can do a particular revision in two days as opposed to two weeks, do it. Any extra steps or delays will increase the cost of your book to the public and may, therefore, jeopardize sales.

Book Design Decisions

Standard publishing procedures leave authors out of book design decisions. Publishers believe authors lack the necessary knowledge and experience to provide useful ideas in this relatively sophisticated area. There are, of course, exceptions. Many smaller and specialized publishers have learned to welcome author participation, and some even use this flexibility as a means to attract authors dissatisfied with the more rigid approach of larger houses.

With books of certain types, such as photography and poetry, you may consider your participation in discussions about format, composition, and reproduction processes to be essential. If so, your right to participate should be formally and mutually agreed upon as early in the publishing process as possible. It is best to do this at the contract stage. Otherwise, you may find yourself shut out.

CONFLICT BETWEEN ART AND COMMERCE

As your completed manuscript enters into production, your editor should begin to function as an intermediary between you and the other publishing departments. Problems and differences of opinion on how to solve them are common at this stage. To react to these sensibly and to understand what sorts of requests are reasonable, an author must understand the publishing process.

Let's take a typical example of how problems can develop. The castoff on a book exposing the medical industry, entitled *Pills and Knives,* indicates that if ten paragraphs of text can be eliminated, an entire printing signature can be dropped. (Books are printed in folded sheets or sections called signatures, which consist of sixteen or thirty-two pages.) This will dramatically lower the unit cost of manufacturing and will result in a more competitively priced edition. The editor concludes that the competitive price advantage is much more important, in this case, than saving a few thousand words, and asks the author to cooperate. Attitude is important at this point. The author can dig in her heels and insist on every word being published or can agree to reasonable changes. Of course, what appears reasonable to a publisher may legitimately seem completely unreasonable to an author. We can't tell you much more than to suggest you enter this juncture with an open mind. State your case, but listen to the editor's concerns. With such openness, reasonable compromises can be worked out to mutual satisfaction. The important thing is for everyone in the process to feel that the others are approaching the problem with goodwill.

You should be particularly resistant to the idea that every request for change is an attack by commercial philistines on your work of art. It can amount to that, of course, but often the changes won't impair your work. Getting your manuscript between covers and onto a bookshelf can be a tricky business, requiring your help, and sometimes even a measure of sacrifice. Of course, you will want to protect the integrity of your writing while doing this. Remember, though, that unyielding rigidity may drive up the final price of the book and, perhaps, place it at an unsaleable level. This may even cause your in-house advocates to turn their backs on your book.

Here is an approach to dealing with requests for last minute changes that we have found helpful. First, clarify (remind yourself of) your publishing intent. Obviously, writers of poetry, fiction, how-to, or scholarly books will have different reactions to change requests. Second, ask yourself if your interest is fundamentally or even significantly hurt by what the publisher wants to do. If it is, how might the same result be achieved in a different way? For example, at this stage of the process, it's not uncommon for controversy to occur over whether to include an index. Indexes enhance library and institutional sales. If you feel these markets are important for your book, and the publisher wants to eliminate your index, firmly but politely state your case. If you encounter resistance, try to bargain. For example, you might offer to shorten the index, or perhaps the table of contents and introduction, if they are less important, so the size of the book will meet the publisher's format requirement.

To illustrate further the process of how a book's concept may change at this stage, let's consider a manuscript that, when cast-off, is 352 book pages long. Some of its 352 pages will be derived from drawings and photographs that have been submitted as part of the manuscript. The book is a how-to guide to spelunking, to be published as a quality trade paperback original at an 8½" by 11" size.

Assume that under the original contract, the author supplied all photographs and illustrations, which means that there will be no additional fees for permissions to obtain artwork. And assume that both the editor and the author are enthusiastic about producing the ultimate book on this subject and that the manuscript appears to be more thorough than anything already in print.

The book is now in production. As a result of a production department conference, a memo is written to alert the marketing department and the publisher that if 10,000 copies are printed, and the normal pricing formula is followed, the retail price will be $14.95. The marketing manager responds to this by informing the publisher, and everyone else whose ear he can bend, that the ceiling for this type of book is $12.95. He has arrived at this conclusion by looking at competing books and querying key accounts. In addition, he believes there is a "casual sale barrier" of about $13 for the book. The casual sale barrier is a marketing concept indicating the price level at which a reader with a moderate interest in the field will be dissuaded from buying the book. A price above this subjective and imprecise level would leave only aficionados, who have no concern for the price, as the only audience for the book. In other words, the marketing manager believes only an extremely dedicated caving enthusiast will pay $14.95. He calls the National Spelunking Society and learns that they estimate there are only 25,000 regular cavers in the United States. He also learns that the society has a membership of

8,000 and can sell an average of 800 copies of a new book to its members in a single year through its newsletter.

Armed with these facts, the marketing manager is even more convinced a problem exists. If there are only 25,000 dedicated cavers (some, he has been told, spend so much time in caves that they don't read at all), and an organization of 8,000 members can sell only 800 copies, sales of perhaps 3,000 to 4,000 copies would be possible. Based on a 10,000-copy first run, the publisher would have 6,000 copies left over. Clearly, something must be done to widen the market.

The editor is summoned and the situation is explained. Although she defends the book as written, she is reluctantly convinced that it is in everyone's best interest to compromise a little. It is up to her to convince the author to change the format of the book, or, as the marketing director says, "Change the package because the numbers don't work."

There are two ways costs can be reduced. One is to cut back on photographs or drawings, which are more expensive to produce than text, and the other is simply to shorten the book. The editor suggests a combination of both techniques. Why not cut some of the more redundant illustrations and photographs? This will not only save money in photo preparation but leave more room for text. Next she suggests cutting the text about 15 percent, which means that less type will need to be set. Overall, she estimates that if this is done, the book will fit into forty-eight fewer pages, thus saving one-and-a-half printing signatures. As a result of these savings, and a willingness of the publishing company to bend the usual pricing formula a little, the price can be dropped to $12.95.

The editor's hardest job will likely be convincing the author to cooperate. His help will obviously be needed to make the cuts. If the author cooperates at this stage, the editor and the rest of the people concerned with the project at the publisher's end will normally bend over backward to cut as little as possible, as painlessly as possible. However, if the author refuses to cooperate, and acts as if the editor is little more than a front for the philistines in marketing, the book may develop a nasty reputation within the publishing house. It will get published eventually, maybe even uncut at $14.95, but no one is likely to continue to support it enthusiastically.

Variations on this theme occur throughout the publication process. The important thing for an author to understand is not so much specific ways to handle particular problems, but a general conviction that it is important to work out production difficulties harmoniously. In doing this, try to make yourself available to as many of the people actually solving the particular problem as possible. Work with your editor, but politely insist that you be included in the broader dialogue.

A rough sketch, if not a portrait, of the problem areas that often separate an author from the publishing people he or she must work with is emerging. United by a common love for books and ideas, these two groups are often divided by the myths that surround both publishing and writing. We believe an individual author, armed with knowledge, goodwill, and determination to make the effort, can cut through these difficulties. If you need an incentive to do this, let us again remind you that, as a general rule, a book's future has been determined well before the first copy leaves the bindery. As an author, you should insist on forming and maintaining a good relationship with the publisher. If the publisher needs reasonable help anywhere in the complicated process of turning a manuscript into a book, you should attempt to rally to the joint cause. This doesn't mean giving in to the publisher's every demand—the author knows her work and the field best, and there are times when it is in everyone's best interest for the author to stand ground. The trick, from the author's point of view, is to be forthcoming, agreeable, and sympathetic to the publisher's needs while maintaining the integrity of the work.

In order to appreciate the general contours of the publishing process, let us examine a typical case history through this personal account of a first-time nonfiction author:

> Getting the contract was, oddly enough, the easiest part. I was approached by a consulting editor who knew I had given extension workshops in holistic health; she had been hired by a major publisher to help expand the adult education market as part of the textbook division's massive new program to find new audiences to make up for the dwindling college market. This consultant showed my prospectus to the publisher. Everyone was enormously enthusiastic; they offered me a standard textbook contract. I was elated. Even though I knew the book would probably have general trade interest, I was pleased to be part of a new publishing venture undertaken by an established publishing house.
>
> Writing the book was hard, demanding work, but it also gave me great satisfaction. I delivered the finished manuscript on schedule. While things had been going smoothly at my end, however, things were in flux at the publisher's. As I was finishing, I learned that my editor, who had been so enthusiastic about the book, had left, and I was turned over to her assistant, a young man fresh out of college who I felt was part of a holding operation as far as the whole series was concerned. That young man left shortly thereafter, and as a result my book became something of a stepchild. It was technically transferred to a senior editor, although it clearly did not command her interest or support. Later, I learned she was almost exclusively concerned with developing an exercise book. I felt quite bitter that I had held up my end of the bargain exactly, only to find the publisher uninterested. When this same editor

told me that the company decided to scrap the adult education program and my book was in limbo (still under contract, but no longer part of a publishing program with money and muscle behind it), I was furious.

After calming down, I decided that if my book was going to get anywhere—either with the publisher or with the outside world—it would have to be largely through my own efforts. In this connection, I enlisted the aid of an able book publicist. We met and mapped strategy. Our campaign was first designed to win goodwill at the publisher's and get to be known favorably (not just as a crank or complainer) to as many people in the house as possible; second, to demonstrate that the book had genuine possibilities, particularly as a trade book; third, to arouse interest—and eventually sales—through the media.

I started by sending out copies of my manuscript to eight people with either respected academic connections or public names, or both, asking for endorsements. I got four "no" responses, two "I'd love to read and comment, but I'm too busy," one person who liked the two chapters he'd read but refused to make a comment for print—and one endorsement from a person who combined a lot of popular appeal with a solid academic background. This was exactly what I needed for a quote on the back cover of the book.

Next I decided not to leave the senior editor's presentation at the trade sales conference to chance. I wrote a six-page set of author's notes, describing the contents of the book, its selling points, the major markets for the book, and my promotability as an author. Some of the publisher's catalog copy was later drawn from this piece, and it was reportedly "very well received" by the trade sales force—the people who would have to get my book into general bookstores. With the growing awareness that this was indeed not an academic textbook but a popular interest book, the publisher's design department came up with a bold cover. Several polite phone calls from me didn't hurt.

In addition, I worked up my own review list to supplement the publisher's list. I wrote for and got permission to handle first and second serial rights when it became clear the publisher had no interest or time to devote to this enterprise. I sent off copies of the front matter to seventeen general and special interest magazines, and so far have received interested responses from several large circulation magazines and have placed one major excerpt.

Once the prepublication phase is over, I'll hire a local media consultant, not to do the work for me (a local media campaign can cost several thousand dollars) but to give me the names of people I can contact as my own publicist. This will be hard work, and will call for different energy from the solitary, thoughtful work of writing, which I prefer, but I'm convinced that in these days of quick turnover in publishing, when only the blockbuster books get star treatment, I must do it if I want my book to sell. In fact, I have reluctantly committed myself to a new slogan: "Publicize or perish."

SELLING BOOKS: THE BOOK MARKETING PROCESS

The Importance of Marketing: How Books Are Sold

You need some background information on book marketing to appreciate the environment in which you and your publisher's marketing department work. Each year, over 50,000 books in all categories are published in the United States. As with any such crowd, there is tremendous competition for space. In the book business, perhaps the most important type of space is shelf space in the bookstores. But there are other space considerations, too: review and publicity space in media outlets, space on library order sheets, and so on. Of course, the most crucial space is that which you and your publisher must try to make in the reader's book-buying budget.

Unfortunately, the sheer number of books published isn't the only negative statistic with which your book will have to contend. In recent years, bookstore sidelines have proliferated, and 10–20 percent of the typical store's inventory now includes nonbook products such as posters, puzzles, and the like. Similarly, competition for the consumer home entertainment (or self-instruction) dollars has come to include video- and audiotapes, software, and other new products and new media. Increasing concentration of ownership at the retail bookstore level is also a serious and growing problem. As bookstore chains continue to replace smaller, independent stores, book buying becomes increasingly centralized in the hands of a few people. Computers tell these people which books are selling in large numbers, and they make their stocking decisions accordingly. The result is chain stores that shelve many copies of a relatively few titles, and at least some publishers who try to publish only what the chains will buy. Or, to put this another way, if two buyers from two major chains don't think your book will sell well, you may find yourself completely shut out of more than 2,000 bookstores.

Fortunately, the homogeneous nature of the chain booksellers has resulted in some countervailing trends. Specialty bookstores dealing with specific subjects (science fiction, mountaineering, or murder mysteries, for example), and smaller specialized publishers, are very much on the scene. While you, as an author, may be able to do little to influence a large chain to buy your book, there is a great deal you can do to help with marketing your book through special interest networks. Your knowledge should be able to help your publisher reach the publicity channels or sales outlets that will bring your book to the attention of the readers who will be most interested in it.

Before we deal with the details of book marketing, let's examine a primary book marketing principle. A successful marketing plan focuses on numerous specific, identifiable groups, and moves gradually toward the more amorphous general interest buyer. This plan seeks to convey the important and unique aspects of the book: a concise profile of product benefits. This profile of product benefits has come to be known as the "sales points" of a book. The marketing plan can be viewed as a series of ever-widening concentric circles whose influence permeates outward. Your goal is for a number of small circles to begin to connect so that together they have major impact. The idea, of course, is that when a number of forms of promotion begin to work together, they can produce an effect far greater in scope than that produced by uncoordinated efforts.

Let's stick with the concentric circle image for a moment. The first one begins at your publisher. It starts with your editor and widens to other departments, reaching its furthest extension in the sales force. From there it encompasses the bookstore buyers, who in turn make your book available to the public. Another circle involves key opinion leaders and special interest groups who care about your subject matter. This is your first effort eventually to inform a larger public. Your promotion circle widens when you next get the word to all sorts of general print and broadcast publicity outlets. Advertising is another marketing circle. It is best used to give the promotion campaign direction and thrust, as well as to alert interested readers.

At a certain point, when enough books are in the hands of enough people, promotion should become self-generating. People will see the book on bookstore shelves or in the hands of friends and relatives. Others will hear or read about it. Since one kind of medium usually takes the others seriously, a good print review may lead to talk show invitations and so on. A real take-off point occurs at somewhere between 50,000 and 100,000 copies of the average trade book. In the mass market format, it seems to take somewhere between 250,000 copies and a half-million copies. Once this level is reached, it sometimes seems that the whole world wants your book. Of course, smaller versions of this synergistic process in specialized subject areas, such as technical science and art criticism, are possible at much lower sales levels. No matter what the book, however, the idea is the same—ever-widening groups of interested readers find out about the book.

NOTE FOR THE SHY AND RETIRING • Lots of people who write books can't stand the idea of publicizing them. The whole public relations process repels them. Obviously, there is nothing wrong with this attitude in the abstract. It can, however, cause real problems between publisher and author if you wait to reveal it until the day your book is published, when you refuse to show up for the press party. If you don't want to help publicize your book, say so early and often (write it into your contract). If the publisher goes ahead knowing of your feelings, there should be no bitterness later. For the purposes of the rest of this chapter, we will assume you are open to at least some public relations chores.

Book Advertising

The publisher's consumer advertising is an area of dissatisfaction for many authors. Unless a book is a big seller or "lead" title, consumer advertising is considered by publishers to be among the least effective methods of launching a book. As the name implies, a lead title is the expected sales leader in a group of books released during the same time period. Lead titles generally absorb the publisher's consumer display advertising budgets. In rough terms, the overall advertising and promotion budget for most titles is placed at 10 percent of the expected sales revenue of the first printing. Some publishers spend considerably less than this. If an average trade book has a first printing of 10,000 copies and the average sales discount is 45 percent off the cover price of $14.95, the overall ad and promotion budget will be set at just under $9,000. If you look at a book as a "new product" in comparison to any other industry, $9,000 would not even be a respectable amount for preliminary market research.

Looking at the problem from another perspective, $9,000 becomes the total amount of money your publisher uses to influence the buyers for 8,000 retail bookstores, 50 major wholesalers, thousands of public, college, and specialized libraries, college professors or high school teachers, subsidiary rights buyers, and readers to select, stock, or buy your book. So advertising used to influence the trade and the public at large must be highly selective. Of necessity, it must take a backseat to less expensive but equally effective means of influence, such as book reviews.

Most authors, unfortunately, see large print ads for lead titles and feel that their book is being slighted. The realities of publishing are such that display advertising is not a cost effective means of launching the great majority of books. It is the exception rather than the rule. If your publisher takes this position, chances are that your book is not being slighted but is merely being handled realistically within the context of trade practice.

Before publication, most books receive advance advertising exposure in trade magazines in order to alert buyers. Trade advertising influences the "sell-in" (stocking decisions). Consumer advertising or promotion influences the "sell-through" (consumers' purchases). The leading trade magazines are *Publishers Weekly, Library Journal, American Bookseller* and *Booklist*. Many stores or associations of stores issue catalogs in which publishers may purchase advertising space. These catalogs (known as gift catalogs) may be mailed to an individual store's best customers or given away in the store itself. The association's catalog may offer individual stores the opportunity to imprint their name on the catalog and will often insert the catalog into a special issue of a local newspaper. The bookstore chains have their own catalogs and insert them into national magazines. These catalogs influence stocking decisions (and function as trade advertising); they reach the consumer as well. In recent years, such catalogs have proliferated. After publication, some small consumer notification ads may appear in specialized magazines, or co-op (cooperative) ads with bookstores may appear in newspapers. A common industry practice, co-op ads are placed by the retailer, and about 75 percent of the costs are paid by the publisher. Ads of all kinds are subject to what is called the "echo effect." For example, a buyer may see a coupon ad in a magazine but elect to buy the book at a local bookstore. Thus the number of coupon responses might be low, but other sales may "echo" into bookstores.

The Author's Roles in the Marketing Plan

Marketing concerns all aspects of reaching potential readers. Publicity is the part of the marketing process where the author has the greatest impact. Here your enthusiasm, specialized knowledge, and interest—all the ingredients that helped you to create your book—can be extremely productive. There are literally dozens of things you can do, through your publisher and by yourself, to enhance the sale of your book. Your editor, of course, should ask you to convey your knowledge to the publicity and sales departments. Depending on your skills and the subject of your book, you may also be asked to do interviews and other publicity tasks. If you have the inclination—and even if you don't, but you want your book to do well—you will want to take an active role in getting your book into the hands of eager readers. Commonly, publishers will do more to promote books whose authors are generating publicity.

The Author's Questionnaire and Beyond

About the time you deliver your finished manuscript, you will be asked to fill out an author's questionnaire. Your editor probably already knows most of the important information requested by this form, and you may be tempted to give it extremely cursory treatment. Don't. This questionnaire will help shape the publicity and sales attention devoted to your book. It will be—or should be—read by people throughout the company. In big houses, some of these people may never have met your editor. With smaller publishers, the questionnaire may be done less formally. In either case, fill out the form seriously and keep a copy. A sample questionnaire is reprinted in Appendix F.

The questionnaire will show you that you have lots of additional information that could help sell your book. This isn't surprising—you know your own area of expertise much better than any editor will ever know it. After all, you wrote the book on the subject. Supplement, if necessary, by providing the following helpful information:

MEDIA CONTACTS • Your personal contacts can help a book get reviewed or place an excerpt in a magazine, even if your new book is not in the specific area of the reviewer's or magazine's interest. For example, if you did a cookbook several years ago and know the food editors of a number of newspapers and magazines, these people may help get your new mystery book on top of the book reviewer's pile. Don't be shy about asking your friends and acquaintances to be advocates on your behalf.

REVIEW COPY TARGET LISTS • Give the publicity or marketing department a list of specialized publications in your subject area, or publications that are interested in you, such as your college alumni magazine. These publications should receive a review copy, press release, and possibly even paid ads. Give the publicity department as much detail as possible, including names of individuals, complete addresses, phone numbers, circulation, and any other relevant facts and figures. As an expert in the field, you obviously know more than your publisher does. For example, the author of a recently published computer book personally contacted 100 publications having to do with computers. He wrote to some, called others, sent book excerpts and articles to more. His book was a big success, at least in part, because of his initiative.

COLLEGE ADOPTIONS AND PROFESSIONAL INTEREST • Furnish the college sales department of your publisher (if there is one) with a list of courses that might use your book as supplementary reading. If appropriate, provide a list of professors who should get examination copies of your book. Be sure to include a list of appropriate academic journals and professional association newsletters for possible advertising and review attention. Many journals of this type have resource listings or a "books received" column. While not as powerful as full reviews, such listings may help to bring your book to the attention of readers with special interests.

COMPETITIVE SITUATIONS • Informing your sales and publicity departments of competitive books will serve several functions. A competitive book will help generate interest in a subject area, and an informed sales force can capitalize on this promotional opportunity. If the competition is threatening, they can devise strategies to make your book stand apart.

OTHER INFORMATION • Basically, anything can be used to describe or help sell or promote your book—your education, cities where you are well known or connected, special exhibits or professional gatherings in your subject area, your organizational or association memberships, and other similar data. The points on publicity and nonbookstore sales in this chapter may also be viewed as supplemental information to the author's questionnaire.

SUMMARY • The important points to remember about the author's questionnaire are that it comes in to the publisher early in the process and lays the foundation for future efforts. Make the questionnaire and the supplemental information you provide as complete as possible, even if you repeat this information (which is likely) later in the publishing process.

OBTAINING ADVANCE ENDORSEMENTS • Because of the critical timing element in publishing—so many independent steps are happening at once—you will often be in the best position to obtain advance endorsements (also known as "cover blurbs"). While these aren't essential to certain types of books, they can often be a big help for most. A reader interested in science fiction, for example, can't help but be impressed if someone of the stature of Isaac Asimov says your book is excellent.

First, talk to your editor and make sure endorsements are welcome. Then make copies of your manuscript (possibly at your own expense, if your publisher won't reimburse you) and contact experts in your field. Do this as soon as you have a finished or even a half-finished manuscript. If you wait too long, you may find someone has designed the cover before your endorsements can be of use. The marketing department may solicit blurbs, as may your editor, and they may tell you, "Oh, we'll take care of that." But if you can get endorsements on your own, do it. If you doubt the wisdom of this, scan new books in bookstores and see how many have no endorsements at all. Time is important, since there are so many delays possible between your soliciting blurbs and your endorser's writing them. Only if you take charge of this process yourself can you be assured of making the stringent deadlines. Also, the marketing department uses early endorsements in catalog copy, sales presentation materials, and announcement ads for the trade. So early endorsements can be a crucial part of getting a book off to a good start.

In addition, you should give the publicity department a list of notable individuals in your field who might read your galleys and give your book further advance endorsements. Annotate this list by describing your relationship with the potential endorser and what you would be willing to do to facilitate the contact. For example, "Robert Anton Wilson, well-known futurist, author of eight novels, four works of non-fiction, one of the founders of the Institute for the Study of the Human Future, personal friend. I will call ahead."

A dramatic example of the impact of endorsements is found in the best-selling self-help book, *How to Be Your Own Best Friend*. Originally self-published, the book was written by two psychologists who happened to have many celebrities as clients. Endorsements by playwright Neil Simon and author Nora Ephron, among others, helped give this book the momentum needed for commercial success, and Random House took over publication.

PUBLICIZING YOUR BOOK

The Importance of Publicity

The importance of publicity in all of its forms, from book reviews to TV talk shows, cannot be overstated. Because of its role in generating interest in a book and because of its cost-effectiveness, publicity remains the primary tool for book selling today. As we have stated before, any small media influence you can bring to bear will have the possibility of sparking larger interest in your book. As your media exposure begins to develop, avail yourself of the advice of your publicity department. There are many things to learn: What wardrobe colors work well on television? How can you deliver your message in a concise and memorable way? If, for some reason, expert advice on how to be a successful interview subject is not forthcoming from your publicity department, seek out the advice you need, from another author, a journalist, a talk show producer, or an independent publicist.

In some cases, when their publisher's efforts falter, authors hire their own publicists to campaign for them. This requires an investment on the author's part and may extend to local, regional, or even national publicity. The cost varies but commonly falls into a range of $500 to $1,200 per locality, plus expenses. Besides the cost, if you're contemplating hiring your own publicists, you should check with your publisher's publicity department to avoid damaging relationships or duplication of effort. Whether you undertake publicity efforts on your own behalf or hire an independent publicist, coordination with your publisher's publicity department should be of prime concern.

Personal attention and contact can often help publicity efforts. After you receive a review or are the subject of an interview or feature story or have appeared as a guest on a talk show, it is a good practice to send your own personal note of acknowledgment. This will help spread goodwill on your behalf.

Coordinating Publicity with Your Publication Date

Your book's publication date is usually six weeks after bound books arrive at the warehouse. A later publication date allows books to reach the market and be in stores all over the country, so ads, reviews, and publicity can be timed properly. If you are going to publicize your book—whether you do it yourself or are on a tour scheduled by your publisher—the three-month period following your publishing date is the best time to promote the book. It is important to coordinate with your publisher and be available for publicity activities at this time. If you're doing it on your own, this is the time to work fast. The performance of your book in the first three months of its official life will often determine the shape of its publishing outcome. Remember, books perceived as strong by publishers, publicists, reviewers, booksellers, and readers will command the necessary resources and space to make them strong. Of course, some books do build slowly, as ever-widening circles of interested people become aware of them. In a sense book publishing is a race between the ever-widening circles of interested readers and the steadily contracting circles of available distribution.

A Word on Author Tours

Like consumer advertising, author tours are usually reserved for lead titles. This has been especially true in recent years, as lodging and transportation costs have dramatically increased. However, if you are planning a trip for business or personal reasons and are willing to promote your book, it would be a good idea to inform your publicity manager as far in advance as possible. If you are paying your own transportation and lodging costs, your publisher might be more interested in helping you get publicity bookings.

Getting Your Book in the News

What is newsworthy about your book? What is newsworthy about you or about how your book came to be written? Does the information contained in your book fit within a larger context of events? For example, is your gardening book, which advocates landscaping with resource-saving plants, part of a larger scheme for energy conservation? News angles help the publicity department shape press materials to create what is known as "off-the-book-pages" publicity. More than a simple book review, off-the-book-pages coverage makes hard news (time-dated) or soft or feature news (not time-dated) of your book and brings attention to it.

Working with Booksellers

You may directly influence the sale of your book by learning how to deal with bookstores. Unfortunately, a great many authors do nothing at all to aid bookstore sales, contenting themselves with checking to see if their book is in the store and complaining to their friends if it isn't. Often this behavior is a manifestation of one of the most basic human debilities—shyness. If this chapter does nothing else, we devoutly hope it convinces you that it makes sense to learn how to triumph over shyness and put some positive energy into trying to sell your book.

When dealing with bookstore contacts, or with any other promotional contacts, remember these two underlying principles: (1)"working the corners," which means that no activity, regardless of how small, will fail to influence the publishing chain of events; and (2) "snowballing," which argues that a number of small acts to help sell your book can snowball into a real success. Now let's get to some specifics.

There are approximately 8,000 bookstores in the United States. Several thousand are chain stores and several thousand are specialized, but no matter where you live, you will have some access to general trade bookstores carrying new books. Many of these are open to special promotions involving local authors. Often independent booksellers will recommend a new book to a customer who they know has a specific interest or taste. This practice has become known as "hand-selling."

As *American Bookseller* magazine noted:

> When you [the bookstores] promote local authors, everyone benefits. The authors get more community recognition and a chance to see old friends . . . The bookstores get sales, good community relations, and general goodwill created with the authors and the public.

Suggested Bookstore Contacts

INTRODUCE YOURSELF • Bookstore owners and employees are interested in books and authors. They will almost always order a number of your books if they know you will help promote sales. An energetic local author can become a valuable sales point for a local bookstore. By personal contact, you may influence the store owner to place your book face out instead of spine out, or have it moved to a display table in the front of the store. By offering creative suggestions (with diplomacy and tact), you may even encourage a window display.

SET UP A BOOK SIGNING • One traditional way to sell books is to do an autograph party or signing in a local store. Your publisher will likely help you arrange a signing, but if you do it yourself, let your editor, publicity manager, or sales manager know. They may help with publicity. Variations on this theme, such as in-store demonstrations, lectures, and slide shows, can also be effective. Unless you are something of a celebrity, an activity more unique than signing books may stand a better chance of drawing people to the store. For example, storefront omelet cooking might attract a crowd. (This, of course, presupposes you have written a cookbook.) The things to remember are that novelty and action form the attraction.

HELP PUBLICIZE YOUR SIGNING • Tell your friends and relatives. The best way to do this is with printed invitations. In addition, assist the store in publicizing the event. This may mean helping to send out press releases or calling local radio and TV people. Call your local paper personally. If they have a calendar of events, be sure you are in it. Again, let your editor know what you are doing. The publisher may provide advertising support.

KEEP TRACK OF SALES • Drop in and see how your book is selling.

EXAMPLE • Sara, a newly published novelist, set up several book signings in local stores. Soon after publication, one store told her that they could not reorder her book because it was out of stock with the distributor. The novelist immediately phoned her publisher to determine whether books were available. She learned the small first printing had sold out. Because formal sales reports were not in yet and the book had not been widely reviewed, the publisher had not decided whether to go back to press. In order to help influence the decision, the author phoned bookstores and the publisher's own sales managers in different parts of the country. In effect, she conveyed verbal sales reports to the publisher and encouraged reorders. This little flurry of enthusiastic activity influenced the publisher. The book went into a second printing.

BOOKSTORES AREN'T THE ONLY PLACES TO SELL BOOKS

As the book market becomes more competitive, nonbookstore marketing takes on new possibilities. Generally, secondary marketing applies to nonfiction subjects, so if your book is nonfiction, you should furnish the sales department of your publisher with a list of nonbookstore marketing ideas. For example, if your book deals with gardening, you might go to a garden shop that sells books and ask the owner where he gets them. Is there a distributor of such books? Does the garden shop belong to an association of garden shops? What are the trade associations and trade journals? Are there directories? Membership lists? Lists of distributors of garden books? Lists of mail-order catalogs that include garden books? Is there an association of garden writers? Are there conferences and exhibits of writers, enthusiasts, retailers, wholesalers, and so on? Basically, you want to find out how merchandise and information flow in the gardening world.

Your research should be designed to give your publisher's marketing department, or in some cases, the special sales department, the specific information needed to mount a marketing campaign in what is very likely a completely new area of distribution. Your local library can help your research considerably. Of course, you will want to tell your publisher what you are doing so you don't repeat work already done. Never rely on a marketing department statement that they will do something soon, however. Do it yourself. Your energy is far more likely to spark the whole project.

Special Sales

Nonbookstore sales (usually lumped together under the title "special sales") are a relatively new area of major concern for trade publishers. Traditionally, special sales departments consisted of one or two relatively junior members of the publishing team. Recently, however, a number of outstanding sales successes outside bookstores have made publishers realize that special sales opportunities are almost limitless and include every conceivable type of environment (from a mail-order catalog to a cruise ship). As a result, most publishers are putting increased energy and resources into their special sales.

Nonbookstore sales for a publisher can mean getting shelf space in an environment where there are fewer competing products and, they hope, where there are a greater number of buyers interested in the book's subject. For example, *National Home Center News*, a biweekly industry newspaper, recently reported that "how-to" book sales have become big business for home improvement centers. Such special sales accounted for over 30 percent of the total sales of books on home improvement. Every person who walks into a hardware store or a home improvement center is a potential buyer of home improvement books. Similarly, trail guides and other books on the outdoors may sell better in a wilderness supply store than in a traditional bookstore.

However, there may be some disadvantage to some types of special sales, as far as an author is concerned. Often, to get books into nonbookstores, a publisher will have to deal with a wholesaler who services that type of account (e.g., a business supply jobber to get books into office and stationery stores). Sometimes, a sales rep's commission must be paid, too. This can result in selling books at higher than normal discounts. For the publisher, this may also create a disincentive: each sale may cost more than usual and may make the cost of reaching this new market uneconomical. As we learned in Chapter 1, extraordinary discounts may mean an author's royalty rate will be cut in half by most book contracts, unless the author makes a more advantageous deal. Even if this isn't possible, however, most authors will want to help their publisher pursue special sales opportunities. After all, a book sold in a gardening, mountaineering, or office supply store, on which an author gets a reduced royalty, is better than no book sold at all.

How can you help with special sales? First, find out who your publisher's special sales people are and establish a good relationship with them. Find out what they plan to do. Then pass along your suggestions.

Rather than asking, "Wouldn't it be great if barber shops carried my book on eyebrow trimming?" get the names and locations of major barber shop wholesalers and talk to people in the business to find out what is possible. Above all, respect the value of the time of the people with whom you are dealing. Emphasize that potential high-volume special sales opportunities exist. Commonly, this translates into dealing with wholesalers, not individual retail establishments. Once lined up, these specialized wholesalers should be included in sales promotion plans. Often they haven't carried books before and will need a lot of encouragement. Working with your special sales department, try to contact a specialized wholesaler to develop promotion plans. Perhaps you can plan a series of in-store events, such as signings, demonstrations, or lectures, with the accounts of the wholesaler. This makes the sales efforts of the wholesaler more complete. Suggested bookstore contacts (which appear later in this chapter) also apply to special sales retail outlets.

Another way to overcome the high-cost-of-sales problem is to suggest ways that your book may be sold with other titles on your publisher's list. Here your specialized knowledge is important. Become acquainted with all of the books on your publisher's back list. Inform the sales manager and the special sales departments of the other titles that you feel could be sold jointly with your book. Because the back list may be large, you may be able to make this determination better than the special sales manager. This will be an advantage to your publisher and lessen the costs per sale in reaching new markets.

Premium Sales

Special sales also include premium sales in which books are purchased in quantity for "giveaway" (not for resale) by businesses interested in generating goodwill. A bank, for example, might give away a book on social security to every customer over sixty who adds to or opens an account. If you have ideas in this area, check them out with your special sales department, but be ready to do some legwork yourself. The author who berates her publisher for not trying to sell larger numbers of books in specialized markets, but does nothing about it, is twice a fool.

Direct Sales

Trade shows, conventions, and other gatherings of people interested in the subject of your book can also generate direct sales and be good places to line up sales outlets. Become acquainted with schedules of conferences, exhibits, workshops, and professional gatherings in your subject area. Your publisher may or may not be as well versed as you are. Once informed, however, your publisher should help you arrange to display books and supply book order forms. If you attend such an event, you will have the option of bringing your own display copies and order forms if the event is outside your publisher's promotional priorities. Often you can contact the organizers of the convention and offer to put on a workshop or lecture at low cost, or even for free. This will get your name and the name of your book into the convention schedule and can be a big factor in getting the word out to important opinion leaders. Sometimes local bookstores can be persuaded to sell books at these events.

Selling Your Own Book

Many authors of nonfiction books give lectures and talks or teach courses in their subject areas. Many localities have education exchanges, adult education, or college extension groups that welcome courses by people who have written books. Such activities not only help publicize books but can directly add to your income. People taking your course will probably be interested in what you have written and will buy books on the spot if you bring some with you. We find that autographing books and giving a small discount (perhaps 10 percent) works wonders. You should be able to buy books from your publisher at a 40–50 percent discount (see Chapter 1, page 46), so your direct sales add enough money to your teaching fee to give you a fairly lucrative day—and increase your book's circulation as well.

Word-of-mouth is the most potent form of sales catalyst for a book, and lectures and courses are a good channel for increasing it. Sending a note about your book to the right people at publication time can greatly augment the possibilities for word-of-mouth. Alerting your friends, relatives, and professional contacts can also help. If you have been teaching or giving courses, this could extend to a mailing list you have been compiling over several years. To increase word-of-mouth, "work the corners." Notify your campus newspaper or alumnae association and any professional hobby, recreational, social, or civic organizations you belong to.

Of course, if you are doing any writing for periodicals, have your byline or biographical blurb identify you as the author of your book. Here again, many magazines will allow you to list an address where people can buy the book. This could be your publisher's direct order information and address. With your publisher's permission, you may wish to list your own. You may want to rent a post office box and make up a name for your book promotion sales business to keep your writing and sales lives separate. If you do, take the time to understand how the tax law affects your business—you may be pleasantly surprised by how many of life's minor expenses are now legitimately considered business expenses. For more information on running a small business, see *Small Time Operator: How to Start Your Own Small Business*, by Bernard Kamoroff (order information is in the Resource Directory, Appendix A).

If your publisher will not sell you books on favorable terms, or if you simply do not wish to undertake direct sales, ask your publisher to furnish you with order forms you can give to potential buyers when you speak or lecture. If these order forms are not available from your publisher, make some up yourself. This method doesn't sell nearly as many books as selling them directly, but it will produce some sales. Again, local retailers may want to get involved.

When you are trying to think of more creative ways to sell your book, don't overlook the experience of others. Networking with other authors can provide aid, comfort, and all sorts of good ideas in conducting your own publicity efforts. Veteran authors will usually give you the benefit of their experience, shortcuts, and media contacts. Often they can supply much needed prepublication endorsements.

You don't necessarily have to limit yourself to authors who write on similar subjects, although that's a good place to start. Investigate writers' associations. Consult *The Writer's Resource Guide* (see Resource Directory for bibliographic details) for a list of such organizations devoted to travel writers, outdoor writers, garden writers, and so on. Other, more general, writer's organizations exist and may also be found in the Resource Directory. Look into regional organizations. If there are no writer's groups in your area, why not form your own?

If you make a good contact or many good contacts with writers of books on the same subject as yours, consider helping them sell their books directly in exchange for similar help from them. For example, if you sell your book at your workshops or courses, you might hand out an order sheet for several other books as well. As long as the other books are good, you are doing everyone, especially your author friends, a service that they will probably be delighted to reciprocate.

LIBRARIES

Are there special libraries, such as law or medical libraries, that might have an interest in your book? If so, furnish your publisher (library sales department) with a list of them, and of exhibits and media as well. Your publisher will handle the main channels of library sales once informed of the potential library market. Library trade magazines (such as *Library*

Journal) will receive a review copy or ad, and major library sales will be solicited or undertaken through library wholesalers (like Baker and Taylor). The smaller, specialized libraries and the specialized journals and exhibits that librarians read or attend may fall into your area of responsibility. If you have an opportunity to attend any gatherings of librarians, major or minor, do so. Librarians love books (some even love authors), and a little personal attention goes a long way. Find out if your local library schedules author events and volunteer for one.

SUBSIDIARY RIGHTS ACTIVITY AS A PUBLICITY FUNCTION

At the time of publication, your publisher may inform you that certain specialized book clubs have selected your book. Similarly, newspapers or magazines may excerpt your book on a first or second serialization basis. In both cases, the actual earnings may be quite low. These subsidiary rights activities don't produce much money, but they promote your book. First, an outside, independent entity has endorsed the book. This endorsement will be used by your publisher to influence buyers and may become part of your book's trade ad and sales presentation material. Second, book club announcements, excerpts in newspapers or magazines, adaptation to audiovisual or computerized formats, and other subsidiary rights publicity have some effect on bookstore sales.

Subsidiary rights activities help influence all of the concentric circles of book publishing—your publishing house, the trade, and the book-buying public. As we noted earlier, and cannot overemphasize, a book that is perceived as being strong will command the resources and space to become strong.

PUTTING IT ALL TOGETHER: THE AUTHOR'S CAMPAIGN

Encouraging Your Publisher to Support Your Work

Your publisher builds a marketing plan for your book. The plan may be formal or informal, depending mostly on the size of your publisher, and it will include a budget. As Jim Foster, a former marketing executive with Harper and Row, aptly stated, "Fiscal responsibility dictates that all books be treated alike with respect to budgetary guidelines. Publishing responsibility dictates that all books be treated differently."

As the publishing process unfolds, the basic marketing plan will be altered. It will expand to meet initial successes and contract to a bare minimum if your book is perceived as unsuccessful. The marketing plan will not discriminate between your and any other title on the list from a budgetary viewpoint. How complete a realization of its unique aspects (Jim Foster's reference to "publishing responsibility") is carried out by your publisher will depend in part on how successfully you communicate with your publishing contacts. From another point of view, the budgetary amount will give you some idea of how well your publisher expects your book to do. The higher the budget, the higher on the list your project is. But don't despair if yours is not a big budget book. Big budget leaders comprise, at most, only 10 percent of any publisher's list.

"Working your publisher" is a phrase coined by Jeremy Tarcher, a highly successful trade book publisher, as part of his advice to new authors. Tarcher means that you should work with as many different employees of the publisher in as many marketing activities as possible. This, of course, requires that you be diplomatic and tactful, and replace demands with persuasive suggestions. For example, an author should request (but not demand) to review in advance copy that will appear on the book jacket or in a sales catalog. In addition, as agent Bill Adler states in *Inside Publishing*, "Authors should pay more attention to the catalog copy written by editors for their books. This is very important, since in most instances it is the publisher's catalog that the sales force carries into the bookstores."

You should also cultivate relationships with your publisher's sales representatives. After all, they are the people who physically go into the stores and sell your book. Since these people are located all over the country, your relationships with them will probably have to develop through correspondence, unless you are invited to a semiannual sales conference. Autographing complimentary copies of your book for sales reps may help build goodwill.

It's particularly important to let each sales representative know of any special geographic angle of your book or your personal history. The fact that you went to college in Chicago, grew up on Long Island, have family in Florida, and profiled Montana campgrounds in Chapter 6 can be important in getting your book into the stores. While many authors think this sort of approach falls somewhere between silly and demeaning, anyone who has sold books for any length of time will tell you that "local angles" can be very effective. Repeat this information, even if it appeared in your author's questionnaire or supplemental lists.

According to company policy—which you should clear with the sales manager—you may or may not be able to write these reps directly. If not, you will have to route your correspondence through the central office. No matter. The point is to give every part of the organization as much sales ammunition as you can. If you do this religiously, you will very likely give your book a much higher priority with your publisher.

You can find many other ways to excite your publisher's enthusiasm. For example, as we mentioned earlier, if you know magazine editors in your area of expertise, you may want to contact them directly, describe your book and the possibilities for excerpts, and put them in touch with your editor. It is particularly important to try this when working with smaller publishers that may not have their information-gathering processes organized as formally as larger houses. Sometimes it's a bit of a trick to do this in a way that won't make your editor feel upstaged, but with a little communication and goodwill, it can be done very effectively. In any case, the rule of thumb is to take the initiative and supply as much information as you can, in writing, and to keep a copy. Don't wait to be asked.

Sales Conferences: Arming Your Editor

Sales conferences are primary events in the life of a book. Twice a year (in most cases, although some publishers have three or more), and approximately six months before the publishing season in which a book is to be released, the publisher and editors introduce new books to the sales force. Generally, the two main publishing seasons are spring and fall.

At sales conferences, publishers and editors discuss their initial expectations for each book on the coming list. Although many books perform better or worse than their initial sales conference expectations, it is also true that many books simply go on to fulfill the prophecy that the conference created for them. If the sales conference is held near you, or if there is any way for you to attend and speak on behalf of your book, do so. (In some cases, company policy may prevent this.) The personal attention and the impression you make on the sales force could be a deciding factor for the early momentum of your book. As we have said before, building momentum is important because a book perceived as having strength in the market will command the resources and attention necessary to make it just that.

One of the significant ways publishers determine the initial strength of a book is through what is called the "advance" or "lay-down." This is the number of copies the sales force expects to place in stores through prepublication orders. These back orders are placed before there is any significant response from reviewers, the press, or the public. How favorable an impression at this early stage does your book make on important buyers in the trade?

As an example of the interlocking nature of the chain of events in publishing, the number of advance orders may be determined by the initial response of the sales force at the sales conference. If geography permits, try to meet with your editor (or exchange material through the mail) prior to the sales conference to review the conference materials. You may have something to add that will help make a stronger impression at the conference.

Increasing Publicity Efforts

Most publishers routinely send several hundred review copies of your book to publications that might be interested. As mentioned earlier, you should have given the names of potential reviewers and contacts to your publicity department before your book was published. Now it's time for you to take an active role. No publicity effort is unimportant. Any review or mention in any medium can lead directly to more important coverage. You may wish to run your own local publicity campaign.

Keeping an eye on related news stories is a good practice after your book is published. Providing your publicity department with news clippings that demonstrate fresh interest in your subject area may stimulate additional publicity efforts. Such clippings may also suggest a new topical tie-in for your book, or a bylined newspaper or magazine writer who has a special interest in your subject area and who may want to interview you or write about your book.

Try a similar approach for ads for other books on your subject. Clippings of ads, sent to your publisher's advertising or special sales department, may demonstrate new markets for your book. Here, a tactful "for your information" note is in order.

Running Your Own Local Publicity Campaign

Aside from helping support local sales, one of the benefits of a small, local publicity campaign is the experience you will gain in dealing with the media. If you are asked to publicize your book in a larger context by your publisher, you'll do better if you've already run your own campaign. You can learn firsthand what works and does not work in promoting your book, and you can then pass this information on to the publicity department.

Start by asking your editor or publicity manager if you can get free review copies of your book or copies at a special discount. The next step is to research local newspapers, magazines, and radio and TV stations at your library. If you can, talk to a person in the business (perhaps at your local newspaper) and get some tips. You will want to develop a short press release or cover letter.

Try to arrange a profile or feature story on yourself or your book. Local newspapers are particularly open to publicizing local authors. In general, many newspapers or magazines are becoming more and more involved with lifestyle, self-help, and how-to information. If you cannot place a feature story, try to get your book reviewed.

A good practice is to combine your press release with a cover letter and any reviews or endorsements you or your publisher have obtained. These, combined with a brief biography or list of author's credentials, form the basis of a press kit for your local campaign. Include commonly asked questions about your subject area to help radio and TV interviewers. An alternative is a "hook sheet" that lists interesting information or news angles about your book. Don't forget to include your day and evening phone numbers so someone who wants to do a story can contact you. Then it's stamp-licking time. Pick up some book-mailing bags and send out your book. Check with the post office for fourth class, "book rate" postage.

Finally, be ready to follow up by phone. Media outlets get lots of free books and are often besieged by people looking for free publicity. You have to follow up to be effective.

By the time you get to running your own campaign, you will have previously provided several information packets to your publisher: your author's questionnaire, supplemental lists, a review of catalog copy, endorsements, a review of sales conference materials, specialized lists of markets, media, exhibits, and so on. By this time you will be skilled in communicating the essential sales points of your book. These points are often broken down into three categories of information:

1. Keynote. A one- or two-sentence "sales handle" description of your book.
2. Sales Points. Four or five key points that summarize why your book will fare well in the marketplace: "first book of its kind," "author's credentials," "high local interest," and so on.
3. Summary: A longer, but still brief, summary of your book, with review "nuggets."

Distilling, refining, and weaving these elements into your presentation materials and furnishing copies to your publisher will further aid all publicity and sales efforts.

You can augment your own local publicity campaign by asking the publicity department to furnish you with extra copies of your book's press releases. Since these are generally printed offset and are inexpensive, they can be provided at no cost or minimal cost. You can then use these extra press releases to supplement the publicity department's mailing. If, for example, you are writing a travel guide, your publisher may mail out 500 review copies to book reviewers, media concerned with travel, and media based in the area about which you are writing, as well as your local media. Your publisher may not wish to extend this to selected members of the American Society of Travel Writers, but you could, with press releases, for the cost of postage and envelopes—and you can add a personal note.

An important element of your publicity campaign should involve cross-linking each activity you engage in. For example, stores should be notified of impending media coverage and the media notified of in-store appearances. Local wholesalers should be apprised of both to accommodate sudden surges in demand for your book. Advance letters with follow-up phone calls are sufficient. Of course, everything should be coordinated with your publisher.

In any case, we emphasize that you should keep the publicity and sales department informed about the progress of your local campaign. The coverage you obtain may help your publicity department achieve wider coverage.

Here is a sample solicitation letter, hook sheet, and follow-up letter used by Stephen Englehart, a first-time novelist. It's a bit long, and as such it risks losing the attention of the prospective media contact. The best hook sheets and cover letters should offer highlights and grab attention quickly. However, Englehart's comprehensive hook sheet illustrates the wide range of points that can be used. Obviously, a hook sheet for a work of fiction will be different from one for a how-to book.

Fiction is generally more difficult to publicize than nonfiction. Of course, this assumes that the fictional work is neither a bestseller nor written by a celebrity author. Fiction can be promoted on literary merit, awards garnered, ties to current events, local angles, or human interest. A novel dealing with a fictional volcanic eruption in the Northwest and its impact on society would have fared well if by fortunate coincidence it had been published when Mt. St. Helens erupted. Sometimes the general subject matter can carry the day with a good local hook. For example, a novel with detailed information on trout fishing might garner media attention in those communities that depend on trout fishing for economic survival.

Stephen Englehart's media solicitation letter and hook sheet rely on both local interest and news angles to spark interest in a work of action/ adventure fiction.

STEPHEN ENGLEHART'S MEDIA SOLICITATION LETTER [FICTION]

Dear Interviewer/Reviewer,

Enclosed is a review copy of *The Point Man,* my first novel. Dell is printing 75,000 copies of it, which is double the average for first novels.

The Point Man is about another media sensation, Max August, the top afternoon drive personality in San Francisco, operating out of KQBU (the third AM rocker). But though his show's number one in its time slot, he's in his mid-thirties, losing touch with rock 'n' roll, and wondering if he should move into management. It's at this time that a family heirloom, a carved lion, is stolen from his house. The theft provides a focus for him as he recalls his days as a Point Man—a scout—in the Vietnam War, and he sets out to capture the culprits.

The problem is, he's not dealing with petty thieves; he's up against a complex Soviet espionage operation. And the kicker is that these spies are not just sallow men in trenchcoats, but the first graduates of a think tank which has actually existed in Siberia since 1959; the Institute of Military Parapsychology. In a word, these spies are wizards.

Very quickly, Max August is called upon to use every skill he ever learned in war—and in life—just to stay alive.

The prepublication reviews on *The Point Man* speak for themselves:

"Stephen Englehart writes with his ears, and with his eyes. Few working writers alive have his sense of sound and of scene."—Theodore Sturgeon, the dean of American science fiction writers

"I haven't read a novel like this since *The Exorcist.*"—Robert Anton Wilson, coauthor of the *Illuminatus* trilogy

". . . a first novel that places itself way up there with some of the finest in the genre. *The Point Man* is as exciting a slam-banger as you'll find this year. But it's much more than that." *Twilight Zone* magazine

So—I'm interested in appearing on your show. The enclosed hook sheet gives you some of the specifics I can cover; and I might add that, in addition to my own media work, I've been the subject of a piece on KPIX's Evening Magazine ("Women Characters in Fantasy") and a regular panelist on KQED's discussions of "The Prisoner" series. In other words, I won't freeze up on you, and I won't be boring.

Thanks,

Stephen Englehart

STEPHEN ENGLEHART'S HOOK SHEET

1. The novel takes place entirely in the Bay Area (San Francisco, Berkeley, Hillsborough, Mt. Tam). The climax takes place in The Equinox above the Hyatt Regency's New Year's Eve parties.

2. The main character, Max August, is a Bay Area media man, charting his fate against the Nine Counties rating book.

3. I'm a local author who will be appearing in bookstores throughout the Bay Area and the rest of the West in the coming months.

4. The story concerns international psychic warfare, and is based on factual reports concerning current Russian capabilities. I know those capabilities in detail.

5. Before the emergence of the Soviet Union, Tsarist Russia was widely considered to have a "mystical soul." Shamanism was born in Siberia, and a long line of famous wizards—Rasputin, Gurdjieff, Blavatsky, et al.—came from Russia. I can discuss this.

STEPHEN ENGLEHART'S FOLLOW-UP LETTER

Dear Reviewer/Interviewer:

Just a note to let you know that *The Point Man,* the novel I sent you in September, sold out its first printing of 75,000 in just three weeks. Dell went immediately back to press, and the second printing will be on sale about the time you receive this memo.

The Point Man is the story of a San Francisco disc jockey who is swept up in a scheme by the first of the Russian parapsychological spy teams to destroy the Free World's economy. The *Los Angeles Times* said, "A psi-fi thriller based on the notion that the U.S. and U.S.S.R. are battling a psychic war, *Point Man* is spine-chilling and goose-bumpy. Englehart writes oblique, metaphorical dialogue (the kind people really speak) and he's au courant on his occultism and psi."

But this book sold quickly through strong word-of-mouth, and if you liked your copy I could use your help to continue building interest. I will call you shortly to see if you need additional copies, answer your questions, and discuss the possibility of a review.

Sincerely,

Stephen Englehart

Publicizing Nonfiction

Nonfiction enjoys many advantages for media promotion. It can offer the media the writer's or the book's authority on topical subject matter. Often an author's credentials become as important as her interviewing presence. These may be formal credentials or those created by experience, as a book resulting from a kayak trip up the Amazon, for example. To publicize nonfiction books and authors effectively, information must be tied to current events or concerns or have important human interest or regional appeal. Nonfiction enjoys an additional advantage, because it can be sold through workshops, lectures, and demonstrations. These can be public events in themselves or rendered such (or amplified) through the media.

Energetic and resourceful, Alexander Bove is both a certified public accountant and an attorney in the state of Massachusetts. The author of a respected weekly financial advice column in *The Boston Globe*, Mr. Bove contracted with Simon & Schuster to produce a definitive guide to jointly owned property, *Joint Property*. The cover of Mr. Bove's book, a trade paperback original, featured endorsements from financial editors of the *Los Angeles Times*, the *Wall Street Journal* and *Business Week*. Mr. Bove participated fully in the promotion of his book and offers nonfiction authors the following checklist for self-promotion:

ALEXANDER BOVE'S AUTHOR-PROMOTION CHECKLIST
a.   Order some of your promotional books through bookstores rather than through your publisher. This can generate some extra "sales" but, more important, will let you know when books are actually available in your local stores. That way your other promotional efforts, when timed correctly, will actually produce results.
b.   Talk to the professionals, including, but not limited to, published authors. These professionals can provide you with some important promotional ideas.
c.   Organize a lecture schedule. Include institutions that are both directly and indirectly related to your book's subject. For example, see my attached sample letter to banks.
d.   Send press releases to people on your own mailing list. For example, I sent letters to readers who wrote in to my *Globe* column on both related and unrelated issues to *Joint Property*.
e.   Send letters and press releases (books as warranted) to all related professional magazines and journals. For example, I sent materials to *Estate Planning, CLU Journal, Lawyer's Weekly*.

f.   Make personal telephone calls to every important magazine or other publication following up on your initial contact.

g.   Send thank-you letters to every interviewer (radio, TV, and newspaper/magazine) as a follow-up to every interview.

h.   Make "cold" calls to major outlets to try to get someone interested in publicizing your book. I merely selected a name from the masthead without any further knowledge. My calls included *Reader's Digest* and *Fortune*.

i.   Excerpts of books in newspapers and magazines can be a big help. I excerpted my book in my *Globe* column for several weeks.

j.   Let your publisher's publicity department know you're working hard to promote the book and keep them posted of your progress.

k.   After each tour, or series of media appearances, send your publicist a thank-you note or some other token of appreciation. At this stage, this is the person at your publisher who can help you most.

l.   Write your own reviews for newsletters. Highlight the idea of the book in a feature story format. This may go to the in-house publications of corporations or professional organizations. Mine went to banks, CPA firms, and insurance companies, among others. Sometimes companies have free newsletters for their clients and are always glad to have some new, interesting articles.

m.   Capitalize on every conceivable contact, even if it is self-created. Ask everyone you can think of for a name. Create as wide a contact structure as you can.

n.   Most important, cultivate a relationship with a working professional in the publishing area. This, ideally, would be with someone who works for a publisher other than your own. This contact can be your most valuable for an inside view into the world of publishing.

As you can see from the sample letter reprinted here, Mr. Bove is an adept self-promoter. It is precisely this type of energetic promotion, allied with an appreciation of all the ways in which different types of book promotions work, that gives an author the best chance of a successful publishing outcome. Here, Mr. Bove is attempting to tie his lecture in with broadcast appearances, as well as trying to generate actual sales for his book. Alexander Bove's approach displays important facets of author participation in a successful publishing outcome. Mr. Bove took the initiative and coordinated with his publisher. He pursued details and followed up each step. He solicited and relied on the advice of professionals and, most important, thought of creative ways to bring his book to the attention of the groups of people most likely to be interested in it.

ALEXANDER BOVE'S SAMPLE LECTURE SOLICITATION LETTER

Dear Bank Officer:

Enclosed is a press release describing a book I have written entitled *Joint Property*, which has received very favorable endorsements by the *L. A. Times*, the *Wall Street Journal*, and *Business Week* magazine.

The book discusses in detail the complications brought about by the various forms of "joint" ownership and how they can frustrate trusts and estate plans, and goes on to suggest funded trusts as the primary solution.

I have developed a short seminar on this scenario which may be offered through your bank's trust department to its customers and prospects. The lecture could be coordinated with other appearances I will be making in _____ on television and radio in connection with the current release of my book by Simon & Schuster.

The gist of my talk is to "get out of joint" and into funded trusts, emphasizing the advantages of a corporate trustee. For your future information, I have enclosed a brief biographical sketch.

There is no charge for the lecture (other than my actual expenses), but it is anticipated that the bank will provide a copy of my book (at $8.95 per copy) to each family in attendance.

If you would like to discuss this funded trust seminar further, please write or telephone my office at your earliest convenience.

Very truly yours,

Alexander A. Bove, Jr.

AAB,JR/jas

Enclosures

HOW CHANGES IN THE BOOK BUSINESS AFFECT YOU

With the development of new technologies and media, such as audio, video, CD-ROM, CD-I, and enhanced cable television, new publicity and subsidiary rights options have opened for publishers. The opportunities for reaching focused groups of people have changed dramatically. Recent years have also witnessed the decline of general circulation newspapers and, in turn, their book review sections. In the past, strong reviews had much to do with the success or failure of a book, particularly a work of fiction. Nowhere is this more evident than in the case of the first novel. What would be the fate of a Hemingway or Fitzgerald if he were writing today? Could powerful new voices in fiction be discovered in the dramatic way they were in the past? Or would they merely sell a portion of their first printings and then be consigned to the remainder table, never to publish again?

Although important book review media still exist (the *New York Times Book Review* remains the most powerful), it is evident that publishers will have to change their means of communicating with the key groups of readers who determine the fate of any book. Publishers will probably reach out to types of media different from those they have used in the past. This can already be seen in the case of recording companies, which provide cable networks with prerecorded material, generally free of charge. The cable networks need programming and the recording companies need exposure for new talent. The link-up is natural. The same conditions exist with the increasing number of radio syndicates. In fact, the publicity tour in which an author schedules ten or twenty cities in as many days may recede now that our society is becoming "wired." It won't be necessary to move an author physically from city to city. Publishers in the future will increasingly opt for long-distance radio phone interviews, prerecorded video- or audiotape perhaps beamed by satellite link, and online conferences over computer networks.

There is no doubt that publishing is in a state of transition. The book distribution system is characterized as chaotic and archaic, and thoughtful critics propose many reforms. Some publishers are switching to a distribution system that offers their bookstore accounts a greater discount if the account lets the publisher select the number of books going into the store. In this system the publisher actually writes the order for the store. This new method of generating orders will increase the importance of the perceived reality of any book to a publisher. Hence the author's role in bolstering the image of his or her book to the publisher's sales force will also increase in importance.

Computer technology has changed almost the entire publishing industry. Bookstores now have computers to track their inventory, send electronic orders, and compile customer mailing lists. Publishers market and even sell their books over computer networks. Books can be produced in different formats on demand. Perhaps the most dramatic changes are the new media available to both publishers and authors, including multimedia and online services. To keep abreast of these changes, you would do well to subscribe to *Publishers Weekly* and to discuss the industry in transition with your editor. Taking note of the changing climate will increase your effectiveness in helping your book achieve the publishing outcome it deserves.

CONCLUSION

We've conveyed some of the realities of publishing as a business and how an author may participate in the publishing process. Difficult and complex, the book business has at its heart, in all of its aspects from bookseller to author to publisher, the simple love of books. When this reality is obscured by cold economic facts or by a mere lack of understanding of the other side's point of view, publishing relationships can become adversarial. You should enter a publishing relationship with the utmost faith and optimism, of course, but your experience may be negative if your expectations run much higher than the attainable realities.

In the words of one author:

> In some respects, having a book published is like having a baby, but without the experience of delivery. That is, it is as much a part of you as a child, both physically and emotionally, but someone else delivers it, and you never seem to be able to pinpoint exactly when the delivery occurred. Then, all of a sudden, the process of presenting your child to the world is upon you. As the proud and still confused parent, you barge forward, convinced that your child will change or at least improve the world, only to find that the world (fortunately, with exceptions) doesn't really give a damn, and some of those who see fit to speak to you politely tell you that your child is a worthless nobody.

> If I let myself get discouraged by every instance of rejection or criticism, or every sign of indifference, I might have given up on my book long before I hit a few successful responses. And if I relied exclusively upon my publisher for the success of the book, I would have been further discouraged.

To achieve the best publishing outcome for your book, you must participate actively in the publishing process in as many ways as you can, as early in that process as you can. The guidance suggested in this chapter will not guarantee that your publishing experience will live up to your expectations. However, if you follow these suggestions and, more important, use them as a springboard for your own ideas, you will maximize your chances of publishing successfully. We've offered a taste of the publishing business, to forewarn you of things to come.

The key words to remember are *information*, *cooperation*, and *action*.

INFORMATION • Because publishers deal with so many diverse topics, no one at your publishing house will know as much as you about your subject area. A difficult and complex business, publishing demands that an author understand some of its fundamentals before that author can effectively participate in the publishing process.

COOPERATION • Because adversarial relationships will damage both your book and your goal of reaching as many readers as possible, it's essential that you learn how to get along with your publisher.

ACTION • Because you are the single person with the most to gain, and the greatest knowledge about and the greatest interest in this project, you must invest yourself in the publishing process with the same commitment that you invested in writing the book. Take the initiative and keep it. Remember, a book that is perceived as strong in the marketplace with a promotable and willing author will command the necessary resources and space to become strong.

13

NEW INFORMATION TECHNOLOGIES AND THE AUTHOR

INTRODUCTION

Technology always seems to outpace contracts and the law. Every major information storage medium developed in the last hundred years has brought with it conflict over legal definition and rights. The phonograph record created issues over monopoly control and jukebox play. The audio-tape wasn't exactly a phonorecord, so people argued about whether phonorecord legal provisions applied. The videotape recorder allowed rapid, convenient off-the-air copying of copyright-protected movies. The scanner allows almost any film or printed material to be copied quickly and cheaply. The computer program that produced a screen display was appropriated by some who claimed that, since it couldn't be read by the unaided human eye, copyright didn't apply and they could use it without compensating the developer. And now the Internet, struggling to find commercially exploitable markets, makes available to the world copyrighted content on a scale previously unimagined.

Publishing contracts haven't kept pace.

THE FAST AND EVER-CHANGING WORLD OF ELECTRONIC MEDIA

In 1990 Jack Mingo, author of eleven books including *The Couch Potato Handbook* and *How the Cadillac Got Its Fins*, published *The Whole Pop Catalog*. It was a 608-page compendium of the icons, objects, personalities, trends, fads, and products that reflected post–World War II American popular culture. Six years later, after the book had nearly run its course and had become hard to find in stores, Jack investigated posting his text files into a site on the World Wide Web.

As a first step, he confirmed with his publisher that he held electronic rights. Jack then began investigating the CD-ROM format, figuring its multilevel, nonlinear and encyclopedic nature made it a natural candidate for multimedia presentation. He began systematically e-mailing CD-ROM producers and received a positive response from Maxima New Media. Soon he also began to create a biweekly online posting based on *The Whole Pop Catalog*.

The rewards of electronic media sometimes don't require that much work. One distinguished American publisher in the area of Buddhist studies received an unexpected call from a CD-ROM game producer requesting electronic use rights to a particular photograph of a sacred site in Bhutan. The image conveyed the type of atmosphere and ambiance the game producer wanted to infuse in its dramatic action game.

At other times the new media's surprises aren't so pleasant. Author Jane Yolen discovered on a school's Internet site a summary of one of her children's books—presented as a story the school proudly credited to one of its pupils. That discovery prompted a useful little lesson in the meaning of plagiarism.

Online and multimedia projects are complex enough to require many creative talents, and their revenue potential is seen as so *potentially* large that they can attract many claimants, making the assignment of rights more touchy. For example, a prominent social scientist started to design a "distance-learning course" to be accessed by students online. She chose to sign a contract with a major publisher, one in which the publisher would pay development costs and royalties to both the professor, for authorship rights, and the college, for a license to use its name on the course. However, the school took the position that the professor's work on the course was work made for hire because she did it as an employee. That would mean the copyright in the course belonged to the college, not to the professor. The professor argued, successfully, that her job description did not include preparing distance-learning courses any more than it covered authoring textbooks. In both cases, a professor makes use of college facilities, but in neither case is the creative product considered work made for hire because it is not part of the professor's usual duties.

All of these stories illustrate how electronic rights, in all forms, offer new opportunities to publish books or booklike content for derivative uses of the content of books and for unexpected ways to promote books. That's why the status of electronic rights as a category of subsidiary rights and an option for promotional opportunities is an area of growing importance for authors. This is something to keep in mind when negotiating new contracts, understanding the status of these rights in preexisting contracts, and investigating promotional activities that you, as author, might undertake yourself or suggest to your publisher.

YOUR RIGHTS AND THE PUBLISHING CONTRACT

As Chapter 1 explains, you, as the author of your work, own its copyright from the moment you complete it. From that point on, you enjoy what practically amounts to a monopoly on all rights to exploit that work in its many forms. You have the legal power to transfer those rights to one or many others: book publishers in your country, film producers, magazine publishers, CD-ROM producers, web site owners, foreign publishers, audiotape producers, and the like. You, as the owner of the rights, *license* others to make use of those rights for compensation. Without your license, no one may legally exploit your rights.

The publishing contract is the means by which you make the license with your book publisher. In it, you name the rights you're transferring to the publisher. Those rights will always include book publishing rights, but the other rights listed in the contract—the *subsidiary rights*—vary considerably. The way the copyright law works, the only rights the publisher gets from you are the rights you expressly convey in the contract. All other rights are reserved by you, as the author.

When printing was the only significant medium for book publishing, the task of drafting contracts between publisher and author was relatively easy. Most book publishers didn't anticipate the growth of new media for publication, so most older publishing contracts dealt ambiguously, or not at all, with the possibilities of new and unexpected media.

OLD WINE IN OLD BOTTLES: DEALING WITH THE EXISTING CONTRACT

If you entered into a contract some years ago, read the rights provisions carefully and objectively to see whether they could be interpreted to snare broad or narrow electronic rights. Think back to your negotiation of the contract, and try to remember whether you and your editor talked about electronic rights. If you didn't discuss them and if the language of the contract isn't clear about them and if there's no catch-all rights clause that says you and the publisher will share income from "all rights not otherwise described herein," or words to that effect, then you may have a compelling argument that you never meant to convey electronic rights and have therefore reserved them. This conclusion puts you in a stronger position to negotiate a favorable share of income or a good royalty if your publisher wants to make use of those rights.

THE COSMIC CLAUSE

However, there's a trap for you to anticipate: The contract may subtly cover "all rights not otherwise stated above" and provide a split of income from the exploitation of those rights between you and the publisher. This clause is most likely to appear, not in the formal grant of rights clause near the beginning of the contract, but rather at the end of a long list of rights described in the subsidiary rights clause of the contract (see page 17). In other words, this important grant of rights is buried where you might not notice it, although it may be crucial in a battle over who controls your rights.

For a long time, the usual film and music business contracts contained a clause that might have made you smile when you first read it, but there's really nothing funny about it:

> Artist grants to Producer all rights in and to the Work, now known or hereafter to become known, throughout the Universe.

The purpose of this language was to respond to court cases that occurred early in the century and held that unless a specific exploitable right existed when the parties signed the contract, the creator-owner couldn't have intended to license that right to the company. In response, the recording companies and film studios devised this language, which we call the "cosmic clause." There is a certain poetry about that language, almost biblical in its tone and scope, but for you as the author of a book about to be subjected to limitless time and space, the cosmic clause is a major problem.

First, because by definition the rights in question don't yet exist, there's no way to determine who will be in the best position to exploit them. For many years, book publishers thought so little of audiotape rights that they didn't bother to exploit them at all. The same might prove true of rights now unknown. You might be better off reserving them for yourself, so that you can find the most appropriate licensee.

Second, there's no way to know how the economics of exploiting the rights will develop, so there's no way to judge the fairness of the publisher's formula for sharing income. In the absence of any rational basis for deriving a fair split, the publisher's contract will probably propose an equal share for author and publisher if the publisher is to license the rights to others, or, if the publisher itself exploits the rights, a royalty at the bottom of the scale. Because good contracts are based on the parties' mutual understanding of the underlying realities the contracts are designed to cover, a contract that tries to deal with unknowns in the abstract is not a good contract.

Over the years, other variations on this catchall approach to subsidiary rights have evolved. Some gave names like "mechanical reproduction, photocopying, sound recording, etc." or "data storage and retrieval," to groups of rights and then added the catchall "by any means known or hereafter invented." These are cosmic clauses with less expansive and grandiose language.

ALTERNATIVES TO THE COSMIC CLAUSE

First let's examine common contract clauses that might have an impact on electronic rights of various kinds. Different publishers use different words to identify these varied potential uses of your work, and different publishers read the language in their publishing agreements in different ways—even when the words are similar or the same. For example, "electronic book rights" probably means that the words in the book will be transferred verbatim into electronic storage on disk or online, without significant modification. "Electronic publishing rights," however, might cover adaptation with significant editing or adaptation into a substantially different form of expression, perhaps by changing straight text into an interactive format.

"Data storage and retrieval" is a common phrase that has come to mean the verbatim replication of the book's content in electronic form. Without specifics that extend these rights—such as the "cosmic clause"—the publisher would retain the right to license others to use your work verbatim, online or off, in whole or part. However, you would be free to license others to use derivative or adaptive versions of your work in electronic form. For instance, the publisher could put the entire text of your novel on the Web, but you would control the right to adapt it into an online soap opera. Still, not all publishers use "data storage and retrieval" in this way, so it's important to clarify just what the publisher thinks it's getting from you.

The only way to know what the publisher means is to ask—and you may have to be persistent. Once you get your editor to tell you what's intended by any vague and general terms, make sure you also get your editor to include the agreed definition in the contract. His or her oral description may not help you if your publisher later decides to change the meaning to your disadvantage. If the editor tells you a certain phrase means "verbatim reproduction of the work," ask to insert the word "verbatim."

We repeat—because it's so important and so often ignored by authors and publishers alike: The only way to know for sure what *your* contract means is to ask the publisher, and the only way to make sure the contract will work the way you expect it to work in years to come is to insist that anything ambiguous be made clear *in the contract.* Nothing else counts.

Another problem might arise. If the contract contains a list of several kinds of rights, the publisher might argue that broad electronic publishing rights are included, even if they aren't expressly stated. For instance, if the contract grants the publisher "rights of mechanical reproduction, including photocopying and sound recording," that clause might be interpreted to include CD-ROMs as well. Lawyers call this form of contract interpretation *iusdem generis*, which loosely translated means "more of the same." That is, in a dispute about whether a right not named in the list is nevertheless covered by it, the court would be asked to decide that a general underlying principle that links the items on the list also extends to other, unlisted items of similar type.

Alternatives to very broad, highly inclusive clauses exist. You can insist on deleting the cosmic clause because it's unfair and deals with an economic problem better solved later. Or, you can limit the publisher's ability to tie up those rights without negotiating with you in different ways:

- You can grant the publisher rights in unknown technologies but state that the money-sharing will be negotiated when the publisher wants to exercise those rights.
- You can grant the publisher a right of first refusal (see page 63) for rights in unknown media. That will free you to explore the market if you can't agree about terms when the publisher exercises the first-refusal clause.
- You can limit the time within which the publisher must either exercise or lose rights in a new medium once the technology becomes commercially viable. Once again, it's a good idea to defer negotiations over money until later, because both the market and the actual costs of reaching that market are more likely to be defined by the time the publisher wants to exercise these rights.

Because electronic rights are undeniably valuable, you should not allow courts or fate to determine whether you've granted them to your publisher. Instead, make sure that all rights you intend to grant to the publisher are expressly and clearly named in the contract, and grant only those rights the publisher can and will actually exploit. Reserve all other rights, and include a provision that results in a reversion of any rights you grant if the publisher does nothing with them within a stated period—two or three years after publication of the book is long enough.

NEGOTIATING FAIR ELECTRONIC RIGHTS CLAUSES

Royalties for electronic rights should be comparable to those for books. Your share of subsidiary rights income from an electronic rights license that your publisher grants to a third party should be at the large end of the spectrum: Either 75 or 90 percent of the income from the license should be yours. When your publisher licenses rights to a third party, the publisher's risks are minimized, at least some income is usually guaranteed, and the administrative costs of negotiating the license aren't large.

CD-ROM LICENSES • The consumer market for CD-ROMs based on books has not lived up to its early promise. Over time, publishers and CD-ROM producers discovered that people generally preferred to read text in printed form; however, the CD–ROM augmented printed text with graphics, video, sound, background material, and so on. There are exceptions: Four CD-ROM niche markets have emerged and become stable—reference (particularly encyclopedias), directories (with easy key-word searches through databases), children's (interactive versions of popular works), and, of course, games.

When your publisher licenses electronic rights for a stand-alone product like a CD-ROM, a fair payment depends on how much of your work is used and how much of the CD-ROM content is your material. If the product is based on your work, that product can be subject to a royalty that can be expressed as a percentage of list price or invoice value (net). If a substantial portion of your work is used but it doesn't comprise the majority of the content of the CD-ROM, then a pro-rated royalty can be worked out. When smaller portions of your work are used, a use fee, similar to "rights and permissions," will be negotiated instead of a royalty.

ONLINE LICENSES • Fees for online usage are hard to define now because revenue isn't very predictable yet. Online publishers now have three potential revenue sources: They can sell advertising space on their sites, they can sell subscriptions enabling viewers to visit those sites (a magazine model), and they can charge for each visit or download (transactions). Excerpts of books appear on various Web sites, but these quotations are usually promotional, that is, presented in the context of the book being reviewed and recommended. If an online publisher wishes to post material you've created, it should negotiate the extent of the material, the fees for its use, and the duration of the license. Technology may soon make it possible to base license fees on revenue-sharing or to calculate royalties based on how many people visit the site.

OUT-OF-PRINT CLAUSES • Traditional out-of-print clauses may work for books licensed for CD–ROMs, but they won't work if your book appears online. Traditionally, a book is considered out of print if the publisher no longer offers it for sale and if no licensed edition of the book is offered for sale. This definition creates lots of problems for the author—see the discussion on page 58—but it's absolutely devastating if the licensed edition or the publisher's own edition is available online. In that case, the publisher has no inventory of hard copies to worry about. The online license can remain in effect as long as people can access the book on the network, and there's very little cost to the publisher for leaving it there. Therefore, you need to modify the traditional out-of-print clause to say something like, "The Work will not be considered in print merely because an online version of the Work exists, unless that online version of the Work has produced $500 [or some other amount] in proceeds for the Author in the past year."

NEW MEDIA COLLABORATIONS • One copyright complication may arise if you contribute only a portion of a multimedia work. For example, you might write the story and text of an online game while an artist, an animator, and a musician provide other important content. If that happens, your copyright will extend only to the text, not to the rest of the game. If the work later goes out of print, your reverted rights will be to the text only; the artist's, the animator's and the composer's rights won't belong to you.

In many cases, that won't matter. You'll be legally free to license the rights in the text to another publisher, who will arrange for the artwork. But if the artwork and the text are closely integrated, the value of your text might be significantly reduced unless you and the artist are legally free to work together. If that's what you want, do your best to negotiate a termination and reversion clause that permits you and those who built the multimedia product with you to continue working together to exploit the separate rights. Two or three years after publication of the book is long enough.

As we said earlier, it's best to grant your publisher the right to use or license electronic versions of the work, in whole or part, only in specified, existing formats. You should also be prepared to negotiate whether this grant of rights extends to online delivery and to verbatim usage, derivative works, or both. If the contract does cover derivative or adaptive uses, you should reserve editorial or creative approval over the proposed adaptation.

EXPLOITATION IS NOT A FOUR-LETTER WORD

With markets still developing, start-up costs for multimedia considerable, and Web surfers used to receiving information for free, the most lucrative way for authors to exploit their electronic rights now is in promoting sales of their books and book-related expertise.

Don and Jeanne Elium, authors of a series of best-selling guides on the subject of parenting (*Raising a Son, Raising a Daughter,* and *Raising a Family*), were asked to host America Online's discussion group, "Parent Soup." They answered questions that came in to the service both in real time as "chat" hosts and through message boards that posted questions and answers for a period of time and sparked further discussions. By participating in "Parent Soup," Don and Jeanne found a way to promote their book series and their identities as authors on a regular basis.

Since the Eliums already had a newsletter for their readers and were using this device to build a mailing list, they then took the next step and created their own Web site: "PlanetParenthood.com." They posted their newsletter online, along with information about their books and how they could be ordered. Within four days of establishing their site, Don and Jeanne had received several major offers for speaking engagements.

ONLINE BOOKSELLING AND ITS IMPACT ON YOU AS AN AUTHOR

Online bookselling is a fairly recent phenomenon with two major players taking the lead: Amazon.com and B&N Online (owned by the bookstore chain Barnes & Noble). The Borders chain and the Bertelsmann international publishing conglomerate will soon join them. These entities offer databases of millions of titles and supplementary information on each book supplied by their in-house commentators, publishers, readers, or even by the authors themselves. If you have access to these entities on the World Wide Web, it is possible to check how your book is displayed and what supplemental information is available. And, of course, you can supply your own helpful comments as to how your book's unique approach to a subject area may benefit others.

Consider creating your own Web site. Both large online booksellers have "associates" programs that link with other sites. As an associate, you send customers their way and in return receive a percentage of the proceeds from any resulting sale (and the pleasure of not having to handle orders yourself). Other authors are either selling books online themselves with the consent of their publisher (as an adjunct to sales they may be undertaking at seminars, workshops, or through direct mail) or posting order information for direct sales through the publisher.

With or without bookselling information, many authors look at creating and maintaining a Web site as an extension of a newsletter. If they maintain mailing lists of readers, associations, and organizations interested in their subject area or of people who have corresponded with them or attended an event, they simply post the newsletter in an online format.

Even if you don't want to create and maintain your own Web site, there are still ways to take advantage of the Internet with relative ease. Just as collecting a mailing list is beneficial, so is collecting its online equivalent, an e-mail address list. When activities and important notices or events in the life of your book occur (like a book signing, feature article, or review), you can send a personal e-mail notice to your list. This will supplement other activities that your publisher might be doing and is especially useful after your book has slipped to the backlist.

Using one of the many popular search engines available for the Web, you will discover a variety of references to your book throughout the world. Some of these may be bibliographic, or they may be reviews and recommendations that appear on Web sites that are devoted to your subject area. It's worthwhile to correspond with those individuals or entities that are recommending your book and thank them. Sometimes this may open other doors for you to add supplemental information; at the least, it will increase your online mailing list.

PROTECTING YOUR WORK IN ELECTRONIC MEDIA

While cruising the Web, you may run into excerpts from your book appearing in another context, or a friend may inform you of a sighting. It's possible that the use is one you're glad to see: a brief quote in a favorable review, for example. But it's also possible that you'll find objectionable uses, such as long quotes from a short story or uses that will diminish or kill the market for your book or a derivative work based on it. If so, you face a crossroads for action.

"Fair use" doctrine (discussed at length in Chapter 9) might protect the online use. But while fair-use guidelines extend to online usage, so does the basic protection given your work by copyright law. If someone is making unauthorized use of your material and you don't think the use is fair use, you should notify your publisher and the unauthorized user. Do it in writing so there's a record of your efforts. You may have nothing but an e-mail address for the online abuser, but make every effort to get a street (or "snail mail") address so you can send a cease and desist letter in hard copy. In any event, save and print your notification to the abuser and any responses from that scurrilous person.

Actually, our experience has been that most abusers aren't scurrilous; they're just misinformed or not informed at all about the limits copyright imposes on them. A lot of online users have no background in publishing, and they're wildly excited by the ability to send words or images they consider intelligent, curious, or funny onto the Internet where millions have access to them. A straightforward explanation of why they have no right to use *your* intellectual property in this way is usually all it takes to get an apology and a prompt removal from the offending Web site. Don't be too quick to flame; save the blowtorch for those who don't respond with proper respect for your copyright.

Attitude has a lot to do with the misappropriations of net abusers. Stewart Brand is often misquoted to justify this form of theft. Brand said, "Information wants to be free," as if information had a will of its own. But in the same sentence, or at least in the same paragraph, he said, ". . . and information doesn't want to be free." Brand meant to inform us that information is hard to control, but that control is both possible and necessary when commercial interests are an important motivation for creative work. That is, the author wants to make money, and so does the publisher. Copyright is what makes profit possible, and because most writers aren't independently wealthy, profit is the incentive to create.

It's so easy to take work that belongs to someone else when it appears on the Internet or when a scanner costs less than $100. And there are "avid Internet enthusiasts and a sprinkling of digital age philosophers" who honestly believe "that the new technology makes information distribution so fluid that copyright will cease to exist, and all information should be free."[1] Whether the intentions of the user are postmodern and honorable or merely expedient and dishonorable, you must be alert for abuse. Now if someone has simply appropriated a little of your work— a brief quote or a portion of an image—for a personal Web site, you might not want to kick up much sand about it. But if your material appears on a commercial site or is offered for sale, it's time to rev up the bulldozer.

When an Internet abuser—or a graphic designer who scans an image, modifies it with software, and incorporates it into an ad—takes your work, despite your copyright, and the use isn't a fair use, you've been robbed of something valuable. It's time to send a letter (and perhaps also an e-mail) saying, "Stop, thief!"

A good cease and desist message should identify you, your work, and your position as owner of its copyright. It should specify where and when you found the material being used, state clearly that you didn't authorize the use, and demand that the use stop immediately. Demand,

---

1. Jonathan Tasini, "Cutting through the 'Info Should Be Free' Debate," *American Writer,* Summer 1997. (*American Writer* is the magazine published by the National Writers Union.)

also, that the abuser reply to your message, confirming the removal of your work from the Web site. Here's an example:

> Dear Ms. Guided Soul:
>
> I just learned that you are using significant portions of my copyrighted work, *Reveille at Midnight*, without my authorization, on your Web site, www.purloin.com. I viewed the material there on March 10, 2000. Your use is an infringing use, prohibited by copyright law, which provides penalties for infringement. Please cease and desist further use of my work by any means and remove it from your Web site immediately. Send a confirming message to me at my address above, acknowledging that you have done so.
>
> Sincerely,
>
> Ira T. Arthur

This letter is simple, straightforward, and compelling. It does not threaten legal action, nor does it demand compensation, but it could, by adding these three sentences:

> Because your use is unlicensed and in violation of my rights, I require that you pay me a license fee, equivalent to what you would have paid had you asked my permission to use my work. That fee is $_____. If you don't respond satisfactorily by January 20, 2001, I'll have no choice but to pursue all remedies available to me.

As a practical matter, an abuser who ignores you presents a problem. You probably can't afford to sue, and we can't condone violent self-help. So what can you do? Is the online world bound to be a no-man's-land where the rules of copyright can't be enforced? Are all these new technologies simply providing more ways for a hard-working author to be exploited?

No, you have many resources. You can let the world—at least the part of it that's connected to you electronically—know what's going on. When a good portion of a little humor book called *I Am My Own Best Casual Acquaintance*, copyrighted by Jack Mingo (whom we met at the beginning of this chapter) and Brad Bunnin,[2] appeared on a number of Web sites without attribution or permission, the authors heard about it from dozens of acquaintances. Mingo had been a member of an online writers' news-

---

2. Shanti Goldstein (the Mingo–Bunnin pseudonym), *I Am My Own Best Casual Acquaintance and Other Cosmic Half•firmations* (Contemporary Books, 1994).

group for some years. Members of that newsgroup rallied to support him. Their electronic detective work turned up several other sites containing the funny quotes and revealed which of the offending postings was the oldest. The same technology that made it easy for the purloined postings to spread also made it possible to track that plagiarism.

Mingo and Bunnin sent e-mail to the abusers. They all apologized and removed the material, some promptly and graciously, others grudgingly. Some folks even offered to publish a favorable review of the book—it really is funny—on their Web sites, but none ignored the message that copyrighted work belongs to its owner and that use of the work as electronic information is *not* free.

THE FUTURE OF NEW MEDIA

We're living in an age in which technology is leapfrogging over our expectations. Someone starting a writing career today will almost certainly end up faced with issues of media technology that we can now barely imagine—"holodek rights," for example. But, despite some dire prognoses about the end of authors' rights, the basic principles of copyrights and contracts will still apply. That's why it's so important for you, the author, to control the electronic rights in the work you create with as much care as you control your print rights.

APPENDIX A
Resource Directory

Here are the books, periodicals, and organizations of most use to the working writer. Addresses and telephone numbers were accurate as of this writing, but you may need to do a little research to be sure the information is current.

ABOUT PUBLISHING IN GENERAL

Publishers communicate with each other through trade organizations and trade journals. The most important are the American Bookseller's Association, 828 South Broadway, Tarrytown, NY 10591, which publishes *American Bookseller*, and the Association of American Publishers, 71 Fifth Avenue, New York, New York 10003, which publishes *AAP Newsletter*. Almost everyone in the publishing business reads *Publishers Weekly*. Its subscription department may be reached at Box 1979, Marion, Ohio 43306-2079. A one-year subscription costs $169, but *PW* is available at almost every library. The magazine calls itself "The International News Magazine of Book Publishing," and it is. Trade news, "Forecasts"—brief reviews of forthcoming books—and information about the publishing industry's constant hiring and firing, all make their home in *PW*.

The publishing business—as a subject for books—attracts writers in substantial numbers. Some books are more accurate—and more useful—than others. Even those that are out of print may still be valuable. Here's a selection, among them books that are used in graduate-level courses for the publishing industry:

- *The Art and Science of Book Publishing* (3d ed), by Herbert S. Bailey, Jr. (Ohio University Press, 1990), is somewhat specialized and, perhaps, of more use to the publishing professional than to the writer. Nevertheless, Bailey establishes the parameters for examining the publishing business.
- *The Book Publishing Industry*, by Albert N. Greco (Allyn & Bacon, 1996).
- *Book Publishing: The Basic Introduction*, by John P. Dessauer (Continuum Publishing Group, 1993).

Some older books may help you to understand the publishing industry's economic setting:

- *The Business of Publishing, A PW Anthology* is a collection of *Publishers Weekly* articles about the business edited by Arnold Ehrlich.
- Bill Adler's *Inside Publishing* (Bobbs-Merrill, 1982).
- Thomas Whiteside's *The Blockbuster Complex: Conglomerates, Show Business, and Book Publishing* (Wesleyan University Press, 1981).
- Leonard Shatzkin's *In Cold Type* (Houghton Mifflin, 1982).

The last three above could have been titled *Publishing: Warts and All*.

- *A Writer's Guide to Book Publishing*, by Richard Balkin and Nick Bakalar (Plume, 1994), will help you to understand the relationship between you and your publisher.
- Richard Balkin also wrote *How to Understand and Negotiate a Book Contract or Magazine Agreement* (Writer's Digest Books, 1985), a useful overview of the contract process.

ABOUT BUSINESS

Other books, less specialized, but no less useful, will help you to define and run your business as a writer. Try, for example, *Small Time Operator: How to Start Your Own Small Business, Keep Your Books, Pay Your Taxes and Stay Out of Trouble!* (22d ed), by Bernard B. Kamoroff (Bell Springs Publishing, 1997). Intensely practical, this book is almost sure to save the small businessperson anguish and money.

Nolo Press (950 Parker Street, Berkeley, CA 94710) publishes many books of special interest to writers-as-businesspersons: *Everybody's Guide to Small Claims Court* is one example.

ABOUT SELF-PUBLISHING

If you're tempted to try self-publishing, don't begin until you've read *The Self-Publishing Manual: How to Write, Print and Sell Your Book*, by Dan Poynter (Para Publishing, 1997; P.O. Box 8206-R, Santa Barbara, California 93118-8206). Another extremely helpful book is *The Complete Guide to Self-Publishing: Everything You Need to Know to Write, Publish, Promote and Sell Your Own Book* (3d ed), by Tom Ross and Marilyn Ross (Writer's Digest Books, 1994). These two books should help you recognize, if not avoid, the pitfalls you face. For even more self-publishing titles, write to Padre Productions, Box 840, Arroyo Grande, CA 93421-0840, and ask for its order form.

ABOUT GETTING PUBLISHED

You may choose to concentrate your efforts on getting someone else to publish you. If you do, read *How to Get Happily Published: A Complete and Candid Guide* (5th ed), by Judith Appelbaum (HarperCollins, 1998). Although there's no such thing as a "complete" guide to a field as complicated as publishing, Appelbaum has covered a lot of territory, with candor, she claims. What's more, the book is fun to read. Try, as well, *Beginner's Guide to Getting Published* (Writer's Digest Books, 1994); *How to Be Your Own Literary Agent: The Business of Getting a Book Published*, by Richard Curtis (Houghton Mifflin, 1996); *Be Your Own Literary Agent: The Ultimate Insider's Guide to Getting Published*, by Martin P. Levin (Ten Speed Press, 1996); and *Literary Agents: What They Do, How They Do It, and How to Find and Work with the Right One for You*, by Michael Larsen (John Wiley & Sons, 1996).

Also try *Literary Agents: The Essential Guide for Writers* (Penguin, 1998) by Debby Mayer in association with Poets and Writers, Inc.

Standard reference works, used by writers for decades, include *The Writer's Handbook*, published annually by The Writer, Inc. (120 Boylston Street, Boston, MA 02116), and *Writer's Market*, also revised each year, by Writer's Digest Books (1507 Dana Avenue, Cincinnati, OH 45207). Each book contains a wealth of information about publishers and publishing.

Best consulted at the library is Bowker's annual *Literary Market Place*, known familiarly as *LMP*. *LMP* is bigger and more comprehensive than *Writer's Market* and *Writer's Handbook*; it's designed particularly for the publishing professional.

The Writer, Inc. and Writer's Digest Books publish *The Writer* and *Writer's Digest*, both magazines avidly read by writers looking for help in the form of information about publishers, tips on marketing one's work, and clues about what sells.

ABOUT PUBLISHING LAW

Even for lawyers, the selection of books about publishing law is limited. You will have to visit a library, or even a law school library, to find them.

These books are written for practicing lawyers who, though they have no monopoly on common sense, do guard the keys to the professional kingdom with legal language and a set of concepts all their own. So please be careful if you decide to use these books; their applicability and effects are not always apparent. And be aware that many law books have periodic supplements, sometimes separately bound, sometimes tucked in the front or back of the main volume (these are called "pocket parts"); check to make sure you have the latest of these supplements.

If you're ready to tackle the more abstruse and difficult books written for lawyers—or at least, for those who understand the framework of the law—then you might try *Publishing Law*, by Hugh Jones (Routledge, 1996), or *Cases and Materials on Copyright and Other Aspects of Entertainment Litigation, Including Unfair Competition, Defamation, Privacy* (5th ed), by Melville B. Nimmer (Matthew Bender & Company, 1997). And have a look at the first volume of a three-volume treatise by Alexander Lindey, called *Lindey on Entertainment, Publishing and the Arts—Agreements and the Law*, published by Clark Boardman. Lindey's book, although out of print, is available at law libraries. The book is a "form book," which means it consists mainly of sample forms for contracts, court actions, and so on, with limited annotations. Be warned— these forms are only samples, not models: don't use any forms without careful analysis. Use them, instead, as an example and a guide to what others have done.

Even more difficult to use for lawyers and nonlawyers alike are the course publications of the Practicing Law Institute (New York). PLI, as it's called, sponsors courses for practicing attorneys in a variety of fields, including publishing. The course books are collections of case digests, articles from legal journals, sample forms, and brief commentary. Many experienced publishing lawyers contribute to PLI books. The great strength of these books is that the material they contain is quite current. Their great weakness is their lack of organization. The PLI volume most useful to writers is the coursebook, published about every other year, most recently called *Print and Electronic Publishing: Understanding the Legal and Business Issues for Books and Magazines*. The book covers a wealth of publishing legal problems, including contracts and their interpretation by the courts, copyright matters, defamation and privacy issues, and legal relations within the publishing industry. It's available in law libraries.

ABOUT COPYRIGHT

Most copyright questions will be answered by the publications of the Copyright Office, Library of Congress, Washington, DC 20559. Circular R2, *Publications of the Copyright Office*, contains a brief description of everything available. Order information is included in Chapter 5. The Copyright Office Web site is lcweb.loc.gov/copyright/copy1.html.

See Appendix D for a list of Copyright Office publications. If you need more information, try *A Writer's Guide to Copyright,* a brief but useful booklet published by Poets and Writers, Inc., 72 Spring Street, New York, NY 10012.

Books especially for writers include the following:

- *A Copyright Guide for Authors,* by Robert E. Lee (Kent Press, 1996).
- *The Copyright, Permission, and Libel Handbook: A Step-by-Step Guide for Writers, Editors, and Publishers*, by Lloyd J. Jassin and Steven C. Schecter (John Wiley & Sons, 1997).
- *The Copyright Handbook: How to Protect & Use Written Works* (4th ed), by Stephen Fishman (Nolo Press, 1997).
- *Electronic Highway Robbery: An Artist's Guide to Copyrights in the Digital Era,* by Mary E. Carter (Peachpit Press, 1996). Although written for artists, this is the only book that deals expressly with electronic publishing issues.
- *Nimmer on Copyright* (Matthew Bender Co.). Consult the current edition for an extended discussion of virtually every copyright issue likely to concern you and many you'll have absolutely no interest in pursuing. Melville Nimmer was the lawyer-professor acknowledged to be the national authority on copyright matters, and his son has taken over this classic treatise. The four-volume set almost merits the adjectives "complete" and "comprehensive." This major work has a minor flaw—a poor index. But the detailed chapter subheadings somewhat make up for it. You will find it in law libraries.

ABOUT DEFAMATION AND THE RIGHT OF PRIVACY

Libel and privacy issues are so complex and so likely to cause you expensive problems that we urge you to rely on no book if you think you have a problem. Please use the books we're about to suggest only for general background and as a way to analyze your work to see if problems may exist.

- *International Media Liability: Civil Liability in the Information Age,* by Christian T. Campbell (editor) (John Wiley & Sons, 1997), is very expensive but it is a remarkably comprehensive look at the international legal implications of online publishing.
- For a near-outline approach, read Bruce W. Sanford's *Synopsis of Libel and Privacy* (4th ed.) (Newspaper Enterprises Association, 1991). This booklet was designed for the working writer in a hurry. It's by no means complete, but it should scare you enough to make you careful.
- Finally, The Practicing Law Institute published *Libel, Slander, and Related Problems* (2nd ed.) by Robert D. Sack and Sandra S. Baron. The book contains about 1,500 pages of information about libel, slander, and privacy issues.

ORGANIZATIONS TO HELP WRITERS

Even though writing is a solitary art, you may find help through a number of organizations. We've grouped them in two broad categories: those whose members are writers, and those whose members are lawyers or agents who work with writers.

Writers' organizations include the following:

1. American Society of Journalists and Authors, 1501 Broadway, #302, New York, NY 10036. (212) 997-0947. www.asja.org.
2. The Authors Guild, 330 West 42d Street, New York, NY 10036. (212) 268-1208. www.authorsguild.org.
3. P.E.N. American Center, 568 Broadway, New York, NY 10012. (212) 334-1660.
4. Media Alliance, 814 Mission Street, Suite 205, San Francisco, CA 94103. (415) 546-6334. www.media-alliance.org.
5. National Writers Union, 873 Broadway, Suite 203, New York, NY 10003. (212) 254-0279. www.nwu.org/nwu/.
6. Poets and Writers, Inc., 72 Spring Street, New York, NY 10012. (212) 226-3586. www.pw.org.
7. There are also professional associations of writers working in specific subject areas: Society of Children's Book Writers and Illustrators,

Science Fiction Writers of America, Outdoor Writers of America, and so forth.

Lawyer referral groups include the following:

1. California Lawyers for the Arts, Fort Mason Center, Building C, Room 255, San Francisco, CA 94123. (415) 775-7200. In Oakland: (510) 444-6351. In Santa Monica: (310) 998-5590
2. Lawyers for the Creative Arts, 213 West Institute Place, #411, Chicago, IL 60610. (312) 944-2787.
3. Volunteer Lawyers for the Arts, 1 East 53rd Street, New York, NY 10022. (212) 319-2787.
4. For a complete listing of sources of legal assistance for "financially strapped writers," see "Volunteer Lawyers for the Arts," a round-up of thirty-nine loosely affiliated organizations and institutions in some twenty-three states, in the April 1983 issue of *Writer's Digest*, page 25.

Finally, an organization of literary agents will provide you with help in locating an agent, if not in convincing one to represent you: Association of Authors' Representatives, Inc. (AAR), 10 Astor Place, 3d Floor, New York, NY 10003. (212) 353-3700.

APPENDIX B
A Glossary of
Publishing Terms

Advance: Money paid to an author for publication rights before the author has earned it through sales of the author's work. Advances are usually "recoupable"—to be paid back to the publisher only out of the author's earned royalties.

Advance endorsements: Endorsements obtained from experts in the field or opinion-makers before a book is published. Useful in catalog copy, sales presentation materials; and announcement ads. May also be used on book cover or jacket. (See *Cover blurbs.*)

Advance orders: Number of copies the publisher's sales force expects to place in stores through orders received prior to a book's publication. Same as *Lay-down* or *Prepublication orders.*

Amortization: Reducing (and eventually wiping out) expenditures and/or debts by spreading them out over a fixed period of time.

Author tour: Book promotion tour undertaken by the author.

Author's questionnaire: Request from the publisher to the author for specific items of personal information, such as education, places lived, other books or articles published, and so on. To be used to shape the marketing and packaging of a book.

Back matter: Everything printed at the end of the book after the main body of text. Includes appendices, bibliographies, glossaries, footnotes, and indexes.

Big budget book: Title(s) on publisher's list that will get the most advertising, promotion, and so on. Generally, no more than 10 percent of a publisher's list receives this kind of financial attention. (See also *Lead title*.)

Boards: Thin cardboard material used for paste-up of text and graphic work in book production; from the boards, printing film or plates are made. (See also *Mechanicals*.)

Book club: A membership organization that sells books, often at a reduced price, to its members. Specialized book clubs offer books in a particular subject area, such as law or science.

Book design: The look of a book; specifically, the graphic and physical elements of the book. Generally book design decisions are not made by the author.

Bulk sales: The sale by the publisher of a large number of copies of a book to one buyer, usually at a deep discount. By contract, authors suffer from a substantially reduced royalty on bulk sales because the publisher's profit margin is less than normal.

Castoff: The estimate of the finished book's size, taking into account format, type size, illustrations, and so on. A preliminary castoff is usually produced by the book's editor; the production department is responsible for the final castoff.

Chain buyer: The person responsible for selecting titles for sale in a chain of stores, such as B. Dalton or Walden.

Consumer advertising: Advertising aimed at regular consumer markets; considered to be among the least effective methods of launching most books.

Costs per sale: General figure for costs incurred by the publisher in the course of making book sales to specific types of accounts.

Cover blurbs: Advance endorsements used on the front or back book cover to promote the book.

Cover price: The suggested retail price of a book; usually printed on the front or back cover or the dust jacket. Largely a function of preproduction, manufacturing, and royalty costs, mitigated by the realities of the marketplace. This is a manufacturer's suggested list price. Resellers may, in actuality, set any price they wish. "Invoice price" is the *Cover price* less the *Freight passthrough;* see those definitions.

Echo effect: In book advertising, when one form of promotion (such as a coupon ad in a magazine) not only works on its own merits but also "echoes" by encouraging sales in other areas (such as bookstores).

Escalation: The practice of increasing the royalty rate when sales reach a predetermined level. For example, the basic royalty rate of 10 percent may apply until 5,000 copies of a book are sold, when the rate increases to 12½ percent for the next 5,000, and to 15 percent for all copies in excess of 10,000.

Exhibits: Trade shows, conventions, and so on. Exhibits often create opportunities for direct sales of books.

Freight passthrough, freight allowance: An amount of money added to the basic retail price of a book to compensate the bookseller for the freight or postage he must pay to get the book delivered to his store from the publisher or distributor. Its significance to writers is that although it's included ("buried" may be more apt) in the price of the book, it is excluded when royalties are calculated.

Front matter: Everything printed in the front of the book, before the main body of text. Includes title page, copyright page, dedication, preface, foreword, introduction, and table of contents. These pages are often numbered in lower-case Roman numerals.

Hook (or Tip) sheet: Part of the press kit containing bits of interesting information or news angles about the author or book being marketed. Meant to "hook" the reader into using the information in the press kit or to provide a handy format of information "nuggets" that can be used directly by the medium the press kit was pitched to.

Invoice price: See *Cover price* and *Freight passthrough*.

Kill fee: Payment to a magazine writer, working on assignment, for a story not finally bought and published, in an attempt to compensate the writer for his time.

Lay-down: Number of copies the sales force is expected to place in stores through orders prior to publication. Same as *Advance orders*.

Lead title: Book expected to sell well, which is positioned to lead the other titles on publisher's list. As a "leader," it is expected to pull other titles on the list into the stores.

"Local angles": Information about author or book useful to sales representatives when making sales in a particular territory or to be used by regional media in promotion.

Marketing plan: Publisher's plan for marketing a particular title, including budgeting, staffing, advertising, book promotion, and so on.

Mass market paperback: A small-trim paperback book priced lower than a trade paperback and widely distributed through wholesalers and jobbers to be sold in drugstores, airports, and supermarkets, although also found in bookstores.

Mechanicals: Pasted-up, camera-ready boards containing text and graphics of a book.

Media contacts: Personal acquaintances and friends in the media (radio, television, newspapers, and so on); useful when trying to get a book reviewed or mentioned.

"The numbers": A collection of figures indicating various things, depending on what is under discussion. Can mean the possible audience for a book, the production costs for a book, and so on.

"The package": The format and total look of the book, consisting of the cover design and the copy.

Plant costs: Nonrecurring production costs.

"PP & B": Abbreviation for paper, printing, and binding, the major manufacturing cost in book production.

Premium: Books sold outside normal trade channels to a buyer who plans to give them away as an inducement to buy something else or to join an organization. Royalties on premium books are much lower than normal, because the publisher's profit is reduced on these sales.

Preproduction: The final preparation of the book manuscript, including preparing front and back matter, obtaining illustrations, editing and designing the text itself, and so on.

Prepublication orders: Book orders received before publication, i.e., before any significant response from reviewers, press, or public. Same as *Advance orders.*

"Presold, prequalified" readers: Readers already having a stake in a book's contents; readers who may buy a copy simply on learning that the book exists.

Press kit: Collection of items sent to feature editors, talk show producers, and the like, used to attract media publicity; press releases, hook sheet, copies of reviews, and so on.

Price: Suggested retail, list, cover, and invoice. All but the last refer to the price, printed on the cover or dust jacket of a book, that the retail buyer nominally pays. "Invoice price" is the *Cover price* less the *Freight passthrough;* see those definitions.

Production grant, production advance: Money paid to an author to help defray the cost of producing a manuscript, including, for example, illustrations, graphs and charts, and other special design costs. The publisher pays itself back out of the author's royalties for a production advance, but not for a production grant—which is obviously much better for authors.

Publication date: Official date the book is released for sale, commonly six weeks after bound books arrive at the warehouse. A historic convention of the book trade set to coordinate the availability of product with advertising and promotion.

Publicist: One whose job is to publicize people or things. Also known as a press agent.

Publisher's discount: The amount stated as a percentage by which a publisher reduces the cover price of a book to establish the price at which the book is sold to a retailer. The amount of the discount depends on the publisher, the quantity of books ordered, and the nature of the *Return privilege;* see that definition.

Quality paperback: See *Trade paperback.*

Quote: Final castoff and manufacturing costs estimate.

Remaindering: The publisher's last-resort effort to salvage something from an inventory of books that hasn't sold, by disposing of the books for a pittance to specialists in such books.

Return privilege: The contractual right of a retail bookseller to send unsold copies of a book back to its publisher for credit, if certain conditions are met (minimum time in the bookstore, resaleable condition, prepaid freight). Publishers don't want to pay royalties on a returned book, so they establish a "reserve against returns," which entitles them to keep a portion of an author's royalties for a time—often a long time.

Review copy target list: List provided by author to publicity or marketing department; targets specialized publications in book's subject area or publications that are or might be interested in author (alumni magazine, for example). Provides core list for sending review copies, press release, or ads.

"Revolving door": Slang phrase for the frequency with which editors move from job to job.

Royalty: Payment to the author of a work by its publisher, usually calculated as a percentage of the price of the work.

Sales conference: Regular meeting (usually held twice yearly, but sometimes more frequently) at which the publisher and editors introduce new books to the sales force.

Sales representatives: The people who physically go into the stores to sell your book, collectively known as the "trade sales force."

Secondary marketing possibilities: Nonbookstore marketing possibilities for your book: specialty stores, trade associations, institutions, and so on.

Serialization: The appearance of a work destined to be published elsewhere in a serial publication (such as a magazine, journal, or newspaper, all published in a series of issues). If the work is serialized before publication elsewhere, it's "first serialization"; if afterward, it's "second serialization."

Signature: Folded sheets that make up a section of a book; traditionally multiples of eight pages.

Special sales department: The department of a publishing firm concerned with nonbookstore sales.

Subsidiary rights: All the rights to deal with a copyrighted work *except* the first right sold. Usually, the first right sold is the right to initial publication of a trade book (or a magazine article), in which case subsidiary rights include paperback reprint rights, serialization rights, film-TV-dramatic-recording rights, merchandising rights, and so on. If the initial sale of rights happens to be for a film, then trade book publication rights ("novelization") becomes a subsidiary right.

Talent coordinator: The person connected with a specific television show who coordinates guest appearances.

"The trade": Slang term encompassing the persons and companies in the book business.

Trade book: A book of some production quality, sold through traditional retail book outlets (bookstores). Trade books may be hardbound or softbound; the latter are called "trade paperbacks," or quality paperbacks," and are trimmed to a larger size than mass market paperbacks (defined above).

Trade paperback: Book format; same as a quality paperback, with higher price, better paper, and better binding than a mass market paperback. Sold primarily through bookstores rather than through magazine racks in supermarkets, drugstores, and the like.

Trade publishers: Those publishers concerned with publishing books aimed at a general audience, and sold through retail bookstores as opposed to textbook publishers, and so on.

Trim size: The dimensions of a book. Standard trade book trim sizes are 5½" by 8½" and 6" by 9"; oversize books are 9" by 12" and larger, while mass market paperbacks are 4¼" by 7".

Warranty; indemnity: A promise of special importance and solemnity contained in a contract. Commonly, an author's warranties have to do with the right to make the contract and the assurance that the work won't interfere with anyone else's rights (as by libeling or invading the privacy or infringing the copyright of some third party).

Breach of warranty usually requires the author to indemnify—that is, pay—the publisher for losses caused by the breach.

Word-of-mouth: Oral recommendation of a title, usually on a one-to-one basis. The most potent form of sales catalyst.

"Working your publisher": Phrase coined by Jeremy Tarcher; activity of an author trying to engage as many different people and departments of the publisher in as many aspects of the book's marketing as possible.

APPENDIX C
Publishing Agreements

1. **Major Publisher's Trade Book Agreement**
2. **Independent Publisher's Trade Book Agreement**
3. **Mass Market Paperback Original Agreement—Main Variant Clauses**
4. **College Textbook Agreement**

We've included four versions of typical publishing agreements. None of these agreements is a model for you to follow. None will suit every author or every publisher. But they represent—in concept and language—the agreements you're likely to encounter. And you should be able to do better with your own contract because you've encountered and analyzed those we provide here, using Chapter 1 as a guide, free of the pressure to sign on the dotted line.

MAJOR PUBLISHER'S TRADE BOOK AGREEMENT

AGREEMENT made as of this 12th day of July, 2001, between Insight Publishing, a division of XYX, Inc., a Delaware corporation with its principal offices at 1002 W.23d Street, New York, New York 10000 (hereinafter referred to as the "Publisher"); and Jane James Smith, of 31 Tempest Tost Lane, Lincoln, California 94000 (hereinafter referred to as the "Author").

WITNESSETH:

In consideration of the mutual covenants herein contained, the parties agree as follows:

1.   THE GRANT AND THE TERRITORY

a.   The Author grants to the Publisher and its licensees, for the full term of copyright available in each country included within the Territory covered by this Agreement under any copyright laws now or hereafter in force within the Territory with respect to a book-length work of approximately 60,000 words, with the tentative title *The Living Business* (hereinafter referred to as the "Work"), substantially as described in the outline attached to and made a part of this agreement, the following "Primary" and "Secondary" Rights:

(i)   "Primary Rights":

(a)   "Trade Edition Rights"—exclusive right to publish, or authorize others to publish, hardcover and trade paperback (softcover editions distributed primarily through hardcover trade channels) editions of the Work.

(b)   "Mass Market Reprint Rights"—exclusive right to authorize others to publish softcover editions of the Work to be distributed primarily through independent magazine wholesalers and to direct accounts.

(c)   "Book Club Rights"—exclusive right to authorize book clubs to print and sell the Work.

(d)   "General Publication Rights"—exclusive right to publish, or authorize others to publish, condensations and abridgments of the Work; publication of the complete Work or selections therefrom in anthologies, compilations, digests, newspapers, magazines, and other works such as a textbook; and in Braille.

(e)   "Transcription Rights"—exclusive right to use the Work, or any portion thereof, in information storage and retrieval systems whether through mechanical or electronic means now known or hereafter invented, including, but not limited to, sound recordings; programs for machine teaching, ephemeral screen flashing or reproduction thereof, whether by printout, photoreproduction or photocopy, including punch cards, microfilm, magnetic tape, or like processes attaining similar results.

(f)   "Direct Mail Rights"—exclusive right to sell, or authorize others to sell, the Work through the medium of direct mail circularization or by mail-order coupon advertising.

(ii)   "Secondary Rights":

(a)   "First Serialization Rights"—exclusive right, prior to publication of the Work in volume form, to publish, or authorize others to publish, the Work in whole or selections (including condensations and abridgments) therefrom.

(b)   "Dramatic Rights"—exclusive right to use, or authorize others to use, the Work or any portion thereof (including but not limited to characters, plot, title, scenes) in any stage presentation.

(c)   "Movie Rights"—exclusive right to use, or authorize others to use, the Work or any portion thereof (including but not limited to characters, plot, title, scenes) in any motion picture.

(d) "Television and Radio Rights"—exclusive right to use, or authorize others to use, the Work or any portion thereof (including but not limited to characters, plot, title, scenes) on television or radio.

(e) "Translation Rights"—exclusive right to authorize others to translate the Work in whole or in part, into foreign languages and to publish and sell such translations anywhere in the world.

(f) "British Commonwealth Rights"—exclusive right to publish and sell and to authorize others to publish and sell the Work in the English language in the British Commonwealth as constituted as of the date of this Agreement (excluding Canada and Australia).

b.   Such grant of Primary and Secondary Rights shall be exclusive in the United States, its territories and possessions, Canada, and the Philippine Islands; the rest of the world shall be an open market except for the British Commonwealth, as constituted in the attached schedule which shall be reserved to the Author.*

c.   All rights not specifically granted herein to the Publisher shall be reserved to the Author. Such reserved rights shall include the right to grant to the purchaser thereof the privilege of publishing excerpts and summaries of the Work not to exceed in the aggregate seventy-five hundred (7,500) words, for advertising, publicity, and other commercial use. With respect to the reserved right of publication in magazines or newspapers after book publication, the Author agrees that if any such publication shall be in one (1) installment, not more than two-thirds ($\frac{2}{3}$) of the Work shall be so utilized. In the event of any such publication, the Author shall promptly notify the Publisher thereof and supply the Publisher with two (2) copies of such publication. If any copyright therein shall be registered in the name of any person, firm, or corporation other than the Author, the Author shall promptly deliver to the Publisher an assignment of such copyright. The Author shall not exercise or dispose of any reserved rights in the Work in such a way as to materially adversely affect the value of the rights granted to the Publisher under this Agreement.

2. WARRANTIES AND INDEMNITIES

a.   The Author represents and warrants to the Publisher that: (i) the Work is not in the public domain; (ii) the Author is the sole proprietor of the Work and has full power, free of any rights of any nature whatsoever in any one that might interfere therewith, to enter into this Agreement and to grant the rights hereby conveyed to the Publisher, (iii) the work has not heretofore been published in whole or in part; (iv) the Work does not, and if published will not, infringe upon any proprietary right at common law, or any statutory copyright, or any other right whatsoever; (v) the Work contains no matter whatsoever that is obscene, libelous, in violation of any right of privacy, or otherwise in contravention of law or the right of any third party; (vi) all statements of fact are true or based

---

*Ed. Note: The schedule is omitted.

upon reasonable research; (vii) the Work, if biographical or "as told to the Author," is authentic; and (viii) the Author will not hereafter enter into any agreement or understanding with any person, firm, or corporation that might conflict with the rights herein granted to the Publisher.

b.   If the Publisher makes an independent investigation to determine whether the foregoing warranties and representations are true and correct, such investigation shall not constitute a defense to the Author in any action based upon a breach of any of the foregoing warranties.

c.   The Author shall indemnify, defend, and hold the Publisher, its subsidiaries and affiliates, and its and their respective agents, officers, directors, and employees harmless from any claims, demands, suits, actions, proceedings of prosecutions based on facts which, if true, would constitute a breach of any of the foregoing warranties (hereinafter collectively referred to as "Claims") and any liabilities, losses, expenses (including attorneys' fees), or damages in consequence thereof resulting in a final judgment adverse to them. Each of the parties hereto shall give the other prompt written notice of any Claims and the Author shall have the obligation to defend the Claims by counsel of his selection, satisfactory to Publisher, or settle the Claims, on such terms as may be acceptable to Publisher, holding the Publisher accountable for fifty percent (50%) of any amounts paid on such settlement, for counsel's fees and other legal expenses. If any Claims result (after a trial) in no liability on the part of the Publisher, Author and Publisher shall share equally the expenses of defending against such Claims. No compromise or settlement of any claim, demand, or suit shall be made or entered into without the prior written approval of the Publisher. In the event any suit is filed, the Publisher shall have the right to withhold one-half the payments due the Author under the terms of this Agreement (except any portion of the advance payable under paragraph 7 hereof), up to the amount of Publisher's claimed liability thereunder, as security for the Author's obligations as stated above. The benefit of the Author's warranties and indemnities shall extend to any person, firm, or corporation against whom any such claim, demand, or suit is asserted or instituted by reason of the publication, sale, or distribution of the Work as if such representations and warranties were originally made to such third parties. The warranties and indemnities as stated herein shall survive termination of this Agreement.

3.   THE MANUSCRIPT

a.   The Author agrees to deliver to the Publisher, no later than June 30, 2003, two (2) complete typewritten manuscripts of the Work, acceptable to the Publisher in form and substance and ready to set into type. The Author will also deliver written authorizations for the use of any materials owned by a third party included in the manuscript. The Author agrees that the Author shall have retained copies of the manuscript as delivered to the Publisher. The Publisher retains the final right to determine whether or not photographs are necessary for the Work, and if necessary, how many. If the Author fails to deliver illustrations, photographs, charts, maps, drawings, or the like (hereinafter collectively referred to as "Additional Material") in cases where any of these have been deemed by Publisher as necessary for the Work, the Publisher shall have the right, but shall not be obliged, to cause the same to be acquired or prepared and to charge the cost of such acquisition or preparation to the Author, but the Publisher shall provide the Author, as a grant and not as an advance against royalties, not more than $2,000 to cover the costs of such acquisition or preparation on the Author's timely presentation of invoices therefore. The Publisher shall not be responsible for the loss of or damage to any Additional Material and the Publisher shall be under no obligation to insure same.

b.   If the Author fails to deliver the Work or all Additional Material within the time specified, or if the Author delivers the Work and all Additional Material and the Work or any of the Additional Material is not accepted by the Publisher as being satisfactory, the Publisher shall have the option to terminate this agreement; in which case upon receipt of notice of such termination, the Author shall, without prejudice to any other right or remedy of the Publisher, forthwith repay to the Publisher any guaranteed advance theretofore paid to the Author. Upon such termination and repayment, all rights granted to the Publisher shall revert to the Author.

c.   If, in the reasonable judgment of the Publisher, the Publisher feels that an index for the Work is necessary the Publisher shall engage a skilled person to prepare such index and the cost of such preparation shall be borne by the Publisher.

4.   PUBLICATION OF THE WORK

The Publisher agrees that the Work, if published, shall be published at its own expense and under such imprint as it deems suitable.

5.   THE COPYRIGHT

Unless otherwise agreed to in writing, the Publisher will, in all published versions of the Work, place a Copyright Notice in a form and place that the Publisher believes complies with the requirements of the United States Copyright Law, showing that the owner of the copyright rights in and to the Work is the Author. Such notice shall not be construed as in any way affecting or diminishing any of the rights granted to the Publisher under this Agreement. The Author shall execute and deliver to the Publisher any documents necessary or desirable to evidence or effectuate the rights granted to the Publisher under this Agreement. The publisher shall pay to the Author the Author's share of subsidiary rights earnings within thirty (30) days of receipt of such earnings by the Publisher once the guaranteed advance and any other amounts advanced to the Author have been earned out.

6.   PROOFREADING AND CHANCES IN PROOF

The Publisher shall furnish the Author with a galley proof of the Work. The Author agrees to read, correct, and return all proof sheets within twenty-one (21) days of receipt thereof. If any changes in the proof or the printing plates (other than corrections of printer's errors) are made at the Author's request, or with his consent, the cost of such changes in excess of ten percent (10%) of the cost of typesetting (exclusive of the cost of setting corrections) shall be borne by the Author. The Publisher shall give the Author prompt notice of any amounts charged to the Author under this paragraph 6. If the Author fails to return the proof within the time period specified above, the Publisher may publish the Work without the Author's approval of the proof.

7.   ADVANCE ROYALTIES

The Publisher shall pay to the Author, as a guaranteed advance against all royalties and other payments to be earned under paragraph 8, below, the sum of Ten Thousand Dollars ($10,000), payable as follows: Five Thousand Dollars ($5,000) on execution of this Agreement and Five Thousand Dollars ($5,000) on compliance with paragraph 3 hereof.

8.   EARNED ROYALTIES AND STATEMENTS

A.   Primary Rights:

(i)   For hardcover editions published by the Publisher, the Publisher shall credit the Author's account with the following royalties:

(a)   On all net copies sold, except as provided below, a royalty of ten percent (10%) of the Publisher's United States list price ("List Price") per copy on the first five thousand (5,000) copies; twelve and one-half percent (12½%) on the next five thousand (5,000) copies; and fifteen percent (15%) thereafter. Copies sold pursuant to any other subparagraph of this paragraph 8. (A.) shall not be counted in computing sales pursuant to this paragraph 8.A.(i)(a).

(b)   On all net copies sold where the discount to dealers or others in the continental United States is more than fifty percent (50%) of the List Price, a royalty equal to that set forth in paragraph 8.A.(i)(a) above less one percent (1%) of the List Price; and with each further increase in discount by one percent (1%) of the List Price, the royalty shall be further reduced by one-half percent (½%) of the List Price.

(c)   On all net copies sold for export, a royalty of ten percent (10%) of the amount that the Publisher receives.

(d)   On all net copies sold in any six (6) month accounting period in which the regular sales do not exceed two hundred and fifty (250) copies; provided that such copies are from a reprinting made two (2) years or more after first publication, a royalty equal to two-thirds (⅔) of the royalty specified in paragraph 8.A.(i)(a) hereof. This provision is made for the purpose of keeping the Work in print and in circulation as long as possible.

(e)   On all copies destroyed, given away, or sold at or below cost, no royalties shall be paid. Upon the first occurrence of either destruction, give away, or sale at or below cost, the Publisher shall present the Author with twenty-five (25) free copies of the Work. On overstocks or damaged copies, a royalty of ten percent (10%) of the net amount that the Publisher receives in excess of manufacturing cost, if the Publisher, at its option, disposes of all or a part of the stock at the best prices it can secure.

(f)   On all net copies sold of any cheap hardcover edition published with the prior written consent of the Author that the Publisher publishes at a price not greater than two-thirds (⅔) of the original List Price, a royalty of ten percent (10%) of the amount that the Publisher receives, but if the Publisher, with the prior written consent of the Author, licenses publication of such edition by another Publisher, a royalty of fifty percent (50%) of the amount that the Publisher receives. If the Publisher adjusts the price of copies of the regular hardcover edition remaining unsold in the hands of booksellers to correspond with the price of the cheap hardcover edition, the royalty of such copies shall be ten percent (10%) of the amount that the Publisher receives.

(g)   On all net copies sold direct to the consumer through the medium of mail-order coupon advertising or direct mail circularization, a royalty equal to two-thirds (⅔) of the royalty specified in paragraph 8.A.(i)(a) hereof.

(ii)   For softcover trade editions published by the Publisher, the Publisher shall credit the Author's account with the following royalties:

(a)   On all net copies sold in the United States and Canada, a royalty of eight percent (8%) of the Publisher's United States list price per copy on the first fifteen thousand (15,000) copies and a royalty of ten percent (10%) per copy thereafter.

(b)   On all net copies sold outside the United States and territories under its administration or within the United States for export, or at a price lower than the lowest regular wholesale price through special arrangements with book clubs, charitable, fraternal, or professional associations or similar organizations, or sold direct to the consumer through the medium of mail-order coupon advertising or direct mail circularization, or sold to members or prospective members of book clubs, a royalty equal to two-thirds (⅔) of the royalty specified in paragraph 8.A.(ii)(a) hereof.

(c)   On all copies destroyed, given away, or sold at or below cost, no royalties shall be paid. On overstocks or damaged copies, a royalty of ten percent (10%) of the amount that the Publisher receives in excess of manufacturing cost, if the Publisher, at its option, disposes of all or a part of the stock at the best prices it can secure, after offering the same to the Author at those prices less such royalty.

iii. For other Primary Rights, the Publisher shall credit the Author with fifty percent (50%) of the net proceeds received by the Publisher for the disposition of any other Primary Rights.

iv.   As used herein, the term "Publisher's United States list price" or "List Price" refers to the sale price established by the Publisher before addition of a factor to cover the cost of freight (or handling charges for mail-order sales). This price is not to be confused with "invoice price or consumer price," which includes the factor for freight (or handling charges for mail-order sales) and which appears on the jacket or cover of the Work and may appear in connection with promotion or advertising of the Work.

B.   Secondary Rights

The Publisher shall credit the Author's account with the following percentage of net proceeds received for the disposition of Secondary Rights:

First Periodical Rights fifty percent (50%)

Dramatic Rights fifty percent (50%)

Movie Rights percent fifty (50%)

Television Rights percent fifty (50%)

Radio Rights fifty percent fifty (50%)

Translation Rights fifty percent (50%)

British Commonwealth Rights fifty percent (50%)

The Author shall promptly remit to the Publisher ten percent (10%) of the Author's net receipts from the license, sale, or other disposition of dramatic adaptation, motion picture, television, or radio rights.

C.   Statements

The Publisher shall render to the Author or his duly authorized representative on or before April 30 and October 31 of each year, statements of net sales up to the preceding December 31 and June 30 respectively and, if the earned royalties exceed the guaranteed advance royalties and the amount withheld and deducted by the Publisher pursuant to this Agreement, the Publisher shall make simultaneous settlement in cash. In making accountings, the Publisher shall have the right to allow for a reasonable reserve (not to exceed three royalty periods) against returns. If royalties in excess of the guaranteed advance payment have been paid on copies that are thereafter returned, the Publisher shall have the right to deduct the amount of such royalties on such returned copies from any future payments under this Agreement. The Publisher shall pay the Author interest on any royalty payments accrued and owing but unpaid at the rate of twelve percent (12%) per annum, compounded. And the Publisher's rights under paragraphs 1a(i) and 20 of this Agreement shall be suspended and may not be exercised while any such royalty payments remain owing and unpaid, and shall be terminated if they remain unpaid for two (2) accounting periods. In the event of a Claim against the Publisher that, if sustained, would constitute a breach of any of the Author's representations and warranties pursuant to this Agreement, the Publisher shall have the right to withhold royalties and any other payment that may be due pursuant to this Agreement pending a final determination thereof. The Publisher shall have the right to apply any of said withheld royalties and other payments then or thereafter accruing hereunder in reduction of the obligation of the Author under paragraph 2 of this Agreement. If a suit shall not be commenced for a period of six (6) months from the assertion of a Claim, all withheld royalties and any other payments shall be payable at the end of the next succeeding accounting period.

9.   AUTHOR'S COPIES

The Publisher agrees to present to the Author twenty (20) free copies of each edition of the Work published by the Publisher and the Author shall be permitted to purchase further copies for the Author's personal use and not for resale at a discount of forty percent (40%) from the retail list price, to be paid for upon receipt of the Publisher's invoice.

10.   EXHAUSTION OF EDITION

a.   If the Work goes out of print in all regular United States editions and if the Publisher fails to reprint, or to cause a licensee to reprint, a regular United States edition within six (6) months after receipt of written notice from the Author unless prevented from doing so by circumstances beyond the Publisher's control, the Author may terminate this Agreement by written notice. Upon such termination, all rights granted hereunder, except the right to dispose of existing stock, shall revert to the Author, subject to rights which may have been granted to third parties pursuant to this Agreement, and the Publisher shall be under no further obligations or liability to the Author except that the Author's share of earnings hereunder shall be paid when and as due. If the Work goes out of print, the Author may purchase Publisher's plates, films, unbound sheets, and inventory at Publisher's cost of manufacture, plus freight.

b.   The Work shall not be deemed "out-of-print" within the meaning of this paragraph 10 as long as it is available for sale either from stock in the Publisher's or licensee's warehouse or in reasonable quantities for sale in regular retail sales channels.

11.   INFRINGEMENT OF COPYRIGHT

If during the existence of this Agreement the copyright shall be infringed or a claim for unfair competition shall arise from the unauthorized use of the Work or any part thereof, but not limited to, the format thereof or the characters or situations contained therein, the Publisher may, at its own cost and expense, take such legal action as may be required to restrain such wrong or to seek damages therefor. The Publisher shall not be liable to the Author for the Publisher's failure to take such legal steps. If the Publisher does not take such action within a reasonable time, the Author may do so, in the Author's name and at the Author's cost and expense. The party taking the action shall bear all costs and expenses (including attorneys' fees) and:

a.   If the Publisher takes such action, shall split all recoveries with the Author after Publisher recoups all its costs and expenses; or

b.   If the Author takes such action, the Author shall retain all recoveries.

12.   RIGHTS SURVIVING TERMINATION

In the event of the termination of this Agreement as elsewhere herein provided, any rights reverting to the Author shall be subject to all licenses and other grants of rights theretofore made by the Publisher to third parties, and to the rights of the Publisher to proceeds of such licenses and grants.

13. CONSTRUCTION

This Agreement shall in all respects be interpreted, construed, and governed by the laws of the State of New York.

14. MODIFICATION OR WAIVER

This Agreement may not be modified or altered except by written instrument executed by the Author and the Publisher. No waiver of any term or condition of this Agreement or of any breach of this Agreement or of any part thereof, shall be deemed a waiver of any other term or condition of this Agreement or of any later breach of the Agreement or of any part thereof.

15. NOTICES

Any written notice required under any of the provisions of this Agreement shall be deemed to have been properly served by delivery in person to the Author or by mailing such notice to either of the parties hereto at the addresses set forth above, except as the addresses may be changed by notice in writing; provided, however, that mailed notices shall be sent by registered or certified mail, return receipt requested, with copies mailed to Publisher being addressed: "Attention: XYX, Inc."

16. EXECUTION AND DELIVERY OF CONTRACT

If this Agreement shall not be signed and returned to the Publisher within a period of two (2) months from the date of its transmittal to the Author, the Publisher shall have the option to withdraw its offer of agreement. Nothing contained herein shall be construed to vitiate the Publisher's right to withdraw its offer of agreement prior to delivery of the signed agreement to the Publisher by the Author.

17. CAPTIONS AND MARGINAL NOTES

Captions and marginal notes are for convenience only and are not to be deemed part of this Agreement.

18. ASSIGNMENT

This Agreement shall be binding upon and inure to the benefit of the heirs, executors, administrators, or assigns of the Author, and the successors, assigns, and licensees of the Publisher, but no assignment by either party, other than an assignment by operation of law or by the Publisher to the purchaser of all or substantially all the Publisher's assets shall be made without the prior written consent of the other party.

19. AUTHOR'S NAME AND PUBLISHER'S TRADEMARKS

The Publisher shall have the right to use, and to license others to use, the Author's name, likeness, and biographical material for the purpose of advertising, publishing, and promoting the Work itself, its title, and all material, including the characters, in the Work through their use, simulation, or graphic exploitations on or in connection with merchandise. Nothing in this Agreement shall give the Author any right in or to any trademark, service mark, trade name, or colophon now or hereafter used by the Publisher, nor shall the Author use any such name, mark, or colophon during the term of this Agreement or thereafter, except that the Author may dispose of copies of the Work obtained by the Author from the Publisher pursuant to the terms of this Agreement notwithstanding that such name, mark, or colophon may appear therein when purchased.

20.   OPTION ON NEXT WORK

The Author shall submit his next book-length work to the Publisher before submitting it elsewhere, and the Publisher shall have thirty (30) days in which to make an offer to publish that work provided, however, that the Publisher need not exercise its rights and make such offer any earlier than four (4) months after the publication of the Work. If the Author and the Publisher cannot agree to terms within thirty (30) days after the commencement of negotiations, the Author shall then be free to deal with other publishers, provided that the Publisher shall have the option to obtain the right to publish by matching the bona fide financial terms which the Author shall have obtained elsewhere. The Author shall communicate such terms to the Publisher in writing, and the Publisher shall have ten (10) days after the Publisher's receipt of such communication in which to exercise such option.

21.   INSOLVENCY

If the Publisher is adjudicated as bankrupt or liquidates its business, this agreement shall thereupon terminate, and all rights granted to the Publisher shall automatically revert to the Author.

IN WITNESS WHEREOF the parties hereto have executed and duly witnesses this Agreement as of the day and year first above written.

XYX, Inc.

By _____

President
For Insight Books

_____

AUTHOR

_____

Jane James Smith
Social Security No.: _____

INDEPENDENT PUBLISHER'S TRADE BOOK AGREEMENT

AN AGREEMENT

made between _____(author), a

citizen of _____whose home address is

_____

_____

and _____(publisher) on

_____, 20_____.

THE AUTHOR AND PUBLISHER AGREE THAT

1. The Author will write for publication a work on _____

_____

_____

The Author grants this work to the Publisher with the exclusive right to publish and sell the work, under its own name and under other imprints or trade names, during the full term of copyright and all renewals thereof, and to copyright it in the Author's name in all countries; also the exclusive rights listed in paragraph I below; with exclusive authority to dispose of said rights in all countries and in all languages.

2. The manuscript, containing about _____words or their equivalent, will be delivered by the Author by _____, 20_____.

3. When the manuscript is ready for publication, it will be published at the Publisher's own expense. The Publisher will pay the Author a royalty based on the actual cash received by the Publisher, of 10%.

4. The Publisher will report on the sale of the work on the first of March and September of each year for the six-month period ending the prior December 31 and June 30, respectively. With each report of sales, the Publisher will make settlement for any balance shown to be due.

5. Paragraphs A–P inclusive, on pages 2, 3, and 4 following, are parts of this agreement as though placed before the signatures.

_____

Author

_____

U.S. Taxpayer Identification No.

By _____

A. The Author will deliver the manuscript in typewritten form (or, in the case of anthologies and revisions, in typewritten and printed form), double-spaced on 8½" by 11" sheets on one side only. The manuscript will be submitted in duplicate and a third copy will be retained by the Author. It will be in proper form for use as copy by the printer, and the content will be such as the Author and Publisher are willing to have appear in print. If the Author fails to deliver a satisfactory manuscript on time, the Publisher will have the right to terminate this agreement and to recover from the Author any sums advanced in connection with the work. Until this agreement has been terminated and until such sums have been repaid, the Author may not have the work published elsewhere. The Author will read the proofs, correct them in duplicate, and promptly return one set to the Publisher. The Author will be responsible for the completeness and accuracy of such corrections and will bear all costs of alterations in the proofs (other than those resulting from printer's errors) exceeding 10% of the cost of typesetting. These costs will be deducted from the royalty payments due the Author.

B. The Author will furnish the following items along with the manuscript: title page; preface or foreword (if any); table of contents; index; teacher's manual or key (if requested by the Publisher); and complete and final copy for all illustrations properly prepared for reproduction.

C. The Author warrants that the Author is the sole owner of the Work and has full power and authority to copyright it and to make this agreement; that the work does not infringe any copyright, violate any property rights, or contain any scandalous, libelous, or unlawful matter. The Author will defend, indemnify, and hold harmless the Publisher against all claims, suits, costs, damages, and expenses that the Publisher may sustain by reason of any scandalous, libelous, or unlawful matter contained or alleged to be contained in the work, or any infringement or violation by the work of any copyright or property right; and until such claim or suit has been settled or withdrawn, the Publisher may withhold any sums due the Author under this agreement.

D. The work will contain no material from other copyrighted works without the Publisher's consent and the written consent of the owner of such copyrighted material. The Author will obtain and be financially liable for such consents and file them with the Publisher.

E. The Publisher will have the right to edit the work for the original printing and for any reprinting, provided that the meaning of the text is not materially altered.

F. The Publisher will have the right: (1) to publish the work in suitable style as to paper, printing, and binding; (2) to fix or alter the title and price; (3) to use all customary means to market the work.

G. The Publisher will furnish ten (10) copies of the book to the Author without charge. Additional copies for the Author's use shall be supplied at a twenty percent (20%) discount from the lowest list price.

H. The Author agrees to revise the work if the Publisher considers it necessary in the best interests of the work. The provisions of this agreement shall apply to each revision of the work by the Author as though that revision were the work being published for the first time under this agreement. Should the Author be unable or unwilling to provide a revision within a reasonable time after the Publisher has requested it, or should the Author be deceased, the Publisher may have the revision prepared and charge the cost, including, without limitation, fees or royalties, against the Author's royalties, and may display in the revised work, and in advertising, the name of the person, or persons, who revise the work.

I. The Publisher may permit others to publish, broadcast by radio, make recordings or mechanical renditions, publish book club and microfilm editions, make translations and other versions, show by motion pictures and by television, syndicate, quote, and otherwise utilize this work, and material based on this work. The net amount of any compensation received from such use shall be divided equally between the Publisher and the Author.

The Publisher may authorize such use by others without compensation, if, in the Publisher's judgment, such use may benefit the sale of the work. If the Publisher itself uses the work for any of the foregoing purposes (other than publishing), the Author will be paid 5% of the cash received from such use. On copies of the work or sheets sold outside the United States, the Author will be paid a royalty of 10% of the cash received from such sales. On copies of the work sold through any of the Publisher's book club divisions or institutes, or by radio, television, mail-order, or coupon advertising direct to the consumer or through any of its subsidiaries, the Publisher shall pay to the Author a royalty of 5% of the cash received from such sales. If the Publisher sells any stock of the work at a price below the manufacturing costs of the book plus royalties, no royalties shall be paid. All copies of the work sold and all compensation from sales of the work under this paragraph shall be excluded in computing the royalties payable under paragraph 3 above and shall be computed and shown separately in reports to the Author.

J. If the balance due the Author for any settlement period is less than ten dollars, the Publisher will make no accounting or payment until the next settlement period at the end of which the cumulative balance has reached ten dollars. If, after the expiration of two years following publication, the sales in any twelve-month period ending December 31 do not exceed a total of 500 copies, the royalty on such sales shall be one-half the stipulated royalty, this reduction in royalty being agreed upon to enable the Publisher to keep the work in print as long as possible. The Publisher may deduct from any funds due the Author, under this or any other agreement between the Author and the Publisher, any sum that the Author may owe the Publisher. When the Publisher decides that the public demand for this work no longer warrants its continued manufacture, the Publisher may discontinue manufacture and destroy any of all plates, books, and sheets without liability to the Author.

K. The Author agrees that during the term of this agreement the Author will not agree to publish or furnish to any other publisher any work on the same subject that will conflict with the sale of this work.

L. This agreement may not be changed unless the parties to it agree in writing.

M. This agreement shall be construed and interpreted according to the laws of the State of New York and shall be binding upon the parties hereto, their heirs, successors, assigns, and personal representatives; and reference to the Author and to the Publisher shall include their heirs, successors, assigns, and personal representatives.

N. The Publisher agrees to make an initial payment to the Author as an advance against royalties of $2,000, payable as follows: $1,000 upon the signing of this agreement and $1,000 upon acceptance by the Publisher of the completed manuscript in a form, style, and content acceptable for publication; provided, however, the Publisher may retain for its own account the first $2,000 otherwise due the Author under the terms of this agreement. The terms of this paragraph shall not apply to revised editions of the Work.

O. If a completed manuscript, acceptable to the Publisher, shall not have been delivered by _____ or within an additional ninety-day grace period, by reason of the Author's death or otherwise, the Publisher may terminate this agreement, whereupon all monies paid to the Author shall then be repaid to the Publisher. The terms of this paragraph shall not apply to revised editions of the work.

P. Upon written request of the Author after the book has been declared out-of-print, the Publisher agrees to revert all rights back to the Author.

MASS MARKET PAPERBACK ORIGINAL AGREEMENT—MAIN VARIANT CLAUSES

Mass market paperback original contracts typically contain only a few clauses that differ from trade book contracts. The clauses you're likely to encounter include a revisions clause allowing the publisher to change the title of the work; a vastly different royalty schedule; a clause providing damages if the publisher fails to publish your manuscript, once accepted; a clause requiring you to notify the publisher if your work is published in another edition before publication of the mass market edition; and a limit on the advertisements the publisher may include in your book. Each of these clauses appears below.

Revision

Publisher may revise or change the title of the Work and may upon notifying the Author make deletions and revisions consistent with reasonable standards of publication. The Author agrees to assist Publisher with any such revision or change in such a manner as to complete the same within the period of time deemed necessary by Publisher.

Royalties

i.   On United States Sales—

Eight percent (8%) of the retail cover price on the first one hundred thousand (100,000) copies sold.

Ten percent (10%) of the retail cover price on all additional copies sold thereafter.

ii.   On Foreign Sales and Sales to Bona Fide Book Clubs—

Six percent (6%) of the United States retail cover price on all such copies sold.

Failure to Publish

If Publisher fails to publish the Work within eighteen months from the date of acceptance of the completed manuscript by Publisher, Publisher's right to publish this Work pursuant to this Agreement shall terminate and revert to the Author. The parties furthermore agree that the only damages recoverable by the Author shall be confined to the advance of Five Thousand Dollars—($5,000)—paid or payable to the Author by Publisher and that no other damages, actions, or procedures, legal or equitable, will be claimed, instituted, or maintained by the Author against Publisher.

Prior Publication

Author shall notify Publisher promptly of any publication of the Work prior to Publisher's publication date and shall furnish Publisher with such copyright notices, credits, or registered assignments of copyright as may be deemed necessary for protection of Publisher's edition of the Work.

Advertisements

Publisher may not include any advertisements in its edition of the Book without prior written consent of the author, except for "house ads" for and listings of other Publisher books, and advertisements for science fiction book clubs and science fiction magazines, which ads may appear either before or after the text, and which shall not require the Author's approval or consent.

COLLEGE TEXTBOOK AGREEMENT

Textbook agreements tend to be a little shorter than trade book contracts because subsidiary rights are of less significance and therefore require fewer words. One great difference between the two kinds of contracts lies in the royalty provisions: textbook royalties are calculated on the publisher's cash receipts, whereas trade book royalties are based on cover price. Another difference is the treatment accorded competing works. Textbook authors need and receive the right to put their expertise to work in other publications. Publishers need protection against unfair competition. The clause in the contract below attempts a compromise.

PUBLICATION AGREEMENT

Made between Alfred Autorite (Author) and Morningstar Press, Inc. (Publisher) on March 15, 1988.

The Author and Publisher Agree That:

1. The Author will write for publication a work on United States Government. The Author grants this work to the Publisher with the exclusive right to publish and sell the work under its own name and under other imprints or trade names, during the full term of copyright and all renewals thereof, and to copyright it in the Publisher's name or any other name in all countries; also the exclusive rights listed in Paragraph I below; with exclusive authority to dispose of said rights in all countries and in all languages.

2. The manuscript, containing about 225,000 words or their equivalent, will be delivered by the Author by January 15, 1990, in form and content acceptable to the Publisher.

3. When the manuscript is ready for publication, it will be published at the Publisher's own expense. The Publisher will pay the Author a royalty, based on the actual cash received by the Publisher, of fifteen percent (15%) from sales of the first fifteen thousand (15,000) copies sold; seventeen percent (17%) on the next fifteen thousand (15,000) copies sold; and eighteen percent (18%) thereafter.

4. The Publisher will report on the sale of the work in March and September of each year for the six-month period ending the prior December 31 and June 30, respectively. With each report of sales, the Publisher will make settlement for any balance shown to be due.

5. Paragraphs A through O, inclusive, on pages 2, 3, and 4 following, are parts of this agreement as though placed before the signatures.

_____

Alfred Autorite, Author

_____

Morningstar Press, Inc.

By _____

A. The Author will deliver the manuscript in typewritten form (or, in the case of anthologies and revisions, in typewritten and printed form). The manuscript will be submitted in duplicate and a third copy will be retained by the Author. It will be in proper form for use as copy by the printer, and the content will be such as the Author and Publisher are willing to have appear in print. The Author will read the proofs, correct them in duplicate, and promptly return one set to the Publisher. The Author will be responsible for the completeness and accuracy of such corrections and will bear all costs of alterations in the proofs (other than those resulting from printer's errors) exceeding ten percent (10%) of the cost of typesetting. These costs will be deducted from the first royalty payments due the Author.

B. The Author will furnish the following items along with the manuscript: title page; preface or foreword (if any); table of contents; index; teacher's manual or key (if requested by the Publisher); and complete and final copy for all illustrations properly prepared for reproduction.

C. The Author warrants that he is the sole owner of the work and has full power and authority to copyright it and to make this agreement; that the work does not infringe any copyright, violate any property rights, or contain any scandalous, libelous, or unlawful matter. The Author will indemnify, and hold harmless, the Publisher against all claims, suits, costs, damages, and expenses that the Publisher may sustain by reason of any scandalous, libelous, or unlawful matter contained or alleged to be contained in the work, or any infringement or violation by the work of any copyright or property right; and until such claim or suit has been settled or withdrawn, the Publisher may withhold any sums due the Author under this agreement.

D. The work will contain no material from other copyrighted works without the Publisher's consent and the written consent of the owner of such copyrighted material. The Author will obtain such consents and file them with the Publisher.

E. The Publisher will have the right to edit the work for the original printing and for any reprinting, provided that the meaning of the text is not materially altered.

F. The Publisher will have the right: (1) to publish the work in suitable style as to paper, printing, and binding; (2) to fix or alter the title and price; (3) to use all customary means to market the work.

G. The Publisher will furnish ten (10) copies of the book to the Author without charge. Additional copies for the Author's use shall be supplied at a twenty percent (20%) discount from the lowest list price.

H. The Author agrees to revise the work if the Publisher considers it necessary in the best interest of the work. The provisions of this agreement shall apply to each revision of the work by the Author as though that revision were the work being published for the first time under this agreement. Should the Author be unable or unwilling to provide a revision within a reasonable time after the Publisher has requested it, or should the Author be deceased, the Publisher may have the revision prepared and charge the cost against the Author's royalties, and may display in the revised work, and in advertising, the name of the person, or persons, who revise the work.

I. The Publisher may permit others to publish, broadcast by radio, make recordings or mechanical renditions, publish book club and microfilm editions, show by motion pictures or by television, syndicate, quote, and otherwise utilize this work, and material based on this work. The net amount of any compensation received from such use shall be divided equally between the Publisher and the Author. The Publisher may authorize such use by others without compensation, if, in the Publisher's judgment, such use may benefit the sale of the work. If the Publisher itself uses the work for any of the foregoing purposes (other than publishing), the Author will be paid five percent (5%) of the cash received from such sales. If the Publisher sells any overstock of the work at a price below the manufacturing costs of the book plus royalties, no royalties shall be paid. All copies of the work sold and all compensation from sales of the work under this paragraph shall be excluded in computing the royalties payable under paragraph 3 above and shall be computed and shown separately in reports to the Author.

On international sales of the work or rights thereunder, the Publisher will pay the Author as follows:

1. On sales of the Publisher's edition of the work outside continental United States, the Publisher will pay the Author a royalty of ten percent (10%) of the actual cash received by the Publisher from such sales of copies of the work or sheets.

2. On foreign-language editions of the work published by others, on any English-language reprint edition especially low priced for sale in underdeveloped countries and published by others, and on other subsidiary rights sales outside the continental United States, the net amount of any compensation received from such use shall be divided equally between Publisher and Author.

K. If the balance due the Author for any settlement period is less than ten dollars, the Publisher will make no accounting or payment until the next settlement period at the end of which the cumulative balance has reached ten dollars. When the Publisher decides that the public demand for this work no longer warrants its continued manufacture, the Publisher may discontinue manufacture and destroy any or all plates, books, and sheets without liability to the Author.

L. The Author, without the Publisher's prior written consent, shall not, nor shall he permit anyone else to, publish or otherwise reproduce or communicate in any media now known or later developed any portion of the work or of any other version, revision, or other derivative work based thereon. The Author may, however, draw on and refer to material contained in the work in preparing articles for publication in scholarly and professional journals and papers for delivery at professional meetings.

The Author, without the Publisher's prior written consent, shall not prepare or assist in the preparation of any other work that might in the Publisher's judgment interfere with or injure the sale of the work, except that the Author may without regard to such restriction contribute a single chapter or article to one or more collective works.

M. This agreement may not be changed unless the parties to it agree in writing.

N. This agreement shall be construed and interpreted according to the laws of the State of New York and shall be binding upon the parties hereto, their heirs, successors, assigns, and personal representatives; and references to the Author and to the Publisher shall include their heirs, successors, assigns, and personal representatives.

O. The Publisher agrees to pay to the Author an advance against royalties of $12,000, payable as follows:

Six thousand dollars ($6,000) within thirty (30) days of receipt of signed contract; three thousand dollars ($3,000) on receipt of first draft; three thousand dollars ($3,000) on acceptance by the Publisher of the complete manuscript. The terms of this paragraph shall not apply to revised editions of the work. This advance will be refunded by the Author in the event the Author does not submit a manuscript acceptable to the Publisher in accordance with paragraph 2 of this Agreement.

A five hundred dollar ($500) nonrecoverable GRANT-IN-AID for manuscript preparation shall be paid by the Publisher to the Author upon submission of invoices. The terms of this paragraph shall not apply to revised editions of this work.

Author, Alfred Autorite

Social Security No.

Citizenship

Domicile

Date of Birth

Morningstar Press, Inc.

By _____

APPENDIX D
Copyright Material

1. Publications on Copyright
2. Copyright Act Comparison Chart

The following publications may be obtained from the Copyright Office. Order by writing to:

Information and Publications Section, LM-455
Copyright Office
Library of Congress
Washington, DC 20559

Forms Hotline
NOTE: Requestors may order application forms at any time by telephoning (202) 707-9100. Orders will be recorded automatically and filled as quickly as possible. The Copyright Office Web site is:

lcweb.loc.gov/copyright/copy1.html.

APPLICATION FORMS

For Original Registration

Form TX: for published and unpublished nondramatic literary works

Form SE: for serials, works issued or intended to be issued in successive parts bearing numerical or chronological designations and intended to be continued indefinitely (periodicals, newspapers, magazines, newsletters, annuals, journals, etc.)

Short Form/SE
and
Form SE/Group: Specialized SE forms for use when certain requirements are met

Form PA: for published and unpublished works of the performing arts (musical and dramatic works, pantomimes and choreographic works, motion pictures and other audiovisual works)

Form VA: for published and unpublished works of the visual arts (pictorial, graphic, architectural, and sculptural works)

Form SR: for published and unpublished sound recordings

For Renewal Registration

Form RE: for claims to renewal copyright in works copyrighted under the law in effect through December 31, 1977 (1909 Copyright Act)

For Corrections and Amplifications

Form CA: for supplementary registration to correct or amplify information given in the Copyright Office record of an earlier registration

For Continuations

Form CON: Universal continuation sheet for use with all forms except Short Form/SE, Form SE/Group, and Form RE

RE/CON: for continuation of Form RE, space 5

Other Forms for Special Purposes

Form GR/CP: an adjunct application to be used for registration of a group of contributions to periodicals in addition to an application Form TX, PA, or VA

Form MW: for published and unpublished mask works

COPYRIGHT INFORMATION KITS

Each Copyright Office information kit contains material on the particular kit's title, including, as appropriate, circulars, announcements, and application forms. When ordering, **indicate kit number.**

THE 1909 ACT VS. THE 1976 ACT (A COMPARISON)

	ACT OF MARCH 4, 1909	*ACT OF OCTOBER 19, 1976*
SUBJECT MATTER	Protects "writings" of an author. Writing has been interpreted as requiring fixation in a tangible form and a certain minimum amount of original, creative authorship. [Section 4]	Protects "original works of authorship which are fixed in a copy (material object, other than a phonorecord, from which the work can be perceived, reproduced, or otherwise communicated, either directly or with the aid of a machine or device) or a phonorecord. [Sections 102(a), 301, 101]

14 classes of works enumerated:

Class A—Books, including composite and cyclopedic works
Class B—Periodicals, including newspapers
Class C—Lectures, sermons, addresses (prepared for oral delivery)
Class D—Dramatic or dramatico-musical compositions
Class E—Musical compositions
Class F—Maps
Class G—Works of art; models or designs for works of art
Class H—Reproductions of a work of art
Class I—Drawings of plastic works of a scientific or technical character
Class J—Photographs
Class K—Prints and pictorial illustrations including prints or labels used for articles of merchandise
Class L—Motion picture photoplays
Class M—Motion pictures other than photoplays
Class N—Sound recordings [Section 5]

7 classes of works enumerated:

1. literary works
2. musical works, including any accompanying words
3. dramatic works, including any accompanying music
4. pantomimes and choreographic works
5. pictorial, graphic, and sculptural works
6. motion pictures and other audiovisual works
7. sound recordings. [Section 102(a)]

The Register of Copyrights to specify classification for registration purposes only. Classes will be:

Class TX—for claims in nondramatic literary works, other than audiovisual works, expressed in words, numbers or other verbal or numerical symbols or indicia.

ACT OF 1909	*ACT OF 1976*
	Class PA—for claims in musical works, including any accompanying words; dramatic works, including any accompanying music; pantomimes; choreographic works; and motion pictures and other audiovisual works.
	Class VA—for claims in pictorial, graphic, and sculptural works.
	Class SR—for claims in works resulting from the fixation of a series of musical, spoken, or other sounds, but not including the sounds accompanying a motion picture or other audiovisual work.
"New versions"—"compilations, abridgments, adaptations, arrangements, dramatizations, translations or other new versions when produced with the consent of the copyright owner." [Section 7]	"Compilations and derivative works." (Derivative work is defined as every copyrightable work that employs preexisting material or data.) Consent of the copyright owner is not a condition of protection; copyright protection "does not extend to any part of the work" in which the preexisting material "has been used unlawfully." [Section 103]

STANDARDS OF COPYRIGHT-ABILITY

Product of case law. Work must represent an appreciable amount of original, creative authorship. Original means that the author produced it by his own intellectual effort as distinguished from copying from another.	Legislative reports accompanying Public Law 94-553 indicate that the standards of copyrightability remain unchanged.

	ACT OF 1909	*ACT OF 1976*

ELIGIBILITY

ACT OF 1909

The following works are eligible for copyright protection in the United States:

1. Works by United States citizens;

2. Works by an author who is domiciled in the U.S. on the date of first publication;

3. Works by an author who is a citizen of a country with which the U.S. has copyright relations;

4. Works first published in a country other than the U.S. that belongs to the Universal Copyright Convention.

Works by authors that are stateless—status of these works is unclear. Copyright. Office registers these claims under its rule of doubt. [Section 9]

ACT OF 1976

All unpublished works are eligible for copyright protection in the United States.

If the work is published, it is eligible for U.S. protection if one of the following applies:

1. On the date of first publication, one or more of the authors is a national or domiciliary of the U.S., or is a national or domiciliary, or sovereign authority of a foreign nation that is a party to a copyright treaty of which the U.S. also is a party;

2. If on the date of first publication, one or more of the authors is stateless;

3. If the work is first published in the United States or in a foreign nation that on the date of first publication is a part of the Universal Copyright Convention;

4. If the work comes within the scope of a Presidential proclamation. [Section 104]

OWNERSHIP AND TRANSFER OF OWNERSHIP

ACT OF 1909

Copyright vests initially in the author

Joint works—There is no statutory provisions but courts have held that, in the absence of an agreement to the contrary, joint authors will be deemed as tenants in common. This means that each owns an undivided interest in the entire work and each has an independent right to use or license the entire work. There is no definition of a "joint work" and courts have defined this extremely broadly and eroded the original concept.

ACT OF 1976

The original source of ownership is the author. [Section 201(a)]

"The authors of a joint work are co-owners of copyright in the work." [Section 201(a)] A work is defined as joint when the authors collaborate with each other or if each of the authors prepared his or her contribution with the knowledge and intention that it would be merged with the contributions of the other authors as "inseparable or interdependent parts of a unitary whole." [Section 101]

ACT OF 1909

Work made for hire—The statute provides "the word 'author' shall include an employer in the case of works made for hire." [Section 26] There is no definition of a work made for hire in the law. Courts, however, have generally said a work prepared by employee within the scope of his employment is a work made for hire. Important factors include the right of the employer to direct and supervise the manner in which the work is performed, payment of wages or other remuneration, and the existence of a contractual arrangement concerning the creation of the work. Many "commissioned" works have been considered works made for hire.

Copyright said to be indivisible; transfer of anything less than all of the rights was a license. Only transfers of ownership (assignments) had to be in writing and be signed by the party granting the transfer. [Section 28] Assignments should have been recorded in the Copyright Office. [Section 30]

ACT OF 1976

"In the case of a work made for hire, the employer or other person for whom the work was prepared is considered the author . . ." [Section 201(b)]

Work made for hire is defined. For a commissioned work or one prepared on special order, only certain categories can be works made for hire. Also, the parties must expressly agree to this in writing and both parties must sign the document. [Section 101]

Copyright is made completely divisible. [Section 201(d)(2)] Transfer of ownership is defined as an assignment, mortgage, exclusive license of any of the exclusive rights comprised in a copyright, whether limited in time or place of effect. Transfers must be in writing and signed by the party making the transfer. [Section 204] Transfers should be recorded in the Copyright Office. [Section 205]

Transfers made by authors on or after January 1, 1978, otherwise than by will, may be terminated after a certain period of time. The notice of termination must be filed by certain specified people no more than 10 nor less than 2 years before the date of termination. The notice must comply in form, content and manner of service with regulations the Register of Copyrights is to prescribe. [Section 203] Termination of the grant may be effected notwithstanding any agreement to the contrary [Section 203(a)(5)]

	ACT OF 1909	*ACT OF 1976*
SECURING COPYRIGHT PROTECTION	For unpublished compositions that are registrable, it is the act of registering a claim in the Copyright Office that secures the copyright.	The act of creation and fixing the work in a copy or phonorecord secures the copyright. [Section 301]
	For published works it is the act of publication of the work in visually perceptible copies with the required notice of copyright that secures the copyright. The notice must appear in a location specified by the law, e.g., for a book either upon the title page or the page immediately following. [Section 20] Promptly after publication, a claim should be registered in the Copyright Office. [Section 13] If a work is published without an acceptable notice, copyright protection is lost and cannot be regained.	
DURATION	For *unpublished* works the term is exactly 28 years from the date of registration; a renewal claim may be filed in the 28th year in which case there is an additional term of 28 years. Copyright protection will expire either 28 or 56 years from the exact date of registration.	For works created on or after January 1, 1978, the term of copyright will be:
	For *published* works the term is same as for unpublished works except the term is measured from the date of first publication. [Section 24]	1. life of the author plus 50 years.
		2. joint works—life of the last surviving author plus 50 years.
		3. anonymous, pseudonymous works, if the name of the author is not revealed in Copyright Office records, and works made for hire—100 years from creation or 75 years from first publication, whichever is shorter. [Section 302]
		For unpublished works created, but not registered before January 1, 1978, the term of copyright is the same as for works created after January 1, 1978, *except* there is a guarantee of protection until December 31, 2002. [Section 303]

	ACT OF 1909	*ACT OF 1976*
		For works under statutory (federal) copyright protection on December 31, 1977—if copyright is renewed during the last (28th) year, then the term will be 75 years. [Section 304]
		All terms will run out on December 31st of the year in which they would otherwise expire. [Section 305]
NOTICE, WHEN REQUIRED	The required notice of copyright must be affixed to each copy published or offered for sale. [Section 10]	The required notice of copyright must be placed on all visually perceptible copies and phonorecords of sound recordings that are distributed to the public under the authority of the copyright owner. [Sections 401, 402]
FORM OF NOTICE	For works other than sound recordings: the word "copyright," the abbreviation "Copr.", or the symbol "©" accompanied by the name of the copyright proprietor and the year in which copyright was secured by publication (or, in some cases, registration). (There are certain exceptions to this basic rule.) [Section 19]	For visually perceptible copies: the symbol © (the letter C in a circle), or the word "copyright," or the abbreviation "Copr."; and the name of the copyright owner, or a recognizable abbreviation or a generally known alternative designation, and the year of first publication. [Section 401]
	For sound recordings: the symbol ℗ (the letter P in a circle), the year of first publication of the sound recording; and the name of the owner of copyright in the sound recording, or a recognizable abbreviation or generally known alternative designation of the name. [Section 19]	For sound recordings: same as the Act of 1909. [Section 402]
PLACEMENT	Specified by type of work—e.g., for a book or other printed publication, upon the title page or the page immediately following . . . ; For music, upon the title page or first page of music . . . [Section 20]	For visually perceptible copies— "reasonable notice" of the copyright claim. Copyright Office regulation will include examples of reasonable placement and affixation of the copyright notice. [Section 401]
	For sound recordings—"reasonable notice" of the claim to copyright. [Section 20]	For phonorecords of sound recordings—same as the previous law. [Section 402]

	ACT OF 1909	*ACT OF 1976*
EFFECT OF OMISSION OR ERROR IN NOTICE	If the notice is omitted or contains a serious error, copyright is lost and cannot be regained.	If the notice is omitted or there is a serious error, there is no effect as long as the claim to copyright is registered in the Copyright Office before or within 5 years of publication without the notice and a "reasonable effort" is made to add the notice to copies that are later distributed in the U.S. [Section 405]
DEPOSIT	"Promptly after publication, two copies of the best edition" are to be deposited with an application and fee of $6.00. Thus, registration and deposit are joined. [Sections 13, 215]	Within three months after the work has been published with a copyright notice in the U.S., the copyright owner should deposit two complete copies or phonorecords of the "best edition." "Best edition" will be determined by the needs of the Library of Congress. The Register of Copyrights may, by regulation, exempt any categories of material from this requirement, or require deposit of only one copy or phonorecord with respect to any category. Alternate forms of deposit may also be allowed. [Section 407]
	Failure to deposit the required material after a "demand" by the Register of Copyrights can result in the copyright becoming void. [Section 14]	Failure to deposit the required material within three months after the Register of Copyrights makes a written demand will subject the copyright owner to fines. [Section 407(d)]
REGISTRATION	*Unpublished* works that are subject to registration one complete copy of the work in legible notation must be sent to the Copyright Office with a properly completed application and a fee of $6.00. Phonorecords are not acceptable as deposit copies of the underlying works they embody. [Section 12, 215]	Registration for both published and unpublished works is entirely permissive. There are, however, substantial inducements to register. [Section 408(a)] *Unpublished* works—one complete copy or phonorecord must be sent with the appropriate application form and a fee of $10. [Sections 408, 709]

ACT OF 1909

Published compositions—two complete copies of the best edition as first published must be sent to the Copyright Office with a properly completed application and a fee of $6.00. The first published edition of a work registered in unpublished form must be registered again. [Sections 12, 13, 215]

ACT OF 1976

Published works—two complete copies of the best edition (or in the case of works first published abroad or contributions to collective works, one complete copy) with an appropriate application and a fee of $10 must be sent to the Copyright Office. [Sections 408, 708]

The Register of Copyrights, by regulation, can require or permit the deposit of identifying material instead of copies, or the deposit of phonorecords rather than notated copies. The Register may also allow the deposit of one copy rather than two and provide for a single registration for a group of related works. [Section 408]

COMPULSORY LICENSE TO USE COPYRIGHTED MUSICAL COMPOSITIONS ON PHONO-RECORDS

The copyright owner of a musical composition has the exclusive right to make or license the first recording of the work.

Whenever the copyright owner of a musical composition has used or permitted his work to be recorded then anyone else may make "similar use" by complying with the compulsory license provisions of the law.

The copyright owner of a musical composition has the exclusive right to make or license the first recording of the work.

Once phonorecords have been distributed to the public in the U.S. under the authority of the copyright owner, the work becomes subject to the compulsory license.

The compulsory license is available only if the user's primary purpose is to distribute the phonorecords to the public for home use.

The compulsory license includes the privilege of making a musical arrangement of the work to the extent necessary to conform it to the style or manner of interpretation of the performance involved; the new arrangement cannot change the basic melody or fundamental character of the work. The arrangement is not subject to protection as a derivative work unless the copyright owner expressly gives his consent.

ACT OF 1909

Compulsory licensee must send to the copyright owner, by registered mail, a notice of his intention to use the music; a copy of that notice must be sent to the Copyright Office for recordation.

Once a copyright owner records or licenses his work for recording, he must file notice of use (Form U) with the Copyright Office. Courts have held that the copyright owner cannot collect royalties for any infringing records made before he files this notice. [Sections 1(e), 101(e)]

On the 20th of each month, the compulsory licensee must account to the copyright owner of the music. He must send the required royalty of 2 cents for each "part" manufactured.

ACT OF 1976

To obtain a compulsory license, the user must send a notice of his intent to the copyright owner. It must be served before or within 30 days after making and before distributing any phonorecords. This notice must comply in form, content and manner of service with regulations prescribed by the Register of Copyrights. A copy of this notice need not be sent to the Copyright Office.

To be entitled to royalties the copyright owner must be identified in the registration or other public records of the Copyright Office.

If the registration or other public records of the Copyright Office do not identify the copyright owner and his address, the notice should be filed with the Copyright Office.

Failure to file a notice of intent forecloses the possibility of a compulsory license.

Compulsory licensee must pay 2¾ cents or 1½ cent per minute of playing time or fraction thereof, whichever is larger, for records that are made and distributed.

Royalty payments are to be made on or before the 20th day of each month. Each payment must be under oath and must comply with the requirements of the Copyright Office regulations.

The Register of Copyrights, by regulation, is to establish criteria for the detailed annual statements of account which must be certified by an independent Certified Public Accountant.

The notice of use (Form U) is no longer required. [Section 115]

APPENDIX E
Permissions Guidelines*

WHEN DO YOU NEED PERMISSION?

Any material in your book that is borrowed from another source may require written permission. The goal is to distinguish between material that can be used without obtaining written permission and material for which such permission is necessary. These guidelines should help you decide the majority of cases; if in doubt; feel free to ask us.

Using material without the need to obtain permission is called "fair use." Your use of the material is considered "fair" to the original copyright holder. This is a marvelous privilege that can save you lots of time and work, but you need to use it carefully. Fair use is defined in terms of the proportion of the whole work being used. *The Chicago Manual of Style* (Chicago University Press, 1982) tells us that

> an author should not quote at such length from another source that he diminishes the value of that source . . . proportion is more important than the absolute length of a quotation: to quote five hundred words from an essay of five thousand is bound to be more serious than to quote the same number of words from a work of fifty thousand.

---

*WARNING! These guidelines are those adopted by just one publisher. They are not definitive. They do not represent the final, reliable, authoritative word on the subject. Each publisher may provide you with its own guidelines, which may differ substantially from these.

Even if you decide that certain material constitutes fair use, you will still need to provide a full credit line for it in your book.

Quoted material from books, magazines, and so on (fiction and nonfiction): Follow the rule of thumb for fair use, given above. As a rough estimate, a quote under five hundred words from a book or under fifty words from a magazine article can be used freely.

Poems, plays, songs: You need to get permission for as little as a single line of poetry or of a song, and for any part of a music score.

Photographs and artwork (including cartoons): All will require the permission of the copyright holder. Sometimes rights are controlled by a photo agency, a cartoon syndicate, or the magazine where the illustration appears. Sometimes it is the artist who holds the copyright. You may be required to estimate the proportion of the book page that the illustration will fill (full page, one-half page, one-third page, and so on).

In rare cases, photographs or artwork may be in the public domain (no one holds right to them). Please don't make this assumption without checking with the source.

Tests, quizzes, figures, charts, tables: These require permission, and they usually stand out in text as entities in themselves, so you can't miss them. If a chart or table is redrawn to the extent that the original concept or form is not immediately recognizable, permission may not be necessary.

News articles: Straight news articles (not features) of any length can be used safely after three months. This does not include any article that is syndicated, under a byline, or individually copyrighted—for example, a "Dear Abby" letter or regularly syndicated column.

Material published or copyrighted by the U.S. government (pamphlets, brochures, and so on): You don't need to apply for permission to quote from these, but again it's a good idea to cite the specific source.

Dictionary definitions: These do require permission and a full credit line.

FINDING THE COPYRIGHT HOLDER

For each piece of material requiring permission, determine the source or copyright holder and the correct address. In books, this information appears on the back of the title page; in magazines and journals, it is usually on the title page or table of contents pages. To save time and trouble, try to find out the name of the person who should receive your request—sometimes this means calling before you send it out.

SENDING OUT REQUEST FORMS

These should be sent as early as possible, even before you send the manuscript to your publisher. Unfortunately, obtaining a necessary permission sometimes takes four to six months. Use the attached letter as a model and type it on your own letterhead, leaving spaces for the addressee and the material you need. Do the same with the release form. Run off a supply of each form, and you're ready to begin.

For each permission, follow these steps:

- Fill in the blanks, citing the fullest information you have about the source (author, title, publisher, date, page numbers).
- Date the letter!
- Add an identifying number in the upper right-hand corner (chapter and page number, or figure number).

Send the following:

- One copy of the letter.
- Two copies of the release form (one for the addressee to keep).
- One copy of the requested material, as it appears in its original source.
- (If possible) a self-addressed stamped envelope (SASE), or business reply envelope. This really speeds the reply. Your publisher can sometimes provide SASEs if you request it.

KEEPING A RECORD

The best method we've found is to keep a log, or a chart, of permissions requested. Use the one on page 338 as a model. You'll probably also need to keep a copy of the requested material as it appears in its original source. This is where those identifying numbers come in handy—they can easily coordinate with the chart, in sequence.

FOLLOWING UP THE REQUEST

If you receive a tentative reply:

- Sometimes the addressee wants to be sure you are agreeable to his terms before actually granting permission. If the fee, credit line, and especially the rights are acceptable to you, phone or write back and let the person know. You may need to sign his permission form and send it back.

If you are told to write elsewhere for all or some of the rights you need:

- Send the forms and other material again to the new person.

If you don't receive a reply in a reasonable length of time (two to three weeks):

- Try to call the person. Often he will cite terms over the phone, then send you the paperwork. If you can't get a phone number, write again.

NEGOTIATING FOR PERMISSION: CONDITIONS AND PROVISIONS

In the great majority of cases, permission will be granted under certain terms and conditions. Some of these are fairly standard and accepted throughout the publishing realm; others are determined by the circumstances of the individual permission and may be negotiable. Here are the most common conditions:

- Credit line. This is not only standard and accepted, it makes your use of copyrighted material legal. We always use the information provided by the copyright holder, sometimes rearranged for consistency within the book.
- Permission fee. This is an accepted condition of many kinds of permission, and the copyright holder has the right to set any fee. In most cases, however, it is negotiable. Be aggressive! If you feel the stated fee is too high for the amount or type of material you're using, contact the person or company who set the fee and explain your point of view. At this stage, especially, it helps to deal with a specific person.

Publishers and agencies usually charge by the page for quoted material from books, and the fee is likely to range from $5 to $30 per page, depending on the value of the material and the extent of the rights they are granting. For individual photos, artwork, tables, and so on, a flat fee is usually charged. Poetry and songs are often charged by the line.

- Free copies. Both publishers and individuals are apt to ask for a free copy of your book when it is published. If this condition is specified in writing, on the permission form, your publisher might be willing to send the book when it is available (this does not come out of your royalties).

WHAT RIGHTS DO YOU NEED?

Our current policy is to request full rights—for translation into all languages, for worldwide distribution, for all future editions of the book, and for all possible subsidiary or promotional uses in connection with the book. This way, we are covered for any future situations (foreign translations or subsidiary rights sales of your book).

The copyright holder you contact initially may not hold full rights and may refer you elsewhere for rights governing certain areas of the world. You'll need to send a second request for the additional rights.

Often the copyright holder may not wish to grant rights for "all future editions" and will limit permission to "this edition" or "first edition" or "one-time use." This means you must obtain permission again when you publish a new edition.

Date _____

I am preparing a book to be titled _____

to be published by _____ in

_____, 20_____. I would like to request permission to use the following

material in this book:

_____

_____

Appropriate credit will be given for the use of this material. If you do not control the necessary rights, please let me know whom to contact.

For your convenience, a release form is attached, in duplicate. Please sign and return one copy to me. Your prompt consideration of this request will be greatly appreciated. Please respond by our deadline of _____.

Sincerely,

RELEASE FORM

I (We) grant nonexclusive all-language world rights to _____
_____ to use the following material:

_____
_____

in (title) _____

by _____

including all editions and all possible subsidiary and promotional uses in connection
with this work.

I (We) require that you print the following credit line:

_____
_____

by _____
date _____

RECORD OF PERMISSION REQUESTS

BOOK TITLE

#	DESCRIPTION OF MATERIAL	OWNER OF RIGHTS (name, address, phone)	REQUEST MAILED	REPLY REC'D	FEE	TERMS & CONDITIONS: CREDIT LINE

APPENDIX F
Author's Questionnaire

This questionnaire provides the publisher with information for publicity and marketing. The more complete the answers, the better job the publisher can do. See Chapter 12 for more about how to work with your publisher.

AUTHOR'S QUESTIONNAIRE

TITLE OF WORK: _____

FULL LEGAL NAME: _____

NAME AS IT WILL APPEAR ON BOOK: _____
(If different from above)

SHOW HERE THE WAY YOU WISH YOUR NAME TO APPEAR ON THE COPYRIGHT:

_____

Is this name a pseudonym? _____

HOME ADDRESS: _____

HOME TELEPHONE: _____

OFFICE OR ALTERNATE PHONE NUMBER: _____

OFFICE OR ALTERNATIVE ADDRESS: _____

DATE OF BIRTH: _____

PLACE OF BIRTH: _____

CITIZENSHIP: _____

SOCIAL SECURITY NO.: _____

OPTIONAL:

RELIGIOUS APFILIATION: _____

FAMILY: _____

IF RELEVANT:

BRIEF SUMMARY OF EDUCATION: _____

HONORS, PRIZES: _____

BRIEF SUMMARY OF PRINCIPAL OCCUPATIONS, WITH APPROXIMATE DATES: ____

_____

OTHER AREAS OF INTEREST OR STUDY: _____

Please list chronologically the locations you have lived in for six months or more.

_____

_____

If possible, please list any local newspapers or publications to whom a release and a copy of your book should be sent, including the person it should be directed to, if known:

_____

_____

Countries in which you have traveled or resided (six months or more) with approximate dates:

_____

_____

Please list any organizations you may be affiliated with which may prove fields for publicity or sales for your book. If known, please provide the names of persons within these organizations to whom information should be directed:

_____

_____

Please list your other books, specifying publisher, date of publication, and type of book, along with any interesting details of these books' publishing histories (book club adoptions, foreign editions, dramatizations):

_____

_____

Please list major articles you have had published, with publishing details as above. Are you a regular contributor to any particular periodicals?

_____

_____

Please list any similar books you know of which may compete with your book and describe how your book is different:

_____

_____

For potential publicity purposes, what has been your broadcast (radio, TV) experience, and in what media do you feel most comfortable and effective?

_____

_____

What lecture experience have you had, and, if pertinent, would you be interested in making any personal appearances on behalf of your book?

_____

_____

Please provide, if possible, a select list of publications or persons who might be provided with advance galley proofs in order to solicit prepublication quotes:

_____

_____

Please list persons who would have a strong interest in your book, and be in a position to do something to help it, so that an advance copy might be sent to them. Include media commentators, critics, booksellers, other authors, prominent acquaintances, and so on:

_____

_____

Please provide a brief, informal, anecdotal autobiography résumé, including any details that might be of interest to the press and the reading public:

_____

_____

What other writing are you currently engaged in?

_____

_____

How do your writings usually evolve? What are your writing habits?

_____

_____

Please attach, if possible, glossy prints of at least two recent photographs for distribution to the media and possible book cover use. Informal pose, with good contrast and definition, is best suited for publicity. Please be sure the photographer will allow reproduction of the photograph without payment of a fee.

If you have any suggestions concerning the promotion of your book, we would be happy to discuss them with you. Thank you for your assistance.

INDEX